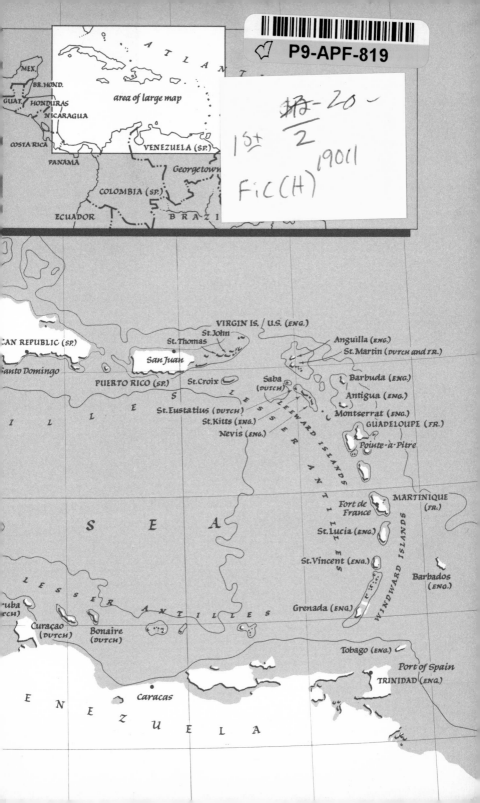

From the Green Antilles

FROM THE GREEN ANTILLES

Writings
of the Caribbean

EDITED AND WITH INTRODUCTIONS BY

BARBARA HOWES

THE MACMILLAN COMPANY · NEW YORK

First Printing

The Macmillan Company, New York
Collier-Macmillan Canada Ltd., Toronto, Ontario
Library of Congress catalog card number: 66-10593
Printed in the United States of America

ACKNOWLEDGMENTS

Acknowledgments and thanks are due to the authors for permission to publish their stories in this anthology. Grateful acknowledgment is also made to the following for permitting stories to be reprinted.

English Section

"Missing the Sea" by Derek Walcott from *Selected Poems,* by permission of Farrar, Straus & Company, Inc. Copyright © 1962, 1963, 1964.

"B. Wordsworth" by V. S. Naipaul from *Miguel Street,* by permission of the publishers, The Vanguard Press; © V. S. Naipaul, MCMLIX, and André Deutsch Ltd.

"A Village Tragedy" by John Hearne, reprinted from *The Atlantic Monthly,* by permission of David Higham Associates, Ltd., London.

"The Wind in This Corner" by John Hearne, reprinted from *The Atlantic Monthly,* by permission of David Higham Associates, Ltd.

"Taxi, Mister!" by Daniel Samaroo Joseph, reprinted from *Bim,* by permission of the editors.

"A Day in the Country" by Ismith Khan, reprinted from *The Colorado*

Quarterly; copyright © 1962 by the University of Colorado, Boulder, Colorado, by permission of John Schaffner, Literary Agent.

"A Requiem for Dan'l Moore" by V. S. Reid, reprinted from *The Tamarack Review,* by permission of the author.

"My Father's House" by V. S. Reid, reprinted from *Focus,* by permission of the author.

"The Snag" by Frank A. Collymore, reprinted from *Bim,* by permission of the editors.

"Listen, the Wind" by Roger Mais, reprinted from *Focus,* by permission of Mrs. Jessie Dayes, literary executor.

"I Hanging On, Praise God!" by Austin Clarke, reprinted from *Bim,* by permission of John Johnson, Esq., Agent.

Section #11 of *In the Castle of My Skin* by George Lamming, reprinted by permission of Michael Joseph Ltd., London.

"The Sun Was a Slaver" by Karl Sealy, reprinted from *Bim,* by permission of the author.

"Sunday with a Difference" by A. N. Forde, reprinted from *Bim,* by permission of the author.

"Cane Is Bitter" by Samuel Selvon from *Ways of Sunlight,* reprinted by permission of John Schaffner, Literary Agent.

"My Girl and the City" by Samuel Selvon from *Ways of Sunlight,* reprinted by permission of John Schaffner, Literary Agent.

French Section

"To Celebrate a Childhood," Parts I, II, and III, by St.-John Perse from *Eloges,* translated by Louise Varèse, by permission of Bollingen Foundation.

"Elisa the Hustler" by Pierre Duprey, from the French text in *Le Rendez-Vous* edited by Françoise Mallet-Joris, by permission of the author.

"Vacation at Monte-Bello" by Gilbert du Chambertrand, by permission of the author.

"The Umbrella Lady" by Florette Morand from *Biguines,* by permission of the author.

"Up in Smoke" by Clément Richer, by permission of the author.

"The Submarine" by Philippe Thoby-Marcelin, by permission of the author.

"The Wake" by Magloire-Saint-Aude from *Veillée,* by permission of the author.

"The Gift" by Joseph Zobel, by permission of the author.

"Calderon's Revolt" by Raphaël Tardon, by permission of the author.
"Memorandum on My Martinique" by Aimé Césaire from *Cahier d'un retour au pays natal*, translated by Lionel Abel, reprinted by permission of Présence Africaine.

Spanish Section

"Wake for Papa Montero" by Nicolas Guillén from *Anthology of Contemporary Latin-American Poetry*, ed. Dudley Fitts, by permission of New Directions.
"The Beautiful Soul of Don Damián" by Juan Bosch, reprinted from *New Writers*, by permission of the author.
"Something to Everyone" by Eliseo Diego, by permission of the author.
"How His Excellency Spent the Time" by Eliseo Diego, by permission of the author.
"*Allies* and *Germans*" by Lino Novás Calvo from *Antologia del Cuento en Cuba*, ed. Salvador Bueno, by permission of the author.
"Josco" by Abelardo Díaz Alfaro from *Antologia de Autores Puertorriquenos, III*, ed. Concha Meléndez, by permission of the author.
"The Innocents" by Pedro Juan Soto from *Spiks*, by permission of the author.
"Twelve Corals" by Carlos Montenegro from *Antologia del Cuento en Cuba*, ed. Salvador Bueno (1902-1952), by permission of the author.
"Turtle's Horse" by Lydia Cabrera from *Cuentos Negros*, by permission of the author.
"Walo-Wila" by Lydia Cabrera from *Cuentos Negros*, by permission of the author.
"The Purple Child" by Emilio S. Belaval from *Antologia de Autores Puertorriquenos, III*, ed. Concha Meléndez, by permission of the author.
"Return to the Seed" by Alejo Carpentier from *Short Stories of Latin America*, ed. Arturo Torres-Rioseco by permission of Las Americas Publishing Co.
"The Child's Gifts: A Twelfth Night Tale" by Tomás Blanco from text published by Aldus Printers, c 1954 by Tomás Blanco, by permission of the author.

Dutch Section

"The Gaucho" by Cola Debrot, by permission of the author.
"My Monkey Weeps" by Albert Helman, by permission of the author.
Section #10 of "Weekend Pilgrimage" by Tip Marugg from *Weekend*

Pilgrimage, by permission of Hutchinson & Co. (Publishers), London.

"Aunty Da" by Boeli van Leeuwen from *De Rots Der Struikeling,* by permission of P. N. van Kampen & Zoon N. V., Amsterdam.

"The Precious Stones of Uncle Brink" by René de Rooy from *Tongoni,* by permission of the author.

Acknowledgment is gratefully made to the "Foundation for the Promotion of the Translation of Dutch Literary Works" for permission to print all Dutch material.

I would like especially to thank the following, without whose advice and encouragement this anthology would never have been completed: Frank A. Collymore, Mrs. Helen C. Cook, Hubert Creekmore, Mrs. Gloria Egui, Mrs. Marie-José Renaudie Jones, Mrs. Harriet de Onís, Dr. J. J. Oversteegen and Nick Vandemoer.

and there are witchcrafts of color. Looking down the narrow, steep street opening to the bay, I see the motionless silhouette of the steamer on a perfectly green sea,—under a lilac sky,—against a prodigious orange light." On the return trip, as they sailed at nightfall toward St. Lucia, he added, "And you behold before you a geological dream, a vision of the primeval sea: the apparition of the land as first brought forth, all peak-tossed and fissured and naked and grim, in the tremendous birth of an archipelago."

And it is true—the West Indies do exert a singular fascination. Having lived for a while in Guadeloupe, one wants both to return and to go on to Martinique; having spent a month in Barbados, one is drawn back there, but also on to St. Vincent, to Dominica, the Grenadas—each is so different, with its complex of history, of races, of conquest, of tongues piled as high as its peaks; each so individual in the flavor distilled from its past and from its natural beauty, established there all by itself between sun and sea.

Most of the islands underwent a series of invasions, from that of the earliest Arawaks, a peaceful Indian tribe, to the warlike Caribs, who came originally from the rain forests of South America; then the Europeans, in waves, Spanish, French, English, Dutch, briefly the Swedes, the Danes, pushing each other out, returning to fight again. St. Lucia, for instance, underwent all of fourteen changeovers. The struggle for power in Europe was mirrored in miniature in the West Indies.

A turning point for the future of the islands came in 1640, with the introduction into Barbados of sugarcane. This led, inevitably, to the development of the plantation system, the search for vast reservoirs of cheap labor—the slave trade. Between 1708 and 1766, Barbados alone brought in 150,000 Africans. The appallingly high mortality rate, both en route and after arrival, called for ever more thousands. It was not until 1834–1838 that this trade was abolished in the British possessions; not until 1863 in the Dutch. Two hundred years of slavery, three hundred years of colonialism, have bitten deep into the psychology of the islanders; in the Lesser Antilles, indeed, 95 percent of the population is of Negro origin.

Speaking of the general outlook for the English-speaking West Indian writer, L. Edward Brathwaite, an acute critic, writing in the Barbadian quarterly, *Bim,* No. 37, has this to say: "The dichotomy"

INTRODUCTION

The psychology of islanders—island psychology—this is the core of Caribbean literature. An island, clearly, is a small self-contained unit which knows its own boundaries, its own nature, its own idiosyncrasies. People who live on islands know each other, and are in touch with what is going on over in St. Peter's Parish, or in Morne-à-l'Eau, or across the way in Bonaire. One can feel very quickly at home on an island, for its physical and psychological characteristics are there available to the interested observer, but on the other hand one may in time feel cramped, hemmed in, even claustrophobic; the very familiarity of everything becomes a burden and a limitation; then one longs for the anonymity of a great city or the standpoint of those who live on a continent. These two opposite views of island living have had a tremendous influence on the writers who have come to maturity in their volcanic or coral confines.

Between the Atlantic Ocean and the Caribbean Sea, in a long arc stretching down as if to point the way from Florida to Venezuela, lie the islands of the West Indies. They are, in fact, peaks of submerged volcanoes which, in their staccato fashion, form a sort of interrupted chain linking the two continents. The larger, Cuba, Hispaniola—which houses both Haiti and the Dominican Republic —Jamaica, Puerto Rico make up the Greater Antilles; the Lesser Antilles, far smaller, range from Guadeloupe with its 680 square miles down to many a jutting rock, touched only by an occasional seagull. Rising from an undersea ridge, these islands exhibit a wonderful variety of structure: the mile-square islet of Redonda, for instance, lifts itself to a height of 1000 feet above the sea, while Dominica and Guadeloupe boast peaks nearly 5000 feet high.

The beauty of the islands in this great chain can scarcely be described. Lafcadio Hearn, that sensitive traveler, attempts it successfully in his *Two Years in the French West Indies*. Writing of a trip in the summer of 1887, he says, "It is sunset as I write these lines,

CONTENTS

(between the desire to leave and the desire to stay) "is still there. It is a permanent part of our heritage. It comes, in a way, as an almost physical inheritance from Africa where, in nature, drought and lushness, the flower and the desert, lie side by side. It is a spiritual inheritance from slavery and the long story before that of the migrant African moving from the lower Nile across the desert to the Western ocean only to meet . . . a history that was to mean the middle passage, America, and a rootless sojourn in the Caribbean sea. . . .

"This dichotomy expresses itself in the West Indian through a certain psychic tension, an excitability, a definite feeling of having no past, of not really belonging . . . and finds relief in laughter and (more seriously) in movement—dance, cricket, carnival, emigration. This is why, perhaps, the best West Indian stories have been picaresque. . . ."

Due to the heavy history of the islands—"the same slave land that once claimed their ancestors like trees," in George Lamming's phrase —social protest in one form or another is a frequent theme, a vigorous, at times bitter, effort on the part of the writer to make his predicament, and the predicament of the transplanted African felt.

Another theme is the sheer physical exuberance of nature in this semitropical area. "The West Indian is a creature of the sun and sea," as the Barbadian writer John Wickham says, and nature has far more influence here than in many other parts of the world— on the fisherman casting his net in the shallows as well as on the most elegant of insular societies such as is presented so brilliantly in Patrick Leigh Fermor's novel *The Violins of St. Jacques,* that marvelous evocation of plantation aristocracy on the eve of the eruption of the volcano. One has only to reread the *Eloges* of St.-John Perse, saturated as the poems are by the beauty and color of his early memories of Guadeloupe, to feel this involvement with the natural world.

These islands have seen the greatest cultural and social extremes; the planters and their ladies tried often to outdo high life in the mother country itself: Paris in Morne-Rouge (Martinique), London in Bridgetown (Barbados), where the statue of Nelson seems almost to nod in the hot sun; and then, in contrast, existence in the poverty-ridden villages clinging like barnacles to the dry steep hills of Haiti, the voodoo drums sounding at nightfall—an atmosphere compounded of folklore and magical influences. Also there is the level of trade, the heavy labor for uncertain markets, the search for new ways to balance the often faltering economy in these densely packed little islands.

And in language, too, there is great variety. First the official language, which in many cases changed back and forth with the fortunes of war, and then the local language, a linguistic stew made up of scraps of English, French, Spanish, Indian, African words, spiced with anything else that was handy, and served up, in the interests of communication, in differing forms on islands perhaps no more than sixty miles apart. Living languages, in any case, forged by necessity. And this mixture of cultures produced their counterpart in legends, especially in Martinique, drawn from deeply fed layers of imagination.

Fundamentally, whatever his present degree of independence, the West Indian writer looks to the mother country: the English-speaking writer to London, the French to Paris, the Dutch to Amsterdam and the Spanish to a degree to the major centers of Latin America. Between them, culturally speaking, and the United States, hangs some sort of Cane Curtain; the American reading public will come to hear of a very gifted writer from Trinidad, say, only after he has made a name for himself in England. There are no regular publishing houses in the islands, with the exception of Puerto Rico and Cuba, and it follows that the artist of talent must seek out the larger world where publication, and the judgment of his peers, is possible.

But to move to London, for instance, as Mr. Brathwaite points out in an article, "The New West Indian Novelists," *Bim,* No. 31, "is to become divorced from one's roots. That is, not only from one's source material . . . but from that special criticism and appreciation which . . . only the writer's own 'home' public can provide. . . . Will West Indian novelists continue to emigrate to London and produce rich and lively first novels, and then settle down to the dull, soulless task of repeating the performance and scraping the memory dry? . . . Will they be able to settle in London and still continue to write good West Indian novels? Or will a new generation soon arise, determined to build here, on our soil?"

This is the major question which haunts the island artist; he reacts to it in various ways, but there is not one who does not feel it, whether he be black, of Indian origin from Trinidad, or white. The very fact of living in a small place makes the creative man's need for a larger experience of the world a necessity. The majority, certainly, of those writers who have had some success are now expatriates.

One further point might be made about the West Indian writer of African origin. Compared to the Negro writer in America, the former has a distinct advantage, and it is, I think, clearly shown in his work. As Mr. Lamming says in *The Tamarack Review,* Winter, 1960: "The West Indian, however black and dispossessed, could never have felt the experience of being in a minority . . . This numerical superiority has given the West Indian a certain leisure, a certain experience of relaxation among white expatriates; for the West Indian has learnt, by sheer habit, to take that white presence for granted . . ." This may account for a quality of soundness, of being as it were at home with themselves, that is apparent in most writing from the Caribbean. Problems there may be, and indeed are, but the artist is not himself fighting in the same way as the American Negro a mountain of prejudice.

Of course the distances between the islands cannot be measured in miles alone. The current relation to the world of the writer in Cuba, for instance, is vastly different from what it was a few years ago, and very different from that of some counterpart in Curaçao. Cuba, Puerto Rico, and the Dominican Republic have also a literary history behind them, something that can scarcely be said of the smaller islands, which only recently have come up with their literary *naissance.* Another aspect of this distance is the difficulty one has in procuring, or even hearing about, worthwhile books and magazines. Many of the stories in this volume are hidden away in out-of-print literary quarterlies which are practically unavailable; and in fact most of the writers have never before been printed in English or in the United States.

The basis of selection for this anthology was essentially literary and imaginative excellence; to think in other terms would be to downgrade the talent available. But another criterion was variety. With so many islands represented, each affected by many different influences, inevitably one would search out many facets, a complex whole.

One thing they all seem to have in common: vitality, a range of talent. A great deal is going on; writers of stature have emerged and more are emerging. What Mr. Wickham in a recent article identifies as the essence of the West Indian is "a quality of intimacy," an honesty and openness which accords well with the creative spirit; this quality "is not separatist in intention," he says, "but arises inevitably from the traffic of a small population living an open life in the bright searching light of the sun." The writer, from the microcosm of his island, reaches out beyond it to the macrocosm of the world. That there is so much talent and intelligence here is our great good fortune.

English Section

INTRODUCTION

In the English-speaking islands, especially in Jamaica, Barbados, and Trinidad, the literary history of the last twenty years has been one of extraordinary development. " . . . it was not until the Second World War," writes L. Edward Brathwaite, in an article on the new West Indian novelists, "that there was brought into focus a process that was going on unnoticed all the time, all over the region: an *intellectual* revolution: in which British West Indians discovered that they had not only political and social sensibilities, but they had *souls* as well; that this region possessed a light and heart of its own that ought to be seen and heard. And it was within this new intellectual compulsion that West Indian literature, as we now understand the term, came into being."

Two giant steps toward forming the necessary climate for the developing writer were taken in 1942; one in London, one in Barbados. The B.B.C. inaugurated, in that year, its "Caribbean Voices" program, most ably edited first by Una Marson of Jamaica, then by Henry Swanzy, an English intellectual who did a great deal to encourage a whole literature-in-progress. In Barbados, the literary magazine *Bim* (Bim—a native or inhabitant of Barbados, sometimes referred to as Bimshire) embarked on what has turned out to be a long career. Edited by Frank Collymore, whom Mr. Brathwaite calls "perhaps the greatest of West Indian literary godfathers," this remarkable magazine is now in its twenty-first year, and has provided a generation of writers with the opportunity of its pages.

In Jamaica, in 1943, came *Focus,* edited by Edna Manley, wife of the then Premier; the three large issues of this magazine introduced the early work of many now well-known men. In 1945, A. J. Seymour brought out the first issue of the British Guianese magazine *Kyk-Over-Al* (from the name of an old Dutch fort), which also was to continue for a number of years. One might mention, too, that both *Kyk-Over-Al* and the *Caribbean Quarterly,*

3

published by the University College of the West Indies in Mona, Jamaica, produced generous special editions devoted to West Indian poetry. With these serious organs of communication available, the stage was set.

The first fruit of the intellectual revolution-to-be was the appearance in 1949 of *25 Poems,* by Derek Walcott, without any doubt the most remarkable poetic talent the English islands have produced; and *A Morning at the Office,* by the Guianese writer Edgar Mittelholzer.

Although the English look on British Guiana as part of the Caribbean chain, I have decided to limit this volume to stories from the islands themselves. Various talented writers from that country, such as Mr. Mittelholzer, Jan Carew, Wilson Harris and E. R. Braithwaite, must therefore regrettably be excluded. (In the case of Surinam, I have made an exception, due to the fact that it is by far the largest territory under Dutch influence.)

In the period just after the war other writers of importance emerged, among the most talented being V. S. Reid, whose *New Day* is a powerful tale of the Morant Bay Rebellion in Jamaica in 1865; Reid has presented this story in a curious blend of biblical and colloquial rhythms of speech, quite unlike ordinary conventional writing, which, whatever its final effectiveness, had a liberating effect on himself and on writers to come; it was no longer necessary to stick to a formal pattern and the resources of dialect were made available to all who could use them.

Samuel Selvon, of East Indian origin, as is about a third of the population of Trinidad, is a remarkable talent; his sensitivity and gaiety lead him, as it were, straight to the heart of his characters. He writes of the rigid society of the transplanted Indians, or of Trinidad young men whose vivid sense of life redeems the coldness of London, with verve and a sort of picaresque grace. These differing worlds live side by side in his stories in *Ways of Sunlight* or *The Lonely Londoners,* as they do in *Turn Again Tiger,* a novel.

Roger Mais, also of Jamaica, published his first novel, *The Hills Were Joyful Together,* in 1953. Two novels, and two years, later, he was dead. Mais's work is clearly along the line of that passionate social protest so much more strongly marked in Jamaican than in Barbadian or Trinidadian literature. He wrote powerfully of lives lived in huts surrounding a yard in present-day Kingston: "A prickly lime tree struggled up from among the earthed-in, seamy, rotting bricks in the yard; it stood against the northern row of wooden shacks right outside the room where the three Sisters of Charity lived, and crooned and gossiped and cooked and sing-sang sad hymns of wailing the livelong day. . . ."

Three other writers of special interest are John Hearne of Jamaica, V. S. Naipaul of Trinidad—the latter, like Selvon, of East Indian origin—and George Lamming of Barbados. All these men are distinctive and distinguished figures, and they bring to their work the individual flavor of their home islands. Read *The Autumn Equinox* or *Voices under the Window,* or any other of John Hearne's novels, and this will be clear; they may, too, as Frank Collymore noted, provide the best introduction, for the non-West Indian, to this literature.

V. S. Naipaul's supple and ironic style makes him one of the most sophisticated and perceptive of writers. His *A House for Mr. Biswas* or the short stories in *Miguel Street* lead one inevitably to his other books—among them his recent *An Area of Darkness* dealing with his first encounter with India—which have about them also a subtle influence from his Indian origin; a flavor one does not find elsewhere.

Then, George Lamming, whose semiautobiographical, strong, and lyrical first novel, *In the Castle of My Skin,* appeared in 1953, is unquestionably a major talent. He is a poet also, as is clear from the intensity and power of his prose.

There is another tradition of good writing that stems from or is due to the islands: that of travelers who over the years have been captivated by this part of the world. Viewers from without they are, but passionate viewers. *At Last,* written by the English writer Charles Kingsley some ninety-odd years ago begins—"we, too, were crossing the Atlantic. At last the dream of forty years, please God, would be fulfilled, and I should see . . . the West Indies and the Spanish Main. From childhood I had studied their Natural History, their charts, their Romances, and alas! their Tragedies; and now, at last, I was about to compare books with facts, and judge for myself of the reported wonders of the Earthly Paradise." A remarkable recent achievement should also be mentioned: Patrick Leigh Fermor's *The Traveller's Tree,* which causes the islands of the West Indies to work in the imagination for long after. Perhaps one never gets over this book, or forgets it—as one never forgets the islands themselves, once one has known them.

Derek Walcott

MISSING THE SEA

Something removed roars in the ears of this house,
Hangs its drapes windless, stuns mirrors
Till reflections lack substance.

Some sound like the gnashing of windmills ground
To a dead halt;
A deafening absence, a blow.

It hoops this valley, weighs this mountain,
Estranges gesture, pushes this pencil
Through a clear nothing now,

Freights cupboards with silence, folds sour laundry
Like the clothes of the dead left exactly
As the dead behaved by the beloved,

Incredulous, expecting occupancy.

V. S. Naipaul

B. WORDSWORTH

THREE beggars called punctually every day at the hospitable houses in Miguel Street. At about ten an Indian came in his dhoti and white jacket, and we poured a tin of rice into the sack he carried on his back. At twelve an old woman smoking a clay pipe came and she got a cent. At two a blind man led by a boy called for his penny.

Sometimes we had a rogue. One day a man called and said he was hungry. We gave him a meal. He asked for a cigarette and wouldn't go until we had lit it for him. That man never came again.

The strangest caller came one afternoon at about four o'clock. I had come back from school and was in my home clothes. The man said to me, "Sonny, may I come inside your yard?"

He was a small man and he was tidily dressed. He wore a hat, a white shirt, and black trousers.

I asked, "What you want?"

He said, "I want to watch your bees."

We had four small gru-gru palm trees and they were full of uninvited bees.

I ran up the steps and shouted, "Ma, it have a man outside here. He say he want to watch the bees."

My mother came out, looked at the man and asked in an unfriendly way, "What you want?"

The man said, "I want to watch your bees."

His English was so good, it didn't sound natural, and I could see my mother was worried.

She said to me, "Stay here and watch him while he watch the bees."

The man said, "Thank you, madam. You have done a good deed today."

He spoke very slowly and very correctly as though every word was costing him money.

We watched the bees, this man and I, for about an hour, squatting near the palm trees.

The man said, "I like watching bees. Sonny, do you like watching bees?"

I said, "I ain't have the time."

He shook his head sadly. He said, "That's what I do, I just watch. I can watch ants for days. Have you ever watched ants? And scorpions, and centipedes, and *congorees*—have you watched those?"

I shook my head.

I said, "What you does do, mister?"

He got up and said, "I am a poet."

I said, "A good poet?"

He said, "The greatest in the world."

"What your name, mister?"

"B. Wordsworth."

"B for Bill?"

"Black. Black Wordsworth. White Wordsworth was my brother. We share one heart. I can watch a small flower like the morning glory and cry."

I said, "Why you does cry?"

"Why, boy? Why? You will know when you grow up. You're a poet, too, you know. And when you're a poet you can cry for everything."

I couldn't laugh.

He said, "You like your mother?"

"When she not beating me."

He pulled out a printed sheet from his hip pocket and said, "On this paper is the greatest poem about mothers and I'm going to sell it to you at a bargain price. For four cents."

I went inside and I said, "Ma, you want to buy a poetry for four cents?"

My mother said, "Tell that blasted man to haul his tail away from my yard, you hear."

I said to B. Wordsworth, "My mother say she ain't have four cents."

B. Wordsworth said, "It is the poet's tragedy."

And he put the paper back in his pocket. He didn't seem to mind.

I said, "Is a funny way to go round selling poetry like that. Only calypsonians do that sort of thing. A lot of people does buy?"

He said, "No one has yet bought a single copy."

"But why you does keep on going round, then?"

He said, "In this way I watch many things, and I always hope to meet poets."

I said, "You really think I is a poet?"

"You're as good as me," he said.

And when B. Wordsworth left, I prayed I would see him again.

About a week later, coming back from school one afternoon, I met him at the corner of Miguel Street.

He said, "I have been waiting for you for a long time."

I said, "You sell any poetry yet?"

He shook his head.

He said, "In my yard I have the best mango tree in Port of Spain. And now the mangoes are ripe and red and very sweet and juicy. I have waited here for you to tell you this and to invite you to come and eat some of my mangoes."

He lived in Alberto Street in a one-roomed hut placed right in the center of the lot. The yard seemed all green. There was the big mango tree. There was a coconut tree and there was a plum tree. The place looked wild, as though it wasn't in the city at all. You couldn't see all the big concrete houses in the street.

He was right. The mangoes were sweet and juicy. I ate about six, and the yellow mango juice ran down my arms to my elbows and down my mouth to my chin and my shirt was stained.

My mother said when I got home, "Where you was? You think you is a man now and could go all over the place? Go cut a whip for me."

She beat me rather badly, and I ran out of the house swearing that I would never come back. I went to B. Wordsworth's house. I was so angry, my nose was bleeding.

B. Wordsworth said, "Stop crying, and we will go for a walk."

I stopped crying, but I was breathing short. We went for a walk. We walked down St. Clair Avenue to the Savannah and we walked to the racecourse.

B. Wordsworth said, "Now, let us lie on the grass and look up at the sky, and I want you to think how far those stars are from us."

I did as he told me, and I saw what he meant. I felt like nothing, and at the same time I had never felt so big and great in all my life. I forgot all my anger and all my tears and all the blows.

When I said I was better, he began telling me the names of the stars, and I particularly remembered the constellation of Orion the Hunter, though I don't really know why. I can spot Orion even today, but I have forgotten the rest.

Then a light was flashed into our faces, and we saw a policeman. We got up from the grass.

The policeman said, "What you doing here?"

B. Wordsworth said, "I have been asking myself the same question for forty years."

We became friends, B. Wordsworth and I. He told me, "You must never tell anybody about me and about the mango tree and the coconut tree and the plum tree. You must keep that a secret. If you tell anybody, I will know, because I am a poet."

I gave him my word and I kept it.

I liked his little room. It had no more furniture than George's front room, but it looked cleaner and healthier. But it also looked lonely.

One day I asked him, "Mr. Wordsworth, why you does keep all this bush in your yard? Ain't it does make the place damp?"

He said, "Listen, and I will tell you a story. Once upon a time a boy and girl met each other and they fell in love. They loved each other so much they got married. They were both poets. He loved words. She loved grass and flowers and trees. They lived happily in a single room, and then one day, the girl poet said to the boy poet, "We are going to have another poet in the family." But this poet was never born, because the girl died, and the young poet died with her, inside her. And the girl's husband was very sad, and he said he would never touch a thing in the girl's garden. And so the garden remained, and grew high and wild."

I looked at B. Wordsworth, and as he told me this lovely story, he seemed to grow older. I understood his story.

We went for long walks together. We went to the Botanical Gardens and the Rock Gardens. We climbed Chancellor Hill in the late afternoon and watched the darkness fall on Port of Spain, and watched the lights go on in the city and on the ships in the harbor.

He did everything as though he were doing it for the first time in his life. He did everything as though he were doing some church rite.

He would say to me, "Now, how about having some icecream?"

And when I said yes, he would grow very serious and say, "Now, which café shall we patronize?" As though it were a very important thing. He would think for some time about it, and finally say, "I think I will go and negotiate the purchase with that shop."

The world became a most exciting place.

One day, when I was in his yard, he said to me, "I have a great secret which I am now going to tell you."

I said, "It really secret?"

"At the moment, yes."

I looked at him, and he looked at me. He said, "This is just between you and me, remember. I am writing a poem."

"Oh." I was disappointed.

He said, "But this is a different sort of poem. This is the greatest poem in the world."

I whistled.

He said, "I have been working on it for more than five years now. I will finish it in about twenty-two years from now, that is, if I keep on writing at the present rate."

"You does write a lot, then?"

He said, "Not any more. I just write one line a month. But I make sure it is a good line."

I asked, "What was last month's good line?"

He looked up at the sky, and said, *"The past is deep."*

I said, "It is a beautiful line."

B. Wordsworth said, "I hope to distill the experiences of a whole month into that single line of poetry. So, in twenty-two years, I shall have written a poem that will sing to all humanity."

I was filled with wonder.

Our walks continued. We walked along the seawall at Docksite one day, and I said, "Mr. Wordsworth, if I drop this pin in the water, you think it will float?"

He said, "This is a strange world. Drop your pin, and let us see what will happen."

The pin sank.

I said, "How is the poem this month?"

But he never told me any other line. He merely said, "Oh, it comes, you know. It comes."

Or we would sit on the seawall and watch the liners come into the harbor.

But of the greatest poem in the world I heard no more.

I felt he was growing older.

" 'How you does live, Mr. Wordsworth?' " I asked him one day.

He said, "You mean how I get money?"

When I nodded, he laughed in a crooked way.

He said, "I sing calypso in the calypso season."

"And that last you the rest of the year?"

"It is enough."

"But you will be the richest man in the world when you write the greatest poem?"

He didn't reply.

One day when I went to see him in his little house, I found him lying on his little bed. He looked so old and so weak, that I found myself wanting to cry.

He said, "The poem is not going well."

He wasn't looking at me. He was looking through the window at the coconut tree, and he was speaking as though I wasn't there. He said, "When I was twenty I felt the power within myself." Then, almost in front of my eyes, I could see his face growing older and more tired. He said, "But that—that was a long time ago."

And then—I felt it so keenly, it was as though I had been slapped by my mother. I could see it clearly on his face. It was there for everyone to see. Death on the shrinking face.

He looked at me, and saw my tears and sat up.

He said, "Come." I went and sat on his knees.

He looked into my eyes, and he said, "Oh, you can see it, too. I always knew you had the poet's eye."

He didn't even look sad, and that made me burst out crying loudly.

He pulled me to his thin chest, and said, "Do you want me to tell you a funny story?" and he smiled encouragingly at me.

But I couldn't reply.

He said, "When I have finished this story, I want you to promise that you will go away and never come back to see me. Do you promise?"

I nodded.

He said, "Good. Well, listen. That story I told you about the boy poet and the girl poet, do you remember that? That wasn't true. It was something I just made up. All this talk about poetry and the greatest poem in the world, that wasn't true, either. Isn't that the funniest thing you have heard?"

But his voice broke.

I left the house, and ran home crying, like a poet, for everything I saw.

I walked along Alberto Street a year later, but I could find no sign of the poet's house. It hadn't vanished, just like that. It had been pulled down, and a big two-storied building had taken its place. The mango tree and the plum tree and the coconut tree had all been cut down, and there was brick and concrete everywhere.

It was just as though B. Wordsworth had never existed.

John Hearne

A VILLAGE TRAGEDY

The old boar slashed Ambrose Beckett across the top of his thigh, almost severed his private parts, and dragged three feet of his gut out on the tip of one tusk. It was done between one brazen squeal and another, while Ambrose Beckett still turned on the wet clay of the path and before the echo of his last, useless shot wandered among the big peaks around the valley.

The men with whom Ambrose Beckett had been hunting turned and saw the ridge-backed, red-bristled beast vanish like a cannonball into a long stretch of fairy bamboo. Before they reached him, they saw Ambrose Beckett's wildly unbelieving face, like gray stone beneath the brown, and the dark arches of his spurting blood shining on the wet dull clay under the tree ferns. Then he had fallen like a wet towel among the leaf mold, clutching the clay in his slack fingers, with one distant, protesting scream sounding from the back of his throat.

They bandaged him, after stuffing, inexpertly, bits of their shirts and handkerchiefs into his wounds. Nothing they did, however, could stop a fast, thick welling of blood from where he had been torn. And no comfort could stop his strangled, faraway screaming. They made some sort of stretcher from two green branches and a blanket. They covered him with another blanket and began to carry him across the mountains to the village. The trail was very narrow, and the floor of the rain forest was steep and wet. Each time they slipped and recovered balance, they jolted the stretcher. After a while, they forced themselves not to shudder as Ambrose Beckett screamed. Soon he began to moan, and the slow, dirty blood began to trickle from his mouth, and they knew that he would never reach the village alive.

When they realized this, they decided to send Mass' Ken's half-witted son, Joseph, ahead of them to tell the doctor and the parson. Joseph was the biggest idiot any man could remember being born in the village. He inhabited a world of half-articulate fantasy and ridiculous confusion. He was strong enough to kill a man with his hands, and he wept if a child frowned at him. In Cayuna, the children do not, as yet, throw stones at their naturals, but they tease them, and often Joseph, who loved to wait outside the school and watch the children going home, would be seen crouched between the roots of the cotton tree, weeping disconsolately because the boys had scowled as they passed and said, "Joseph! What you doin' here, man?" He could learn nothing, and remembered little from one minute to the next unless you dealt him a blow across the head when giving him the simplest instructions. But he was marvelous on the mountains: tireless as a mule and much faster.

Now, with Ambrose Beckett dying on the blanket, the men standing around gave Joseph his instructions. "Doctor!" said Mass' Ken, his father, and cuffed him across the head. "Doctor! You hear?" He hit him again. "Tell doctor an' tell parson dem mus' come quick. Tell dem come quick, you hear! Tell dem Mass' Ambrose sick bad. Sick! Sick! You hear!" Joseph's big, stone head rocked again under a blow, and his odd, disorganized face closed its askew planes into a grin of pure understanding. He went off among the huge trees and thick wet bush and into the mist. When he had gone ten steps they could no longer hear him.

It was twelve miles and four thousand feet down to the village, and he did it in four hours. At ten o'clock that night he started to bang happily on the door of the manse and kept it up until the Reverend Mackinnon put his head out of the window. When he heard the shutter slamming against the wall, Joseph ran to the middle of the lawn, capering and shouting.

"What?" called the Reverend Mackinnon. "What is it, Joseph?"

He could see nothing but a vague, starlit blur, bounding up and down on the lawn, but he recognized the manner and the voice. Joseph jumped higher and shouted again, his voice tight and brazen with self-importance.

Finally the Reverend Mackinnon came downstairs and cuffed the boy until he became calm. Then he got the story.

"Doctor!" he said, turning Joseph around and giving him a push. Leaving the parson, Joseph ran across the damp Bahama grass of the lawn to where he could see the deep yellow of a light in one window of a big house along the road. Doctor Rushie was still up; it was one of the nights that he got drunk, as he did, regularly and alone, twenty times a month.

"Good God!" said Rushie. "How far up did it happen?"

Joseph gestured. Distance, except in terms of feet and yards, was not of much importance in his life.

"Have you told parson?" the doctor asked. He was drunk, but not much. Had the news come a little later he would have been very drunk and quite incapable. He went to the window and bawled for his servant. "Saddle the mule," shouted Doctor Rushie, "and put on your clothes. Bring a lantern. Hurry up!"

In about five minutes the doctor was riding out of the village, with his manservant trotting ahead, the circle of light from the lantern sliding quickly from side to side across the path and making the shadows of the hillside and valley drop deeper. There was a stand of golden-cup trees along this stretch of the bridle path, and the dropped fruit broke wetly under the hoofs of the mule, and a thick, sugary scent came up on the cold air, cutting through the hot, oily smell of the lantern.

They overtook the Reverend Mackinnon, who had no manservant and who was riding his stubby, gray gelding alone in the dark. By the lantern light Doctor Rushie could see the parson's very pale long face and his lank gray hair fallen across his forehead and full of burrs from the long grass of the steep bank beside the narrow path.

"You've heard?" the doctor said. It was not really a question, and they were riding on in the darkness behind the bob and sway of the lantern while the parson was nodding his head.

BACK on the road, Joseph sat on a big stone outside the doctor's house. Nobody had told him what to do after delivering his messages, and he felt confused and restless. The doctor's house, and the Reverend Mackinnon's, were up the road from the village. Neither man had thought to inform the people down there as to what had happened on the mountain. Soon Joseph rose from the stone, ran down to the village, and began to race about the street from side to side, talking loudly to himself. It was not long before he had awakened every household within sound of his voice.

"Joseph, you bad boy," screeched Mr. Tennant, the schoolmaster. "What are you doing here? At this hour." Joseph flapped a big dirty hand at him excitedly. "Boy, if I bring a switch out to you . . ." Mr. Tennant said. Joseph shot away down the street like a dog, but he continued to talk very loudly.

Mr. Tennant, with a tight, moist smile on his plump lips and carrying a long supplejack cane, came from his house. Joseph bolted for the shoemaker's doorway. Only Elvira, Joseph's smallest sister, could get as much sense from his clogged speech as quickly as Mass' Emmanuel, the shoemaker.

"Joseph," said Mass' Emmanuel, as the natural found refuge in his doorway, "why you not sleepin', eh? What a bad boy. I've a good mind to let teacher flog you."

He put an arm across the boy's trembling shoulders and drew him close.

Joseph told him about Ambrose Beckett, imitating with great vividness the terrible, ripping twitch of the boar's head, writhing enthusiastically on the ground to show what it had been like with Mass' Ambrose. Mass' Emmanuel translated as people began to come from the houses. Then they all looked up to the hill at the other end of the village, to where Ambrose Beckett's house stood. They began to move toward the house.

"Lawd King!" said Miss Vera Brownford. "Fancy! Mass' Ambrose! A fine man like dat. Poor Miss Louise!"

She was the center of the older women of the village as they went up the hill to the house where Ambrose and Louise Beckett had lived for thirty years. Vera Brownford was ninety-eight or maybe a hundred. Perhaps she was much more. Her first grandchild had been born before anyone now alive in the village, and only a few people could still remember her, dimly, in early middle age. Her intimate participation in every birth, death, and wedding was, for the village, an obligatory ritual. She had lived so long and so completely that she had grown to want nothing except freedom from pain. She had even transcended the brief, fierce resurgence of the child's longing for recognition which had assailed her again when she was about seventy. At times the shadow line between life and death was not very distinct to her expectation, her desire, or her feeling, but she understood the terror and confusion that the crossing of the line brought to those younger than herself. And understanding this, she gave comfort as a tree gives shade, or as a stream gives water to those who fetch it, with a vast, experienced impartiality. It was her occupation.

Among the younger men and women Joseph was still the center of interest as they went up the hill. His mime performance of

Ambrose Beckett and the boar had begun to acquire the finish of art. In all his life he had never experienced such respect for his ability and knowledge. He was almost gone out of his poor mind with happiness.

"Joseph," said Mass' Emmanuel suddenly, coming back down the path which was leading them to Louise Beckett's darkened house, "Joseph. I forget. We gwine to need ice fe' pack Mass' Ambrose. Tell dem to give you ice. Ice, you hear. At Irish Corner."

He gave a five-shilling note to the boy and hugged the huge, smoothly sloping shoulders and smiled at him. Only for two people, Elvira and Emmanuel, would Joseph remember anything unaccompanied by a blow.

Joseph turned and raced down the path. He seemed to weave through the murmurous crowd like a twist of smoke. Before he was out of earshot they heard him singing his own chant, which was a mingle of all the hymns and songs he had ever listened to. He was always adding to it, and though it had no more conscious structure than a roll of thunder, it had a remarkable pervasive quality, coming to you from a dozen points at once, with odd limping echoes.

THE Reverend Mackinnon and Doctor Rushie met the party of returning hunters about five miles from the village. They heard the dogs barking and saw the lantern lights jump along the pines on the saddle between the peaks ahead of them. This was on the side of a great valley, on a trail worn through a stretch of ginger lilies. The night was very cold, and mist was coming down from the sharp, fuzzy peaks and piling into the valley below, and the air was full of a thin spicy tang as the hoofs crushed the long ginger-lily leaves against the stones.

"Ho-yah!" shouted the doctor's manservant when they saw the lights. "Is dat you, Mass' Ken?"

"Yes." The answer rolled back slowly, thin and lost in the air of the huge valley. "Who dere?"

"Doctor. Doctor and parson. How Mass' Ambrose stay?"

"Him dead!"

He was dead, right enough, when the two parties met. In the glare from the lanterns his skin was the color of dough and earth mixed, quite drained of blood. The blankets between which he lay were dark and odorous with his blood. His mouth had half opened, and one eye had closed tightly, twisting his face and leaving the other eye open. It gave him an unbelievably knowing and cynical leer.

"Well, I'll be damned," Doctor Rushie said, and then, seeing Mackinnon's face, "Beg your pardon; but look at that."

"Look at what?" the Reverend Mackinnon said stiffly. He had never liked Rushie much, and now he did not like him at all.

"His face. How many dead men have you seen?"

"I don't know. As many as you I suppose."

"Exactly," Doctor Rushie said. "Probably more. But how many have you seen die with one eye closed? You know, it's generally both eyes wide open. Sometimes both closed, but not often. Damned odd, eh?"

"I hardly think it's important, doctor," the Reverend Mackinnon said. His long, ugly, Scots face was tightly ridged with disgust. Only the presence of the villagers kept him polite.

"No," the doctor said, "it's not important. I just noticed it. Well, no point hanging around here. Let's get him home, eh?"

Going down the track, the doctor and the parson rode behind.

"What a dreadful thing to have happened, eh, doctor?" said the Reverend Mackinnon. "I can hardly believe it."

He always felt guilty about not liking Doctor Rushie; and he constantly asked himself wherein he as a minister had failed to contact the drunken, savagely isolated creature who rode behind him.

"I can believe it," the doctor said. "Do you know how many ways the world has of killing you? I was adding up the other night. It comes to thousands. Simply thousands."

The Reverend Mackinnon could find no answer to this. There were answers, he knew, but none that he cared to risk with the lonely, brutal man who, more or less, cared for the health of their village and a score of other villages in the district.

He's not even a very good doctor, the Reverend Mackinnon thought, and felt a cold flush of shame because the thought gave him satisfaction.

"He was such a strong, vital man, too," the Reverend Mackinnon said a little later. He was unable to bear the night with the mist blowing damp and cold across his face, and the bobbing lanterns lighting up the silent men as they scrambled awkwardly with the stretcher on the narrow track.

"He was a strong man," the doctor said dryly.

"Why, the other day I saw him clearing that land of his up by the river, with his sons. He was doing twice as much as they," Mackinnon continued.

"Oh, he was a good farmer, all right," the doctor agreed, in the same dry tone. "He ought to have been, with what he had acquired these last few years. He knew what he wanted, all right."

"He was an example to his community," Mackinnon said with solemn emphasis. "God-fearing and responsible. An example. If only he had had an education. They would have made him a justice of the peace. He was an example. A Christian example."

"Well, maybe the boys will become examples, too," the doctor told him.

"The boys," said the Reverend Mackinnon, "the boys have fallen far from the stem. Thomas has his father's sense of duty, but he is weak. Weak. And Sidney cares only for himself, his pleasures, and his land. He caused Ambrose Beckett a great deal of worry. Which one of them do you think will get the holding, eh? Thomas or Sidney?"

"Couldn't say," the doctor replied. "I was only Beckett's doctor, not his lawyer. Probably they'll have equal shares. He had enough, God knows, for these parts."

The Reverend Mackinnon frowned and shifted uneasily in the saddle. Oh, God, he said to himself, make Thomas get the holding. He looked somberly over the nodding head of his beast and at the vague blur of the stretcher. The men were moving fast now, because Ambrose Beckett was dead and they could heave the stretcher about quickly.

Twenty years before this, Ambrose Beckett had rented land from the church. It was the first move in a program which had made him the largest peasant farmer in the parish. It had been good land, and he had paid a good rent. But since the war, when everything had gone up, the rent had fallen to a fraction of the land's value, and the Reverend Mackinnon had been looking for some way to increase it. He was, essentially, a timid man, who felt courage and confidence only on Sunday, when he stood unassailable in the pulpit, beyond interruption, with God and the Hosts at his back.

His method of attack in the matter of the rent had been to mount a series of hints. Veiled and offhand at first, they had evolved, after three years, into frequent references about the difficulties and embarrassments of a priest in the modern world. Pride and timidity had kept him from stating an open claim. These and the reasonable certainty that Ambrose Beckett would, at first, refuse to pay more. Would refuse with the plausibility and righteousness of a man who valued an acre, really, more than he regarded a wife and who knew his own usefulness as a parishioner.

I am not covetous, the Reverend Mackinnon told himself in the darkness. I do not want it for myself. But the manse is falling to bits, and if I send Jean home next year she will need clothes. Perhaps two sets within the year; girls grow so fast at her age.

Given time, he knew, he could have persuaded Ambrose Beckett. It would have been painful, but it would have come. Now he would have to begin again with the sons. If Thomas were the heir, it would be easy. He was a gentle, almost girlish lad, very devout and proud of his family's influence in the church. But Sidney. Sidney would be difficult. Difficult and slow. And arrogant. He had always treated the Reverend Mackinnon with a casual politeness more infuriating than hostility. A bland indifference which only on occasion became genially ferocious. The afternoon, for instance, when Mackinnon had caught him making love to a little East Indian girl under a huge rock by the river. The lad had raised his head from beside the girl's blind, contorted face and stared at the parson with cool, amused malice. And the next day, Sunday, while Mackinnon was preaching a sermon on the sin of fornication, he had looked down from the pulpit to the front pew where Ambrose Beckett sat in a hot, high-buttoned black suit among his family and seen such a sparkle of conspiratorial intimacy in Sidney's eyes that he had floundered in his speech.

WHILE they were bringing the body of Ambrose Beckett down from the mountain, Joseph had reached the market town of Irish Corner. He knocked on the zinc fence around the shop until the Chinese keeper came down and a small crowd gathered. Then he told the story of Ambrose and the boar again, giving a really practiced and gigantic performance. He had great difficulty in making them understand what had happened, or what he wanted, but they finally got it. Then they cut a great block of ice, wrapped it in a crocus bag, hoisted it onto his head, and set him on the road back to the village.

He had hardly stopped running since the late afternoon, and he streamed with sweat as if he had been put under a hose; but he was not tired and he was crazy with excitement. He had never played such a central part in anything before.

Suddenly he slowed his long, effortless jog trot up the steep road. He stopped. The ice in its wrapping of crocus bag was cool and wet between his hands and on his huge, idol's head. From his great, heaving lungs there burst an ecstatic grunt. Ice . . . ice . . . *ice*. If he got back quickly, they would chip a white, glittering, jagged lump for him. A piece with a point around which he could curl his tongue. A bit to hold above his opened mouth, so that the cold, unimaginable drops would hit the back of his throat. A bit with edges he could rub across tightly shut eyelids and then feel the cold water drying on his skin. He danced with happiness, balancing the huge block as if it were a hat. As far up as his village, ice was still a luxury for all but the doctor, who had a machine which made ice cubes.

THE people at Ambrose Beckett's house heard the dogs as the men came up the hill. Louise Beckett rushed from the house and down the path toward the light from the lanterns. When she saw the stretcher she began to cry and moan wildly, covering her face and clutching her body. Her two sons came close to her.

"Mother . . . Mother," Thomas said. He embraced her tightly and began to cry too.

Sidney put his arm around her shoulder and said softly: "I will take care of you, Mother. I will take care of you. Don't cry. Don't cry."

Inside the house, the body was laid out on the kitchen table. The table was too short, and the feet hung over the edge. Doctor Rushie shut the people out and by the light of four lamps sewed up the hideous openings in Ambrose Beckett's body. Once during this operation he spoke, as if to the corpse. "You poor devil," he said, "this must have hurt like blazes. But the other thing would have hurt you more, and it would have lasted longer."

Outside, in the tiny stiffly furnished drawing room, Vera Brownford sat on the old-fashioned horsehair sofa. Louise Beckett sat close up beside her, resting her head on that old, indestructible breast which, thin and hard as a piece of hose pipe, was yet as hugely comfortable as a warm ocean.

"Cry good, child," Vera Brownford said. "Cry good. If you don't cry you will get sick. Oh, Lawd, it hard to lose a man. It hard to lose a good man like Ambrose. Cry good, child. It much easier."

The old, dry voice flowed smoothly, uttering banalities that sheer experience gave the weight of poetry. Louise Beckett cried noisily.

The women of the village stood around the sofa; the men gathered near the door and outside, each group around one of the hunters, who told in whispers what it had been like. The children waited on the fringes of each group; some of them looked with wide stares toward the locked kitchen door.

The Reverend Mackinnon hovered between the men and the women. Finally he went across to Louise Beckett. "Louise," he said, "you must take comfort. Remember your beloved husband is not gone. He only waits for you in our Master's house. He was a good man, Louise. A true Christian man. Take comfort in that and in the promise of everlasting life."

Louise Beckett raised her stunned face and looked at him from red eyes. "Thank you, parson," she whispered, and burrowed her head against Vera Brownford's breast.

Among the men, Sidney was saying in a hard unbelieving voice: "Jesus, it happen so quick. I tell you, Mass' Emmanuel, it happen before we even see it."

"How things happen so, eh?" Emmanuel said. "Truly, it is like the Bible say: in the midst of life we are in death."

"That is true, Emmanuel," said the Reverend Mackinnon, joining them. "That is very true." He laid a hand on Sidney's shoulder and gave it a little squeeze. "But remember, as Christians we need not fear death if we live so that death finds us prepared for God. We must remember the life God showed us through His only son, and, in our turn, live so that each day we can say to ourselves: Today I did God's will."

He looked closely at Sidney as he spoke, but the young man's face was closed, sullen with grief, unreadable.

Mr. Tennant, the schoolmaster, cleared his throat. He thought very highly of the Reverend Mackinnon, but he also felt that, in the village, he should reinforce the parson. Provide the practical epilogues to the more refined utterance of the church.

"It is you and Thomas now, Sidney," Mr. Tennant said. "You must act like men. Work the land as diligently as your father. Look after your good mother ..."

They heard a hard, heavy grunting outside in the dark, and then Joseph stepped into the room. He was lathered about the lips, with sweat and water from the ice mingled on his face and staining his clothes. Everyone stopped talking when they saw the ice.

Mass' Ken, Joseph's father, took the boy by the arm and led him into the bedroom. Four of the men who had hunted that day with Ambrose Beckett followed him. They stripped the clothes and mattress from the springs and spread old newspapers under the bed. They unwrapped the coarse, shaggy crocus from the ice, and one of the men split it into five great lumps with an ice pick. Then they spread old newspapers on the bare springs and waited awkwardly in the half-dark of the little bedroom where Ambrose Beckett had lain with his wife for thirty years.

Outside, one of the younger men who had been on the hunt laid his hand shyly on Sidney's arm. "Sidney," he said, "I sorry, you see. If it was me own Papa I couldn't sorry more. Lord, Sidney, don't worry. I will help you. You gwine to need anoder man fe' help you wid dat lan' you an' Mass' Ambrose was clearing. What you gwine to put in it, bwoy? It is one nice piece of ground."

Tears shone in Sidney's eyes. He was remembering how powerful and comforting his father had looked in the sunlight as they cleared the land by the river. His friend's words were sweet and warm and made him feel comforted again.

"T'ank you, Zack," he said, "t'ank you. Thomas an' me will need a help. Papa did want to put citrus in dat piece. Dat is de crop pay well now, you know. Since de war over, everybody want orange oil again."

Thomas looked suddenly and with disturbance at his brother.

"When Papa say we was gwine put citrus in?" he asked. "You know we only talk about it. Las' time we talk, you remember I say we should plant ginger. I like ginger. It safe."

"Everybody plant ginger, Thomas," Sidney said gently and inflexibly. "Papa did always say too much ginger was gwine to kill de small holders. Time some of us plant somet'ing else."

The door to the kitchen opened, and they saw Doctor Rushie framed in the opening, with the lamplight yellow behind him. Sidney and Thomas, Mass' Ken and Emmanuel went into the kitchen and brought the body out. Some of the women began to wail. Louise Beckett set up a long howling cry and ran across the room. She held the dead face between her hands. She was twitching like an exhausted animal.

"Mass' Ambrose," she cried, "Mass' Ambrose."

After they had packed the body among the ice lumps, the Reverend Mackinnon led them in prayer around the bed. Then the people started to go home. All went except Vera Brownford and three of Louise Beckett's closest friends, who stayed to watch the body.

It was now the blackest part of the morning, before the sun began to touch the mountaintops and make the sky glow with pink and green.

The Reverend Mackinnon went home and tiredly unsaddled his stumpy gray gelding. He went up to bed and thought about the gentle, exhausted wife he had buried two years before, and worried about the plump, soundly sleeping daughter a hundred miles away in boarding school.

Doctor Rushie went home, and his manservant led the mule away while the doctor sat down to finish the bottle he had been drinking when Joseph came. He thought about the wounds in Ambrose Beckett's body and whether, if he had got to him right away, he could have saved a life. He thought, also, about the sliver from Ambrose Beckett's rectum which he had sent down to Queenshaven for analysis a week ago and which, he was sure, showed the beginnings of cancer.

Lying in the bed they had shared from childhood, Sidney and Thomas clung to each other and sobbed in the painful, tearing manner of grown men. In between grieving for their father they argued fiercely and quietly as to the wisdom of planting citrus or ginger.

In the room with the body, the women sat and watched. Once Louise Beckett leaned forward and touched the damp sheet wonderingly.

"Mass' Ambrose?" she asked softly. "You gawn? You really gawn?"

In the kitchen of his home, Joseph snuggled into bed beside Elvira, his little sister, and began to cry bitterly. She woke when she heard him crying and asked him what was the matter. He told her how he had run all the way to Irish Corner, and back, with the ice, and of how no one had thought to give him a little piece. The ingratitude and thoughtlessness of the mourners shocked the little girl profoundly. She wiped the tears from his big, sweaty face and hugged him, rocking him in her thin arms and kissing him with little quick maternal pecks.

Very soon he was fast asleep.

John Hearne

THE WIND IN THIS CORNER

In the middle of the morning we drove out of the low, scrubby Queenshaven Hills and into the Braganza plain. It was very hot and dry outside, but in the car, going fast with the windows open, the heat was only pleasant: a warm, thick-textured rush of air, smelling of baked brick and a peppery grass tang of the deep country. Charlie McIntosh was driving us in his car, the big, always dusty, hard-used Buick that had covered every road in Cayuna bigger than a bridle path; I was sitting behind with my forearms resting on the back rest of the driver's seat; and Roger Eliot sat beside Charlie.

"Well, it's a good day for it," Roger Eliot said.

"A good day for what?" Charlie McIntosh asked, before I could nudge him to keep quiet.

"A good day for murder," Roger told him. "I don't like committing murder in bad weather. That spoils everything. Don't you think so, Charlie?"

"Cho, God!" Charlie muttered. He was the older man but he sounded like a boy who has gone too far with adults and has been brutally snubbed. "You don't have to talk like that, Roger. It's not funny."

His florid pleasant face was hurt and very Jewish, and as he squirmed in his seat, I felt the big car surge forward on a burst of new speed. Charlie always finds comfort and release, in any situation that seems to go beyond his grasp, by driving too fast, or by swimming furiously across harbor in which there are barracuda, or by getting drunk in a dozen widely separated bars, driving too fast to each of them.

"How are the other assassins?" Roger said and turned to look back past me and through the rear window. "Good. They're still keeping up. We won't have to do all the knife work alone."

"It might help if you shut up, Roger," I told him. "None of us is going to enjoy what we have to do. So why not stop whining as if you're the only one who hates it?"

28

His small green eyes were somber and forbidding as they turned to me, and his long, pale, ugly face was too vivid and yet empty. It reminded me of the sad, dangerous face you see, sometimes, when a man has been smoking ganja and feels all his connections with other men are down and is getting ready to kill or maim simply to assure himself that the gap he senses can be bridged. I made a fist and punched Roger gently on the shoulder and smiled. Sometimes people like Charlie and me, in the party, tend to forget how young Roger Eliot is. He is so good that it is easy to forget.

"Go on," I said. "I know what the Old Man means to you. But what about us, eh? You think we don't feel it too?" He made a wry, tired grimace of disgust and turned away and looked before him again. We were traveling through the cane fields now but from the rear window I could still see the hills, close behind us and faded by the long dry season. They were a dusty gray-green, stark and inhospitable under the glowing sky. Where the road had been laid across the saddle there was a white gash of limestone looking strangely alive against the bleached-out, dehydrated bush of the hill slope. The other cars were strung out along the straight road: Osbourne's Riley and Douglas' black Jaguar close together, and a good way behind, Dennis Broderick's old station wagon trailing a lot of dirty blue exhaust. The canes were all around us, close packed, tawny with the sun, stretching for ten miles down to the coast where the sky above the swamps was gray and hazy. The pink earth from the fields was dusted on the black road, and occasionally, as the trees churned the soft surface, a tickling earth smell mingled with the sharpness of hot asphalt would swirl briefly about the car.

"Do we have time to stop for a drink at Sherwood Bridge?" Roger asked me.

"Sure," I said. "Do you need one?"

"Good God, yes, man. I don't want to go into him cold. Do you?"

"No," I agreed. "A drink would be a good idea. Get rid of this lead in my stomach. We don't want to get caught up in Sherwood Bridge, though. How long since you've been there?"

"About three months," Roger said. "When I was speaking at the agricultural show. But it's Charlie's territory. When were you over last, Charlie?"

"Ten days ago," Charlie told him. "There shouldn't be much to hold us up today. They won't have many new things that need listening to. Besides, it won't be a bad thing for Eugene to show his face. He's been so busy in the Eastmoreland divisions he hasn't had time for Braganza."

"How's he doing in Eastmoreland?" I asked. "Are we going to win down there?"

"You tell me," Charlie said. "Does anybody ever know how Eastmoreland is going to vote? Jesus, I'm glad I don't have to fight the election down there. Those Eastmoreland boys kiss you on Monday and hang you on Tuesday, and nobody ever knows why they do either."

"They're not the only ones," Roger said. His voice wasn't pleasant. It was flat and too precise and full of that angry sadness I had seen on his face. "When it comes to kissing and killing, we're doing all right, aren't we, Charlie?"

I saw Charlie's hands tighten on the wheel. He had big hands, firmly fleshed and virile like the rest of his body, covered with reddish freckles and a thick pelt of fine dark hairs. When he turned his face briefly to Roger, the full red lips were thinly compressed and the heavy bar of his mustache made a melancholy, decisive sweep across his profile.

"When we stop at Sherwood Bridge," he said, dead and even, "you can take the car and drive back to town. Tony and I will go on with Eugene. If you don't want to do this, then you can back out now. Do anything you want but for Christ's sake stop all the bull-shit. I've had enough. You hear me?"

"Me too," I said. "I know Charlie and me and the rest of us are pretty coarse, Roger, compared with you, but just stop reminding us how sensitive you are, eh."

The strange thing about it was that I think we all knew what we were trying to do. We were trying to get angry with each other so that when we reached the Old Man there would be enough anger left for us to do the job properly.

"Oh, shut up, both of you," Roger said. He passed his hand roughly over his pallid, heat-shiny face. "Let me think what I'm going to say to him. You have any cigarettes left, Tony?"

"Sure," I said, and smiled at him as he turned round and took one from the packet. "Take it easy, boy. We've given you a nasty job, but take it easy."

"You want me to do it?" Charlie asked. "I'll do it, Roger. It ought to have been me from the beginning. Not you. It was a son-of-a-bitch trick asking you to tell him."

Roger looked at him sideways and gave a warm, harsh snort of laughter.

"You know something, Charlie," he said. "You're a nice old bastard. Only your mother and I know it, but you're all right. No. I'll do it. I have to."

"Let me do it," Charlie said. "It ought to come from me."

"Don't be damn silly," Roger said. "Of course I have to do it. If you or Tony or Eugene, or any of the others, initiated this it would finish him. When he thinks of the party and the movement now it's your faces he sees. All of you who were with him from the beginning, or who went to prison with him during the war. No, you couldn't do it. When I do it, I'll be speaking for the new guard, eh, for the hard young professionals who hope to govern this bloody island after the election. He'll understand that—just. I hope."

We drove on into the hot, sharp-shadowed plain. Nobody wanted to say anything more. We had said it all too often before this Sunday morning, and no amount of talking had made it any easier.

At Sherwood Bridge we stopped beside the yellow plastered wall of the Chinese grocery; when we climbed from the car and stood on the gritty pavement, the heat rose from the concrete and enfolded us. The water in the gutter ran slimy and tepid around the tires of the Buick, and a bright dense glare was flung into our faces from the whitelimed wall of the courthouse across the street. The little town had the dreamy, suspended feeling of Sunday morning and a church bell somewhere sounded thin and lost in the still air. In about a minute the first people began to gather round us, and by the time the other cars turned into the street there was a good crowd on the pavement outside the grocery. If only half of them meant to vote for us, it was still good to see that so many had collected so quickly.

There was a lot of excitement when Eugene Douglas' gray lion head emerged from his car, and further excitement, but lesser, when Osbourne and Broderick pulled up. Listening to the voices, I realized that unless the party did something very foolish we were in this time. Even allowing for the fact that this was the Old Man's parish, there was a note of recognition and pleasure in the voices that I had been hearing now for the last two months in other districts. It came from something more than the Old Man's personal influence, and we all had waited a long time for that sound from a crowd.

We went from the pulsing heat of the pavement into the green, bottle-glimmering coolness of the bar. Yap, the grocer, was standing behind the scarred wooden counter and smiling as he saw the crowd coming after us. Everyone was talking at once and somebody put a glass into my hand and Yap looked at me, pointing to a bottle of soda on the counter, and I nodded and he opened it, and handed it to me over the shifting heads. I splashed a little into the drink I had been given and watched the dark amber of the rum turn to pale gold and gave the bottle into a hand that reached out from the crowd.

This was the sort of gathering in which you realized how good Roger Eliot was. As I talked to the people around me, I could see him in the middle of his group, very tall, white-faced, with that distinctive, bony ugliness, turning from man to man unhurriedly. Each response was certain and intimate and you knew that he enjoyed this campaigning in the grass roots as most men enjoy being with a pretty woman. This was his gift. One of his many. Charlie McIntosh had it too, by background training and because being with the crowd made him feel happy, but he would never have, in addition, the cold, legalistic authority that Roger could turn on in the House like the controlled, merciless bursts from a machine gun. In the House, apart from the Old Man, the only person who carried more sheer weight was Eugene Douglas, and then only because he had more experience and had been with the Old Man from the very beginning. And nowadays when you sat in the visitors' gallery, facing the opposition benches, and saw Roger Eliot and Eugene Douglas lounging side by side, each with that bleakly exultant histrionic barrister's keenness on his face, you realized that Roger was the greater man. He was greater because he was younger and we had given him a party and a machine to inherit. Sometimes, I wondered if we had asked too much of him too soon. It seemed to me that a lot of youth and a lot of gentleness had vanished from that intense, tautly preoccupied face while none of us was really looking.

He began to tell a clever and destructive story about the government and even the men talking with Eugene stopped to listen. I had heard it before, but listening to him tell it I found myself grinning. It was all very personal and rather obscene, as stories like that tend to be in Cayuna. We all pretend to be outraged when we hear them against ourselves, and then we start digging up one about our opponents. When he had finished the laughter crashed around us like surf.

"Den tell me, Mr. Eliot," one of the men said; he looked like a cane worker or a small farmer, in for the day. "How we gwine do when election come? Who gwine win dis time?"

Roger grinned and pushed him roughly, like a father pushing a grown son with affection. Nobody else but Charlie or the Old Man could have done it in quite that way without patronage.

"Who gwine *win?*" he mocked the man, and appealed theatrically to the crowd. "Who gwine win? You hear him? We going to win, of course. How you can ask a damn fool question like that, man? Lord, but we getting some milk-an'-water workers in the party nowadays. Who gwine win?"

He clapped the man on the shoulder, hard, and grinned down at him, enjoying what he was doing so genuinely that the man grinned too, with delight and confidence, as the rest had already begun to chuckle and repeat what Roger had said.

When it was time for us to go, the men in the bar came out to the pavement and watched us getting into the cars. They were very pleased that we were going on to see the Old Man, and they waved us down the street until we turned the corner by the Methodist church.

Beyond the church there was an iron bridge spanning a shallow, dirty green river; sugar cane began on the far bank of the river and the great column of the sugar factory chimney towered red and harsh into the deep, soft sky. We could see the clean shimmers of heat rising from the road.

Two miles from Sherwood Bridge, Charlie turned the Buick into a pink, rocky side road, and as the big car lurched and jolted in the ruts, I could see, in the driving mirror, the others following. On the left there was a big dried-out pasture with the Old Man's famous mules grazing on the dusty stubble, along with four lordly jacks and seven swollen mares. In the field on the left there was a stand of heavy maize and another of dense, cool-looking tobacco. Then the road began to rise a little and there, just under the crest of the hillock, was the Old Man's house, and the Old Man, who must have heard the cars, standing against a pillar at the head of his steps, lifting his hand as we drove into the yard and parked in the shade of a breadfruit tree.

"Well, gentlemen," he said, and came halfway down the steps to meet us. "What an unexpected pleasure. Charlie, you young scoundrel, I knew you were coming. But not everyone else."

The great, square, cropped head moved forward on the enormous neck as he squinted into the yard to where Eugene Douglas, Broderick and Osbourne were getting from their cars.

"Eugene!" he called as he took my hand and Roger's simultaneously. "I almost didn't recognize you. I thought you must have left the island. . . ."

"D.J.," said Eugene and came up and put his hands on the Old Man's shoulders "How are you? I've been out of town every time you've come up. Things are tight in Eastmoreland and All Souls. We're going to need you in both places before the election. If we don't get at least one set of seats from those two we might lose again."

"We'll get 'em," the Old Man said crisply. "I promise you that. We have to, eh. We can't lose this time. Twice is as much as anyone can afford to lose in Cayuna. After that you're bad luck."

He stood, still holding Eugene by the arms, and smiling at us with the slight half-twist of his lips that, for as long as we could remember, had always accompanied his brief, almost aphoristic lectures on the strategy of practical politics. Each of us there, except Roger Eliot, could have written down about two hundred sentences, nearly proverbs, with which for over thirty years the Old Man had taught all he had learnt.

"No, gentlemen," the Old Man continued. "We cannot lose this time. Do not even entertain the idea. Now let's go in and spend a proper Cayuna Sunday morning. Good Heavens, but it's splendid to see you all like this."

He turned and led us up the broad steps: a short bow-legged old man, with immense shoulders and a back as broad as a bank door, who yet managed to appear of a height in a crowd of tall men. Always, in the past, when you had bent your head to talk to him you had felt as if he were making the concession. And now, as I watched his stiff-collared, immaculately linen-suited figure between the bright-patterned, fluttering sports shirts and casual slacks of Roger and Eugene, there was still enough of the old demonic authority left to make those two towering men appear somehow slight.

"Mildred!" The marvelous gong of a voice carried through the darkened, cool rooms of the old house. "Mildred, we have guests. Tell the girl to bring ice and all the rest of it. Come, gentlemen. Draw up your chairs here. The wind in this corner is always cool for some reason. Some accident of architecture. On the hottest day it's always pleasant here. I know how you Queenshaven people complain about our Braganza heat. It makes men, though. You need a furnace for a good sword."

Watching us as we drew the wicker chairs into a semicircle on the broad, wooden veranda, his old, wildly seamed face was firm and glowing with happiness. The huge, deerlike eyes sparkled. Once those enormous liquid eyes and that compactly massive, squat body had been very nearly irresistible. All over Cayuna, now, you could see men and women, of all colors, with those same brown pools that beautified the plainest face, and with those same sloping, heavy shoulders.

"D.J.," Charlie said, "you have any of that whisky you gave me when I was over last week? Jesus, but that was a whisky, man. Don't give it to these crows. They wouldn't appreciate it. Save it for you and me."

The Old Man laughed: an emphatic, musical bark. He glared at Charlie with a furious love that became suddenly too naked to witness without embarrassment. From the beginning, he had respected Eugene and Osbourne as nearly his peers, or been fond of those like Broderick and myself, but it had been Charlie who filled his hunger for the legitimate son he had never been able to have. Now there was only his daughter: a gray, plump woman called Mildred; silent and distant like so many country spinsters.

"Any of that whisky?" the Old Man said. "Charlie McIntosh, you're a damned blackguard, as I've always maintained. Gentlemen, that person you see making himself at home on my veranda came here last week and under the pretense of talking party business filled his gut with over a quart of the whisky I keep for important guests. . . . Mildred, for God's sake, child, where is the drink? You want these poor men to die of thirst?"

He raised his voice to an unconstrained shout, and rubbed his hands hard together as if crushing his pleasure to get its essence. Then as the maid came out with the drinks and Mildred followed her, he sat down. We rose and Miss Mildred nodded to our greetings with a disdain that we knew was not directed at us personally but at whatever fate or chance had caused men to leave her alone with only a genially tyrannical old father to care for. She saw to the maid as the girl set the big mahoe tray with its load of bottles, glasses, and a bowl of ice on the low veranda table. They both went inside again immediately. The maid was a big clumsy-looking girl, not wearing shoes, so I knew she must be from far back in the country, probably from the St. Joseph mountains. She seemed to be very apprehensive of Miss Mildred.

"Now," said the Old Man. He was alight with anticipation. Talking and drinking were two of the four or five things he had always liked doing best. He took us all in with one quick, hot glance. "Charlie, my boy, work for your living. Find out what these gentlemen would like and give me a whisky and water. You know how I like it."

"Yes," Charlie said, under his breath. "Five fingers of liquor and the dew off a blade of grass."

"What's that? What did you say?"

"Nothing, D.J. Nothing. Just thinking aloud."

"I hope so. I hope that was all."

I felt the smile on my face become unbearably strained and looked at Roger desperately, begging him in my mind to say what he had come to say and stop this ritual exchange between Charlie and the Old Man. Roger was carefully mixing himself a rum and ginger ale, not waiting for Charlie to help him, and not looking at anybody. You could sense the crushing Braganza heat in the bright yard, but the wind in the corner of the veranda was cool and gentle. As the Old Man had said it would be. As I had known it would be. I had sat here often enough. After a long time Charlie gave me my drink.

"Here's to victory, D.J.," I said, and lifted my glass.

"I'll drink to that, Tony." He smiled, raising his glass first to me and then to the others, and then ran his square-tipped, coffee-brown fingers energetically through the cropped, silver lawn of his hair. "My God, I'll drink to that. It's been a long time, eh? Thirty years. You boys were in your twenties. And Roger . . . were you born yet, Roger?"

"Yes," Roger told him. "I was born. I wasn't taking much notice you understand, but I was born."

"My God," the Old Man said again. "Sometimes it seems like thirty centuries and sometimes like thirty months. I used to think I was mad sometimes. Expecting this damned island to want independence. You remember what they called us then? 'The black man's party.' Well, if we never win an election we can be proud of that. There isn't a politician in the island now who wouldn't like to have that title for his party. That's our doing."

"You know what the government boys have started calling us these days?" Eugene asked him.

"No. What?"

"The white man's party. I heard Gomez saying that over in Eastmoreland the other day."

The Old Man threw his head against the back of his chair and laughed. The wickerwork gave that peculiar shushing creak of straw as the chair shook under him.

"Why?" he asked, and chuckled again. "Why?"

"Oh, because of Roger, I suppose. Charlie, too, if you count Jews. Mostly because Fabricus is standing in Eastmoreland and is being very popular. It's his old parish, you know? Before he came to Queenshaven. He's beginning to frighten the government now, so Gomez decided to use his color against him."

"Lack of color, you mean," the Old Man said with delight. "Good. That's what I like to hear. Black man's party. White man's party. Jew man's party. Chinaman's party. They'll soon run out of labels. Each time they clap another one on us, it means we're hurting them somewhere."

"We've got them running, all right," Charlie said, "but it's going to be close. They could edge us out yet."

"Close!" the Old Man said. "Of course it's going to be close. But it's our election. I can smell it. If we get in this time, and the next, we're set for a long innings. Good God! After thirty years' fighting, to sit with men like you on a government front bench."

He leaned forward and gave his empty glass to Charlie. The stretched, deeply grooved skin of his face was burnished with the drink he had just taken. Charlie mixed him another quickly and he leaned back again. The long stomach was quite flat under the gleamingly starched linen waistcoat, and in the irreducible, worn bronze of his face, the eyes were much too young and adventurous.

Now, I said to myself, now, Roger. He's given you the cue. Say what you have to say. For all of us. If you don't say it now, when will you ever say it?

I heard the shallow heave of Eugene's breathing beside me. Broderick's fat yellow face was beaded with little unattractive drops of sweat. Charlie was a still, untidy heap in his chair, and Osbourne had begun to finish his drink in small, ridiculous sips.

"Look, D.J.," Roger said. "We haven't come out just to finish your liquor. We want to talk a few things over with you. Election business. And about afterwards."

His precise and resonant lawyer's voice was a little high. He looked into his drink, then swallowed half of it.

"Of course," the Old Man said. "I have a number of points I want to raise myself. I shall be putting them before the executive, officially, when we meet in Queenshaven next week, but so many of you are here this morning that I'd like to discuss them now."

"What we had in mind—" Roger said.

"I made a memorandum," the Old Man said. "Mildred was typing it for me last night. I'll go and get it. . . . Gentlemen, your glasses are empty. Charlie McIntosh, you dog, see to your duties or I'll cut you off with a shilling."

He stood up and his stiffness in getting from the chair was barely perceptible. And then we were looking at each other and listening to the slow, decisive footsteps going across the wooden floor of the old-fashioned drawing room.

"He never even listened," Roger said. "Has he ever listened? He's run this damned party so long he thinks it's his personal property. There's no easy way out of it now, Eugene. I'm going to give it to him straight. He won't understand it otherwise."

"He *was* the party," Broderick said sullenly. "He was all the party this island had when you were still wetting your pants, Roger. When I was half your age, he was burning up Cayuna like a bush fire. He has a right to say his say. More right than any of us. My God!"

Roger turned on him with the speed of a biting dog, and I could almost touch the relief and eagerness with which he fastened on a cause for anger. On the excuse for any heat that might drive him through what he had to tell the Old Man.

"Right, Broderick," he said. "You do it. Or don't let's do it. Just as you all please. Say the word, gentlemen, and I'll stop where I started and we'll listen to what he has to say, as we always have. . . ."

He was shaking with desolate rage.

"We'll listen," Eugene said quietly. "We'll listen as we always have. And we'll learn something, as we always have. But not until you've told him he can't stand for election again, Roger. Not until you've told him that he has to leave the House. That's what we came out here for, and you are going to do it, aren't you?"

"Yes," Roger said, and the word was rough with the violence of his conflict. "Yes, I'm going to tell him what he should have realized for himself. But I don't want any of you old comrades-in-arms looking at me as if it's all my idea."

"Nobody is doing that," Charlie said heavily. "Just do what you have to and get it over. It's going to be kinder that way."

Then we heard the Old Man's emphatic footfall coming back across the drawing room. He stood in the doorway studying two closely typed pages of foolscap, his rolled-gold spectacles pushed up on his forehead. God knows why the Old Man had ever worn spectacles. His vision hadn't altered much between seven and seventy-five. But he wouldn't read the posters on a wall without an elaborate performance of taking out the ancient, faded almost colorless, morocco case, removing the spectacles, putting them on carefully, and then, as carefully, pushing them up on his forehead, almost to the hair line. This had become part of his legend. Cartoonists used it. Little barefoot boys in the street acted it. Visitors to the House stayed to see it. It hadn't done us any harm at all.

"Gentlemen," the Old Man said, "I was considering our tactics the other night." Still studying his sheets he stepped onto the veranda and settled in his chair with a grunt. "I feel that we are going to need more emphasis in the north. Much more than we've given it up to now. It has always been our weak spot and we've always dodged it. Not any more though, gentlemen. We're going to take the fight to them—"

"D.J.," Roger said; his voice was calm now, and weary, but suddenly assured. As he sat there, leaning forward with his elbows

on his knees and holding his glass in both hands, I could see two
hectic smears of color along the cheekbones, beneath the very
pale, normally waxen skin. "D.J., before you get on to the general
plan of the campaign, there is something we'd like to discuss. It's
very important."

The Old Man looked up, the frowning flicker of his impatience
merely suggested within the lustrous vitality of his eyes, like the
lightning you thought you saw behind the mountains at night.
"Certainly," he said to Roger. "We have all day. You're all staying
to lunch, by the way. I've told Mildred. What's come up, Roger?
You sound worried." He sprawled easily, in that long familiar
slouch of confident readiness, his face tightening into a still, sharply
edged cast of experienced attention, the face of an old hunter to
whom any problem is a repetition of one known long ago and yet
one needing care because some detail is always new. "Elections!"
he said happily. "They always bring more trouble than any blasted
thing I know. Even women. They're the price we pay for being
politicians."

"D.J.," Roger asked him, "have you ever thought of giving up
the House? Giving up parliamentary work, I mean, and using
yourself on the trade union side?"

"Giving up the House?" We sat in a sort of hypnotized absorp-
tion as we watched bewilderment and then exasperated dismissal
of an unworthy waste of time struggle for place in the Old Man.
"Roger, boy, what the hell are you talking about? If that's what's
on your mind, I'll settle it right away. No. I've never thought of
leaving the House." He gave a short bark of laughter, half annoyed, half indulgent. "Not until the people of Braganza parish vote
me out, at least. And they've been sending me up for thirty years
now. What in God's name brought this on?"

"You," Roger said. "And the elections. And thinking about you
after the elections."

"And what I'd be doing in trade union work at my age," the Old
Man said, ignoring him still with the same wry anger that was no
more than the quick reflex of a stallion at stud, "I don't know.
What's the matter, has Brod been neglecting his duties there?" He
winked at Broderick, who was the leader of the trade union congress that during the years had grown into affiliation with the
party, and Broderick grimaced back at him stiffly as Roger got to
his feet. He stood deliberately, and the three steps he made along

the veranda and the three steps back were deliberate also, controlled and almost pensive, and when he stood above the Old Man, I thought, "Merciful Heavens, he looks just like the Old Man did that afternoon during the war when they came to arrest him for sedition as he left the House." And it was true. Roger as he stood there, elongated rather than merely tall, grotesquely thin, hunched in his bright shirt like a harlequin in the mime, all knobs, angles and elbows, with his tapered yet ugly hands jammed into his trouser pockets, was invested with the same moment's quality that I had seen on the Old Man when they arrested him, politely enough and on the steps outside because members were immune while the House sat: a quality at once angry and serene, dispassionately implacable with the sense of utter conviction.

"D.J.," Roger said. "Will you listen?" And the Old Man looked up quickly, as the weight of that charged voice roused in him his first serious apprehension. "Yes," the Old Man said. "Go ahead, Roger."

"We're asking you to resign your seat," Roger said. "To resign and not make it an official executive matter. We want you to join Broderick in the trade unions and do the sort of field work you still do better than anyone else. The executive want you to present them with your resignation when you come up next week."

"The executive," the Old Man said. "I didn't know the executive . . ." His voice had become thick and uncertain and when I saw the papers in his hand begin to shake I looked away. I didn't want to look at the others. "The executive," the Old Man said again, and then harshly, astonishment, not protest, but stark incomprehension, lending strength to the uncertain voice, "Why? I must have a reason for this." The great eyes as they stared at Roger were dulled, opaque and absolutely still and his face had a livid rigidity, as if he had gone beyond a point of disbelief to where the personal shock was much less than a sense of awed encounter with some fathomless and abstract phenomenon. "Why?" he demanded.

"Because we are going to win this time," Roger said, "and you could not stand five years as chief minister. No, listen, D.J. Let me finish." He was pleading and almost anxious now, hurrying what he could into the destruction we had chosen him to commit. "Do you have any idea what we're going to have to do in the next five years, after we get in? What sort of mess we have to clear up?

There's five hours' paper work a night for any minister. Let alone the business in the House during the day. Half the year we'll be beating around Europe and America raising capital investment. Off one damn plane, into another, living out of suitcases, fighting it out at all-day conferences for an extra million dollars. Do you really think you could do that, D.J.?"

The Old Man's gesture was unthinkably distant and disinterested.

"I believe," he said conversationally, almost absently, "that I have proved my capacity for work in the past. Go on. I should like to hear this to the end."

His gaze traveled to each of us, with a flat, bleak absence of surprise that was far worse than recognition of treachery. It was then, I think, that the necessary, hungrily sought anger that had eluded Roger all morning finally seized him.

"Listen!" he shouted. "Listen, D.J." Not pleading and anxious now, but shivering in an ecstasy of inextricable rage and sadness. "You can't do it. You know you can't do it. However much you want to. It's a government you'll have to lead in October, not a radical opposition. You'd last a year, maybe two, and then you'd have to go. And even then you wouldn't have done your work properly. Well, we're not going to waste you like that, you hear? What you started in this island and what you built with us is too good to throw away. We want to use you where you'll do a job on the sugar estates or on the wharves, and among the fishermen. That's what you know. That's what you can do standing on your head. Tell me that isn't so. Tell me that isn't so, if you dare."

"I don't agree," the Old Man said.

"You don't agree." It was hard to tell whether the rasp in Roger's voice was savagery or tears or triumph. "Of course you don't agree. Not now. You want to be on the front bench with us. That's what you saw thirty years ago. A front bench with men like Eugene and Charlie and Tony and me. Well, you've got it for us. But it's not for you. And you'll know it tomorrow. You probably know it already because that's the sort of man you are. If you weren't, do you think I'd be standing on this blasted veranda saying what I've just had to say?"

He was bent over, folded from the waist in that slightly incredible fashion of the immensely tall whose skeletons seem to struggle for release from the too scanty flesh, as if he were not bent but suspended from the ceiling by a wire attached to the base of his spine; his face, thrust close to the Old Man's, suffused now with the uncontainable mixture of sadness and pure fury, compelling from the Old Man, now, by some sheerly visible, silent and terrific explosion of will, an acknowledgment not only of those truths by which he had taught us to live in our work but of how well he had taught those truths to us, both men locked and isolated within that explosion of shared service, love and integrity of purpose, neither man conceding one particle of his anger or sorrow or stubborn righteousness until reluctantly, tentatively, then with sudden and prodigal generosity, the will of the older man recognized the faith behind the will of the younger, recognized that and saluted, also, what it must have cost a man as yet so young and vulnerable.

"Good God, boy," the Old Man said softly, "don't stand there like that. I feel as if you're a tree about to fall on me. Sit down."

Roger sat, in the slow careful fashion of a man who has been exhausted to a point where he dare not trust his muscles to perform the simplest action. As slowly he took his right hand and a handkerchief from his pocket and wiped the film of damp and grease from his face. He grinned lopsidedly at the Old Man. It was a hot day. Such as you get only in Braganza. In the middle of the cane fields, on the south side of the mountains, cut off from the northern trades and too far from the sea to catch the breeze. Even in this corner of the Old Man's veranda you could feel a declaration of heat, distinct and independent, parasitically attached to the accidental current of cool air.

"I did not realize," the Old Man said, "that this was the feeling of the executive. Of course I shall be proud to accept whatever you may suggest. Gentlemen! Your glasses are empty again. There is plenty of time for another before lunch. Charlie!"

His gaze, withdrawn but courteous, roved across our circle, not so much repudiating contact as, for now, impervious to what might mistakenly be offered as a substitute. Passed round us until it rested on Roger where he sat wrapped in his own exhaustion like a Mexican in his blanket.

Hot, I thought, dry hot. No rain. Much more of this and the Old Man will have to buy grass from the hills for his mules and his jacks and those mares in foal.

I don't know why this occurred to me then. Perhaps to protect me from an act of intimacy we had all witnessed but from which all but two of us had been excluded.

Daniel Samaroo Joseph

TAXI, MISTER!

HEY! Taxi, mister! Last car for town tonight. It late like hell. You
won't get another car leaving San Fernando. Come in, neh, man!
Going right away. I have four passengers already . . . is only you I
waiting for. Good, come in. Ease up inside there, partner. Don't
shut the door so hard. Jeez! Four slam like that and all the money
I working for go in glass. Okay, all set now. Port of Spain direct.
Okay, take it easy; I won't kill all you. I know this road to a tee;
on it for more than six years; never make an accident. Who, me?
Nah, man. This same car? Bounce a cart last week Friday? Oho, it
wasn't me driving it, man; was my brother. You find he resemble
me? Yes, somebody find so too. But he can't drive like me. I . . .
Jeez! What the hell wrong with he? Coming so fast and he won't
dip he light. Ah bet that's a English car with they twelve-volt
lights—they bright for so. When you see them fellars coming so
fast is because they done pass the police jeep down the road. I go take
it easy myself; I ain't want no case tonight. Hear how sweet the Chev
running? Watch how she making Pointe-à-Pierre on high and I
never touch the engine since I have it, and she still burning forty oil.
But is the gas what does cut me skin. These people in Trinidad
good wutless, you know; they making the gasoline here and they
still charging more than everybody else. Everything raising; money
hard to get and work harder. Even sweet drink and all going up.

Look that fellar there stopping me. Ah better pick him up. He
never to get nothing to carry him down after this. What happen,
friend? Where you going? Town? Dollar. Yes, I know this is Cali-
fornia . . . you know is after eleven already? Dollar or you see your
tail till morning. Okay, see you then. That's the trouble with—
What happen? Why he won't make up he mind? Come quick, pal.
Put your grip in the trunk. It could open; the lock break. Make
yourself small inside there. Close the door easy. Lewwe go. You see
for yourself, friend, you find out it don't make no sense to hang
around there the whole night.

All you does find it so hard to pay the fare. Me never to take a chance for nothing. Just so one night I pick up a fellar near Chaguanas. I had five passenger already and it was late, near midnight, when he jump out the bush on the side of the road and call on me to stop. I was full already and I didn' want to stop, but all the passenger in the car say they sorry for the fellar, and to stop. So I stop. When the fellar come up he say he only got one shilling if I go take that. Well, I in this taxi work million years and I know all them kinder tricks. People try telling me is they last twelve cents and they last shilling. Me ain't come here yesterday, nah; I born and grow up in this Trinidad and that kinder ole talk never get me.

You see any time I passing through Couva right here by the police station I always remember the coffin ah see in the middle of the road. As soon as the car light shine on it two fellars in black pick it up and walk away with it. At first I say it was police, but ah see them walk cross the road and go in the cane field on the other side. Who, me? 'Fraid spirit? You talk smart. We ain't in business with obeah people at all. I catch enough hell from them. Me father dead with a spirit, and a sookooyant used to suck me sister till she come thin like a matchstick. Lemme done with this talk; me don't want to call spirit, eh? Any of all you have a cigarette there? Ah feeling for a smoke; ah forget to buy in San Fernando. Who say that? Is you, friend? You charging me wrong. Me ain't like all them other fellars who does drive taxi. I does always buy me own cigarettes. First time ah run short. Right, nah, forget the match. Ah go use the lighter in the car.

Yes, I was telling all you bout the fellar who stop me one night near the bridge going up Chaguanas. Just now ah go show all you the place ah pick him up. He telling a man like me is the last shilling he got. I say, "Okay, pal, if you won't ease me up is your funeral," and ah start to pull out when a ole fellar in the car, one of the passenger, tell me I mustn't be so hard on people on the road, and when I do good for people they go do good to me. . . . Look, is right here ah pick up the fellar. . . . Well, me ain't believe in all this do-good foolishness. It don't work out. I ain't know. It must be all right for other people, but I tired do for people, and when ah take stock in the long run is me what does pay for it again.

So I turn to the passenger what telling me 'bout doing good and ah say, "Listen, mister, when the police hole me for overloading, you think I go tell them they must do good to me and lemme go?" Ah never hear that in forty-four years. Them police on this road too thirsty. They doesn't want no nancy-story at all. From the time they hold a taxi man is because he done try. The magistrate don't forget to pepper we skin. Then ah tell the passenger if you talking so much 'bout doing good, do good yourself. If you so sorry for the fellar as you say, well, pay the extra fare for him, and done the ole talk right there. What you say, friend? Because me ain't taking no chance for nothing. He ask me how much more, and when he hear is only thirty cents more, he say he loaded; he go pay. Well, what the hell I care who pay, once I get the right amount.

So the fellar get inside and we making road for town. Up to today any time I pick up anybody on the road in the night I always remember that night. Is about four years now that happen.

You see this Caroni big bridge? For a big bridge so, I find it too narrow. One day a fellar was coming here in a new car he just take out from the agent and he was going hell hard when he reach this bridge. Another car was on the bridge already, so he had to stop; but you should know he mispitch and he land straight down in the river. He lose he car and he was damn lucky he not lose his life too. Anyhow he come out all right in the whole thing. It was a private car, and how! You don't know insurance give him a new car! That is something I don't understand. A poor man like me have a car, and because I making a living with it running hired, they won't give a full insurance on it. When I in a accident is my tail where does have to pay for it. As soon as a fellar that have money damage he car, insurance glad like hell to give him a new one. Well, they say the more you have, the more you does get.

Anybody for San Juan? Who, you, friend? I thought you say you was going to town. Okay by me, but is the same dollar, you know. How you mean? No. They ain't have no schedule on this road at all. Ah sorry, friend.

Well, as ah was saying, ah pick up the fellar and we making good for town. All the road the fellar who say he like to do good, the same fellar who paying the fare for the other fellar giving me a long story about how I must treat people good and a lot of pep talk. Me ain't paying he no mind. I drive me car and come right into town. When we reach the railway taxi stand, time come for the fellar who say he loaded to pay. He cry out somebody thief he wallet. He say he had twelve dollars and some small change in it. It was in he breast pocket. Well, I turn on the house light and we dig up all over the car but nothing doing. The fellar start to kick up ole Harry. I myself vex too bad because ah in to lose all round: he own fare and the extra thirty cents he was paying. I ask him what we go do. Do? He say we go find that wallet tonight if we have to search all the passengers.

Well, to tell you the truth, for all the noise ah does make, me don't like that kinder talk. Searching passenger! That is police work. So I tell him lewwe go to the police station and report the whole thing. He say he don't want to go to the police; they go keep him back too long; he busy. Lewwe stay right here and search the rest of them. But I make up me mind already, and ah shove in a gear and we went straight to St. Vincent Street headquarters.

When you crooked you good crooked, you know. You say you getting out at San Juan, pal? This is you stop. Anything in the trunk? Wait lemme see if is a dollar. People tired passing all kinder ole foreign money on me head for a dollar. Okay. Oho! You want to hear what happen?

Well, you go laugh at me. You should know when ah reach headquarters ah find out ah get stick big, big. The fellar who say he lose the wallet was a ole thief. The police know him long time. He never own twelve shilling in he life, far less twelve dollars. So I lose the dollar fare from he and the extra thirty cents he promise to pay for the other fellar.

And that ain't all. The police buss a charge on me for overloading on the bargain. I went quite in the station with the six passengers I had. That is what does happen when you do good. Okay, friend. Thanks. See you again.

Port of Spain direct!

Ismith Khan

A DAY IN THE COUNTRY

Whenever the rain came pelting its pitchfork tines through the night like that, it slipped in under the covers, up through the mosquito nets, and slid into the pores of wood in the flooring. I could rub away the wood of the windowsill with my fingers, texture it between thumb and index finger as though the loose pulp were part of the rain. The crisp white curtains which hung like stiff embossed parchment, scratching the windowsills like birds' claws, the night before now hung limp, awkward, and misshapen because the land at Tunapuna, where my uncle lived, was low and already soaked.

On these mornings, the chimney of the kerosene lamp, which gleamed the evening before, accumulated a wide ring of dark brown soot around its neck so that the lamp gave off a mellow bronze light in the little room my cousin and I slept in with its old gramophone of dark mahogany, old brown photographs of uncles, aunts, and grandparents on the center table, and the ornate glasses and cups whose only function was to rattle as they jogged each other with a strange and eerie ring whenever there was a mild tremor of earthquake in the middle of the night. I had asked my cousin once what the glasses on the cabinet reminded him of and he said old people who smelt like the dust that collected in them. They had, on nights like this, reminded me of all the far countries of the world which we had seen in pinks, purples, greens, and blues on the large map in the Tunapuna school, and in my own way I had come to think that those glasses and dishes which were of the same color as the countries on the map had come from them. I think I also felt that to tell this to my cousin would make me seem very foolish. He was twelve, and I ten, and then too, he already had a bicycle and a pair of long pants which he could wear on Sundays.

As I lay in bed I could hear the long broken threads of gray water falling on the galvanized roof, sliding along its grooves into the spout, then into the great "copper" which my uncle kept at the corner of the house outside in the yard. It was overflowing now, and as I lay awake I wondered what would happen to the spiders and the spider webs under the huge copper, which stood a few inches above the ground on boulders buried in the earth.

The light outside was turning as pale a pink as snail shells, the sky filled with a similar translucence of the shells down by the sea, and the house, although still dark, was filled with light from the kerosene lamp, which still burned. The rain would clear up in an hour or two, the sun would come out and make the wood on the windowsill crisp again. It would be a crystal-clear Saturday and you could tell it already.

"Rajo . . . Rajo," I heard my aunt calling, "time to get up. Is Saturday, you know."

My uncle only groaned a few times while she went busily moving about the little house softly on her bare feet. And although you could not hear her footsteps, you could hear the pictures on the walls shake gently as the house moved on its loose foundations like a toy house put together by stacking cards one on top of the other, awaiting a real earthquake which never came.

One of the boys from the village who had gone to America to study engineering warned my uncle about the house and its foundations. But my uncle, who read everything from *Automobile Manufacturing in 1880* to *Inscriptions on Ancient Tombstones in the British Isles,* explained to the young engineer that the house was now settled and had "give" to it, and would therefore never collapse.

"But this man like to sleep an' sleep . . . Rajo . . . AY RAJO! Saturday come! Wake up an' open the shop befo' people come and catch you in bed. You ain't have no shame or what?" my aunt called a little more forcefully.

My uncle had sworn that she had a clock built into her head, and a long time ago when roaches stole into their alarm clock and ate through its white paper face, he never bothered to get a new timepiece. It still stood on the shelves of the shop, its white face mottled brown and disintegrating a little more each year, its dust falling into a small neat pile behind the glass, keeping its perpetual and awkward-looking five past four, so that you could not help but wonder just what the state of this household was on that particular day when the clock had stopped.

First there were sounds of a cutlass chipping away at boxwood, making fine long splints which my aunt would arrange like a bird's nest in the center of a bed of black charcoal in her earthen fireplace. And now, perhaps because the coals and the kindling were damp, there was the wonderful aroma of breakfast spreading through the house, of its fire being built, and that aroma was enough to make our mouths water with anticipation of what wonderful things the fire in the kitchen would yield up.

This was our signal to get up too or my aunt would be rapping on the door with her wooden pot spoon. I think that my cousin Kemal had had a few whacks with that very spoon many a time, although I doubt it would happen during my stay for the August vacation from school. My cousin and I were up and we made for the kitchen, where the air was warm and not quite so damp, our towels wound around our waists like loincloths, but before we could investigate what was for breakfast, we had our orders from my aunt.

"March out! March out!" she ordered, her pot spoon held high, pointing in the direction of the copper in the yard, which could be seen through the small window in her kitchen. And so, out into the rain, each armed with cups made from milk tins we "marched out" to take our morning baths, dipping water from the overflowing copper and pouring it over our bodies.

As the water hit Kemal's body, he jumped up and down trying to make as loud a noise as he could with his feet, slapping hard on a piece of old board that squelched in the wet earth. "Don't jump," came an order from my aunt, whose head disappeared again in the kitchen window. I thought I saw Kemal's body stop in mid-air for a second at the command, then come down slowly to earth again . . . to writhe only as the cold rainwater washed over his body, raising each fine hair to a bristle. When we had dried ourselves and come into the kitchen, my uncle was brushing his teeth in a slow circular motion, using a fresh hibiscus stem which my aunt had cut from their fence in front of the house. He looked out into the gray light, dipping his toothbrush in a mixture of salt and ground-up charcoal on the windowsill. There was a peculiar leisureliness about him that was a pleasure to watch, especially beside **my aunt**,

who moved swiftly, her white orhani and white skirt flying as she
darted this way and that. I had heard my grandfather say long ago
that her sternness and her swiftness came from the fact that she
was a peasant girl and was used to hard work and early rising on
the sugarcane plantations. And indeed, she resembled some of the
goddesses in the Indian paintings which hung on the walls of their
home, painted in dark purples, with large breasts and hips and feet
formed with arches and toes like sculpture which pointed upwards
like hers did as she took each long striding step.

"Chan, Kemal, Rajo," she rapped on the table for attention and
with her eyes pointed out to us where we should each sit. My uncle
moved slowly to his seat, almost with a kind of defiance of the
haste which all her orders automatically inspired. They spoke very
little, and yet they seemed to have a quiet kind of language going
on between them which they alone understood. We had placed
before us a roasted eggplant with a clove of garlic peeping out of
it, and at its sides were six singed tomatoes, which were also in the
hearth, steaming as their aroma rose in the air. Our cups were
already filled with dark brown cocoa, which she roasted and
ground herself. My uncle began by scooping out the insides of the
eggplant, then peeling the tomatoes, which he crushed up in a bowl
with some raw onions, while my aunt kept turning the last of the
"rotis," round flat breads which she roasted in the open fire.

It was now time to open up the shop with its thousands of
items: foods, medicines, hardware, toys. There were safety pins,
balloons, aspirin, butter, rice, dried codfish; there was a cake of ice
outside in front of the shop for the sale of aerated drinks. The shop
itself was quite simple. No one remembered how it had started in
the village, but how my uncle and aunt came by it was through my
grandfather, the ancient head of a large family of thirteen sons and
three daughters. My uncle Rajo, it seemed, long ago wanted to
become an engineer, go abroad and study in different countries,
but my grandfather, who felt that some of this great tribe should
remain always close to the soil, the people, the country districts,
had decided one day that Rajo should stay while others did other
things. He bought the place, had a house built onto its side, found
a "good hardworking girl" from the sugar estates, and moved Rajo
out of the family home into his own, equipped with everything:
wife, furniture, all the way down to the safety pins and the alarm

clock on the shelf of the shop. No one disappointed the old tyrant, and Rajo, just as was predicted, soon got used to shopkeeping. He learned what to purchase, and got other items as well. The shop consisted of a long wooden counter, under which were the opened bags of rice, flour, sugar, salt, their tops rolled up like shirt sleeves as their contents emptied. On the counter stood the scale with its bright brassy weights, its scoop polished from the contin-ual rubbing of peas, rice, and other goods, which left it dazzling. At the far end of the counter was a great chopping block, the trunk of an old tree, on which dried cod, Tasso, a kind of dried horse-meat, smoked herring, and other things were cut up and sold by the three cents' worth.

All of these dried fish and meats were favorites of the peasants, who were fed on them when they were brought to Trinidad to work as cheap labor on the sugar plantations, and although they had now shifted over from sugarcane to the oil refineries a few miles away, their taste for the old foods of their indentured parents and grandparents still lingered on. The back of the shelves from floor to ceiling were stacked with tinned milk, salmon, sardines, cans whose labels had fallen away long ago, slates piled high, pencils, erasers, celluloid windmills, brooms, sunglasses . . .

As the morning opened, vendors from the nearby villages came and began unloading their produce in front of the shop. They spread down sugar sacks and arranged their tomatoes, eddoes, cassava, okra, string beans, mangoes, and oranges in small heaps. In short, my uncle's shop was a small bazaar on Saturday, which was payday at the oil fields. People came with their entire families to do their shopping. They argued, fought, told stories; some of them even came to look for prospective brides and grooms for their children. All along the front of the shop, on the inside, were piled high the unopened bags of sugar, rice, flour, and often after the day's work was done, it was not unusual to find that children who were put to sit on the sugar bags had dug small holes into them and eaten away the sugar, nailful by nailful, while the shop hummed and no one was looking their way. My cousin's job at one time was to keep an eye on all this, but now that his parents could use him behind the counter, they had to be content with shouting warnings at a guilty-looking face high up on the burlap.

"You want to eat up all of the profits in this shop or what?" my aunt would shout at some little mole who burrowed away at the sugar, but my uncle, who parried all her statements like a good stick fighter, would ask point-blank, "How much sugar you think that child could hold in he stomach?" Then they would go back to waiting on their respective customers.

As the numbers rose, the voices rose. All but my aunt's—her cool cutting voice would silence the shopful of screaming buyers. She would stop pouring rice into the scale from her scoop, look ten people over, then say, "You think I is God with a dozen foot an' hand or what?" My uncle, meanwhile, went about selling in his own leisurely way, talking to each customer about all the complex machinery that they had at the refineries, or then he would be prescribing medicine for someone's child who had the five-day fever, and then again, if it were someone's donkey that was ill, it was not beneath his calling to prescribe for the animal too. And we two boys alike ran up and down between the counter and shelves filling orders. "A penny baking soda," and we would rush to the bin where the little parcels had been wrapped up in brown paper during the week when the sun was hot in the streets and only a bicycle passed, or a donkey cart, and there was nothing to do but wait for evening, when someone who had forgotten something, or who had run out in the middle of cooking dinner, would come in to make a purchase.

Later on in the day, when the crowd had reached its peak, my cousin would start running wires here and there. He had fixed up a radio to work on batteries and put an extra loudspeaker outside for the crowd, who peered incredulously into the small bowl of the loudspeaker as though they could see the faces of the people in those wonderful places from which they sang, talked, and played music.

I moved about in the crowd outside when the rush in the shop began to die down, and always among the vendors there were old farmers with hard hands and sun-cracked faces who would offer me some fruit or delicacy which they had brought to sell on Saturday. I had the feeling that they looked upon me with a kind of pity, that I should come from the city of Port of Spain, with its confusing streets, automobiles, bicycles, tramcars, and people constantly on the move, and they would ask questions of me about the city as if to confirm the doubtful things they had heard.

"You mean to say that you have light dat work by a wire? . . . an' all you have to do is twist something an' it will go—whole day–whole night?"

"Whole day–whole night," I would acknowledge, and they would wag their heads and go away.

My cousin meanwhile would be polishing up his bicycle. He was the only boy in the village who had one. If any of the little ruffians from the sugar sacks came over and stared, even from a proper distance from the bike, my cousin would chase them away unless they were ready to pay a penny for a ride on the handlebar while his parents weren't looking. He would get a can of Brasso and shine up each spoke, then he would wash out the chain in kerosene from the shop. Sometimes he had the whole bicycle apart, rolling the tiny glistening ball bearings in his hand. "One of these days you goin' to break up the bicycle for good," his mother would shout, but my uncle, who was sure that the bike would always be put back together again, would mumble under his breath, "It ain't break he breakin' it—is *fix* he fixin' it . . . and *clean* he cleanin' it."

As evening approached, the noise and the shrill voices quieted. Customers who waited to come in at this hour were more leisurely, as if they had put off their visit to the shop till that time when they could stretch it out long, calling out their items from atop the sacks piled up across from the counter, punctuated by long silences as they tried to think of anything that they had forgotten. "Let me see now . . ." they would say as they enumerated on their fingers all of the things they had already bought with a feeling that the things they forgot would spring into their minds as they ran through their purchases. "Let me see . . . let me see . . . rice? flour? sugar? oil? aha! aha! . . . I did know I forget something . . . nails! Gimme a pound of one-inch nails. It have a mongoose eatin' up the chicken an' dem and I want to fix up that old chicken coop before the brown hen hatch." And then, someone who overheard this remark would add, "Is mongoose I hear you say mongoose? Must be is the same mongoose that uses to eat up Ram Singh chicken an' dem." And then my uncle would be drawing up the diagram of a mongoose trap for them on a sheet of brown wrapping paper.

But when the evening came, my aunt brought the lamps into the shop, where the conversation flowed like oil from a drum, and in her own quiet way, as she went about trimming the wicks, cleaning out the chimneys with old newspapers, you could tell that, beneath her busyness and her intent look at the shiny glass chimneys, she was enjoying each moment of the day, each word of conversation, as the light fell outside into that early darkness that tumbles into night all of a sudden. And when she was finished with the lamps, she hung up the two large ones in the shop, then struck a match to them, and suddenly everyone was surprised to find that the day had slipped by so softly that no one had noticed the thinning out of the light. My cousin was getting his flashlight ready for the night too. It was a kind of weapon he had against something indefinable in the darkness. Whether it was the weight of the long flashlight or the brilliant beam of white light in the black countryside where the land seemed so old and filled with secrets, I do not know, but there was in the possession of a flashlight like his something that was near to magic, and even grown men who could not afford its luxury looked at Kemal with a special kind of respect.

There is always someone who loses track of the sound of time flowing past; not even the finest instrument is without flaw, except perhaps my aunt, as my uncle swore. And her large dark sorrowful eyes would start and look up as she polished her chimneys when the first cricket, off key, off time, started screeching outside. With her eyes, she as much as said "It ain't evening yet . . . why you don't wait!" But then other small beasts hissing in the bushes and ditches, who were not sure of the time themselves and did not wish to be left out of the vast symphony that was beginning, soon began half-heartedly to sing their song of evening and the dying of the sun, and by the time the first fireflies came out of the darkness, the night was one great sound that seemed to envelop the world, and there was no single place, no bush nor hedge, where you could go and turn the leaves upside down and find the throat of one single voice, for they were everywhere and sometimes you began to feel there was nothing outside at all, but only the sound of the earth rolling slowly through the vastness of its mysterious void, like they said in school.

Was it this that my grandfather had listened to long ago? Was it this that he wanted some of his great tribe of a family to remember and to listen to? This song of evening coming home to Tunapuna, where the land was low and wet and where Rajo had become a shopkeeper? And after all of the talk of the gallons of oil, after all the speeches of how hot they could make something and how white it would glow in the heat, there was a strange and mysterious look in Rajo's face, as if he were listening to the evening. He would stop whatever he was doing and listen as if someone were calling him from far away; then he would say, "Yes . . . yes . . . aha . . . aha . . . !" then would come back to Tunapuna and the shop and the smell of sugar sacks and salt codfish and Saturday.

But his was not the only face on which this strange confusion was pictured. It was so with some of the people who came to the shop. They had worked on their small plots of land, planting sugarcane or vegetables, selling their produce by the wayside, and then suddenly they were working the bizarre machinery that stood like lordly giants in the fenced-off refinery, lit up by night to show off some arrogant splendor in the bright silver-painted tubes coiling around and about, great tiered wooden structures with water flowing through them making the sound of waterfalls, and giant ball-shaped tanks standing on tiny feet in acres of green grass. In the faces of men and women in the shop at this hour of the day was something incongruous, something like the look of a frightened child, as unrelated as the bare-chested peasant in his fraying trousers swiping at grass around the huge tanks of gasoline in the landscape that made the passerby on a bright sunny day wonder who was here first, the great silver orb . . . or the grass cutter? And who would be here last?

When the late customers reluctantly left the shop for their little mud huts buried in the bush, my uncle slapped his palm on the counter, kicked his legs high in the air, and skipped over the counter as light as a kite.

"You playin' young an' strong," my aunt would say, glancing quickly up at him as he startled her. "When you sprain your back an' take sick in bed don't say I didn't warn you." He was a man who was neither old nor young, and he could cross that border line from one moment to the next. He was our age just then, Kemal's and mine, and we had the feeling that he did it to show us that he was still a boy.

There were two heavy wooden crowbars that wedged into hinges on the doors of the shop, then slipped into deep holes in the walls. It would take dynamite to open those doors from the outside, for the shop was built like an ancient arsenal in the days when the Spaniards held the island, scattering forts and fortresses throughout the countryside. As my uncle closed the heavy doors, the wide bar of light falling on the ground outside narrowed slowly, then was gone. The wooden bars were slipped into their hinges and holes, and then there was a feeling of safety and warmth inside, for outside now there was only black night and the earth with all its secrets of massacres and mutilations, slavery and Spaniards, and old English bones buried there to sleep forever. And now we were counting out the money. Two-shilling pieces, shillings, half shillings, and large copper pennies and cents, all placed in their separate piles. My uncle would remove one coin, scrape it with his fingernail, flip it in the air and listen to its ring, then pound on it with one of the brass pound weights. If it stood all these tests, it was put back in the piles of silver. If not, my uncle would throw it to my aunt and she would give the coin a few tests of her own, and my uncle, waiting her verdict, would ask "Counter-feet?" I had always thought that my uncle invented the word "counterfeit," that it had in some way been related to the counter in his shop, on which many worn-down coins were nailed through their centers because they were "counter-feet."

A strange silence would then fall across the shop as we ate our dinner that evening in the midst of all those bags of flour, rice, and all those pins and hair clips from all the world, which had come, as if miraculously, to haunt my uncle's shop in this silence of lamplight, breathing out their odors. The soaps, perfumes, candles, and now and then a quick waft of new white bolt-cotton, in which people would bury their dead, and if you went close enough to the shelves there was the smell of funerals, the smell of eau de Cologne which everyone used at funerals, and dark brown butter in ten-pound tins from Australia, and lard as white as cotton in great wooden kegs, and spices from India in dozens of jars, each one filled with its own aroma, blending together to make that one odor that everyone knew was curry, and the smell of onions and garlic drying on the string suspended from the ceiling.

My aunt would go back and forth from her kitchen to the shop with a small kerosene lamp, bringing whatever dishes she had fixed for her men for dinner, and we all had a peep into them, naming off each item as she opened the dishes. "Ahhhh . . . rice." "Ahhh . . . fried okra with salt fish." "Ahhhhh . . . goat curry." "No," my aunt would say, "guess again." "Lamb curry." Then we would all get ready to have our special Saturday dinner, which meant that we could have along with our regular meal anything that we relished in the shop.

"What about a can of sardines?" Kemal would offer. My uncle nodded and he was up and opening one of those small flat cans that could fit into the palm of your hand, with small silvery fish in oil. "Lime! wait, lime for the sardines," my aunt would say, running back into her kitchen. And then, after we were busy eating again I would ask, "How about some of those salt biscuits?" and Kemal, with his mouth full, would grunt um . . . hmmm . . . um . . . hmmm and pry open that large drum, and before he could return from the far end of the shop with the biscuits, my aunt would say, "And bring some of that nice brown butter too. It does go well with the biscuit."

When dinner was over, my aunt took the dishes and piled them up slowly. It was the one day of the week when she left her dish washing for the morning. My uncle rolled some of the coins into long tubes of paper, then put the money in a small rusted iron vault under the counter. The vault itself was hardly any guarantee of safety for his money, but it would take several strong men to move it away, and it was on the strength of this that he felt safe from robbery, since both he and Kemal had opened the vault with a two-inch nail that had been flattened on the train lines.

The rest of this evening was ours, mine and Kemal's, to do with as we pleased. There was a traveling tent theater that was showing an American film about two miles away in the direction of the oil-field refineries. Kemal hitched to his bicycle the small wheelbarrow in which I rode and we made our way noisily through the black countryside, the wheels of the metal cart rattling the stars loose from their cold and solitary hinges, the long white beam of his flashlight cutting a sharp bright cone as we moved. When we got to the small tent, there was another bazaar spread out. People were roasting ears of corn on charcoal braziers, and the wonderful aroma of many delicacies frying in cauldrons of coconut oil filled the air. A peanut vendor with a shrill whistle steaming and shrieking barked his goods. Everywhere there were trays of fruit and homemade candy.

As we came riding in like two lords, Kemal ringing the bell all the way, people cleared a path for us as they stared in confusion at our strange contraption. We moved about in the crowd, filling our pockets with all the sweetmeats and tidbits that we would need to sit through the hour and a half. Then we joined a group of boys who were playing a game for grains of roasted corn. The banker held a number of roasted-corn grains in his closed hand, and each boy tried to guess the right number. If you guessed ten grains and were wrong, you had to pay ten. But if you guessed the right number, you got ten times that number of corn grains and you also became the banker. We had just lost for the third round when someone came through the crowd ringing a school bell, shouting, "Picture show startin' . . . picture show startin' . . . picture show startin' . . ." Everyone was making a run for the first rows, where the picture was largest and heads would not get in the way, but the first row was already filled with those who sat there and waited while someone else went out to make their purchases.

The ground was still soaked from the rain of the night before, and the wooden folding chairs in the tent sank in deeper and deeper as we rocked back and forth on them, and when the picture stopped at the end of each reel, there was a burst of noise, shouting and talking and calling out to friends, which took several minutes to quiet down after the next reel was running. Now and then the old watchman from the oil fields who had a policeman's uniform went up and down the aisles playing his flashlight in the faces of a row of noisy boys or girls who would not quiet down, and when the noise got completely out of hand the film was stopped and six naked light bulbs that hung from the roof of the tent went on until silence was resumed. Through the hour and a half that the film ran, people kept going in and out. Someone would shout from outside the tent, "Aye, Rani . . . Rani . . . your moomah want you to come home right away." If there was no stir in the crowd and the voice still kept calling, people would begin to call out inside the tent, "Rani . . . Rani . . . who name is Rani here? Why you don't go on home an' see what you moomah want?" Or perhaps someone had brought a young child who started crying during a noisy battle or a scene with gunplay. Then they would be the target of the crowd. "Take dat child out. Take dat child out," they would shout, until some mother sheepishly stole out of the tent to quiet her crying baby.

When the show came to an end, the lights were put on again and an old scratched record of "God Save the King" blared forth from the two loudspeakers in front of the screen, on which was flashed a picture of King George with a benign smile on his lips and a long row of medals across his breast. Little boys with their dark brown broomstick legs sticking out of shorts stood up, staring at the King as the trumpets blared and the drum rolls crackled in the speakers and the policeman went about shouting, "Stand up . . . Stand up! You can't hear they playin' 'God Save the King'?" If anyone had fallen asleep on the chairs, the policeman was doubly annoyed, and he rapped on the backs of chairs shouting, poking, threatening arrest if proper respect was not paid to the King. There was a scuffle at the far side of the tent, and although we were warned to avoid fights and trouble of any kind we went to investigate. Before we could squeeze through the crowd, we heard an angry voice shouting. "And what the hell the King ever do for me—tell me dat," a man was saying to the policeman who hovered about him to make the arrest. "He curse the King. That what this vagabond do. He ain't show respect for the King and dat is against the law." The policeman addressed the crowd while the man stood about with his gleaming cutlass threatening to chop anyone who dared to touch him. "Come on," Kemal said, pulling at my arm, "let we go before bad bad trouble start."

We ran out to the shed where the bicycle was and raced away from the thickening crowd. I felt strange and bewildered, as though we had betrayed the man who stood alone with his cutlass, and I was wondering what happened to him, if they were going to lock him up in jail because he did not respect the King.

The wheels of the cart seemed to find all the holes and pebbles on the road and my teeth felt like the pebbles under the metal wheels each time I opened my mouth to talk to Kemal. The noise the cart made was so loud I knew that he would not be able to hear me until we stopped. And when we finally did, I could not understand why the countryside was so still. In the distance was the one-room railroad station with a light in its window and the two glistening steel tracks disappearing in the distance. I had heard stories from my grandfather of how the police came around on horseback in the old days whenever there was an uprising among the peasants and a small-scale massacre was in progress over some similar incident. I thought that the railroad station might be set on fire . . . that soon we would be hearing gunfire from the direction of the oil fields.

The house was in a dim light as we entered on tiptoe and went to our room. I heard my aunt cough, clear her throat, then ask, "Kemal? Chan? Dat you?" "Yes," we answered, and we stretched out on our beds feet to feet. I was feeling a strange kind of excitement as though the policeman were after us. I could tell that Kemal was excited too, although he did not say anything.

"Kim, you sleepin'?"

"No . . . you?"

"No . . . why?"

"That was a good picture, eh?"

"Boy, that picture was hearts. You see how them people up in America and all them big big places does live."

"Yes, but you don't think . . ."

"Boy, is so I want to live. Just like that! No mosquito, no dark, no pitch-oil lamp."

"Kim . . ."

"What?"

"What about that man?"

"Who? The fellar in the film? Boy, is so it is in America."

"You see how that fellar invent the telephone and he get to be a great man? I want to go up there one day and do something like that. No more small Island for me. Soon, soon, soon as I grow up I leavin' . . . leavin' for good."

Silence.

"Chan, you sleepin' . . . you gone and sleep-away on me, man?"

"No."

"What you goin' to do when you grow big?"

"I don't know."

"Boy, how you don't know . . . you ain't see with you own two eye how them people livin' up in them big big countries?"

"Yes."

"And you don't want to go way and do something?"

Silence.

"Chan, wake up . . . wake up, man. How you could sleep-away like that?"

"I ain't sleepin'. I listenin' to you."

"And what you think . . . boy, you lucky to be living in **Port** of Spain and not here in the bush."

"But I like it up here. . . ."

"Hey, man, what you say we ask your parents and mine to let we exchange places."

"All right. First thing tomorrow morning."

"Chan . . . Chan . . . what you thinking?"

"I was thinkin' that I wonder why that fellar didn't want to show respect for the King."

"The man was a damn blasted fool. That was all."

"No, Kim. I don't think so. I wonder why he do a thing like that . . . and why they want to put 'im in jail? Kim . . . Kemal?"

Silence.

"Kemal?"

The full moon had come out in the sky now and the country road lay like a pale blue ribbon in the night, as though all the people all over the world had gone to sleep forever. The people in the film, the people who made the safety pins and eau de Cologne, the people in Port of Spain . . . and the policeman. But the man with the shining cutlass? Where was he sleeping now?

V. S. Reid

A REQUIEM FOR DAN'L MOORE

TOMMY MOORE lay between the sheets and thought that
At a quarter to seven in the morning when day breaks upon the
roofs of East Town and the yellow sunlight leaking down the
wall is hot and eager as a wish in hell, then the bells and steam
whistles of the Quarter rip you to pieces.
He rubbed his eyes and murmured something sleepily and thought
that
At a quarter to seven in the morning when the allnight seller of
banana fritters fattens her cheeks to puff out the oil lamp, the
thlack thlack you hear under the hurrying feet is the street-
sweeper's longhandled broom snatching at the gutter to put into
heaps
empty beer cans grumbling and lurching illtemperedly out of
the way
twists of fruit peel crushed by a thlack to a hearse for a foolish
cockroach
cigarette ends puffed lovingly down to the gentle fragment
broken bricks that in the fight last night were more powerful
than an arm.
He stretched and dreamily remembered the slim little fishermen
who with their twinkling knives had fenced the cops from his
brother, and in his head he swore like them, thinking
At a quarter to seven the cracked old bell in the boatyard rattles
your teeth as he tells his lazy caulkers it's time to be at the tar and
oakum. And that other one, the wide-mouthed one in the tannery
loosens her tongue in a clangor and empties your head of sleep.
Then it is the turn of the steam whistles at the Ice Company and
the railroad roundhouse and McGaffey's foundry to lace you with
their whips, ordering you to open your eyes and smell the stinks
of the tannery.
And with the sleep still knotted in his limbs, young Tommy Moore
opened his eyes and thought

I'll lay on my back looking up at the ceiling and say Good Morning, Ceiling. What a shame it is that the mice have picked up soot from the kitchen and blackened your face with their shoes as they walk upsidedown through that hole to their own houses.

And when he heard the noises outside in the street, Tommy Moore groped drowsily around in his head and said to one of the noises

Good Morning Jim the Donkey, hauling Milk Headley's cart going by in Fleet Street and telling me good morning back by the flapping of your ears.

Good Morning Carpenter Mahoney-O.

Your hammer falls thickly now, Carpenter Mahoney-O. You've bought the rosettes of purple satin and you're nailing them on the inside of the coffin so the dear old one will rest softly—

And then he was bolt upright, last night flooding into his mind and saying the good mornings quicker now, like this

Good Morning, Room.

Good Morning Soap and Towel and Toothbrush.

And in the shower, shivering as he looked up, he said

Good morning Shower.

Please to kill me Shower.

And the cold water fell and killed him.

Johnny the Poet had a message for his friend Tommy Moore and so he climbed the fence at the back of No. 11 and hooked his insteps to the top bar of the fence and leaned forward until his balance broke and he hit the side of the house on his hands and chest. Now he was looking down through the bathroom window grinning at the antics of his friend and he called through the rush of water,

"Skunky small one?"

Tommy Moore turned his soapy face upward. He was used to being summoned this way by Johnny. No going to the front door for the Poet.

"The Piano Mover wants to see you. You know the Mover? He was the crook who knew the police would have Jimmy Lovelace even before we found it out. You remember the Mover? You remember Jimmy Lovelace?"

A hammer knocked in Tommy Moore's narrow chest. Who in East Town could forget Jimmy Lovelace? He was martyred by a policeman's bullet. They held the wake for Jimmy Lovelace in Solomon's Yard where they dock the schooners coming in with salt and turtle from the Cayman Islands. And who would not remember forever the mullets which had been cooked in oil until the bones vanished into an idea under the tongue? The bread had been baked in the shapes of cherubims so that Jimmy Lovelace would have an easy time at the Gate; for would St. Peter not have looked down and seen that the friends of Jimmy Lovelace ate food of holy figures for the good of his soul?

A Coromante girl named Kedala had led the singing at the Wake. And the Poet who was older than Tommy Moore had observed that you knew her for Coromante by the hard curve of her flanks and the wing-slant to her eyes and her skin the sweet sable your fingers whimpered to stroke. And nobody in East Town would ever forget that

> sweet Jimmy Lovelace
> blessed Jimmy Lovelace
> holy Jimmy Lovelace

who had emptied a burlap bag full of half bricks on the heads of the constables before they were forced to shoot him, was that night as much martyr as St. Stephen under the stones.

"The Piano Mover has news about your brother, the celebrated Dan'l Moore," Johnny the Poet said. Sunlight slanted down on the side of his face and lit up the malice in it. "He's down by the Marine Board full of news about your brother from Walker the Policeman."

The Piano Mover was a brokendown old thief who now cleaned the police barracks for his keep. But he still retained his loyalty for East Town, shedding the pieces of information that could help a man on the run. Tommy Moore whinnied a small cry as he dived for the shower cock. He toweled fast and, the skin wet yet, he drew on his clothing and raced through the yard. Aunt Caro's suspicious yell hit him on the back of the head and he turned and flailed a hand at her, begging her to be quiet for no matter that it was daylight, Walker and his dirty policemen were no doubt about and abroad. He fled into Fleet Street among the fast-walking people, their heads full of clocks.

The railroad men in blue dungarees hurrying to beat seven o'clock.

Dockyard men in navy canvas shoes softly racing to flog seven o'clock.

He wiped his face with the tail of his shirt and swarmed swiftly past them. He slowed at the corner of Harbour Street, edged his head past the angle of the Marine Board Building and rolled his eyes along the pavement until he saw the down-at-heels police regulation boots worn by the Piano Mover. His head down in the secretive way he figured a man needed to act if he would outfox the constabulary, he slid to the sidewalk and sidled his bottom along it toward the boots. The black leather boots waited for a lull in the traffic of seven o'clock feet and then spoke.

"Take this to your aunt Caro Moore," said the boots. "Tell her the police have put capture-at-any-cost against Dan'l Moore's name."

At the mouth of hell, Tommy Moore asked shakily: "Is the sergeant that was knifed dead, then?"

"Maimed until they can patch him up," the Piano Mover said, his eyes inside the crowd. Nobody could link him with the little boy sitting on the sidewalk near his foot. "But you can tell Caro the policeman will live."

The Poet, panting from the chase after his friend, slipped up beside Tommy Moore. "Who has the case?" he asked the Piano Mover, making ready to punish Tommy Moore for outdistancing him so badly through the crowd.

"Who the hell but Walker," the Piano Mover said impatiently.

"And Walker is a hanging man," the Poet said in a hollow voice as he pushed Tommy Moore to the brink.

A *hanging man,* cried Tommy Moore in his head. The man who had led the Good Friday raid on Sugarfoot Hogarth's gang. And because of Walker's raid, they had hanged Hogarth and buried him with his feet pointed south.

It had been a battle to talk about from the first spring of the fists-O.

Hogarth had been in the ring, a smart man with his fists as he was with his dandy linen suits. And his gangsters were also strong men of repute with the iron knuckledusters, and tonight, as all East Town saw through the half-opened blinds of their windows, they fought like the holy hosts. But a plank did for a policeman and they hanged Hogarth at the next Assizes and buried him with his feet pointed south and not east as one would a Christian.

"It's seven o'clock, gotto go to work," the Piano Mover said, stepping down into the crowd. And the boots firm and heavy on his feet, he thought he walked with a policeman's stride, but those who saw him saw a shuffling old man swinging his arms foolishly light for such a poor walk.

But the Piano Mover strode proudly on, thinking how fine it was to be going to work and not hiding from the police like Dan'l Moore.

V. S. Reid

MY FATHER'S HOUSE

WE called our beach Boscobel. This was because my head for history reminded me that the English Prince Charlie, when he was a-running from the wars, found refuge in a hollow oak at a place called so. This beach was the oak of my hope and the name strode easily into my mind.

Meanwhile, we studied the sea.

And, O the early weeks at Boscobel; the walls into which we ran our heads!

For at the top of our mind was the conviction that this fishing would not be much of a task. There could be *nothing* to putting a bait on your hook and dipping your hook over the side. When enough fish had been caught and sold, the nets would be bought; then it would be easier still.

Just throw your net over the side and haul them in, Fisher Labe.

Aie.

Then, as for the oaring. Could there be a hardship to a grown man's plying of eight foot of balanced wood through water? Hardship, your granny.

But I remember now the grin on Nicky Ffolkes when he watched the cocky nods we recruits gave as we talked of our plans around the cooking fires after vespers. How that, soon, we would earn enough to each build his house and have our women with us. Our memories went stumbling down rough roads when such talk came up. And I knew well this inner ache, how it opened into bitter flowers at our talk.

But could I have them marrying on the poor strength of Boscobel? Without proper arrangements for their living? And make of this beautiful beach, a show of leaning hutments? And their women quarreling over their washtubs because their poor larders would not settle their distempers?

Wait and wait, I tell them. A *Rae Town* must no' come to my Boscobel.

68

But back to Nicky Ffolkes. By virtue of the knowledge of fishing he had, Ffolkes grinned his mean amusement at us. His navel-string was buried under a rock in Great Pedro Bay of St. Elizabeth Parish. He knew long ago how the calluses would have to come to our palms and be grown over again before we could break our nets with a heavy catch.

And true enough. For by the time we had sense enough to cover our hooks with skill to suit bold water or shoal, we also had sense enough to know why Peter the Fisherman earned such strong remembrance for his oathing. As for the use of the oar!

I sat still on the thwarts with shame when I viewed the ease with which Nicky Ffolkes played the wood in the water, while I, known to men for my strength, furiously fought to keep from kicking backward each time my oar dipped.

So it was not as Murph hoped. We fished, but not with the sort of luck we liked. Hunger loved our kitchen. A thin smoke coming through our chimney only once a day as we lived on coffee and flour cakes. But men in need quickly knuckle down. By the third month we were baiting with more success and by summer we were bawling at the cooks if for any reason the morning meal was late.

But still the going was slow since there was little coin to put by for the purchase of our first net. And so, how we came by the first net, I will tell of presently.

Of Cobina, I heard no word.

But those times when Murph went to the city to pay a mite on the interest on our mortgage, I am certain he saw her. I have heard him, more than once, telling perhaps for my hearing, what a blessing it was to be fishing an open beach with blue sea for floor, bluer sky for roof and trees about for walls, while others fished out of a beach that had warehouses fouling their elbows, and sand the color of a Port Said hotel sheet.

I know he talks of Cobina at Rae Town and nobody could tell by the smooth of my face how I am thinking that the day is coming when I will beat Murph with my fists sure as Gabriel's judgment day.

Cobina is my light and my anguish. And who the hell is Murph in my life?

Should I reach into the room of my soul and borrow the words of King David? The words of Shepherd David are for a man's employment when there are no others to tell what should be said. And . . . it was in his longings that much of King David's eloquence struck.

As the heart panteth after the waterbrooks, so thirsteth my soul . . .

There is no blasphemy in me. In chapel I will swear it.

Our seine, the first big seine with Canadian cork floating the guy and iron cleats at the boat's gunwale and two hundred feet of manila for the draw, did not come from fishing. It came this way.

Now you must know that there is a need for hallelujah in my people. Batter down their walls and double their burdens, their songs will flourish in the ruins. No exception with our company at Boscobel.

There were songs for the boating and songs when we lay back on the ropes which pulled in the roundwood from the bush for our huts.

There were songs to ease the long march to town with our catch, and songs for high noon and the smell of sun in the trees.

But the singing we made at the close of each day was the finest singing of all.

O, man. We took the lean things of the day and packed them into our hopes for tomorrow and laughed at the full hampers we saw.

There would come first, the humming, lifting to a stronger murmur when one of the tunes caught our fancies. The voice which claimed the commencement of the tune would then take up with the words—and then off were we fifty in such a hunt for harmony that often you would pause to listen at the glory around you. To gape at the richness of it. This was the case one day.

The hot old sun was fast losing his heat back of the hills and the sea washed up the beach the way it does at evening, with a flurry on the sand like the brush of sticks over a thwarted kettledrum. With Murph watching my hands for faults, I was learning to bend a strip of bamboo to a broken fish pot. Near me, Joe Black drove nails into the soft wood of a bollard pin. Beyond us were the others, backs leaned to the blockhouse or fallen into such groups as they disposed.

Three or four tunes had been worked about, when, from Rich Beamish and Bully Fergusson, who were skewering mussels from the shells for our sun-up fishing, was coming a hymn which was catching our ear. And one by one, we were leaving off our own tunes to join in this air.

"Lead, Kindly Light," it was. A hymn of humility and strength.

Then as our voices joined, tenors, working up to their notes and bassos looking down their chests, I nodded at Joe Black, who carries magic in his fingers. So that, out he went quickly to the flank, turning like a fugleman to face us, and his hands came up.

His hands drew our eyes to them, for a mason of fame is Joe Black the way he molds voices with his hands. There were altos and sopranos standing in now, carrying the hymn with certainty. We made the notes move into each other with warmth and understanding for the next, and, in the fifth line where for many strong bars there is a unison for all, O, man, we were noble.

And then the hymn ended and we were still awhile as we waited for the glory to drain out of us so we could be men again.

Presently, I had Murph's elbow in my ribs. Up went my eyes to his pointing finger and followed the slant of it to where an automobile had halted in the road. Huge and shiny it was, of more wealth than those others which used to pass along the road. My eyes sharpened and I made out a driver sporting a visored headgear and three faces staring at us through the window at the rear.

"Hi, be they tourists?" Nicky Ffolkes asked generally. "I used to see tourists in St. Elizabeth Parish, as many as ever. The men wear knickers and berets like French sailors."

"And the women wear knickers and berets but you know they are women because they cover their knickers," Johnny M'Cook said.

A hail from the car. I held up my hand to still the laughter.

"Bravo! Bravo!" the shout went. I rose and removed my straw hat and bowed—for I believe in manners.

"Tell them 'tis the Don Cossack choir performing blackface, Sarge," Johnny M'Cook's strong whisper came to me. Likely, this lad will joke at Old Nick when he raises the fork for him. But he is a good man, this M'Cook. I tell him to put his foot in his mouth; but not unkindly. He was in my platoon at Tobruk.

I watched the men in the car as they seemed to talk among themselves.

"I say, come down here!"

It is a voice full of authority. It is evident he is not used to disobedience and I barely remember I am no longer in khaki or doubtless my heels would have clicked. But I held my footing.

"Tell the General 'tis a camp of Commies, this is, Sarge," Johnny said in advice. "Tell him it's the officers who must come up to us now."

"You there—I want to talk to you!" There is impatience in the shout.

Then I could not stop the thin and angry Richard Beamish before he had insulted the stranger.

"Well then, crawl up to us on your belly, Great Slug!"

There was a great howl of laughter from the men at Beamish's sudden bellow.

Beamish has twice been a corporal and twice has he been court-martialed. There have been times when I think something must be wrong inside of him, for army beef has not filled him out and his anger comes on him anytime. I began walking down the hill then, for the lads had offered an insult to the strangers. I stepped down into the road, went to the door of the car, and politely told them how-de-do.

The man at the end nearest me, with authority spluttering from his tongue, was Squire Groves, a justice of the peace as he told me when he had asked how dared us use such words to him. The others were younger with less fat on their chins. Madding to let go of their laughter, they are. Garvey and Flynn were Americans, from the easy drawl of their tongues—but Irish as a sprig of shamrock from their names and the laughter bubbling back of their eyes. They are staying at a hotel in Montego Bay, taking the sun and sea. And now they are driving back from the city with their friend, the Squire, who was a white man of our island. Nobody had to tell me that Squire Groves was a man of heavy purse, with more title deeds to his name than were required for a shroud.

I hear his spluttering quietly enough, for he has not got the gift of abuse as us brown men of the island.

"How would you like to bring your choir to Montego Bay?" Flynn asked me. "We could arrange it with the management and I am sure the folks staying at the hotel would make it all right for you."

Well then.

From soldiering to farming to fishing to performing. I grinned deep inside and there was no waiting in my mind. Our fobs needed the coin. And if Providence chose to bring it to us through Bishop Newman's hymn, then should I argue with the mystery of it?

I laugh to think that I should argue with the mystery of it.

Hear me, to Flynn: " 'Tis a long march to Montego Bay, Mr. Flynn."

He waved his hand like a turtle flapping at low tide. "That need not be your worry. We could send a truck for you and the men. How about, let's say Sunday evening?"

I said, "Sunday then," with an end of talking about it in my voice.

But when I looked back to Squire Groves, his eyes were going over me like a company commander at morning inspection.

"You're an ex-soldier," he clapped firmly on me. "Disbanded?"

I cannot help the ramrod King George has fitted to my spine. It is my belief it will always be there to mark me as a man of khaki and brass.

"That is so, Justice Groves," I said respectfully.

"Hmm," he gave me for reply, his eyes yet hot with wrath. "Is this your land?"

Brusqueness rode suddenly down to me. "On lease," I snapped. A color sergeant is a man of responsibility and even fresh young lieutenants show respect to him.

"How did you get to it?" he barked. This? A slap on my face at the unbidden poverty which showed plainly in my gear. But I have dealt with fresh officers before.

"A road smote cunningly through openings in the mountains and took us down to this beach, Justice," said I, the mock most clear in my manner.

Garvey and Flynn hooted quickly and shut up.

He was a man who had never had other men laughing at him. Not to his face anyway. Beamish had led the lads into an earthquake of a deed and Squire Groves was flung all topsy-turvy.

"Who is the owner of this beach?"

I do not know the owner. And I am not worried about it except if we cannot pay the rent and the bailiffs come. Murph's is the head for such business and I say praise his genius.

But even had I known the owner, I believe I would have answered Squire Groves as I did.

"A—*gentleman*," I said and stepped back from the car.

He must have been a good judge of men to have acquired his heavy purse. He must have read the storm rising in me. He rapped the door of his car and signaled his driver to go. The Squire dislikes me. He's roped to the eyes with it. I gave him my most gifted grin.

"Sunday, soldier!" the one called Flynn shouted back out of the dust. And I stood and waited for the lads crowding down the hill to the beach.

So that was how we came to sing in Montego Bay that Sunday evening. It was Murph who suggested that we shake out the old uniforms for the performance. We had few pieces of sound clothing between us, but the tunics in the kitbags were sound. So, we shook them out and used cookhouse ash to shine the buttons.

But there was little joking between us as we brought back the old glisten to the buttons. I believe we were silent because we were rubbing the rust from our memories too.

Not a pip less than a thousand were on the smooth grass in front of the hotel the evening we sang. Overseas people they were, mostly from America. Flynn had made them put up a stage, with some palms in pots about. I grouped the lads out of sight while I took a peep at them. They were chattering enough to shame a company of washerwomen. Down in front I saw the ugly fatness of Squire Groves, the man who had asked "disbanded" with relish.

As to the jokers facing the stage—well, Charcoal Cossacks, some said of us. The Bronze Bellowers of Boscobel, others said. The Growling Guardsmen, came out of the wings. I would have given half of our fees to have had the blue-gold-scarlet of our full-dress Zouave to put around my lads now. But we would do with what we had.

So I had the lads divide to right and left of the stage, while Chippy Dale, with his bugle, crouched behind a palm. Then at a lift from my hand, there came from Chippy the sweet flourish of the reveille, and on the last high note, Murph from the left and I from the right, marched onstage at the head of our platoons to the rousing tune of "The British Grenadiers."

Aie, then. The noise of their approval was salve to any bruises their name-calling had caused the lads.

We stood to attention before them. I made a little talk to tell these foreigners who we were and what the ribbons on our chests meant, the lads behind me standing to such statues as the fine men outside the gates of Buckingham Palace in London. After that, I stepped back into the ranks and left our glory to the hands of Joe Black.

We sang for our want of new huts with white Spanish walling and mahogany floors waxed to a wonder with the cerosee bush and binded thatch for the roof thick as your arm and a half.

We sang for two more canoes cut from cottonwood and braced with mahoe and a deck-over prow to ice our catch.

We sang for a seine net, No. 6 thread, and for a dozen throw nets for inshore tobacco money.

And, more than all, we sang to leave the blockhouse and be bedded under our own roofs with our women.

And we had them rapt and in our pockets.

There were the songs of the Irish and the Welsh, which the younger lads had learnt from us who had campaigned with these soldiers. There were the hymns which most of our boys had been learning even before we could talk. And we gave them a psalm of Shepherd Davie, that forty-sixth, which goes "God is our refuge and strength." We left the chant pathways to speak it, with a great rustling in our throats, the piece about the river in the city, then mounted into the chant again to end it. And every man jack of us nursed the feeling in our bones that we had rolled up the ill luck which had slowed us at Boscobel and flung it far away.

Afterwards Joe Black let fall his hands and stepped back into ranks with us for some of the songs of our island. We shook and bothered them with a number of devilish *mentos* which made the women move their hips and the men grin around their cigars.

Such as "Brown Skin Gal" and "Manoel Road" and "Mango Walk" and "Hol' Hard, Mattie," and several of the tunes that tickle.

Until at last when we became statues again and Chippy Dale had blown the notes of the last post, and we had in prayer and for forgiveness chosen "Lead, Kindly Light" for our retreat, we marched from the stage amid such an uproar nobody could hear our boots.

Frank A. Collymore

THE SNAG

MARK woke, stretched, rubbed his eyes, and yawned. At first he wondered where he was. He missed the iron rails and solemn little brass knobs of his own bedstead. Then, as he looked around the room, at the sloping roof of the attic with the myriad twisted rusty nails patterning its whitewashed surface like so many strange insects, at the chest of drawers, at the tin washstand with its basin in which squatted a shamelessly naked ewer, he remembered; he was spending a week with the Aunts.

And this was the second day. It was the first time his parents had allowed him to sleep away from home all by himself, and he was utterly and completely happy. Mother hadn't been keen on it, but Father had stood up for him manfully: "He's getting to be a big boy now, pet," (he certainly was—seven years old last Saturday!) "and you mustn't mollycoddle him too much. Besides, think how glad Jane and Judy will be to have him." Eventually it had all turned out satisfactorily. Not without a deal of incomprehensible fuss, Mother had brought him over yesterday, and, after many last-minute instructions and many embarrassing hugs and kisses, had gone, leaving him for the first time alone.

Not that the place was strange, of course. Mark knew Graham Lodge almost as well as he knew his own home. He had often spent days there. The house, old and rambling, was a couple of miles out of town; there were odd corners and unsuspected little flights of stairs almost everywhere; outside there was nearly an acre of wasteland once you got beyond the prim rows of garden beds and the tiny orchard—a thrilling country which bravely withstood the challenge of repeated exploration: there were so many things to be seen, so many things to be done!

Mark sat up. Now he could look right through the tiny window over the weathered shingled roof, on to the treetops aback of the house. They were enjoying themselves immensely, tossing in the breeze like horses all harnessed up and waiting to be given the

76

word go. Downstairs he could hear windows and doors being opened, voices, and other sounds of matutinal activity. The call of the morning was imperative. He scrambled out of bed, and, after the hastiest of toilets, was soon stepping cautiously down the rickety flight of stairs from the attic. He tiptoed past the bedrooms—Mother had warned him that Aunt Judy disliked her morning sleep being disturbed—through the wide-open dining room, out onto the wide bricked veranda that faced the rising sun. It was lovely there. You could look over the old wooden paling and the bread-and-cheese hedge past the dense clumps of neighboring trees to the low-lying hills a mile or two beyond.

The wind was busy this morning. From the tall whitewood tree near by, it was wafting a flurry of little winged seeds that spun round and round in the air as though they were alive; it was causing the gate that led to the backyard to sway to and fro with a series of brisk little explosions; and a rooster crossing the graveled path was undergoing a severe strain to his dignity with all his tail feathers blowing the wrong way; and on the wayward breeze rose and fell, plaintive in its loneliness, a long bugle call.

On Mark's right was a bit of wasteland sheltered in the hollow of an abrupt declivity. Once they had dug marl from it, but now it was chock-full of weeds and green-smelling bushes; a few anemic banana plants stuck up here and there, and crazy festoons of some luxuriant creeper added to its charm. The Indians Mark had killed there! And the lions and bears! He heaved a deep sigh of satisfaction. All this was his to enjoy for a whole week.

The garden gate exploded with somewhat greater violence, and a stocky well-built young Negro of twelve or thirteen carrying two buckets of water came through it sideways.

Mark rushed down the veranda steps.

"Hello, Joe!"

Joe, the yardboy, flashed a bright grin at him. "Hey, Masta Mark, you up early enough!"

Joe was Mark's favorite at Graham Lodge. The aunts were all very well in their grown-up way, Cookie was good-natured and could be depended upon to dispense secret samples of Aunt Jane's jams and jellies, and Martha the housemaid could be enticed in to singing folk songs for you on occasion, but Joe was the only one you could be really chummy with. He could tell the most entrancing stories about Brer Rat, could make kites, catch birds . . . do all sorts of things that really mattered. He had numerous chores to perform, and Aunt Jane saw to it that his time was not wasted; but whenever Mark paid a visit, it was understood that he had a right to his company for some part of the day.

"Did I tell you I was going to be here for a whole week?"

Joe deposited the buckets and filled the watering can before replying. That was a provoking characteristic of Joe's; he was so very deliberate in everything he did.

"Miss Jane tell me yesterday. Thought you had forget we. And Christmas come and gone."

There seemed to be some implied reproof in this remark, which set Mark wondering, but just then Aunt Jane appeared. She was wearing a large straw hat, pulled down over her ears and fastened under her chin with bits of tape, and her black, beady eyes shone brightly from beneath the overhanging brim. "Joe, Joe, what's become of you? Those snapdragons . . ."

Then she caught sight of Mark.

"Well, well, somebody's up very early. Have you had your tea?" And she stooped and presented a lean weatherbeaten cheek, which Mark dutifully pecked.

"And did you sleep well, dear?"

"Uh-huh," he replied, surreptitiously wiping his lips with the back of his hand.

"How many times have you been told not to say 'uh-huh'? Gracious, look at your hair!"

Unable to comply with her request, he ran his hand through it. He was sure he had brushed it.

"You can't run around looking like that. Come with me, dear." And grasping his hand she led him up the steps, through the dining room, into the large dark bedroom where the gigantic mahogany bedstead towered like a four-master at anchor. From the dressing table bristling with long-necked bottles and pincushions she extracted a yellow potbellied brush and a sinister-looking comb.

"Please let me do it, Aunt Jane."

Aunt Jane had a way of holding you under the chin and setting to work with such efficiency that she often brought tears to your eyes.

"Nonsense, Mark, you never brush your hair properly."

Mark submitted with a sigh. Aunt Jane was rather a problem anyway. She had little or none of the ineffective fussiness or submission to masculine whims so characteristic of grown-up ladies; there was something ruthless and forthright about her. Even her laugh, though she laughed but seldom, was gruff. Mark always pictured her in his private romances as the captain of a pirate ship. Yes, you had to watch your step with Aunt Jane. It was she who issued all orders at Graham Lodge and, what was more, saw that they were carried out to the letter. She was much older than Mark's mother, her sister, as was also Aunt Judy. They were both unmarried, and Father always referred to them as the old girls. But whilst Father always pooh-poohed Aunt Judy's suggestions, he usually paid attention to what Aunt Jane had to say.

When Mark visited Graham Lodge, Aunt Jane was a perpetual reminder that nothing could ever be perfect. There was always a snag somewhere.

"There," she said, giving a final whoosh of the brush to Mark's unruly curls. "Quite happy?"

"Uh-huh."

"I told you not . . ."

"I mean yes, Aunt Jane."

"And have you been to say good morning to Aunt Judy?"

"No. I thought she was asleep. Mother said . . ."

Aunt Jane chuckled. "No, dear, she doesn't sleep quite as late as all that. She's been reading her prayers. Come."

Aunt Jane ushered him into an adjoining bedroom. It was much smaller than Aunt Jane's, as was also the bed. Mark had often reflected how strange this was, for Aunt Judy was much larger than Aunt Jane. She was almost twice her size. She had a deal of faded fluffy brown hair, a roundish chubby face, and, goodness, what an expanse of bosom! This was usually bedecked with an array of brooches, from one of which, when she was neither reading nor crocheting, dangled a pair of gold pince-nez. Why she preferred them to spectacles Mark could never discover, for they were always becoming entangled with the brooches and could never be induced to remain for any appreciable length of time on her pudgy nose.

She was sitting in a low armchair and reading from an unattractive moth-eaten volume entitled *Sermons from Stones*. She closed it as they entered, removed the pince-nez, moored them to one of the brooches, and held out her arms.

"And how is my Diddums this morning?"

Her Diddums, disdaining to reply, and keeping a wary eye on the brooches, allowed himself to be embraced.

"Why 'stones'?"

"Stones? . . . Oh, that's just a metaphor."

"A meta . . . What's a meta . . . ?"

But that wasn't so easy to explain. "Well, it's from Shakespeare, you see, and what he meant was that one can find the most beautiful things in the most commonplace surroundings. . . . Music, for example . . . Listen to the wind in the trees . . ."

"Tea's ready, Judy," interrupted Aunt Jane. "Come along or you'll be getting wind in your stomach presently."

"Jane, Jane!" Aunt Judy's reproof was valiant, but she was still chuckling when they sat to tea.

Early morning tea was a misnomer at Graham Lodge for they always drank coffee. Rich brown coffee together with slices of thickly buttered toast, greasy flakes which flew off when you bit into them and made a pleasant mess of your face and hands. They were so messy this morning that Aunt Jane's ministrations were again called upon, and Mark found that the application of so much soap spoiled the lingering flavor of the coffee. Another snag, he thought.

But out-of-doors, he was soon carefree and happy. He was filled with the gaiety of the young morning. He raced, he danced, he sang, he chased the rooster (pompous ass) around the yard, teased Cookie by making sorties upon her and slapping her broad bottom, he snatched off Joe's cap and tossed it onto a branch of the lignum vitae tree . . . and by way of reparation persuaded Aunt Jane to surrender Joe to him for a game of Indians.

At "breakfast," which was at eleven o'clock, he was ravenous. There were flying fish so thickly covered with bread crumbs and egg batter that they seemed twice their usual size, coo-coo and okras, roast yam . . . He sighed with mixed feelings when it was all over; he'd had to refuse a second helping of guava jelly.

Aunt Judy wiped her lips with the large stiff napkin and leaned forward, her pince-nez tinkling upon the empty coffee cup.

"We're going to have a lodger, Mark. Did Mother tell you?"

A lodger! He looked up inquiringly. He didn't quite know what a lodger was.

"Yes. An old lady is coming to stay with us. To live here."

"Who?"

"She's . . . she's an old, old friend of ours. Papa . . . and Mamma were very fond of her."

Aunt Jane was scowling, and at Aunt Judy's last remark uttered a little growl of annoyance.

"Have I said anything I shouldn't, Jane?"

"Stick to facts, stick to facts," Aunt Jane grunted.

"That's all over and past, Jane. Forgiven." Then addressing Mark again, "Yes, she's coming to stay here with us."

"Why is she coming, Aunt Judy?"

"Because she's old and she's all alone. She has no one else to go to. All these years she's been living with her sister. And now she's gone."

"Where?"

Aunt Judy pointed to the ceiling and Mark looked up apprehensively.

"The Lord has called her home."

Aunt Jane grunted again.

"She's very old," Aunt Judy continued. "She was very fond of . . . of Papa, and now she has nowhere to go. Nowhere." She shook her head sadly.

"And when is she due?" (Mark's father worked in a shipping office.)

Aunt Judy smiled. "She's not a vessel, dear, but she's due, as you say, this afternoon. Your Uncle William is bringing her over."

"She's very old," Aunt Jane said warningly.

"Very, very old," emphasized Aunt Judy. "You've probably never seen anyone quite so old. You mustn't go asking her questions. She's eighty-nine."

Eighty-nine! Mark's eyes opened wide.

"She's rather hard of hearing," Aunt Jane added, "and she can't see very well."

"Is she . . . is she alive?" asked Mark, and then blushed the moment he'd said it, it was so absurd.

Aunt Judy's titter was lost in the guffaw that escaped from Aunt Jane.

"Alive! Of course she's alive."

"The things a child says."

"I mean . . ." But Mark couldn't quite express what he'd wanted to say. The conversation left a sense of unease in some corner of his mind.

Mark couldn't get Joe to play with him after breakfast. The lodger's room had to be made ready. It was comfortable but sparsely furnished, and an old cupboard had to be emptied and a few oddments shifted. It was great fun to help moving things from the cupboard, whose contents he had often speculated on. Stacks of letters, faded photographs of quaintly attired dead-and-gone relatives, scentless sachets, an old and extremely complicated mousetrap, a couple of Indian chisels, an entrancing book with cuts of skeletons and people's insides, which was all too quickly snatched away from him, broken china ornaments, an old rag doll . . .

Luncheon, lemonade and bread and butter, was a scrappy meal in between the bustle, and afterward, all preparations made, they sat in the drawing room. Aunt Judy set to work on her latest bit of crochet, Aunt Jane read a day-old newspaper and hummed some half-forgotten tune at intervals, Mark lay on the rug. It was too warm to play outdoors; besides, Joe had been dispatched on some errand and wouldn't be back until nearly four o'clock. Then he'd dress and he and Joe would roam about on the strip of windblown pasture aback of the house and—he looked across at Aunt Jane half-expecting her to read his thoughts—and pick dunks. Eating of dunks was, if not exactly forbidden, at least severely frowned upon. They were supposed to be extremely indigestible.

Mark found the drawing room mysterious, mysterious and faintly hostile. It was not gay and cheerful like the dining room; there were no windows giving onto the open sky. There were heavy curtains that masked the doors leading to the front veranda, faded reddish curtains that swelled and bulged importantly at the slightest breeze. All the furniture in the room seemed important and forbidding and alien. The elaborately carved chiffonier at the far corner of the room was the most aloof and superior of them all. And at night when the big brass hanging lamp was lit, and shadows lurked in the depths and corners of the room, you couldn't play at

Bears or Shipwrecks or anything like that, for you never knew what might hear your howls and come creeping, creeping softly from the dark recesses of the chiffonier to investigate. Only the rug was friendly and openhearted, the old rug with the twisty pattern of roses and . . . "Nearly four o'clock, Mark! Wake up, wake up! Time to dress."

And then when Joe had finished watering, away through the hedge onto the open pasture, where they rambled, picking and eating dunks to their hearts' content; then they lay in the sweet-smelling stubbly grass and Joe related once again the old stories of Brer Rat and the other animals.

The shadows lengthened, the sky changed from powder-blue to gunmetal; marauding bats were weaving a crazy pattern overhead . . .

When they returned Mark was greeted by Aunt Jane: "Wherever have you been, child? Uncle William wanted to see you before he left. He doesn't like driving in the dark. Come on in and meet Miss Martha."

"Who?"

"Don't you remember? The old lady. Come along, now. Remember, she is very old."

It was just six o'clock, and in the early January dusk the drawing-room lamp was shining wanly. In the far corner of the room beside the chiffonier a figure was seated, a figure that seemed too fantastic to be real.

Mark came to an involuntary halt and had to be pushed forward by Aunt Jane.

When they reached the figure, Aunt Jane bent over it and shouted in its ear, "This is Mark, Miss Martha! Mark! Carrie's boy!"

Miss Martha's head moved slowly around. In the brief while that ensued as she turned her head, a picture of her intense decrepitude was painted indelibly upon the screen of his memory. He saw a huddled, almost shapeless form, clad in some stiff shiny black material. From the white lace collar of the dress protruded a small shrunken head upon whose sparse silver hairs was perched a little lace cap with black ribbons. The face was scored with countless crisscrossing wrinkles and was of the color of wax. The bluish eyes, sunk far back in their sockets beneath the bony ridge of brow, were covered with a strange whitish film; the withered, puckered mouth was trembling.

Miss Martha's head moved slowly around with a swaying, halting approach. Mark clutched Aunt Jane's hand. He felt cold with horror.

"It's Mark. Carrie's son."

A look of understanding passed over the blank features. The lips mumbled.

"Carrie's son?"

"Yes, Miss Martha."

With all his soul he prayed she wasn't going to kiss him: O God, don't let her, don't let her.

Possibly the prayer was heard, for Miss Martha stretched out a hand, hitherto concealed by a black shawl Mark had not observed, a wasted, gnarled hand upon which were bunched bluish snaky veins that seemed to have been pasted on the withered flesh.

The hand moved blindly toward him. "How are you, little Mark?"

Aunt Jane gathered the groping hand in one of hers and with the other pressed Mark's into it.

But for the kindly tone of Miss Martha's voice he would have cried out at the impact of that clammy grasp.

"How are you, little Mark?"

He saw the quavering lips take upon them the tracery of a smile.

"Well, thank you, Miss Martha," he heard himself saying.

Miss Martha's other hand came out of its hiding place and passed tremblingly over his hair.

"A nice curly-headed boy, Carrie's boy," she mumbled, turning her sightless eyes toward Aunt Jane.

Mark felt his insides being torn between horror and an inexplicable overwhelming sadness. Tears sprang to his eyes.

Aunt Jane touched him on the shoulder.

"Run away now, dear. Go and call Aunt Judy for me."

Mark was unusually silent for the rest of the evening. Miss Martha was led to her room early and did not dine with them. After dinner he did not go into the drawing room. It was more hostile than ever tonight. When the dining table had been cleared and the porcelain lamp set upon the checkered tablecloth, he remained there looking through some old illustrated papers until bedtime.

Aunt Jane went upstairs with him, helped him put away his clothes, reminded him to say his prayers, tucked him in bed, and bade him goodnight.

He fell asleep almost immediately.

The moon had risen and the room was filled with an unusual pale radiance when he awoke. He had been dreaming. Miss Martha had been chasing him round and round the house. At last she had caught him and had sat upon his stomach. He could feel the weight of her there still. It was surprising how heavy she was. He was terrified. He wished he was back at home. He began to cry. He tried not to. But soon he had forgotten he was a big boy and was yelling at the top of his voice, "Mother, Mother, don't let her!"

Presently Aunt Jane opened the door, set down the smoking oil lamp upon the chest of drawers, and, looking unusually large in her long frilly nightgown, was bending over him.

"Mark, Mark, stop that howling. Whatever is the matter?"

The strangeness of Aunt Jane's attire and the novelty of seeing her hair done up in two spiky plaits reassured him somewhat. The crying stopped, but big sobs came up and burst inside him.

"Miss Martha," he said. "She was chasing me."

"Nonsense. You've been dreaming."

He continued to sob, and Aunt Jane smoothed his hair. She sat with him for a long time until at last he no longer felt frightened. And now he wasn't sleepy. He wanted to talk.

"Aunt Jane, does everybody have to get old?"

"Well, we all like to live as long as possible."

"But do we have to get old like Miss Martha? Do we?"

"Not always. But never mind that now."

"But do we, Aunt Jane? Will you get old like that? And Aunt Judy? And Mother? And Father? . . . And me?"

Aunt Jane fidgeted. "Go to sleep now, dear. It's very late."

"But why do we have to get old and look like that? It's awful, Aunt Jane."

"Go to sleep, there's a good boy. Very few people ever reach that age."

Mark was silent for a little while. Then: "I hope I die pretty young, Aunt Jane."

"Nonsense. Nonsense. Go to sleep."

Again Mark was silent. But his stomach began making gurgling noises and he rubbed it contemplatively.

"Have you got a pain in your tummy?"

"Miss Martha sat on it."

"Mark!"

"Yes, Aunt Jane?"

"You've been eating dunks again."

"Yes, Aunt Jane." Very faintly.

"Many?"

He considered the question drowsily. It couldn't have been Miss Martha after all. Perhaps it *was* the dunks. How old Miss Martha was, though . . . She was so old, so old, so very old . . .

"How many did you eat, child?" Aunt Jane insisted. Really, how anyone could eat those horrid frothy things . . .

Yes, Miss Martha was old, old . . . so very old. . . . How old had they said she was? . . . She was . . . she was . . .

"Eighty-nine," he murmured as he dropped off to sleep.

"My God!" ejaculated Aunt Jane. "Really, Mark, I must forbid—"

But on hearing his deep regular breathing she broke off and a smile spread over her stern old face. She stooped over and kissed his forehead.

She straightened herself, crossed over to the window and looked out on to the moonlit peace of the night. She sighed. Mark's questioning had come as a grim reminder of the toll taken by the passing years. Not so long ago she had watched Miss Martha dancing with Papa on just such a night as this. She had been beautiful then. Well, it was for Papa's sake she was with them now. Mamma would understand. And in a few years' time she, too, if she didn't die in the meantime, she too would be an old, old woman like Miss Martha. Time spared nobody.

She came back to Mark's bed and looked down at him. He was so young, so full of life . . . And downstairs, Miss Martha. And poised between them, but slipping dangerously over to the wrong side, herself. Ah, well, there was always a snag somewhere.

She took up the lamp, gave Mark another glance, closed the door behind her, and slowly creaked her way downstairs.

Roger Mais

LISTEN, THE WIND

THE banging of the shutter had kept her awake all night. It was a hinged jalousie, and the lower hinge was broken. The wind took it and rattled it and let it go until she was on the point of dropping off to sleep again, then it would shake it and bang it with tremendous thuds against her half-consciousness, until she wanted to get up and scream.

Joel's form stretched out beside her with an abandon of limbs that sprawled heavily and only occasionally twitched with little starts and prods against her side, filled her with a sort of dull resentment . . . that the slamming shutter that wrung tortures out of her should leave him so peaceful, so blissfully undisturbed.

Joel's gentle snoring was another prod against her peace of mind . . . that he could be so full of slumber, so unconscious of her burden of sleeplessness.

Tomorrow he would mend the broken shutter . . . always it was tomorrow. She smiled deeply—down inside herself. Joel's face bloated and sagging with the relaxation of total sleep, tugged at the involuntary strings of her sense of humor . . . made her aware of him as part of that self she had found in the wonderful merging of their two selves . . . as though she had given birth to that new, rapturous idea of Joel with the smooth, bloated cheeks of a boy—like the one you see sometimes on Valentine cards, with such ridiculously inadequate wings and a ridiculous little bow and arrow.

The round, jolly impudence of that face sharing her pillow, as he always did while hugging her in a close embrace, she found urgent of her uttermost compassion, sympathy, understanding. That was why Joel, pretending to be smart and full of worldly wisdom, and full of big ideas of things he was always on the verge of pulling off that would bring the stars down about their feet and set them up for life in the midst of a heaven of fulfillment, never really cheated her of her simple, yet sublime, understanding of Joel—an understanding that was more than half pure adoration.

87

It was at times like this, when she came into a kingdom of her own, peopled with herself and Joel, and intimate with the little imps of laughter that shook within her, that she could smile deep down within herself . . . a woman with a secret . . . an enigma to the neighbors, because in spite of all their unkind gossip and forebodings of evil, she still kept her secret, and it defeated them, thwarted them, so that their tongues were robbed of that spell of evil that drips with slander and gossiping—like a scorpion that has been deprived of its sting.

The banging of the shutter jerked her out of unconsciousness, just as she was dropping off again.

All night long she lay awake and listened to the gossip of the wind. Strange how tonight the wind was full of foreboding . . . like the tongues of those gossiping old women—only worse, much worse, for the words that told of the evil to come were her own words, shaped in her own consciousness.

She turned over on her side and tried not to listen to the things that the wind whispered about the trees outside, that the wind against the banging shutter was telegraphing to her waking brain.

Tomorrow was washday. She would take the large round bath pan full of washing down to the river, where all the women of the village would be. Above the noise of the paddles with which they beat the clothes, with the soap in them, against smooth, round boulders to get the deep dirt out of them, would be heard the tongues of the women, the cruel tongues that tore secrets from the innermost recesses of homes and spread them out before the world as washing was spread upon the river bank; the idle tongues, never for a moment quiet, that slavered over another's wounds with gloating and laughter.

But her secret would be locked tight within her breast, and she would smile deep down inside herself. That smile would be etched upon the corners of her mouth, but that would only be a reflection of the other, just as the white shifts of the women shone up at the men passing over the bridge above, from the placid surface of the pool.

The hearty cries of the younger women and girls who had waded higher upstream to bathe naked under the shadows of some trees, reached her in occasional gusts. Once there was a wild scattering of shrill laughter, and little shrieks of terror that were without sincerity, as some young men, for the mischief of it, sauntered down to the pool where they knew the girls were bathing.

There was a bold exchange of challenges, retorts, spiced with elemental, good-natured teasing, that would have sounded coarse to the ears of their more sophisticated sisters. But these black girls were of an innocence and naïveté that defied the conventions of what was regarded as the licence that might be allowed between men and women. The nakedness of their bodies, under the frankly covetous stares of the men, left them not one scrap ashamed. Their hiding behind boulders and frantic splashing of water to form a curtain around them, was not because they were ashamed to be caught thus, without their clothes on, but in reproof of those impudent young men who would reveal the secrets of their bodies' loveliness.

She had left Joel at home busy working out the details of his latest scheme to get his hands on to a lump of cash so he could go into business like his uncle, who was making a fortune out of buying produce from small settlers and selling it to the big merchants in the city and, more recently, had even been exporting it himself.

He had armed himself with hammer and nails with the intention of mending the broken shutter. He was all contrition in the morning when she told him of her sleepless night.

He found the ladder in the fowl house; the fowl had been using it as a roost. It too needed mending. As she was going out with the pan of washing on her head, he had just looked up from the ladder, his mouth full of nails, and waggled the hammer at her.

A gaunt old woman with the stringy, pimpled neck and sharp face of a crow, was saying in her cracked voice, that had an edge to it that reminded one of a saw, "He'll break your heart, my fine hussy. You take my word for it. He'll spoil your sweet face for you, and that smile too."

A stout woman laughed. Her strong arms were bare to the elbows, and she was wielding a paddle with savage grunts that seemed to indicate the satisfaction she got out of pounding at something . . . anything.

"That Joel of yours needs a strong woman to make a man out of him—to make him do something besides fritter away his time with women and dice. None of your milk-and-water kind for him, honey. After the first flavor wears off, he'll be sorry he ever tied himself to you, because you're the sort of weak creature that will never do no good to him. When he was foolin' round my Estelle— now there was a gal would have been a match for him—I told him straight he'd have to get a real job first, or else work the land his father left him. That sent him on his way. Then he took up with you."

She plied her paddle with powerful strokes, as though driving home her words.

It was getting dusk when she left the river with her burden of clean linen heaped up in a white bundle that flowed over the rim of the pan. She walked with the grace of a goddess, balancing her load upon her head with a perfect sense of rhythm, going up even the steepest incline.

She had to hurry home in order to prepare supper in time.

They were vultures, all of them, great flapping black vultures circling above the still-living flesh upon which they hoped to feast.

The sound of an ax met her as she was coming through the gate. Somehow that sound cheered her. It was Joel splitting firewood to cook their supper. The steady rhythm of the ax contrasted comfortingly with the quick feminine staccato thwacks of the women's paddles that still echoed about her ears. It was a homely agreeable sound. The slow smooth rhythm of it flowed about her, filling her breast. She smiled deep down inside her, taking out her secret as she did in quiet moments of revealment like these, to look at it with wonder, and a sort of gentle longing.

She sought to reconcile all things with the quotient of that . . . the fixed and constant idea of him that she held in her mind's ideal imaging . . . that rapturous idea of *her* Joel that she kept locked away in the secret place of her heart . . . the revelation of him that looked up at her and made demands upon all her woman's store of compassion and faith and understanding. . . . How could she make these things known to those soulless harpies who would rob her of her happiness for the barren satisfaction of knowing that she too had succumbed to the dross and canker of uninspired living. . . .

She cooked rice cakes and dumplings and set them before him with a hash made from what was left of Sunday's joint.

He ate ravenously without saying much. He was thoughtful and subdued this evening as though he had something on his mind. She recognized the mood. It meant that he was being driven by his thoughts into channels of exploration down which her simple mind could not follow him. When he tried to explain his plans to her, her inability to keep pace with his nimble thinking irritated him. She had learned, when he had moods like these, not to ply him with questions.

She thought, with that secret smile of hers, that those other women would have construed it differently. Their suspicious minds would instantly have accused him of infidelity. They would say, "He got some mischief on his mind. Ten chances to one it's another woman he's thinking about." But she knew differently.

He said, suddenly pushing his plate away from him, "Why the hell you don't say something, instead of just standing there, staring at me like an idiot all the time? God, I didn't know I was marrying a dummy, a woman without any mind of her own!"

He pushed the chair away from under him so savagely that it was overturned, and strode past her through the door. She felt as though he had struck her.

Numbed, unthinking, she started mechanically to clear the dishes from the table.

Hours later, as she lay awake in bed, the portentous stillness of night suffocatingly thrown about her, shutting her off from those emotions that moved deeply within her like currents of tide and wind moving across the face of the deep, she heard him coming up the path, singing lightheartedly as though he had not a care in the world.

She heard him stop just outside the door of their bedroom and remove his boots. He came into the room in his bare feet, so as not to awaken her. She felt his breath on her cheek as he bent over to kiss her long and tenderly.

She longed with all her heart to take his head upon her breast then, to tell him that all was right and as it should be between them . . . that she would not have had anything of all that changed.

She was surprised that he should have been able to fall asleep so soon, so soundly, leaving her, a little shaken, a little bewildered, with a feeling of unfulfillment, on the brink of this new and wonderful revelation of himself. Almost she could have been the tiniest bit resentful of this . . .

And then she too slipped quietly into the unconsciousness of sleep. How long she slept she did not know. It may have been an hour or a matter of moments. She was awakened by the banging of the broken shutter that Joel had set about mending that morning. It went through her with a nerve-racking insistency, until her body became numb and feelingless under the bludgeoning of that dreadful sound.

And the wind spoke to her . . . telling her wild and terrible things . . . telegraphing them to the sounding board of her unconscious self that translated those ominous whisperings and noises into words, heavy with portent. . . .

And all that night she lay awake and listened to the wind.

Austin Clarke

I HANGING ON, PRAISE GOD!

"Gawd bless my eyesight! Clemintine!"

"Pinky! The Lord have His mercy, child, I seeing right?"

"Yesss! How long you here in Canada?"

"Child, I here now two years running 'pon three. But I didn't know *you* was up here, too! What the hell bring you in this godforsaken place though?"

"I come up 'pon the Scheme. The Domestic Scheme. First little break in my whole life. And I glad for it. But I hanging on, meanwhile."

"You damn right to hang on. 'Cause you know as well as I do that there ain' no particular bed o' roses back where we come from. You could live donkey years back in Barbados, and 'cepting you have godfather or iffing you been to Queens College, or maybe you learn little needlework, you ain' getting *nowhere*. But how you making out?"

"Child, now and then. Today, I up, tomorrow, I down."

"Well, since I meet up with you, you might as well come and see where I lives. You ain' in no hurry, though? 'Cause you don't look like no Canadian what always rushing, running, turning their blood to water, they in so much o' hurry!"

"To tell you the truth, I come downtown to buy two-three item for the Missy, and . . ."

"How you and she gets along?"

"Betwixt me and you, I don't care much for working for these people. They *too* smart! They counting ever' grain o' rice, and watching ever' slice o' bake pork you put 'pon that table. But they want to go to the Islands, and then they would see *how* smart they is!"

"I list'ning."

"Well, this lady I works for . . . up in that place, Forest Hill Village, where all the rich-able Jews does live. . . . Clemintine, you never see so much o' money in your born days! But they *tight!*"

"You ain' lie, darling."

"Child, as I standing up here with you in this subway place, I ain' lying. I tell you. . . . well, since I been working off my tail for her, three years! she ain' give me one blind cent more than the two hundred dollar a month, what I start out with! All kind o' Jamaican gal, who you know can't touch me for the way I does set table with knife and fork . . . they getting all up in the three hundreds, and . . ."

"You kidding!"

Child, you gotta open your two eye wide, wide wide, in this country, yuh! If not, these people jook them out! And I complainin' to her 'bout how the hot stove giving me pains right up in my shoulder blade, all 'cross my back, in me stomach-bone, when the nights come. I catching more cold than what John read 'bout. Can't get a decent night's sleep, I so damn stiff all over my body from standing up at the hot stove, the ironing board . . . scrubbing the damn floor . . . kitchen floor, bedroom floor, living room, pantry. You see me here? Well, I don't know how I keeping the little fat God give me on these bones! All these years, and only two hundred dollars a month."

"You look good, though."

"Nobody mind you. You pulling my legs."

"We getting off at the next stop."

"You living 'pon Bloor Street?"

"Three months now. I can't take on the Missy quarters, soul. Nine o'clock I goes up, and I sits down and face them four bare walls. Prison walls I staring at, all the time. It have television, radiogram, record player. You can't ask for more comforts. But it lacking in something basic. It ain' have peace and happiness! You remember back home, when we was working out for them white people in the Garrison Barracks, how when the evenings come, we could stroll round the Garrison Pasture, or the Explanade? Maybe go for a bus drive and let little o' Silver Sands sea breeze blow in we face? Well, that don't happen here! No place to go. Nowhere to enjoy weselves. All we doing is making money. And nothing, nowhere to spend it. . . ."

"Don't talk so loud, the man in front list'ning. . . . You been going church lately?"

"Hold over. Lemme tell you something. I get *saved*."

"No! Clemintine, you lie!"

"Shhh! The whole streetcar ain' talking to you, woman. Only me talking to you. Yesss! I meet my Savior, soul. Is the onliest salvation what going to help soften my burdens, and my troubles. I looks at the situation this way: I here in Canada three years now, going 'pon four. After work, I changes my clothes and sits down in that Baptist church 'pon Soho Street, and praise my Gawd. Is the onliest salvation I sees in this place. I can't say I going looking for friends. Friends does bring yuh grief!"

"You couldn't be serious, though?"

"Don't let we pass the stop. We getting off at the next one. Look, sweetheart, I come in this place with the '57 batch o' girls. And when that big ugly man down at the Negro Citizens Place finish greeting ever'body, and showing we 'bout Toronto, loneliness step' in. Loneliness. I up there in Bayview. Nobody to talk to me. Only work. I ain' see a soul my color, saving the other Bajan girl, Babbsie, what works for that nice doctor family. I spraining my brain. Things ain' working out, at all. 'Cause we is womens together. And as womens, we does feel a certain way lonesome when we lonely."

"But how you? Engage' yet?"

"Me, darling? Bother out my soul-case with the niggers in this world!"

"You mean you ain' settle down with a man?"

"And what 'bout you?"

"I have God! And my Bible."

"Uh-huhn? . . . . I had a man once. I come up in Canada. I work hard as hell. And I saying I sending back money to him in Barbados, to help make up his plane fare. Well, eight month pass', and I still ain' hear one word from that brute. I getting ready all the marrieding things: white dress, veil, even the eats and drinks, 'cause I had a wonderful freeness in mind. I prepared. And you know, as the Regulations say, we could married after one year pass'. Well, I so *good* to that man! And he writing me all these love letters, how: "Darling, you leave me down here, and I lonely for you. Your heart in front o' my eyes all the time." And Clemintine, the sweet words! How he miss' me in a certain way and that he hope the reaches of his letters would find me in a perfect state of good health, praise God! Darling, I don't know what them sweet words do to my heart in this cold place, but I pouring all my money in that man hand when the paydays come. Two days after the month end, brisk! I down in the post office taking out money order. 'Cause, blood more thicker than water. And I know how lonely them winter nights is, up here, child; and iffing I could do little goodness for the man who say he love me, well, you ain' see no crime in that, eh? But, child, when I hear' the *shout!*"

"Wha' happen?"

"Man in the States! He grab-on 'pon my money and run to 'Mer'ca!

"Another woman, eh, soul?"

"Some slick Yankee rat turn the man head. And that's the last I hear."

"The dirty, ungrateful rat!"

"Me, soul? I trying to put man outta me mind! . . . . and when I gets that certain feeling, I buys a half bottle o' rum and drinks myself in a nice stupor, up in the Missy quarters, where I safe. And when I get enough 'pon that bank account, it is a acre or two o' land up in Highgate Garden that I after. Nice small stone bungalow, and a nice English Austin car. . . . I fix up for the rest o' me old days. I out-out man outta my life, honey!"

"You playing the fool, yuh, child. How you mean?"

"Well, I say I not *looking* for *no* man. If when I fix up myself good back home, and some retired old gentleman, with a little cash in his pockets, who ain' have no wife, and who ain' looking for bed companion, want little attention and somebody to take care o' him well. . . . *perhaps* me and him could come to a understanding."

"Take off yuh coat, lemme make some tea. I have some rum from home. Want little?"

"A drop in the tea, thanks, so the Missy won't smell it on my breath."

"But I had something to ask you. Who presses your hair? I looking for somebody nice to fix mine. I had such a nice hair-dresser back in Barbados! . . . up 'long Jessemy Lane!"

"I does mine myself. But I could do yours too."

"And bu'n off me two ear hole? I don't know, though, why some o' we girls who pass' the Scheme, don't open up a little nice, hairdressing place?"

"Child . . . heh-heh-heh! . . . . they 'fraid."

"But why we kind always hiding?"

"Ain' no common thing such as hiding, Pinky, darling. I telling you, child, that when you here as long as me or the next one, you going learn that what and what we does with our hair, it ain' no small thing that call for hiding. Them other too malicious. Too fresh! Ever'day, my Missy saying, 'Clemmy, dear, who fixes your hair? My! it's always in place. You uses Clairol or Helena Rubinstein shampoo?' I keeps my mout' shut. Let her take *that!* Now, tell me, what I going go picking my teet' to her, for? I remember one time, I taking my rest period before I go downstairs and put the steak in the oven. I gets so tired in the afternoons! So, I say to myself: 'This place so hot and humid, you better lay down here in your slip.' Well, I can't tell how long I been laying down. But when I open my eyes! Missy standing over me, look, she there, right over me, examining ever' hair in my head! I carry-on so stink, I make myself shame. She says to me, 'But Pinky, I was only trying to wake you. The master coming home early for supper.' And Clem, I take such a turn in her arse, she nearly change her color! I says, 'Well, niggerwoman, you drunk in Hell? Snooping 'bout the little dirty room you give me, and you think I going to smile up in your face and forgive you, as the rest do? Now lis-ten to me. And listten good good good. Mistress Bergenstein, you make this the last time you come in my room! It may be in your house, but the Regulations says this room is mine. Now, you get to-hell outta here, before I hold on 'pon you, and screel out for blue murder!'"

"Heh-heh-heh-heh-heh!"

"You ain' in 'greement with me?"

"That I is, child. She won't come round again!"

"You damn right she never come round again. You gotta make these whores understan' what the position is."

"The tea ready, soul. Help yuhself. . . . Oh, I forget to ask you. You ever get black-eye pea, or dry pea, since you here?"

"Mout' ain' touch little home food since I land up here, saying I bettering myself, child."

"Must get yuh some."

"Mout' watering for little good bittle!"

"When I say one thing, I got to say the next. You intend to stay in the Domestic Scheme, all the time you in Canada? Or you thinking 'bout taking up something diff'runt? Like nurse aid, or nursing assistant?"

"I don't know yet, child. Sometimes, when I realize that Canada ain' mine, I mad to bound back home where people does smile, and tell me good morning. 'Nother time, I takes a look at the situation, and I have to decide to stick it out. 'Cause where in Barbados people like me and you going get television, telephone, carpet 'pon the floor, inside running water from? Is like that, soul. We here, through the tender mercies o' God. He open this door for us. And we gotta thank Him. This Scheme is the best thing ever happen to poor womens like we. Is for that, and *that* alone, we shouldn't complain. Canada ain' no bed o' roses. And since *they* like they ain' want we nowhere in this Christ's world, we have to stick it our wherever the Lord say we going get a little break."

"Is too nice to have somebody . . . one o' your own . . . to exchange a thought or two with, sometimes. I sits there at that third-floor window up in that Forest Hill Village, and I looks down and see all them people, happy happy, and enjoying themselfs, and I ain' part o' that life, at all. I there looking out like I is some damn monkey. Days come and go, and not a friend to pick my teet' with, or swap two ideas. Only people. All these years, people people people, and more people. Ain' a friend. . . . not till I run in you this forenoon down in the subway place."

"Ain't a pleasant existence, at all. . . ."

"More than we mortals can bear! Many's the night when I flood that pillow with tears. Water dropping outta my eyeball like a tap leaking. Cry-water, Clem, tears! 'Cause I don't have a living soul . . . not one living *soul*. . . . to say, 'white in your eyes!' And yet, I earning more money than I ever had hope to work for in all my lifetime back in that island; and still I spending all my young years in a Missy kitchen. Before the Lord's sun rise up from behind the hills, I down there making breakfast. . . . lunch, snacks. Child, you never see a people could eat so much o' snacks in one day! And the suppers at night! They spends all their time eating. Two-pound piece o' steak for a fourteen-year-old kid? Ain' that worthlessness to the height?"

"You is a joker."

"And I sweating off my behind in front o' the hot stove. But what I going do? Pick up myself and say I looking for another job? It don't have no *other* job, darling!"

"Let we talk 'bout something else, child. Them thoughts does make me too blind drunk with vexatiousness. The more I think 'bout these things, the more I want to puke."

"This is nice tea. It bringing the air outta my stomach nice."

"Is the Missy steak you t'ief that giving you gas, soul."

"How yuh like this fur-imitation coat she give me for my Christmas, last Christmas?"

"Missy give you that? You works for a damn fine lady, then."

"She have her bad ways. But yuh can't kill her. Live and let them live, too."

"Can't beat them; have to 'gree with them."

"I hope you ain' thinking I does work for a slave driver."

"I know yuh feelings, darling!"

" 'Cause words does get back to Missy ears."

"You is a woman and a human being. Ever' human being have feelings. Ever' woman is flesh. That is why it so damn hard 'pon we who come up here adventuring in this rough country, without we mens as companions. And I ain' so drunk saying I tangling up with no white mens. Leave that for the Jamaican girls, love. And Canada ain' no featherbed we laying down 'pon."

"Is the Gospull!"

"That's why I telling you, child, looka, *hang on,* you hear me? Hang on! Even if it is by the skin o' your teet', hang on! For I hanging on. I take up the Bible. Not causing I is this big-able Christian-minded person. It ain' true. I like my rum, and my dances. But here, if I don't have Church to look forward to, well . . . Where it have a place for me and you kind to enjoy weselfs? The Granitt Club? The Yacht Club?"

"A shame, a shame! We can't even put on a nice frock and go for even a moonlight walk."

"Venture outta that place the Missy put you in, and see if man don't snatch you up offa the street! Ravage you! This place bad, it wild, savage. You can't trust *nobody.* We in *barracks.* Permanunt barracks. You see that rubber stamp-thing the Immigration People put on we passport when we land? You know what it say? PER-MANUNT! And it mean just that. We permanunt in this hell! . . . but I start out to tell you something else, though . . ."

" 'Bout the church."

"Church? What church? I only going there as I tell you, 'cause it don't have no other place for me to go."

"Hey! I forget . . . what is the hour? It ain' three yet, nuh? Drunk or sober mind yuh damn business. I ha' a work to go to.

"Three? Today, or tomorrow morning?"

"It pass' three?"

"Five o'clock, honey."

"Wuh loss! Look my crosses! The lady waiting for the things . . . well, look, Clemintine, child, me and you going have to get together some time soon, and lick we mout' again. . . ."

"See yuh Thursdee?"

"God willing. . . ."

"Care yuhself. Don't let that Missy put more on you than you able to bear, child."

"Not me, nuh, soul. Dog my age ain't no pup!"

"Well, you hang on!"

"In the name o' Christ! I hanging on, praise God!"

George Lamming

from IN THE CASTLE OF MY SKIN (a novel)

THE surface of the sand seemed much the same the day before, even, sloping and undisturbed. I watched it as though there was an image of the other day which I carried to check the details of this. But only that day had passed and the pebble had gone. It was about the same time the day before when the sun broke through the clouds and the light fell over the sea and the leaves. The sea was steady and dull as it is at dawn and the shore was deserted. It was then that I placed the pebble under the grape leaf, grouped the leaves round it in an inconspicuous heap and left it to wait my return the next morning. There was no one on the shore to see me, and even if I had been seen it wasn't likely that anyone would suspect my intentions. I didn't know myself what my intentions were, but this feeling, no longer new, had grown on me like a sickness. I couldn't bear the thought of seeing things for the last time. It was like imagining the end of my life. Now it had happened again. The pebble wasn't there. I looked again in the hope that I was wrong. I pushed the leaves back and dug my fingers into the sand, but there wasn't a trace of the pebble. Until my touch disturbed the evenness of the slope everything had seemed as it was the day before. The leaves were there in a small heap, slightly shifted by the wind, but there was no evidence that anyone had taken the pebble. I walked away from the spot circling the trees and lifting the branches of the grapevine with my feet. The small crabs crouched into hiding, and when the wind raised the vine I saw pebbles scattered about under the branches, but the pebble I had placed under the grape leaf wasn't there. I knew it, shape, size and texture. I had held it long and seen it closely before putting it away. And on the spot where I had placed it I had seen it more accurately against the bed of sand. For a moment I wondered whether the waves had washed up overnight, but I couldn't see why that should have happened. The spot which I had chosen was far up the shore. The sea was still the morning I had the pebble and it was as still this morning. Moreover, the sea on this side never ran so far up the shore. I had no overwhelming sense of the supernatural, but I was getting a strange feeling that something had interfered. I didn't know how to relate the situation because I didn't know how I should describe this sense of the other's interference. And in any case no one might have cared to understand why I should have hidden the pebble at all. It seemed rather silly when I thought of telling somebody, and since it was incommunicable to another I got the feeling more acutely of the other's interference. Either the pebble had taken itself away, or something had lifted it from beneath the leaves. It was clear that the sea had played no part. There was nothing I could do but carry the feeling of the other's interference and resign myself to the loss. I looked again, leveled the sand and rearranged the leaves. Finally, I told myself that it was useless to search. The day before I had seen the pebble for the last time. The sun was making a retreat behind the cluster of clouds and I entered the water, dull and wrinkled like a soiled sheet. I watched the light change and the waters part as I waded forward. It was daybreak.

I had no particular liking for pebbles, but I had seen the pebble at the top of a heap of others, bright and smooth in the sunlight. I passed the heap on my way up the shore and again on my way down. Each time I noticed the pebble and thought of taking it away. It seemed a little silly to be worried in this way by a pebble and I tried to think of something else. Then I went on with my exercise up and down the beach, and it seemed the pebble became more and more insistent. It was as though it stood out from the others and asked to be taken away. I ran in another direction and it seemed the heap of pebbles had shifted. I returned to that part of the shore where the real heap was and I decided to put an end to the pebble by taking it away. I spent the greater part of my time throwing it in the air and catching it as it came down. I threw it against the rocks and played with it on the shore. Then I took it into the sea and another game started. I pitched it into the moss over the sand and dived it up. I threw it a yard away and swam under the surface to meet it before it settled on the sand. And this went on until it became other than a pebble. Each time I retrieved it I held it long and felt its shape and saw its texture until it was no longer a pebble. It had become one of those things one can't bear

to see for the last time. I said I would take it home and return with
it the next morning, and then the thought occurred that I should
hide it.

I wasn't sure why I decided on hiding it. At first it seemed that it
would mean more to me if I had been separated from it for a day.
When I returned to take it from the hiding place I would choose,
my enjoyment would have been greater. Then I thought of the risk
of losing it, because it seemed to me that there were certain things
one couldn't lose. Things which had grown on you could be risked
since they had an uncanny way of returning. And above all I had a
vague feeling that there was no reason one should see things for
the last time. I selected the spot and placed the pebble under the
leaf on the even slope. A day had passed. There was no change in
the weather, and the waves were as quiet as ever on this side of the
sea. They rode up gently, tired themselves out and receded in
another form toward the sea. But the pebble had gone. The feeling
sharpened. It had really started the evening before when I received
the letters, and now the pebble had made it permanent. In the
evening I had read the letters and it seemed there were several
things, intimate and endearing, which I was going to see for the
last time. It was very embarrassing when my mother came in and
saw me rereading the letters. I threw them aside and walked out of
the house. At my age I couldn't risk making a fool of myself, and
the safest defense seemed to be a forced indifference. Yet there
was little in the letters themselves to upset me. It was the feeling
which came on when I saw what was going to happen.

I tried to recall when this feeling had started, but that seemed
useless. I could only think of it as a sickness which had spread
through the system, gradual and unsuspected, but certain and permanent. You couldn't bear the thought of seeing things for the last
time, and things included all that had become a part of your affection or anger, or even the vague feelings which you couldn't corner
and define. Things included people, objects, and situations.
Whether you were glad or sorry to be rid of them you couldn't
bear the thought of seeing them for the last time. I remembered
vaguely that something used to happen when as a small boy I rode
in the bus and reviewed the objects and people as they glided by.
The shop and that lamppost and the man who stood at the corner
blank and impersonal. It seemed that the bus was steady while

they slipped past, and I wondered whether I would see them again, and it was difficult to understand why I felt as I did when I imagined that I wouldn't. But the next day I saw them, and the next, and each time the little act repeated itself. Each day the objects were new and the feeling was new, and unless I forced my mind in another direction, I received the thought that I had seen them for the last time. I experienced the feeling in a high degree when I left the village school; and in the circumstances there was no reason to be sorry. The school was a kind of camp with an intolerable rigidity of discipline. The head teacher and all the assistants carried their canes as though they were in danger of attack from the boys, and they used them on all occasions and for all sorts of reasons. Yet the feeling was there. I was seeing the village school for the last time. The teachers shook my hand and wished me the best of luck. And I left with the intolerable feeling that they had somehow gone forever. I recalled the lampposts and the shops and the man at the corner, and I knew that the feeling was not new. That was a situation which I recalled, although I had to tell myself that the feeling was present long before I entered the High School.

Later when Trumper came to say that he was going to America I couldn't bear to look him straight in the face. He had always dreamed of going to America and the dream had come true. He was happy and I was glad for him. He left on a wet morning three years before I left the High School; and although an important difference in our fortunes had forced us apart I went to see him off. We stood on the pier together and watched the ship, which was anchored in the distance. There were hundreds of them leaving for America, and I saw them all less real than Trumper but with the same sickness which the feeling brought on. It seemed I wasn't going to see any of those faces again. Later I returned to the pier and watched the big ship sweep through the night and out of sight across the sea. They were gone. I started to think of Trumper and Bob and Boy Blue, using Trumper as a means of tracing when the feeling had started. Boy Blue and Bob remained in the village, but they had drifted into another world. None of them had gone to the High School, which was the instrument that tore and kept us apart. I started to think of the High School and what had happened to all of us in the intervening years; and suddenly as if by an inner compulsion, my mind went back to the spot under the grape leaf and the pebble which I had seen for the last time. I ducked my head in the water and came up again wet and refreshed.

It was a year or two after the riots and I was eleven. It probably wasn't the way all boys at that age behaved, but when the results of the public examinations were announced and I learnt that I would be going to the High School I was wild with joy. It seemed in a way the only thing I had looked forward to, and when it happened I didn't care what would happen next. It was true my mother had been preparing me for it. For three or four years she had paid for the private lessons which were a preparation for the public examination. At last I had arrived and the world was wonderful. I told Bob and Trumper and Boy Blue and they were as excited. It was as though they were going to trade on the fact that they had a friend in the High School. But my mother saw the matter from a different angle. She said it was nothing more than she expected, and hadn't it happened she would have considered all her efforts and money a waste of time. I became less enthusiastic until the books and the school uniform arrived. These were my first introduction to the High School. There were several books, including some in languages I couldn't understand, and there were books that treated of the subjects which the village head teacher used to call a kind of advanced arithmetic. The books were so many and so large that it wasn't possible to put them all in the sack. When she took me to the High School on the opening day of term we were like refugees burdened with the weight of personal possessions. I strung the black-and-gold tie round my neck, tieing the knot so that both colors showed equally on it. Then I put some of the books under my arm, holding the sack with the others in my hand, and looked at myself in the mirror. I was pleased with what I saw.

But my mother was unsparing. She kept harping on the money she had spent on books and uniform and insisted that if I didn't do well at the High School she would consider everything, scholarship and all, a waste of time. Then there was much talk about the opportunities others had had and wasted, and the opportunity which I would now have to make a man of myself. At times she seemed to take it for granted that I wouldn't do well at the High School, and there followed an unbearable monologue which described the way her money and time would flow into Maxwell pond.

I entered the High School alert and energetic. The surroundings were very exciting. To the west the orchard with its tall green hedge and opposite the playingfield where the groundsman was preparing the cricket pitch. The school was much larger than the village school, and if there weren't more teachers, there was something which made them look more prepossessing. The headmaster wore a parson's collar with a long black gown. He had a large red face with a thick neck and very tiny eyes. When he came out into the school yard with the other teachers it was obvious that he was the chief. He didn't seem to look anybody straight in the face. When they talked his head was raised toward the treetops and when he spoke you got the feeling that he knew beforehand what the other person was going to say and was only being kind enough to let them say it. His manner was often jovial, but never familiar. In many ways he had proved very kind to me.

It wasn't long before I relaxed into an *old boy* at the High School. I grew as callous as most of the others, and played the role which the *old boys* played. You knew the school. You knew what certain masters liked and what others couldn't stand, and you behaved accordingly as you wanted to affect them. One master couldn't bear to hear the boys talk about girls because that sort of talk would sooner or later ruin them. The *old boys* knew this and made it a point of talking about girls when he was present. Another had a liking for chocolates and the *old boys* kept asking him questions about sweets. Sometimes the boys asked questions which to them seemed perfectly straightforward but which irritated the masters. Sir, what did you have for breakfast this morning? Sir, what sort of boy were you at school? Sir, do you dance? Sir, what would you do if you impregnated a girl and you couldn't marry her because you didn't want to marry her? Sir, is it true that masturbation is bad for your health? Sir, is there a God?

This world was different from that of the village school. There was no supervising minister, and although the governor and the bishop were always invited to attend the annual prizegiving, there were no inspectors who gave orders as they did at the village school. To one who was new from the other place the High School seemed a ship with a drunk crew. The restrictions were fewer than those at the village school and the boys seemed happier. And, of course, there was no contact between the two. Education was not a continuous process. It was a kind of steeplechase in which the contestants had to take different hurdles. Some went to the left and others to the right, and when they parted they never really met again. It would have been inconceivable for a teacher at the High School to take a class in the village school, and the teachers at the village school didn't belong in or out of school to the world in which the other teachers lived. The village school and the High School were not only different buildings with different teachers. They were entirely separate institutions.

The High School was intended to educate the children of the clerical and professional classes, while the village school served the needs of the villagers, who were poor, simple, and without a very marked sense of social prestige. When a boy left the village school it was customary for him to learn a trade. And many of the village carpenters and shoemakers were recruited from such boys. They left at fourteen and spent a year at the bench. Within two years they had become men with weekly wages and women of their own. If the boy was clever at the village school, he remained to become what was called a pupil teacher. After he had taken a few preliminary examinations he was given a class. Most of the village teachers were recruited in this way, and it was no wonder the village school should have received within six or seven generations the same kind of instruction in the same way. At the High School the boys never left till they were eighteen or nineteen. Then they entered the civil service or an English university where they read for one of the professions, law or medicine. Those who didn't pass the Cambridge examinations and couldn't enter the civil service or the university were heard of four or five years after they left. They usually went to live with an aunt in New York. The doctors and the lawyers returned to practice in the island and the civil servants seemed to remain all their life under the evergreen trees outside the public buildings. When the clock chimed four in the afternoon they parked on the pavement and watched the buses and the women and the sea which never had anything to say. They were smartly dressed, well groomed and on the whole quite imposing. When you saw them you didn't think the High School had done so badly after all.

Those boys who went from the village school to the High School had done so on the award of the public examinations. There weren't many, and it wasn't easy for them to cope with the two worlds. They had known the village intimately and its ways weren't like those of the world the High School represented. Moreover, it wasn't until they had entered the High School that they knew what the other world was like. They may have heard about it and seen it in buses, at dances, and in the various public departments of the civil service, but it remained foreign. Gradually the village receded from my consciousness although it wasn't possible for me to forget it. I returned to the village from the High School every evening. The men sat around the lamppost talking or throwing dice, and when it was possible I joined them. Now that I was at the High School it was easier to join them, but it was more difficult to participate in their life. They didn't mind having me around to hear what happened in the High School, but they had nothing to communicate since my allegiances, they thought, had been transferred to the other world. If I asserted myself they made it clear that I didn't belong, just as Bob, Trumper, and Boy Blue later insisted that I was no longer one of the boys. Whether or not they wanted to they excluded me from their world, just as my memory of them and the village excluded me from the world of the High School.

It would have been easier if I had gone to live in a more respectable district, but that was beyond my mother's resources. She would have done so without hesitation, but she saw it was impossible and consoled herself with the thought that it didn't matter where you lived. The mind was the man, she said, and if you had a mind you would be what you wanted to be and not what the world would have you. I heard the chorus every day and sometimes I tried repeating it to others. The mind was the man. I remained in the village living, it seemed, on the circumference of two worlds. It was as though my roots had been snapped from the center of what I knew best, while I remained impotent to wrest what my fortunes had forced me into. And it was difficult to say who was responsible. I didn't play cricket at the crossroads as often as I used to because the cricket pitch at the High School seemed to me much better, and since I had a chance of selection for the school team it seemed sensible that I should get used to things like pads and gloves. Bob and Trumper thought otherwise. It wasn't safe for the

High School boys to see me at the crossroads. And we were both right. We met every day and talked, but the attitudes were different. It reminded me in a way of the village head teacher and the inspector. Hidden somewhere in each was the other person which wondered how far the physical surface could be trusted. I had had the last of a certain situation, and I knew the feeling which the letters I received the evening before and the pebble had made permanent. I saw them every day and yet I had seen the last of them. Soon I would see the last of everything.

Sometime later we heard about a war in Europe. The men who assembled round the shoemaker's shop had prophesied it, and the shoemaker, who had never abandoned his friend Priestley, said that that writer had prophesied it too. They said it was the last of the British Empire, and it was another piece of evidence that God didn't like ugly. That was the way they put it. They said the world had become ugly and so had the village. And in fact the village had changed greatly in some ways. But at the High School we had got used to reading about wars in Europe, one of which lasted a hundred years. It seemed that Europe had taken a fancy to war since they even tried to give them decorous names. I recalled that one was called the War of the Roses. It seemed a perfectly natural thing for Europe to have war. The newspapers and the radio reported what was happening in Europe and people seemed very concerned. But at the High School the boys weren't particularly shaken. If we regretted the war it was simply because we foresaw another date added to the intolerable pile which they called history. We received the news with the same curiosity or boredom we had shown when reading Michael John's account of the Norman invasion of England. But the shoemaker's friends were more interested and concerned because they seemed to understand the issues much better. History had quite a different meaning for them. At the High School the battles took place there and then within the limits of the textbook, and it was our business to note and check all the details. The shoemaker's friends couldn't remember many dates, so they talked in terms of vast periods. The shoemaker said once upon a time there was a thing called the Roman Empire and it didn't matter when precisely this thing was. But the thing was real for them. These things had not only happened but they happened for certain reasons. And they knew the reasons.

One morning the boys at the High School were assembled in the hall and the headmaster announced in a very slow and solemn voice that France had fallen. He said it was the greatest threat to civilization mankind had ever known. The school was quiet, and for a moment this war seemed somewhat different from those we had read of. When they were dismissed the boys speculated on the fall of France. They talked about the Rhine and Rhône and some drew small maps of the routes the Germans must have taken. I went home in the evening and told my mother and the neighbors that France had fallen. I looked terribly gloomy and spoke in a voice like the headmaster's. They were very sorry. They didn't know anything about France, but they knew that France was on the side of England, and Barbados was Little England. Three hundred years of unbroken friendship, they thought. They understood what that meant, and the fall of France became their fall as well.

One day shortly after lunch a young man called Barrow walked up the school yard and entered the headmaster's office. He smoked a cigarette as he spoke to the headmaster, and one or two boys who passed by the headmaster's study stole a glance and ran to inform the others. Some of them said they had known Barrow at school and it looked strange to see him smoking in the headmaster's presence. We were a little curious. In the afternoon the school was assembled and the headmaster talked about Barrow. He was leaving in a fortnight to join the Royal Air Force. There were several Barrows, the headmaster said, and the school felt only pride for those who had the courage to follow the motto which was printed on the plaque in the hall: Greater love hath no man than this, that a man lay down his life for his friends. Some of the boys in the upper school started to get the feeling they should become Barrows.

From now on the war had become more of a reality. At the High School a course in military training was started. One of the soldiers from the local army came every evening to train the boys in the use of the Bren and Sten guns. They crawled on their stomachs for hours across the playingfield, carrying the guns pressed under their arms. Some learnt wrestling tactics which they could apply if unarmed they were attacked by the enemy. It seemed very exciting, but for most of them the exercises were intolerably strenuous. The guns bruised their arms, and their knees and elbows remained sore. Then there were parades which lasted for hours and on which some of the cadets fainted. The training seemed terribly rigid. Those who weren't cadets were taught how to conduct themselves if the school was ever bombed. When the whistle went the boys walked out from their classrooms in single file, silent and tense, taking the orders from a member of the imaginary civil defense. We walked toward a wood on the outskirts of the school and stood erect against the school wall. We were told how we should stoop or lie if it were necessary to lower the body. This was very frightening for it had become part of the school curriculum, and it didn't seem that these exercises were being carried out as a joke. Moreover, a rumor had circulated from the shoemaker's shop that there were Germans in the island. It was said that some speaker by the name of Lord Haw-Haw, who did a regular broadcast from Germany, had given the name of the sugar factory in Barbados where the island's surplus food was stored. The Germans knew the layout of the land. This war wasn't history. It was real, and we walked out every morning on the civil exercises saying farewell to the classroom. We expected to hear the bomb fall.

Some of the boys were hardier and tried to make a joke of the others. They said the island was much too small, and the Germans had nothing to gain by dropping a bomb on Barbados. One boy said that although a bomb was a little smaller than Barbados it cost more than all the sugar factories and the stores put together. One bomb could have brought an end to life in Barbados, he said, but the bomb cost so much more than the island, the expense would have been incredibly extravagant. The Germans couldn't afford to indulge in such waste at that stage of the war. Another said he couldn't care less, but he had always heard his grangran say that if you went on crying wolf, wolf, the wolf would one day visit you, and he believed this military training and the civil exercises were just another way of crying wolf, wolf. If he were right the school went on with its cry wolf, wolf, and indeed the wolf did come.

Shortly after four o'clock one afternoon a large merchant ship was torpedoed in the harbor. The city shook like a cradle and the people scampered in all directions. The war had come to Barbados. Many of us flocked to the pier in the hope of seeing the submarine. The shells made a big booming noise and the spectators ran wild with hysteria. They ran a few yards away and ran back as quickly in the hope of seeing the submarine. The ship's hull sank slowly below the surface and most of us had our first experience of seeing a ship go down. She was loaded with cargo, which had not yet been taken off, and the men started speculating on what would happen. The ship sank slowly. For reasons which were never understood the three or four submarine chasers which had always been active were out of order on this occasion. One was floating some yards away from the ship but the propeller, it was said, had been taken out for repairs. The others were in the dock. The people swore the Germans were advantage-takers; and one man said if he had his bathing suit what and what he would do. No one knew whether he was going to have it out with the submarine or the inactive chasers, but he kept on swearing, ". . . would to Jesus Christ I had on my bathin' suit."

But it was only natural in a war that the Germans should do what they did. If Barbados said she was Little England she had to put up with what she got for being what she was. Moreover, it was rumored that when the Prime Minister of England announced the declaration of war the Governor of Barbados, at the request of the people, sent the following cable: "Go brave big England for Little England is behind you." The Germans had no time to make subtle distinctions. A man started to say that it wasn't the Germans at all. He had it from the best authority that the Germans weren't operating in those waters. He was going to explain further when the police strolled up and told him that if he wanted to spend the night with his wife and children he had better shut his mouth. The people were anxious to hear the details since he had only got as far as saying that certain people were trying to get certain ships off the line for purposes of trade between the islands. The man kept quiet, looking, like the others, toward the sinking ship.

The war went on like an exciting habit, while the village and the High School went their separate ways, each like a slow disease. At the High School the usual things were done. Cricket and football replaced the classrooms in the evening, and the interschool athletics were never interrupted. We sank quietly into this life like a crab clawing through filth. But the village was changing in some ways, and with each change I got the feeling which the pebble had made permanent.

So many things were being taken away and the boys' activities changed with each departure. I had a feeling sometimes that the village might get up and walk out of itself. It had receded even farther from my active consciousness, but I knew now that somewhere in my heart, already riddled with fear, ambition, and envy, there was a storage of love for the sprawling dereliction of that life.

One morning I walked through the wood and placed a pin on the train line. I sat beside the rails waiting for the hoot of the engine, and it was like returning to the days before the riots. There weren't any other boys around and if I had not been so excited about seeing the blade I would have tried to find out where the boys had gone. But some time had passed since I had placed a pin on the line, and in a way I preferred to do it alone. I waited for an hour, and then rain fell in a fine clean drizzle and I went home. The train didn't come and it never came again.

It was my last year at the High School when Bob and Boy Blue were recruited for the local police force. In the village this might have been regarded as an improvement on carpentry, but it had disqualified them further from the social layer for which the High School was preparing me. Trumper had emigrated to America and no one could tell what he would become. Most people who went to America in such circumstances usually came back changed. They had not only acquired a new idiom but their whole concept of the way life should be lived was altered. It was interesting to speculate what would happen to Trumper. Mr. Slime had continually raised the question of emigration in the local House of Assembly, and a delegation which was sent to Washington brought back the news that the United States Government would contract a considerable number of laborers for three or four years. The rates of pay seemed fantastic to people like Trumper who had never worked. We parted as friends who had overcome all the little difficulties which the village and the High School had made for us. We were all wearing long pants now, and it seemed silly that we should be worried by the things that kept us apart while we wore short pants. We had promised to forgive and forget.

Bob and Boy Blue had also come to say that they were going into the force with the jocular warning that I would have to be on my *p's* and *q's*. They were the civil guardians of the law. I had remained at the High School.

America. The High School. The Police Force. There were three

different worlds where our respective fortunes had taken us, but
now it was time for me to leave my world. The feeling came back
as sharp as it did when I remembered leaving the village school
and later Trumper's departure. And there was little reason why I
should have regretted leaving the High School. For six years my
life had alternated between boyish indifference and tolerable
misery. I had done badly after the first year and shortly before I
decided to leave there was a request for my expulsion which the
headmaster rejected. He had summoned me to the study and it was
the last of several lectures which I had. He sat behind the large oak
table with his head pointing upward and his short fat fingers
twiddling on his legs. And he told me what some of the masters
had said. It seemed more like a conspiracy than an accusation.
Then he said what I had never been told at the High School. He
said they were trying to make gentlemen of us, but it seemed that I
didn't belong. Immediately I remembered Bob and Boy Blue, who,
in different language, had said the same thing. The headmaster gave
me the feeling that I had made him seem a big failure. It seemed
he had spilled his attention on an undeserving wretch. He said
there was nothing more he could do, and passed me on to the first
assistant who would probably understand me better. There were
times I recalled when I wanted to hate the masters. I didn't know
whether I had been more fortunate than Boy Blue and the others,
but I had a feeling that I wasn't. I tried to think what would have
happened had I become a carpenter or a shoemaker or a pupil
teacher. It was the feeling uppermost in my mind when I was
about to leave the High School. Would it have made any difference
if I hadn't gone? My interest in the games and the people I had
known was exhausted and my feelings were gradually moving back
to the village. It is true I had learnt something of two foreign
languages which I liked, but they didn't seem to apply until I met
the first assistant.

This personal attachment to the first assistant was the only concrete thing for which I could be grateful to the High School. Had I
not gone to the High School we would never have met. I didn't
remember how we met, but it might have had something to do with
a poetry lesson which he was asked to supervise. He returned three
or four times and we had talked. The first assistant was a poet and
actor who could scarcely have been a finer actor, but who might

have been a better poet if he weren't an actor. He was a man of medium height, robust, alert, and energetic. He walked like an ex-football player who couldn't forget the athletic stride. He had a large head with a receding forehead that had got lost in a shock of thin brown hair. The hair was always flying wild, disheveled and resistant. His skin was heavily tanned and his eyes, small and brown, looked down at the nose that came out from beside them like a pleasant surprise. He was over fifty with the look of a man in his early forties, and his face, which was capable of many expressions, sometimes gave you a feeling of unease. He was versatile, sensitive, and cultured. He had a large and carefully chosen library which he had invited me to use. He was always making suggestions for my reading, and he talked about the way people painted and what had to happen before he could write a poem. When visitors called who didn't know me and who might have made me feel uneasy, he gave me a large album which I fingered till they had gone.

I couldn't understand what part he played at the High School for the world of his immediate interests was quite different from what the school knew. He must have been capable of living on different levels and this must have been responsible for the reputation he had of being genteel and accessible. He was a kind of legend in the High School. But the legend had nothing to do with his interests. It related to his gifts of social intercourse. Few had ever seen him angry although it was said that he could be violently angry. From the malaise of the High School I had drifted into the despair of the first assistant's world. Soon I found it difficult to cope with what I wanted. The High School had dissolved into one man who represented for me what the school might have been. It was two years since I had known him well and the keenest result of that attachment was the feeling that somewhere deep within myself or far beyond the limits of this land was a world whose features I did not know and might never grow to understand. He was the High School without the world which it prepared me for. Now I started to feel that I was going to see him for the last time.

The two letters had arrived the evening before, and the feeling was acute. One had come from Trumper, who had written in a way I hadn't thought him capable of and which in fact I didn't quite understand. He had been away three years and the new place had done something to him. The language was not unlike what he was used to speaking in the village, but the sentiments were so different. He had learnt a new word, and the word seemed like some other world which I had never heard of. Trumper had changed. The other letter came from the school authorities in Trinidad. They had confirmed the appointment which I had accepted. I was going to the neighboring island to teach English to a small boarding school for South Americans from Venezuela and one or two other republics. There was something ironical in the choice of this teacher. I thought the masters at the High School would have been a little puzzled and amused when they heard. For a moment I felt like the small boy who had won the public examination to the High School. I promised that I would start afresh, a new man among other men.

Then the pebble returned, present in its image on the sloping sand under the grape leaf, and I thought of them all in turn. Trumper, Boy Blue, Bob. The High School, the village, the first assistant. They had all arisen with the pebble, making the feeling of separation a permanent sickness. The thought of seeing things for the last time. And my mother? She seemed in a way too big for this occasion. I waded out of the water and walked to the rocks where my clothes were bundled. For the last time I looked at the spot where I had placed the pebble, and then quickly turned my thoughts to Trumper's letter. It was difficult to decide which was less perplexing. I repeated the sentence with which he ended the letter. "You don't understand, you don't understand what life is, but I'll tell you when I come and I am coming soon."

Karl Sealy

THE SUN WAS A SLAVER

THE workmen were hurrying homeward, their arms powdered above rough elbows and their black faces smeared with the white stone, the time I took Grandfather's jug of milk for the last time. The red sun was striking upon the rising walls of the chapel's new vestry, and the tops of the dingy trees were the color of honey. But when I reached Grandfather's house the last sun had gone, and in the east was a color like when I tilted the milk so that it stained the glass jar.

My grandfather grumbled because the jug wanted two inches to fill it, and swore that children no longer knew their duty to their parents, and that he'd lick his arthritis and be about and rear his own cow again yet. I told him my father said why didn't he stop being so stubborn and chuck this living alone and come and live with us, but he made a sound with his mouth like a pig feeding and said that he'd never been a trouble to anyone in his life and he didn't plan to be then. He'd been always master in his own house, Grandfather said, and, say help his blest, he'd rather die than be otherwise. More and besides, my grandfather went on, he thought it more proper for a son to come to a father, not for a father to go to a son. If my dad wanted to show gratitude to his old parent, Grandfather said, let him come with his wife and me and make our homes there. But to be ordered around and lorded over in his son's house by a young gal like my mother, it certainly wasn't true, said my grandpa. And I could tell my dad too, Grandfather told me, that if he thought twice about sending him the little milk, say help his blest, he could very well stop that too. Grandfather wouldn't have been put out, he said. He wouldn't even have been surprised, for this generation, he said, was a generation of vipers, and children would rise up against parents.

But when I had lit the lamp and taken the milk from the stove Grandfather called me his own dear Ruth and, hugging me into his side, stroked my head with his hand, the hardness of whose palm I seemed to feel through my hair. And in a voice that was kind like his actions he asked how my dad's canes were looking, and if my mother'd been about as usual that day, and if I would have liked a baby sister like myself or a brother. I told him that my mother had only been just in time to stop Dad and Bert Seale from fighting, for Dad had caught Bert breaking the arrows from our canes. Grandpa said that my father mustn't get himself into trouble with such red trash as Bert Seale, but that all the same Bert knew it was wrong to break the cane arrows, for the water would get in.

Grandpa had just taken the first sip of milk when the first note came from the chapel, and he put his face as though the milk tasted badly and turned his face to the window as though to spit it out, but I knew it was because he didn't think much of Chrissie Coggins as a bell ringer. My grandfather said that if ever in life anyone told me a bell was an ordinary piece of cast metal without soul or power, I should look him in the face, whoever he was, and tell him to his teeth he was a liar. Or if I didn't care to be so straightforward, seeing that I lived only a few inches off the ground, I could tell whoever it was that my granddad said so, and direct the lying rascal where he could be found too.

Grandfather said that Chris Coggins' bell ringing had as much to it as the bell on a wandering wether, and said that Chris'd make the best bell that was ever molded sound cracked. If medicine, or the priesthood, or law was ever in anybody's blood, Grandfather said, bell ringing was in the very bones of our family, and it'd broken his heart when my dad took up mad with this planting, with overhead irrigation and the Lord knew what, and had no time for bell ringing. Grandfather told me of the time when, as a young man, he had gone from parish to parish and listened to a hundred bells, each speaking to him with a sweet different voice; how he had climbed a hundred high steeples and traced with his hands the curvatures of each vibrant bell, until he knew them all like intimate forms.

My great-great-grandfather it'd have been, Grandfather said, who'd made his little piece in cholera by letting it be known that if the right hands were put to the church bells no cholera'd come to the members. And from far and near, grandfather said, the villagers flocked to the old man, dropping their shillings in the jar of vinegar which he kept for the purpose, and praying him to put his hands to the bells of their missions. The old man, Grandpa said, was kept far busier than a doctor, and made more too out of cholera, he'd warrant. For no true member of a church whose bell the old man rang was ever stricken, Grandfather said, only the water-washed Christians. And if I doubted that he spoke the God's truth—for this generation, Grandfather said, was full of disbelief—I could get into conversation with old Clawson Peare, who'd been a young lad in cholera, and whom the Lord seemed to let live to vouch for the truth of such things.

But my great-grandfather, that is, Granddad's father, had the gift of laying restless spirits, Grandfather said. And he wouldn't venture to say that he had made as much out of his gift as his father before him had made out of cholera, but he had managed to buy the spot of land under the house which cholera'd given his forebear. Grandfather said that at funerals his father made no bones of telling the relatives of the dead that while it was, right enough, his duty as sexton to toll the funeral bell, he would not, however, if they were unreasonable, vouch for the peace of their dead, seeing that, in view of their tight purses, he would not, in his bell ringing, employ the uncommon gift which heaven'd given him. And as oft as not, Grandfather said, the dead person's folk were reasonable, for, as oft as not, those who weren't were haunted by their dead and, as oft as not, had to pay my great-grand-dad a bigger fee for laying the restless spirits with his art.

And this gift of laying restive spirits, Grandfather said, had been passed on to him too. He told me of how, when his father had gone to his maker, at the chapel the post of sexton had been given another through favor. But on the night of the birth of the Savior, Grandfather said, above the graves the full moon shone like the heralding angel, while the worshipers were flocking to the midnight mass. But at each entrance, Grandfather said, fear awaited and checked them, for lining the causeways that lead through the thick graves were the dead of a hundred years risen up on that night, Grandfather declared, against the bastardly ringing. Straightway, Grandfather went on, he made his way to the ministering father, who stood perplexed at the approaching hour and the vacant pews, and taking him to a window showed him the thick ghosts and told him just how the affair stood. And when the ground was ripe for a bargain, Grandfather said, he offered to lay the ghosts by the art of his ringing and give the worshipers way, if the sextonship, which was rightly his'n, were gi'n him. So said, so done, Grandfather said. The bargain was struck and no sooner was the bell rope given him than the ghosts sank back to their places. And ever since then, Grandfather said, he'd been ringing the bell of the chapel, until a year or two back when his bad heart failed him.

The sky was a sea, and the sun a white slaver, the time Ruth ran bearing her father's message to her grandpa, that the new baby was a boy. But when she burst in and fell on her knees where the old man slumped in his armchair, shaking him and shouting her news of an heir, she could not rouse him, nor, for that matter, could a million Ruths.

By the time Ruth came into the tower her streaming eyes were shot red like the spent sun. Chris Coggins surrendered the bell rope to her, and, sobbing, she tolled her grandfather to his rest.

A. N. Forde

SUNDAY WITH A DIFFERENCE

THE sun had not yet risen and in the dull morning light the sea was acres of dark color, its greens and blues merging in a gray sheet of water. In an hour's time, I knew, everything would be changed. The sun would set studs of light in the crinkles of the waves, and the sea would separate the shades of green from the shades of blue. The breakers would huff and puff against the rocks or bite into the sand or search the holes and hidings of little fish and crabs and water spiders. It would be very inviting: a playground for the young and careless and idle. And so it always was, every Sunday, weather permitting.

But this was a Sunday with a difference.

The beach was the same, curved like the quarter moon of a fingernail. The waves, as ever, clucked energetically up the gradient of the sand, and the panels of rock on either side of the cove were as solid as time and the erosions of wind and water would allow.

The difference was in the boat which sat high up on the beach, clean and new in the morning sun.

It was to be launched that day.

Early the bustle started. Fishermen in old pants and ragged headgear, helpers, well-wishers prepared the ropes for the launching, each man bent on a purpose, fastening here, tightening there.

Meanwhile the women were fixing a tremendous cook-up for the occasion. Chicken and rice and salt beef and potatoes and peas and plantains were in the pots and the smell was soon rich and plentiful on the air. It seemed to enlarge the feelings so that every man became your brother. Its goodness was overwhelming. Then the rum went from hand to hand and was decanted down the throat from the bottle, or tossed off straight with hardly a grimace.

This was a Sunday for big things. You ate big, you drank big, and if you got drunk everybody would laugh at you for weeks—in a big way. And all because of the new boat, perched on the sand, built by the craft of a carpenter-shipwright and the experience of men whose brains ticked to the rhythm of the sea. This was the moment they had worked and waited for, this was their cumulus, the climax of weeks of labor in which skeletons of wood had been transformed into this creature of the deep, this . . . personality.

It was a small schooner, sturdy-looking. Ropes stretched from it to fixed points on the land and in the sea. The men were preparing to draw it down the gradient of the beach. Smooth round logs had been set in place to guide its passage to the sea.

Perched on a slight elevation, five boys beat out a lively steel band version of "Brown Skin Girl."

The children were all there, getting in the way of the workers, skipping naked in the sea, diving for stones, testing their muscles in sea fights, ducking one another, and shooting water into one another's eyes, feeling the legs of the unwary underwater, climbing on shoulders to belly-land on a rising wave, peering into the brown layers of the sea moss underfoot, making balls out of the wet sand and flinging them into hair and eyes and ears, watching horseflies light on their legs and crushing them with a slap on the flesh, peeping into crab holes and prodding unseen creatures in the earth, picking their way on the rocks and disturbing the white seagulls, searching for "wilks," pulling at the ropes, sliding under them, jumping over them, larking and screaming, tugging and pushing, teasing and giggling, bright-eyed and wet, brown-skinned and dark in a harlequinade by the sea.

I knew Robby well. He was a small chap; about eight, I should think. He swam well, was always "around" the fishermen doing one thing or another, helping them pull a boat ashore or swimming out to one with a fisherman's bundle on his head. His body was spare, economical, and after a swim his ribs stood out against the flesh. His chest was a frame with skin stretched over it. He was a healthy little scoundrel.

There was a dog there that day, a black dog, nibbling at Robby's heels. Robby was running up and down the beach with it; it was a tiny mite with an experimental bark more like a squeak. When Robby was in the sea, it sat on the sand and refused to be decoyed into further fun. It looked lonely then.

The sun grew hotter and the scene on the beach more animated.

The children were bundles of concentrated energy, little parcels of explosive bursting into the sea. The seawater and sweat ran lines along the bare skins of the men who worked in the rising heat, pulling at the ropes, drawing the boat inch by inch down the slope of the beach. The big carpenter and a thin man who seemed to know all about it shouted orders, "Heave now, ease now," and the boat crept or stayed. Sometimes the figures of the men guiding its passage were caught in a stark dramatic stance as they steadied it from going off course. There was something almost cinematic about the mixture of shouts and the heat and the merriment and the sweat and the steaming breath rising from under the pot lids and the male smell of rum and the streaks of white sea salt staining the faces and backs of the men and the sand crushed by heavy feet into hollows and the children squirting their joy upon the sea—and the boat resisting.

Then the men stayed the boat near the water's edge. It was time for the food and drink. Every man grabbed himself a plate filled with the good rich food and ate with a spanking relish. The liquor went the rounds. The children gorged themselves. The women served and ate by turns. Grease shone on fingertips and on mouths and on the wide leaves from which some children ate, and when sand got in the way, it was rinsed off in the sea and the job of feeding begun again.

I remember the boat as I had been seeing it for weeks before this day from across the lagoon; at first a few unseasoned planks appearing in a crude geometry; then the gradual change as its open jaws closed and its flanks were sealed; then the keel. The knocking and planing, the slabbing of the wood, the hammering, the clanging sound of metal, the riveting of bolts, the loud talk and laughter which I could pick up easily as I passed in the rowboat with my friends—all these had given place to this day of consummation, this Sunday with a difference.

Then the eating and drinking subsided and the men rose to crown the day's labor. A tautness suddenly came. The children for once ceased their wild rollicking and the women beside the dying beds of fire wiped their hands or licked their lips. A period of understatement was succeeding the earlier rhetoric of the day. The men took up their positions and waited. Then the wife of the schoolmaster stepped forward and broke the bottle of liquor against the bow of the vessel and the liquid fell to the sand. There was a sudden cheer, the signal for the final effort. The men stood firm, then heaved together, and the boat shuddered at the water's edge. Backs arched in the painful agonizing last pull. Faces grew rigid and the sun struck the sea surface with a savage light.

And the boat slid bulkily into the water.

Then the tightness in the air went loose and the children rushed at the boat, touching it, running their fingers along its sides, pushing it out, falling, slipping down beside it, climbing into it, clinging to the ropes that hung from it, leaping from it, deifying it.

And a fresh breeze sprang up and beat the hot air. It whipped the wave tops into foam and bruised the fists of water. The tide began to heave and pull and the boat, anchored, became a live thing on the back of the waves. The children laughed, flinging themselves asprawl on the sand or tugging at the boat in its new kingdom or dancing in a frenzy on the beach to the pounding rhythm of the steel band.

It was growing on dusk when they saw the dead body. It was Robby. The body was found upside down, wedged between two brackets of rock. There was a wide scrawl of open flesh down the side of his right cheek. The white bone of a rib in his side was showing.

A woman had seen the black dog sitting at the edge of the water alone.

Half an hour later, I looked across the lagoon toward the little cove with darkness settling over it. The sun had left a mere gesture of light at the base of the distant sky. The boat was a shapeless huddle, dark and mysterious.

And I remembered the woman's comment when she had seen the boy's dead body.

"Every boat need a soul," she had said. "Every boat need a soul."

Samuel Selvon

CANE IS BITTER

IN February they began to reap the cane in the undulating fields at Cross Crossing estate in the southern part of Trinidad. "Crop time coming, boy—plenty work for everybody," men in the village told one another. They set about sharpening their cutlasses on grinding stones, ceasing only when they tested the blades with their thumbnails and a faint ping! quivered in the air. Or they swung the cutlass at a drooping leaf and cleaved it. But the best test was when it could shave the hairs off your leg.

Everyone was happy in Cross Crossing as work loomed up in the way of their idleness, for after the planting of the cane there was hardly any work until the crop season. They laughed and talked more and the children were given more liberty than usual, so they ran about the barracks and played hide-and-seek in those cane fields which had not yet been fired to make the reaping easier. In the evening, when the dry trash was burnt away from the stalks of sweet juice, they ran about clutching the black straw which rose on the wind; people miles away knew when crop season was on, for the burnt trash was blown a great distance away. The children smeared one another on the face and laughed at the black streaks. It wouldn't matter now if their exertions made them hungry, there would be money to buy flour and rice when the men worked in the fields, cutting and carting the cane to the weighing bridge.

In a muddy pond about two hundred yards east of the settlement, under the shade of spreading *laginette* trees, women washed clothes and men bathed mules and donkeys and hog-cattle. The women beat the clothes with stones to get them clean, squatting by the banks, their skirts drawn tight against the back of their thighs, their saris retaining grace of arrangement on their shoulders even in that awkward position. Naked children splashed about in the pond, hitting the water with their hands and shouting when the water shot up in the air at different angles, and trying to make brief rainbows in the sunlight with the spray. Rays of the morning sun

came slantways from halfway up in the sky, casting the shadow of
trees on the pond, and playing on the brown bodies of the children.

Ramlal came to the pond and sat on the western bank, so that
he squinted into the sunlight. He dipped his cutlass in the water
and began to sharpen it on the end of a rock on which his wife
Rookmin was beating clothes. He was a big man, and in earlier
days was reckoned handsome. But work in the fields had not only
tanned his skin to a deep brown but actually changed his features.
His nose had a slight hump just above the nostrils, and the squint
in his eyes was there even in the night, as if he was peering all the
time, though his eyesight was remarkable. His teeth were stained
brown with tobacco, so brown that when he laughed it blended
with the color of his face, and you only saw the lips stretched wide
and heard the rumble in his throat.

Rookmin was frail but strong as most East Indian women. She
was not beautiful, but it was difficult to take any one feature of her
face and say it was ugly. Though she was only thirty-six, hard
work and the bearing of five children had taken toll. Her eyes were
black and deceptive, and perhaps she might have been unfaithful
to Ramlal if the idea had ever occurred to her. But like most of the
Indians in the country districts, half her desires and emotions were
never given a chance to live, her life dedicated to wresting an
existence for herself and her family. But as if she knew the light
she threw from her eyes, she had a habit of shutting them whenever she was emotional. Her breasts sagged from years of suckling.
Her hands were wrinkled and calloused. The toes of her feet were
spread wide from walking without any footwear whatsoever; she
never had need for a pair of shoes because she never left the
village.

She watched Ramlal out of the corner of her eye as he sharpened the cutlass, sliding the blade to and fro on the rock. She knew
he had something on his mind, the way he had come silently and
sat near her, pretending that he could add to the keenness of his
razor-sharp cutlass. She waited for him to speak, in an Oriental
respectfulness. But from the attitude of both of them, it wasn't
possible to tell that they were about to converse, or even that they
were man and wife. Rookmin went on washing clothes, turning the

garments over and over as she pounded them on a flat stone, and Ramlal squinted his eyes and looked at the sun.

At last, after five minutes or so, Ramlal spoke.

"Well, that boy Romesh coming home tomorrow. Is six months since last he come home. This time, I make up my mind, he not going back."

Rookmin went on scrubbing, she did not even look up.

"You see how city life change the boy. When he was here the last time, you see how he was talking about funny things?"

Rookmin held up a tattered white shirt and looked at the sun through it.

"But you think he will agree to what we going to do?" she asked. "He must be learning all sorts of new things, and this time might be worse than last time. Suppose he want to take Creole wife?"

"But you mad or what? That could never happen. Ain't we make all arrangement with Sampath for Doolsie to married him? Anyway," he went on, "is all your damn fault in the first place, wanting to send him for education in the city. You see what it cause? The boy come like a stranger as soon as he start to learn all those funny things they teach you in school, talking about poetry and books and them funny things. I did never want to send him for education, but is you who make me do it."

"Education is a good thing," Rookmin said, without intonation. "One day he might come lawyer or doctor, and all of we would live in a big house in the town, and have servants to look after we."

"That is only foolish talk," Ramlal said. "You think he would remember we when he come a big man? And besides, by that time you and me both dead. And besides, the wedding done plan and everything already."

"Well, if he married Doolsie everything might work out."

"How you mean if? I had enough of all this business. He have to do what I say, else I put him out and he never come here again. Doolsie father offering big dowry, and afterwards the both of them could settle on the estate and he could forget all that business."

Rookmin was silent. Ramlal kept testing the blade with his nail, as if he were fascinated by the pinging sound, as if he were trying to pick out a tune.

But in fact he was thinking, thinking about the last time his son Romesh had come home. . . .

It was only his brothers and sisters, all younger than himself, who looked at Romesh with wonder, wanting to ask him questions about the world outside the cane fields and the village. Their eyes expressed their thoughts, but out of some curious embarrassment they said nothing. In a way, this brother was a stranger, someone who lived far away in the city, only coming home once or twice a year to visit them. They were noticing a change, a distant look in his eyes. Silently, they drew aside from him, united in their lack of understanding. Though Romesh never spoke of the great things he was learning, or tried to show off his knowledge, the very way he bore himself now, the way he watched the cane moving in the wind was alien to their feelings. When they opened the books he had brought, eager to see the pictures, there were only pages and pages of words, and they couldn't read. They watched him in the night, crouching in the corner, the book on the floor near to the candle, reading. That alone made him different, set him apart. They thought he was going to be a pundit, or a priest, or something extraordinary. Once his sister had asked, "What do you read so much about, *bhai?*" and Romesh looked at her with a strange look and said, "To tell you, you wouldn't understand. But have patience, a time will come soon, I hope, when all of you will learn to read and write." Then Hari, his brother, said, "Why do you feel we will not understand? What is wrong with our brains? Do you think because you go to school in the city that you are better than us? Because you get the best clothes to wear, and shoes to put on your feet, because you get favor from *bap* and *mai?*" Romesh said quickly, *"Bhai,* it is not that. It is only that I have left our village, and have learned about many things which you do not know about. The whole world goes ahead in all fields, in politics, in science, in art. Even now the governments in the West Indies are talking about federating the islands, and then what will happen to the Indians in this island? But we must not quarrel, soon all of us will have a chance." But Hari was not impressed. He turned to his father and mother and said, "See how he has changed. He don't want to play no games anymore, he don't want to work in the fields, he is too much of a big shot to use a cutlass. His brothers and sisters are fools; he don't want to talk to them because they won't

understand. He don't even want to eat we food again, this morning
I see he ain't touch the *baghi*. No. We have to get chicken for him,
and the cream from all the cows in the village. Yes, that is what.
And who it is does sweat for him to get pretty shirt to wear in Port
of Spain?" He held up one of the girls' arms and spanned it with
his fingers. "Look how thin she is. All that is for you to be a big
man, and now you scorning your own family?" Romesh got up
from the floor and faced them. His eyes burned fiercely, and he
looked like the pictures of Indian gods the children had seen in the
village hall. "You are all wrong!" he cried in a ringing voice.
"Surely you, *bap,* and you, *mai,* the years must have taught you
that you must make a different life for your children, that you must
free them from ignorance and the wasting away of their lives? Do
you want them to suffer as you have?" Rookmin looked like she
was going to say something, but instead she shut her eyes tight.
Ramlal said, "Who tell you we suffer? We bring children in the
world and we happy." But Romesh went on, "And what will the
children do? Grow up in the village here, without learning to read
and write? There are schools in San Fernando, surely you can send
them there to learn about different things besides driving a mule
and using a cutlass? Oh *bap,* we are such a backward people, all
the others move forward to better lives, and we lag behind believ-
ing that what is to be, will be. All over Trinidad, in the country
districts, our people toil on the land and reap the cane. For years it
has been so, years in the same place, learning nothing new, accepting our fate like animals. Political men come from India and give
speeches in the city. They speak of better things, they tell us to
unite and strive for a greater goal. And what does it mean to you?
Nothing. You are content to go hungry, to see your children run
about naked, emaciated, grow up dull and stupid, slaves to your
own indifference. You do not even pretend an interest in the Legis-
lative Council. I remember why you voted for Pragsingh last year;
it was because he gave you ten dollars—did I not see it for myself?
It were better that we returned to India than stay in the West
Indies and live such a low form of existence." The family watched
Romesh wide-eyed. Ramlal sucked his clay pipe noisily. Rookmin
held her youngest daughter in her lap, picking her head for lice,
and now and then shutting her eyes so the others wouldn't see
what she was thinking. "There is only one solution," Romesh went

on, "we must educate the children, open up new worlds in their minds, stretch the horizon of their thoughts . . ." Suddenly he stopped. He realized that for some time now they weren't listening, his words didn't make any sense to them. Perhaps he was going about this the wrong way, he would have to find some other way of explaining how he felt. And was he sufficiently equipped in himself to propose vast changes in the lives of the people? It seemed to him then how small he was, how there were so many things he didn't know. All the books he'd read, the knowledge he'd lapped up hungrily in the city listening to the politicians making speeches in the square—all these he mustered to his assistance. But it was as if his brain was too small, it was like putting your mouth in the sea and trying to drink all the water. Wearily, like an old man who had tried to prove his point merely by repeating, "I am old, I should know," Romesh sat down on the floor, and there was silence in the hut, a great silence, as if the words he'd spoken had fled the place and gone outside with the wind and the cane.

And so after he had gone back to the city his parents discussed the boy, and concluded that the only thing to save his senses was to marry him off. "You know he like Sampath daughter from long time, and she is a hard-working girl. She go make good wife for him," Rookmin had said. Ramlal had seen Sampath and everything was fixed. Everybody in the village knew of the impending wedding. . . .

Romesh came home the next day. He had some magazines and books under his arm, and a suitcase in his hand. There was no reception for him; everyone who could work was out in the fields.

He was as tall as the canes on either side of the path on which he walked. He sniffed the smell of burning cane, but he wasn't overjoyful at coming home. He had prepared for this, prepared for the land on which he had toiled as a child, the thatched huts, the children running naked in the sun. He knew that these were things not easily forgotten which he had to forget. But he saw how waves of wind rippled over the seas of cane and he wondered vaguely about big things like happiness and love and poetry, and how they could fit into the poor, toiling lives the villagers led.

Romesh met his sisters at home. They greeted him shyly but he held them in his arms and cried, *"Beti,* do you not know your own brother?" And they laughed and hung their heads on his shoulder.

"Everybody gone to work," one girl said, "and we cooking food to carry. Pa and Ma was looking out since early this morning. They say to tell you if you come to come in the fields."

Romesh looked around the hut in which he had grown up. It seemed to him that if he had come back home after ten years, there would still be the old table in the center of the room, its feet sunk in the earthen floor, the black pots and pans hanging on nails near the window. Nothing would change. They would plant the cane, and when it grew and filled with sweet juice cut it down for the factory. The children would waste away their lives working with their parents. No schooling, no education, no widening of experience. It was the same thing the man had lectured about in the public library three nights before in Port of Spain. The most they would learn would be to wield a cutlass expertly, or drive the mule cart to the railway lines swiftly so that before the sun went down they would have worked sufficiently to earn more than their neighbors.

With a sigh like an aged man Romesh opened his suitcase and took out a pair of shorts and a polo shirt. He put these on and put the suitcase away in a corner. He wondered where would be a safe place to put his books. He opened the suitcase again and put them in.

It was as if, seeing the room in which he had argued and quarreled with the family on his last visit, he lost any happiness he might have had coming back this time. A feeling of depression overcame him.

It lasted as he talked with his sisters as they prepared food to take to the fields. Romesh listened how they stumbled with words, how they found it difficult to express themselves. He thought how regretful it was that they couldn't go to school. He widened the thought and embraced all the children in the village, growing up with such little care, running naked in the mud with a piece of *roti* in their hands, missing out on all the things that life should stand for.

But when the food was ready and they set off for the fields, with the sun in their eyes making them blind, he felt better. He would try to be happy with them, while he was here. No more preaching. No more voicing of opinion on this or that.

Other girls joined his sisters as they walked, all carrying food. When they saw Romesh they blushed and tittered, and he wondered what they were whispering about among themselves.

There were no effusive greetings. Sweating as they were, their clothes black with the soot of burnt canes, their bodies caught in the motions of their work, they just shouted out, and Romesh shouted back. Then Ramlal dropped the reins and jumped down from his cart. He curved his hand like a boomerang and swept it over his face. The soot from his sleeves smeared his face as he wiped away the sweat.

Rookmin came up and opened tired arms to Romesh. *"Beta,"* she cried as she felt his strong head on her breast. She would have liked to stay like that, drawing his strength and vitality into her weakened body, and closing her eyes so her emotions wouldn't show.

"Beta," his father said, "you getting big, you looking strong." They sat down to eat on the grass. Romesh was the only one who appeared cool, the others were flushed, the veins standing out on their foreheads and arms.

Romesh asked if it was a good crop.

"Yes, beta," Ramlal said, "is a good crop, and plenty work for everybody. But this year harder than last year, because rain begin to fall early, and if we don't hurry up with the work, it will be too much trouble for all of us. The overseer come yesterday, and he say a big bonus for the man who do the most work. So everybody working hard for that bonus. Two of my mules sick, but I have to work them, I can't help. We trying to get the bonus."

After eating, Ramlal fished a cigarette butt from his pocket and lit it carefully. First greetings over, he had nothing more to tell his son, for the time being anyway.

Romesh knew they were all remembering the last visit, and the things he had said then. This time he wasn't going to say anything; he was just going to have a holiday and enjoy it, and return to school in the city refreshed.

He said, "Hari, I bet I could cut more canes than you."

Hari laughed. "Even though I work the whole morning already, is a good bet. You must be forget to use *poya*, your hands so soft and white now."

That is the way life is, Ramlal thought as Romesh took his cutlass. Education, school, chut! It was only work put a *roti* in your belly, only work that brought money. The marriage would change Romesh. And he felt a pride in his heart as his son spat on the blade.

The young men went to a patch of burnt canes. The girls came too, standing by to pile the fallen stalks of sweet juice into heaps, so that they could be loaded quickly and easily on to the carts and raced to the weighing bridge.

Cane fell as if a machine were at work. The blades swung in the air, glistened for a moment in the sunlight, and descended on the stalks near the roots. Though the work had been started as a test of speed, neither of them moved ahead of the other. Sometimes Romesh paused until Hari came abreast, and sometimes Hari waited a few canes for Romesh. Once they looked at each other and laughed, the sweat on their faces getting into their mouths. There was no more enmity on Hari's part; seeing his brother like this, working, was like the old days when they worked side by side at all the chores which filled the day.

Everybody turned to in the field, striving to outwork the others, for each wanted the bonus as desperately as his neighbor. Sometimes the women and the girls laughed or made jokes to one another, but the men worked silently. And the crane on the weighing bridge creaked and took load after load. The laborer manipulating it grumbled: there was no bonus for him, though his wage was more than that of the cane cutters.

When the sun set all stopped work as if by signal. And in Ramlal's hut that night there was laughter and song. Everything was all right, they thought. Romesh was his natural self again, the way he swung that cutlass! His younger sisters and brother had never really held anything against him, and now that Hari seemed pleased, they dropped all embarrassment and made fun. "See *bhai*, I make *meetai* especially for you," his sister said, offering the sweetmeat.

"He work hard, he deserve it," Hari agreed, and he looked at his brother almost with admiration.

Afterward, when Ramlal was smoking and Rookmin was

searching in the youngest girl's head for lice ("put pitch oil, that will kill them," Ramlal advised), Romesh said he was going to pay Doolsie a visit.

There was a sudden silence. Rookmin shut her eyes, the children stopped playing, and Ramlal coughed over his pipe.

"Well, what is the matter?" Romesh asked, looking at their faces.

"Well, now," Ramlal began, and stopped to clear his throat. "Well now, you know that is our custom, that a man shouldn't go to pay visit to the girl he getting married . . ."

"What!" Romesh looked from face to face. The children shuffled their feet and began to be embarrassed at the stranger's presence once more.

Ramlal spoke angrily. "Remember this is your father's house! Remember the smaller ones! Careful what you say, you must give respect! You not expect to get married one day, eh? Is a good match we make, boy. You will get good dowry, and you could live in the village and forget them funny things you learning in the city."

"So it has all been arranged," Romesh said slowly. "That is why everybody looked at me in such a strange way in the fields. My life already planned for me, my path pointed out—cane, labor, boy children, and the familiar village of Cross Crossing." His voice had dropped lower, as if he had been speaking to himself, but it rose again as he addressed his mother, "And you, *mai,* you have helped them do this to me? You whose idea it was to give me an education?"

Rookmin shut her eyes and spoke. "Is the way of our people, is we custom from long time. And you is Indian? The city fool your brains, but you will get back accustom after you married and have children."

Ramlal got up from where he was squatting on the floor, and faced Romesh. "You have to do what we say," he said loudly. "Ever since you in the city, we notice how you change. You forgetting custom and how we Indian people does live. And too besides, money getting short. We want help on the estate. The garden want attention, and nobody here to see about the cattle and them. And no work after crop, too besides."

"Then I can go to school in San Fernando," Romesh said desperately. "If there is no money to pay the bus, I will walk. The government schools are free; you do not have to pay to learn."

"You will married and have boy children," Ramlal said, "and you will stop answering your *bap* . . ."

"Hai! Hai!" Drivers urged their carts in the morning sun, and whips cracked crisply on the air. Dew still clung to the grass as workers took to the fields to do as much as they could before the heat of the sun began to tell.

Romesh was still asleep when the others left. No one woke him; they moved about the hut in silence. No one spoke. The boys went to harness the mules, one of the girls to milk the cows and the other was busy in the kitchen.

When Romesh got up he opened his eyes in full awareness. He could have started the argument again as if no time had elapsed, the night had made no difference.

He went into the kitchen to wash his face. He gargled noisily, scraped his tongue with his teeth. Then he remembered the toothbrush and toothpaste in his suitcase. As he cleaned his teeth his sister stood watching him. She never used a toothbrush; they broke a twig and chewed it to clean their mouths.

"You going to go away, *bhai?*" she asked him timidly.

He nodded, with froth in his mouth.

"If you stay, you could teach we what you know," the girl said.

Romesh washed his mouth and said, *"Baihin,* there are many things I have yet to learn."

"But what will happen to us?"

"Don't ask me questions, little sister," he said crossly.

After he had eaten he left the hut and sulked about the village, walking slowly with his hands in his pockets. He wasn't quite sure what he was going to do. He kept telling himself that he would go away and never return, but bonds he had refused to think about surrounded him. The smell of burnt cane was strong on the wind. He went to the pond where he and Hari used to bathe the mules. What to do? His mind was in a turmoil.

Suddenly he turned and went home. He got his cutlass—it was sharp and clean, even though unused for such a long time. Ramlal never allowed any of his tools to get rusty.

He went out into the fields, swinging the cutlass in the air, as if with each stroke he swept a problem away.

Hari said, "Is time you come. Other people start work long time; we have to work extra to catch up with them."

There was no friendliness in his voice now.

Romesh said nothing, but he hacked savagely at the canes, and in half an hour he was bathed in sweat and his skin scratched from contact with the cane.

Ramlal came up in the mule cart and called out, "Work faster! We a whole cartload behind!" Then he saw Romesh and he came down from the cart and walked rapidly across. "So you come! Is a good thing you make up your mind!"

Romesh wiped his face. "I am not going to stay, *bap*." It was funny how the decision came; he hadn't known himself what he was going to do. "I will help with the crop; you shall get the bonus if I have to work alone in the night. But I am not going to get married. I am going away after the crop."

"You are mad, you will do as I say." Ramlal spoke loudly, and other workers in the field stopped to listen.

The decision was so clear in Romesh's mind that he did not say anything more. He swung the cutlass tirelessly at the cane and knew that when the crop was finished, it would be time to leave his family and the village. His mind got that far, and he didn't worry about after that. . . .

As the wind whispered in the cane, it carried the news of Romesh's revolt against his parents' wishes, against tradition and custom.

Doolsie, working a short distance away, turned her brown face from the wind. But women and girls working near her whispered among themselves and laughed. Then one of the bolder women, already married, said, "Well girl, is a good thing in a way. Some of these men too bad. They does beat their wife too much—look at Dulcie husband, he does be drunk all the time, and she does catch hell with him."

But Doolsie bundled the canes together and kept silent.

"She too young yet," another said. "Look, she breasts not even form yet!"

Doolsie did not have any memories to share with Romesh, and

her mind was young enough to bend under any weight. But the way her friends were laughing made her angry, and in her mind she too revolted against the marriage.

"All you too stupid!" she said, lifting her head with a childish pride so that her sari fell on her shoulder. "You wouldn't say Romesh is the only boy in the village! And too besides, I wasn't going to married him if he think he too great for me."

The wind rustled through the cane. Overhead, the sun burned like a furnace.

Samuel Selvon

MY GIRL AND THE CITY

ALL these words that I hope to write, I have written them already many times in my mind. I have had many beginnings, each as good or as bad as the other. Hurtling in the underground from station to station, mind the doors, missed it!, there is no substitute for wool; waiting for a bus in Piccadilly Circus; walking across Waterloo Bridge; watching the bed of the Thames when the tide is out— choose one, choose a time, a place, any time or any place, and take off, as if this were interrupted conversation, as if you and I were earnest friends and there is no need for preliminary remark.

One day of any day it is like this. I wait for my girl on Waterloo Bridge, and when she comes there is a mighty wind blowing across the river, and we lean against it and laugh, her skirt skylarking, her hair whipping across her face.

I wooed my girl, mostly on her way home from work, and I talked a great deal. Often, it was as if I had never spoken; I heard my words echo in deep caverns of thought, as if they hung about like cigarette smoke in a still room, missionless, or else they were lost forever in the sounds of the city.

We used to wait for a 196 under a railway bridge across the Waterloo Road. There were always long queues and it looked like we would never get a bus. Fidgeting in that line of impatient humanity I got in precious words edgeways, and a train would rumble and drown my words in thundering steel. Still, it was important to talk. In the crowded bus, as if I wooed three or four instead of one, I shot words over my shoulder, across seats; once past a bespectacled man reading the *Evening News* who lowered his paper and eyed me as if I was mad. My words bumped against people's faces, on the glass window of the bus; they found passage between "fares, please," and once I got to writing things on a piece of paper and pushing my hand over two seats.

The journey ended and there was urgent need to communicate before we parted.

All these things I say, I said, waving my hand in the air as if to catch the words floating about me and give them mission. I say them because I want you to know, I don't ever want to regret afterwards that I didn't say enough; I would rather say too much.

Take that Saturday evening; I am waiting for her in Victoria Station. When she comes, we take the Northern Line to Belsize Park (I know a way to the heath from there, I said). When we get out of the lift and step outside, there is a sudden downpour and everyone scampers back into the station. We wait a while, then go out in it. We get lost. I say, "Let us ask that fellow the way." But she says, "No. Fancy asking someone the way to the heath on this rainy night; just find out how to get back to the tube station."

We go back, I get my bearings afresh, and we set off. She is hungry. "Wait there," I say, under a tree at the side of the road, and I go to a pub for some sandwiches. Water slips off me and makes puddles on the counter as I place my order. The man is taking a long time and I go to the door and wave to her across the street signifying I shan't be too long.

When I go out she has crossed the road and is sheltering in a doorway, pouting. "You leave me standing in the rain and stay such a long time," she says. "I had to wait for the sandwiches," I say. "What do you think, I was having a quick one?" "Yes," she says.

We walk on through the rain and we get to the heath and the rain is falling slantways and carefree and miserable. For a minute we move around in an indecisive way as if we're looking for some particular spot. Then we see a tree which might offer some shelter and we go there and sit on a bench, wet and bedraggled.

"I am sorry for all this rain," I say, as if I were responsible. I take off her raincoat and make her put on my quilted jacket. She takes off her soaking shoes and tucks her feet under her skirt on the bench. She tries to dry her hair with a handkerchief. I offer her the sandwiches and light a cigarette for myself. "Go on, have one," she says. I take a half and munch it, and smoke.

It is cold there. The wind is raging in the leaves of the trees, and the rain is pelting. But abruptly it ceases, the clouds break up in the sky, and the moon shines. When the moon shines, it shines on her face, and I look at her, the beauty of her washed by rain, and I think many things.

Suddenly we are kissing and I wish I could die there and then, and there's an end to everything, to all the Jesus-Christ thoughts that make up every moment of my existence.

Writing all this now—and some weeks have gone by since I started—it is lifeless and insipid and useless. Only at the time, there was something, a thought that propelled me. Always, in looking back, there was something, and at the time I am aware of it; and the creation goes on and on in my mind while I look at all the faces around me in the tube, the restless rustle of newspapers, the hiss of air as the doors close, the enaction of life in a variety of forms.

Once I told her and she said, as she was a stenographer, that she would come with me and we would ride the Inner Circle and I would just voice my thoughts and she would write them down, and that way we could make something of it. Once the train was crowded and she sat opposite to me and after a while I looked at her and she smiled and turned away. What is all this, what is the meaning of all these things that happen to people: the movement from one place to another, lighting a cigarette, slipping a coin into a slot and pulling a drawer for chocolate, buying a return ticket, waiting for a bus, working the crossword puzzle in the *Evening Standard*?

Sometimes you are in the underground and you have no idea what the weather is like, and the train shoots out of a tunnel and sunlight floods you, falls across your newspaper, makes the passengers squint and look up.

There is a face you have for sitting at home and talking; there is a face you have for working in the office; there is a face, a bearing, a demeanor for each time and place. There is, above all, a face for traveling, and when you have seen one you have seen all. In a rush hour, when we are breathing down each other's neck, we look at each other and glance quickly away. There is not a great deal to look at in the narrow confines of a carriage except people, and the faces of people, but no one deserves a glass of Hall's wine more than you do. We jostle in the subway from train to lift; we wait, shifting our feet. When we are all herded inside, we hear the footsteps of a straggler for whom the operator waits, and we try to figure out what sort of a footstep it is, if he feels the lift will wait for him; we are glad if he is left waiting while we shoot upward. Out of the lift, down the street, up the road: in ten seconds flat it is over, and we have to begin again.

One morning, I am coming into the city by the night bus, 287, from Streatham. It is after one o'clock; I have been stranded again after seeing my girl home. When we get to Westminster Bridge the sky is marvelously clear with a few stray patches of beautiful cloud among which stars sparkle. The moon stands over Waterloo Bridge, above the Houses of Parliament sharply outlined, and it throws gold on the waters of the Thames. The Embankment is quiet, only a few people loiter around the public convenience near to the Charing Cross Underground, which is open all night. A man sleeps on a bench. His head is resting under headlines: *Suez Deadlock*.

Going back to that same spot about five o'clock in the evening, there was absolutely nothing to recall the atmosphere of the early morning hours. Life had taken over completely, and there was nothing but people. People waiting for buses, people hustling for trains.

I go to Waterloo Bridge and they come pouring out of the offices and they bob up and down as they walk across the bridge. From the station, green trains come and go relentlessly. Motion mesmerizes me into immobility. There are lines of motion across the river, on the river.

Sometimes we sat on a bench near the river, and if the tide was out you could see the muddy bed of the river and the swans grubbing. Such spots, when found, are pleasant to loiter in. Sitting in one of those places—choose one, and choose a time—where it is possible to escape for a brief spell from Christ and the cup of tea, I have known a great frustration and weariness. All these things, said, have been said before, the river seen, the skirt pressed against the swelling thigh noted, the lunch hour eating apples in the sphinx's lap under Cleopatra's Needle observed and duly registered; even to talk of the frustration is a repetition. What am I to do, am I to take each circumstance, each thing seen, noted, and mill them in my mind and spit out something entirely different from the reality?

My girl is very real. She hated the city; I don't know why. It's like that sometimes; a person doesn't have to have a reason. A lot of people don't like London that way; you ask them why, and they shrug; and a shrug is sometimes a powerful reply to a question.

She shrugged when I asked her why; and when she asked me why I loved London, I, too, shrugged. But after a minute I thought

I would try to explain, because a shrug, too, is an easy way out of a lot of things.

Falteringly, I told her how one night it was late and I found a fish-and-chips shop open in the East End and I bought and ate in the dark street; walking; and of the cup of tea in an all-night café in Kensington, one grim winter morning; and of the first time I ever queued in this country, in '50, to see the Swan Lake ballet, and the friend who was with me gave a busker two-and-six because he was playing "Sentimental Journey" on a mouth organ.

"But why do you love London?" she said.

You can't talk about a thing like that, not really. Maybe I could have told her because one evening in the summer I was waiting for her, only it wasn't like summer at all. Rain had been falling all day, and a haze hung about the bridges across the river, and the water was muddy and brown, and there was a kind of wistfulness and sadness about the evening. The way St. Paul's was, half-hidden in the rain, the motionless trees along the Embankment. But you say a thing like that and people don't understand at all. How sometimes a surge of greatness could sweep over you when you see something.

But even if I had said all that and much more, it would not have been what I meant. You could be lonely as hell in the city, then one day you look around you and you realize everybody else is lonely too, withdrawn, locked, rushing home out of the chaos: blank faces, unseeing eyes, millions and millions of them, up the Strand, down the Strand, jostling in Charing Cross for the five-twenty; in Victoria Station, a pretty Continental girl wearing a light, becoming shade of lipstick stands away from the board on which the departure of trains appears and cocks her head sideways, hands thrust into pockets of a fawn raincoat.

I catch the eyes of this girl with my own; we each register sight, appreciation; we look away, our eyes pick up casual station activities; she turns to an automatic refreshment machine, hesitant, not sure if she would be able to operate it.

Things happen and are finished with forever; I did not talk to her, I did not look her way again, or even think of her.

I look on the wall of the station at the clock; it is after half past eight, and my girl was to have met me at six o'clock. I feel in my pockets for pennies to telephone. I only have two. I ask change of a stander with the usual embarrassment; when I telephone, the line is engaged. I alternate between standing in the spot we have arranged to meet and telephoning, but each time the line is engaged. I call the exchange; they ascertain that something is wrong with the line.

At ten minutes to nine, I am eating a corned beef sandwich when she comes. Suddenly now, nothing matters except that she is here. She never expected that I would still be waiting, but she came on the off-chance. I never expected that she would come, but I waited on the off-chance.

Now I have a different word for this thing that happened—an off-chance, but that does not explain why it happens, and what it is that really happens. We go to St. James's Park; we sit under a tree; we kiss; the moon can be seen between leaves.

Wooing my way toward sometimes in our casual conversation, we came near to great, fundamental truths, and it was a little frightening. It wasn't like wooing at all; it was more discussion of when will it end, and must it ever end, and how did it begin, and how go on from here? We scattered words on the green summer grass, under trees, on dry leaves in a wood of quivering aspens, and sometimes it was as if I was struck speechless with too much to say, and held my tongue between thoughts frightened of utterance.

Once again I am on a green train returning to the heart from the suburbs, and I look out of window into windows of private lives flashed on my brain. Bread being sliced, a man taking off a jacket, an old woman knitting. And all these things I see—the curve of a woman's arm, undressing, the blankets being tucked in, and once a solitary figure staring at trains as I stared at windows. All the way into London Bridge—is falling down, is falling down, the wheels say; one must have a thought—where buildings and their shadows encroach on the railway tracks. Now the train crawls across the bridges, dark steel in the darkness; the thoughtful gloom of Waterloo; Charing Cross Bridge, Thames reflecting lights, and the silhouettes of city buildings against the sky of the night.

When I was in New York, many times I went into that city late at night after a sally to the outskirts; it lighted up with a million lights, but never a feeling as on entering London. Each return to the city is loaded with thought, so that by the time I take the Inner Circle I am as light as air.

At last I think I know what it is all about. I move around in a world of words. Everything that happens is words. But pure expression is nothing. One must build on the things that happen: it is insufficient to say I sat in the underground and the train hurtled through the darkness and someone isn't using Amplex. So what? So now I weave; I say there was an old man on whose face wrinkles rivered, whose hands were shapeful with arthritis but when he spoke, oddly enough, his voice was young and gay.

But there was no old man; there was nothing; and there is never ever anything.

My girl, she is beautiful to look at. I have seen her in sunlight and in moonlight, and her face carves an exquisite shape in darkness.

"These things we talk about," I burst out, "why mustn't I say them? If I love you, why shouldn't I tell you so?"

"I love London," she said.

French Section

INTRODUCTION

Antillia was the name accorded, before the discovery of the New World, to a semimythical archipelago or continent presumably to be found somewhere west of Atlantis. It appeared on an anonymous map as early as 1424, and might have been suggested by one of the larger Azores. Columbus, coming upon the middle islands of the West Indian chain on his second voyage, in 1493, gave to them the name in its plural form: Antilles. A long way from the lost continent of Atlantis, but a whole new world indeed.

One fact of importance to hold in mind about the French Antilles is that Haiti, on the one hand, and Martinique, Guadeloupe, and attendant isles, on the other, have had very different histories. Haiti's career has been rough and bloody, with the ravages of invasion and civil war its almost constant predicament. Its early situation as a base for English and French buccaneers has not really changed, except as the racial or political character of the buccaneer has changed. And the warfare between Negro and mulatto has been entirely as savage as any conflict between Negro and white—in Haiti, I understand, thirty-five different gradations of color have been recognized. On the final defeat of the French General Ferrand, Haiti's independence was proclaimed at Gonaïves in 1804. Since then, there has been almost continuous strife, with the mulattoes who leaned culturally toward France endeavoring to maintain their domination, and the far larger black peasant population remaining psychologically and emotionally tied to Africa. From this source, handed down from generation to generation, came their myths and legends, the whole pantheon of native gods familiar to voodoo, their songs and chants, their very sense of rhythm.

"Every third Haitian is a poet," we were told time and again in Port-au-Prince. And this is scarcely an exaggeration, for, in proportion to its population, Haiti since its independence has produced more books than any other country in the Western hemi-

147

sphere—this was true as recently as 1951—excepting the United States.

Throughout the nineteenth century, Haitian writers hewed close to the Parisian literary line, and it was not until the late 1920's that a serious effort was made to deal with the realities of island life. In Haiti, as Edmund Wilson points out in his introduction to the novel *The Pencil of God* ("the pencil of God has no eraser" —a Haitian proverb) by Pierre Marcelin and Philippe Thoby-Marcelin, one finds a people "who are living in imagination in a world of omnipresent myth." For them, he goes on to say, "the immediate thing was the supernatural world . . . and what we call the real world no more than a symbolization of events in the world of religious myth. Thus we find in the novel *Canapé-Vert,*" also by the Marcelin brothers, "that a tree blown down on a drunkard or the bite of a mad dog is not considered a natural accident but appears as a deliberate move in a game of transgression and punishment, of revenge and counter-revenge."

It was at this vast and complex world of *le peuple* that writers in the twenties had the courage to look: such men as Haiti's foremost poet, Emile Roumer, the Marcelins, the novelist Jacques Roumain, the noted scientist Dr. Price-Mars, the writers Anthony Lespès, Jean F. Brierre, Magloire-Saint-Aude, and many more.

Guadeloupe, with its nearby islets, and Martinique have always been part of France, at first as colonial possessions; subsequently, since 1946, each as a department of France. They have, in recent times at least, escaped the disorder that has prevailed almost constantly in Haiti.

Again, as in other islands, literary tradition followed closely behind that of the colonizing mother country; poets and novelists alike reflected the prevailing Romantic or Parnassian influences then current in Paris. In recent times, however, attention has turned increasingly toward the islands themselves, though the writer may live far away, as a glance at the biographical notes for this volume will show. One event of the last few years, by the way, that did much to encourage and liberate the younger poets was the wartime visit of the French poet André Breton, chief architect of surrealism, to Martinique.

And there have been poets of consequence, such as Daniel Thaly, who was born in Dominica, lived long in Paris and London, and then returned to Martinique. Without a doubt the two greatest figures are St.-John Perse (Alexis Saint-Léger Léger) born on an islet off Guadeloupe and winner in 1960 of the Nobel Prize; and Aimé Césaire, of Martinique, whose work first appeared around 1941 in the review *Tropiques,* which he edited in Fort-de-France. The concentrated sensuousness of nature on the islands suffuses the work of both men, however different that work may be.

St.-John Perse

TO CELEBRATE A CHILDHOOD

I

PALMS . . . !

In those days they bathed you in water-of-green-leaves; and the water was of green sun too; and your mother's maids, tall glossy girls, moved their warm legs near you who trembled . . .

(I speak of a high condition, in those days, among the dresses, in the dominion of shifting lights.)

Palms! and the sweetness
of an oldness of roots . . . ! the earth
in those days longed to be deafer, and deeper the sky where too tall trees, weary of an obscure design, knotted an inextricable pact . . .

(I dreamed this, in esteem: a sure sojourn among ecstatic linens.)

And the high
curved roots celebrated
the departure of prodigious roads, the invention of vaultings and naves
and the light in those days, fecund in purer feats, inaugurated the white kingdom where I led, perhaps, a body without a shadow . . .

(I speak of a high condition of old, among men and their daughters, who chewed a certain leaf.)

In those days, men's mouths
were more grave, women's arms moved more slowly;
in those days, feeding like us on roots, great silent beasts grew noble;
and over heavier shadow longer the eyelids that lifted . . .

(I had this dream, it has consumed us without relics.)

II

And my mother's maids, tall glossy girls . . . And our fabulous eyelids . . . O

radiance! o favors!

Naming each thing, I declaimed that it was great, naming each beast, that it was beautiful and good.

O my biggest

my voracious flowers, among the red leaves, devouring all my loveliest

green insects! The shrubs in the garden smelled of the family cemetery. And a very young sister had died: I had had, which smelled good, her coffin of mahogany between the mirrors of three rooms. And you were not to kill the hummingbird with a stone . . . But the earth in our games stooped like the maid,

the one who has the right to a chair when we are indoors.

. . . Vegetable fervors, o radiance o favors! . . .

And then those flies, that sort of fly, toward the last tier of the garden, which were as though the light had sung!

. . . I remember the salt, I remember the salt my yellow nurse had to wipe away at the corner of my eyes.

The black sorcerer harangued in the pantry: "The world is like a pirogue which, turning and turning, no longer knows whether the wind wanted to laugh or cry . . ."

And straightway my eyes tried to picture

a world poised between shining waters, would recognize the smooth mast of the tree trunks, the crow's-nest under the leaves, and the booms and the yards and the shrouds of vines,

where flowers too long

ended in parrot calls.

III

. . . Then those flies, that sort of fly, and the last tier of the garden . . . Someone is calling. I'll go . . . I speak in esteem.

—Other than childhood, what was there in those days
that is not here today?

Plains! Slopes! There
was greater order! And everything was but shimmering
reigns and frontiers of light. And shadow and light in those days
were more nearly the same thing . . . I speak of an esteem . . .
Along the borders the fruit
    might fall
    without joy rotting along our lips.
And men with graver mouths stirred deeper shadows,
women more dreams with slower arms.

    . . . Let my limbs grow and weigh heavy, nourished with
age! I shall not know again any place of mills and sugar cane, for
children's dream, that in living, singing waters was thus distributed
. . . To the right
    the coffee was brought in, to the left the manioc
    (o canvas being folded, o praise-giving things!)
And over here were the horses plainly branded, smooth-
coated mules, and over there the oxen;
    here the whips and there the cry of the bird Annaô—
and there again the wounding of the sugar cane at the mill.
    And a cloud
    yellow and violet, color of the coco plum, if it stopped
suddenly to crown the gold volcano,
    called-by-their-names, out of their cabins,
    the servant-women!

    Other than childhood, what was there in those days that
is not here today? . . .

TRANSLATED BY LOUISE VARÈSE

Pierre Duprey

ELISA THE HUSTLER

WHILE still worthy of her nickname, "the hustler," Elisa had long ago ceased living solely off her charms. In 1942, she was not yet ancient enough to repent and "be converted," to become a pious chair attendant, haunting the church day and night in the hope that her deadly sins might be forgiven.

She was so fat, however, that men were inclined to confide in, rather than court, her, to treat her like a comfortable old granny, instead of a sweet young thing.

Without bitterness, she had given up being the beautiful *doudou* once fought over by Bardurot and Pidier (a well-heeled pair already rivals in the entertainment business) and was resigned never again to be offered a "little apartment," baubles, and gold nuggets from Guiana like those the sea captains, explorers, and even the respectable gentlemen of Fort-de-France used to throw at her feet.

Ah yes, she was past her prime. Her glorious prime! As a consolation, she still had certain sentimental evenings when a blond sailor would spill out his soul in her enormous lap, the admiration of jaded old hands who recaptured their youth in her company, and the impatient curiosity of young bucks to whom mountains of flesh were a promise of ecstasy . . .

Elisa lived in town, near the market (deserted at night) in a wooden house of about her own vintage, a present from an admirer. She liked to think back on those happy days when Negre, Basson, Plissonier, des Marches and that old lecher Marcaton would come to see her, bringing their mistresses and Bardurot, to drink, dance, play cards and carouse. At five in the morning, the last of the tilburys, the first of the baby Peugeots would take these gentlemen home, where, after enjoying a savory *mabillage,* or flying fish stew, they would set off to their respective offices to direct the high finance, the banks, the industry of the island.

Now, instead of rich gentlemen, carousing, games, and dancing, there were uncouth young men who were afraid of their wives, wouldn't support a mistress, and who paid her furtive visits at dusk, calling her to the threshold to find out about a "new girl."

"Good evening, Madame Elisa!"

"Good evening. We haven't seen you in ages. I thought you'd been arrested."

"Don't be funny."

"Won't you come in?"

"No, no. I can't stay. I just wanted to find out if what they say is true."

"Why, of course! Girls don't last long in my house. I have taste; I know how to suit my clients, if I say so myself. The prize pieces get whisked away, but there are always more where they came from. I've taken in a little Negress from Vauclin. . . . A little body, my dear . . . You've heard about the mountains and winds of Vauclin. Well, climbing over those bluffs, she's developed a firm pair of thighs, and the wind has polished her from head to toe. I could go on and on. A pretty little mouth that seems to say 'kiss.' But almost a virgin, so she's pretty wild. . . ."

This always got them, the milksops.

"Oh, really?"

"But you'd better hurry, because Lionel told me . . . you know, Lionel the dentist . . ."

"Don't give the girl a job just yet. I'm off to dinner; I'll be back at nine."

"What a dismal clientele. They eat, one-two-three, without so much as a drink first!"

Elisa had not been boasting; she had good taste. In her house there were none of those wirehaired Negresses, those awkward mustees and moronic half-breeds who gave the profession a bad name everywhere else, degraded the establishment, and did nothing to deserve their fees. Her clientele was therefore enormous, prosperous, and satisfied, her reputation secure. Seafaring gentlemen honored her with a monthly visit, lawyers requested her to arrange meetings, and the major part of her practice was made up of lovers on vacation, at a loss for someone to hold.

Business was excellent; the "children" were grateful, the clients faithful. Elisa had no need to feel envy, to covet her neighbor. Her digestion was good, and she slept the deep, instantaneous sleep of the innocent.

She never got up before eleven. The house was already cleaned, swept, "tidied up," the marketing was done. A tuna-fish casserole was simmering, which she would serve with succulent breadfruit, yams, or at this time of year, with the delicious, sticky, blue-tinted *dachines*. And the children, with no more work to be done, were giggling quietly about this and that.

They would come running for Elisa's *levée*, one bringing her coffee, another a spoon and sugar.

"Good morning, Ma'am Elisa."

"Good morning, children. And how is everyone today?"

"Just fine, thank you. Did you sleep well?" etc.

Polite and solicitous, they all wanted to shine in the eyes of the *patronne*, never to show lack of respect (for which, besides, she would have scolded them roundly).

Then time for gossip.

Without budging from her house, Elisa was better informed than the police commissioner.

"The fish are running. The *Porto-Cabello* is in drydock. Taxi prices are going up. Ernest, the one on rue Louis-Blanc, got in a fight with a drunken sailor. Havert waters his milk. . . ."

When Elisa said "enough" the girls stopped right away and withdrew discreetly to let the *patronne* dress.

Elisa received callers after lunch. At this hour, the children deserved a rest. Between marketing, dusting the piano, scaling the fish, they hadn't had a minute to tell each other their little secrets. So after lunch they would rush up to the attic. There two little rooms were saved for them, too cramped a setting for leisurely passion. Aside from the tools of the trade, a firm bed, an old chipped jug, and a washbasin that was losing its enamel, the rooms had no other decoration but pious prints. The children's belongings, in their straw baskets, had been left for safekeeping with Elisa.

The attic was a paradise for the children. Elisa left them alone, no one could overhear their whispering, and they could confide in one another to their hearts' content.

"Last night I saw you giving the quartermaster of the *Sirocco* sexy looks. I thought you weren't interested."

"But I'm not! I was hoping he would choose you. You can't count on sailors. What I need is someone nice and steady. For the love of Mary, will I ever find a cute little mulatto who knows how to make love and gives me everything I want. . . ."

"When I was in Vauclin, I thought that in town . . ."

"Sweetie, in town it's hopeless. Now and then you find a fellow who knows his business. But then he calls you Juliette or Gertrude, or else cries like a baby. Afterwards he feels ashamed and never comes back. . . . Anyway, the real money all goes to Ma'am Elisa."

"The day before yesterday, in the market, I met a country girl from Diamant. I told her I had a job as a maid in a good family. 'A job?' she said. 'That's a laugh. Since when do maids earn money? You have to be a whore to earn a real living.' Did I get a kick out of that!"

"How many do you think we've had? You arrived a week after I did . . ."

"I was up to a hundred and seventeen, but I lost count the day the schoolboys were here. They kept on coming, one after the other . . ."

"Ah well, it's not money that keeps you happy. Why are you hiding down there at the foot of the bed as though I had the mange? Take a look, silky and smooth, isn't it?"

Meanwhile Elisa was entertaining in the living room. Other ladies as successful as she—old Féfé, from the Terres-Sainville; Red-hot Marie, who had a luxurious but poorly attended establishment; and Paulette-Big-Boobs, who had no qualms about doing a wholesale business, with shifts of sailors, in her shabby hut on the embankment—all came regularly to visit their colleague who had been the most notorious and scandalous beauty of her day.

They chattered, complained about the commissioner who poked his nose into everything, the "children" who were now so demanding—why, they didn't even speak French or walk properly, or know how to keep a man happy, and there they were, asking for everything on a silver platter.

They gossiped. There was the little Lebuc boy's divorce, the sudden disappearance of Madame Félicie-Julienne, the little six-months tummy that Mademoiselle Marbaud flaunted around without even blushing (I ask you, fresh out of the convent!). Everyone got the once-over, top, middle, and bottom drawer, and then, invariably, they began reminiscing: those frisky suitors, gay blades, handsome young squires with watch chains and curly mustaches. They drank hard in those days; they shouted and ate enough for four; they showered a mistress with jewels; what men, in a word! Girls, do you remember?

"They're dead, each and every one: Belon, Tardieu, even Montagne, who had a dozen by his missus and eight on the side. A handsome bunch of rascals!"

"Nowadays, with their sneaky looks and little behinds, all they think of is getting to Paris to try out the Parisiennes, or else they like to talk. God, what a letdown!"

"Not only that, but they're scared. 'If anyone should see me, if anyone should say anything. . . .' Why, they won't even sing for fear someone might recognize their voices. . . ."

"In those days . . ."

And the ladies, in a sea of starched skirts of multicolored madras, frivolous petticoats, relived days gone by, the days of tilburys.

But it was nearly five o'clock, time to get to work.

"My dear, we're not living on our income, alas!"

Saying good-bye took another half an hour.

"If you see Emilienne, tell her I have a deal for her . . ."

"By the way, Paulette, you wouldn't know of a prim salesgirl type, would you? Cute, on the petite side, and really serious about her work? My client means business. . . . A standing appointment . . ."

"Well, I'll see what I can do. I have a real bumpkin on my hands now. Would anyone like to take her off?"

"I just had an idea. Your salesgirl. How about the cashier at Barlando's? She has a most refined little face . . ."

But here was the first customer, already.

"Julie, Marie, come down now, children," called Elisa; and, always a stickler for cleanliness, she added, "Shake off that sleepy look, tidy up, and put on your freshly ironed dresses . . ."

The moment Eugénie arrived, Elisa knew she would have both a willful spirit to tame, and a rich personality to cultivate.

In her modest village of Lorrain, Eugénie had earned the nickname "Syrup."

In war, one lucky deed can make a hero. Not so in the game of love, which demands an unfailing sense of improvisation, endless patience, and the courage to venture far afield. For the cowardly men in the small villages are quite willing to disparage their mistresses, in order to maintain sole rights, just as certain African males choose saucer-lipped mates for their peace of mind.

In spite of men, of their jealous suspicions, their perverted sense of chivalry, Eugénie had been honored with a nickname.

Though the blood of three continents ran in her veins, her magnificent face and figure had suffered none of the cruel surprises of nature, none of the unfortunate omissions which crossbreeding tends to produce.

Her hair was clearly East Indian, straight, black, shiny, and luxuriant. Her eyes were distinctly Asian, tilted upward at the temples. Her Minervan brow and classical nose were a direct inheritance from some Sicilian peddler. Her full lips opened upon gleaming teeth in a wide African smile, and from Africa, too, came her firm, high, and insolent bosom.

It had taken nature perhaps a century to shape such a masterpiece as Eugénie. The same ingredients, combined in a more slapdash manner, might have resulted in a caricature, a grinning monstrosity.

What sort of heart beat beneath her bronze skin? Did the look in her eye, now alert, now bedroomy, betray a stubborn fighter or a *bayadère* resigned to her fate and ready to leap into the nearest harem?

Elisa looked her over for a second with the ruthless eye of the expert.

"Who sent you, black girl?"

"I came to town yesterday. Since I don't know anybody, I started in along the Savane after dinner. I met a man you know, César Quinte-Curce. He told me I'd pick up some dire disease if I worked the Savane, that I ought to enter a respectable house."

"Well, you're a lucky girl to land here, because anywhere else you'd find yourself in the hands of an old pinchpenny who'd give you nothing but drunken sailors . . . A cute little puss, I must say. . . . Where do you come from?"

Here Eugénie balked, and made clear, by drumming up an unlikely story about an alcoholic mother and an abusive stepfather, that she had no intention of laying bare her private life.

Then she added, "I'm not just anybody back in Lorrain. They called me Syrup. So, if I may be so bold, how much will you pay me if I work here?"

Elisa stepped back for a moment, took into consideration this "how much" thrust at her so defiantly, weighed Eugénie's beauty, her evident strength of character, the advantages of adding a pearl to the establishment, the cost of showing her off to advantage . . . and wore her very warmest smile as she announced the usual rate.

"And over and above that, half and half?"

"Now, now, child, let's not be too demanding at first. You'll have some good seasons, and then there will be the gifts that come to you directly. The secret, you see, is not to give the client the works, but to leave him a bit hungry, to see that he comes back, etc. . . ."

"Oh, I know my job. You can count on me. How much is the fee for . . ."

"According to size, as they say on menus. Some go as high as . . ."

"Ma'am Elisa, I'm not lazy, but I don't want to waste my youth piling up gold. I'd rather have two really interesting boys than . . ."

Funny girl, talking about men and the work without embarrassment, the moment she's hired. And yet she's fresh out of the village, where she couldn't have known anything but whispered propositions, secret rendezvous, and not the shameless joys of a house of love. . . .

"You'll make out, girl. You're bright, you have gumption, and you're talented as hell, I'll bet. Just see that you stay."

"Don't worry, no one is going to lure me away with fancy promises," replied Eugénie-Syrup, finally setting down her bundle, then taking off her straw hat.

Eugénie certainly was talented. Two weeks after her arrival Elisa's *salon* was full every afternoon by five o'clock, and not just with chief petty officers and cruise passengers in transit looking for an adventure to tell of back home but with virtually everyone who was anyone in the mulatto society of Fort-de-France.

Right away, Eugénie had proved so maliciously incompetent with undesirable clients that they had complained to the *patronne*.

"A pearl you told me. Why, she's no better than a stick of

wood! She may be beautiful, but that's all the more irritating. . . ."

Elisa could sense that she had less authority with Eugénie than with any of her other girls. She called for her, however.

"Child, there is one thing I don't want around here . . ."

"I know what I'm doing. Why should I fill your house with fussy old skinflints? It wouldn't do a bit of good if I gave them ninety or a hundred percent, or syrup, because their budgets only allow a visit once a week. Let me work on the smart, well-dressed, well-heeled young fellows who act like big shots around the Savane or the drawing room, but get down on their hands and knees for my "Jocelyn Lullaby.""

Elisa trembled for the reputation of her house but did not protest, secretly happy at last to have found a superior kind of girl, in whom she kept discovering mysterious and disconcerting new qualities. And she prayed to the Virgin to keep her vigorous and healthy.

Eugénie was perfectly right. What good were these shabby types, who came for a quickie and three drinks once a week? And who made a big fuss when the rum wasn't the right brand, or when they hadn't been properly "serviced." They arrived with a week of abstinence, silence, and good behavior behind them, and proceeded to release everything that they had repressed. When they arrived, they started out by throwing their arms around the *patronne,* with awful drunken smiles, fumbling, impatient gestures, harmless but noisy swearing . . .

Not so the new gentlemen. Ah, now that was another story!

They all knew one another, and were very courtly. No Tuturs, Totors, Milos and Uncle Pauls. They addressed one another as "my dear fellow," rolling their r's for you in an elegant, flowery French. A delight to the ears! They must all be doctors or lawyers or at least gentlemen who never used coarse words. They would not take off their shoes in the drawing room, pretending to have corns or to feel ill at ease. They talked and laughed pleasantly among themselves, in the clear, youthful voices of society.

They were in another class entirely from those longshoremen who sometimes came to the wrong door, so drunk they confused Elisa with Cut-rate Bertha, took their pleasure with their hats on and left the marks of their hobnail shoes on the sheets.

A month after she arrived in town, Eugénie was no longer just a new name bandied about between friends, but a celebrity sought out by everyone.

A hundred men now knew her, half of whom were the local fast set who established the pace in town.

"What a girl! I'm telling you. Do you remember Pneumatic Cécile, Double-Trouble Annie, Mademoiselle Golden Arrow, and Rose, that big mare who neighed in soprano. . . ? Well, they're nothing compared to Eugénie, just specialists, with a limited repertory. A repeat performance with Cécile was pretty dull. But Eugénie is a genuine artist. She plays by ear, like a dancer doing different steps to the same music . . ."

"Victor wrote a poem about her. It starts with a quotation from Gide:

Let others condemn the bittersweet joys
Of the flesh, the blood, and the senses!

He read it to us yesterday. What a laugh! He's in love with her!"

"What? You live in Fort-de-France and you don't know Eugénie-Syrup? You'd better trot over to Elisa's. You're behind the times, man!"

They were careful, however, not to boast of Eugénie's virtues in front of children, gossipy maids, and women in general, especially those who envied the sudden glory of their rival, only yesterday completely unknown.

Success had not changed cheerful, smiling, impish Eugénie into one of those uppity belles, "God's gift to men," who look down their noses at you and remark insolently, "So that's what you think, is it?"

No, she was still a good girl, full of eager, lively hospitality.

"Well, what do you know! Here's Monsieur Nicolas. Sit down. Let me take your hat. Oh, what a pretty tie! You deserted us, you naughty fellow! We haven't seen you for six months . . ."

The punch was already on the table. "I know you like it dry, with a twist of lemon. And me with all my syrup . . ."

The men smiled, ready to enjoy anything from those firm, tempting lips.

Then there was the fan to be adjusted. And the arrival of a new client with whom Eugénie maintained a shy reserve.

"Come now, Eugénie, it's our old friend Gustave!"

"Oh, I didn't recognize you. Well, in that case, sir, make yourself at home."

She was the very model of the gracious hostess as she dashed about, helped by an ugly, thick-lipped girl with low-slung buttocks, who rinsed off the glasses in the back courtyard.

Elisa sat enthroned in the parlor, the imposing queen mother, before whom all the gentlemen callers had to pass muster.

"Nothing right away?"

"Wait until eight. There's always a lull then, when people go off for dinner. Then we can take care of you in style. Right now, it would have to be a rush job, if you know what I mean."

"Okay."

Very soon, too, as the prices began to eliminate all the ordinary clientele, a certain unspoken code, a social ritual developed. Elisa's house was so illustrious that it became respectable, and fancy gentlemen with lots of gold braid began to risk a visit.

As long as one or two of them were seen there, decent sorts, who took the teasing, the barely veiled attacks on the French government and its faithful bastion, the Navy, without flinching, everything seemed fine. But success is doomed if it stands still, and Eugénie, this girl from the hills, sensed that she had better recruit a fresh set of admirers.

And so her prettiest smiles, graceful undulations, and risqué schemes which had made her reputation were for Messieurs les Officiers, who now had their day, arriving in shifts of five, six, and seven, and soon finding themselves as well treated in Elisa's house as in Toulon or the rue de Siam.

All that was needed was a few prints, flags, color photographs of Nice, of Land's End, of the Roscoff fig tree. This lack was soon remedied, and the former parlor, once adorned with madras, coral, and conch shells, where a scene of St.-Pierre before the earthquake had kept company with a photo of Ernest Renan and a view of the *Renown,* was transformed into a peaceful officer's retreat, with pipe smoking, talk of promotions, a child with the flu, or the latest magnetic mines.

These nautical gentlemen disconcerted Eugénie a bit with their technical or personal chatter, but they were so generous (for fear of being called stingy) that she began to save the most exquisite of her professional talents for them.

They no longer came just Tuesdays or Thursdays, but three or four times a week. There seemed to be an understanding that certain evenings were to be kept open for them, while the Gustaves and Victors of earlier days had to swallow their resentment. Mulatto society, after all, had been but a stepping-stone, and if Eugénie now and then waxed nostalgic over a delicate shade of color, her feminine instinct made her smile at the disappointment she could cause.

Heredity had endowed Eugénie with an amorous nature. Her childhood, on the other hand, between an "unfeeling mother" and a chronically unemployed father, an adolescence deprived of understanding, of sweets, even of the necessities of life, had left her dry of heart, fiercely avaricious, and distrustful of daring schemes that promised mountains of gold in the future for only a few thousand in cash.

She had often seen the wrinkled old hags, pale or swarthy, half fortune-tellers, half procuresses, who roamed from brothel to office, from shack to back storeroom, from chapel to shrine, purveying all sorts of gossip, doing errands, garrulous, parasitic, ubiquitous as bedbugs, busy undermining, with plenty of amens and Hail Marys, the best reputations. These sanctimonious old harridans with their pinched expressions offered investments in Cayenne, life annuities, lovers, and only the most optimistic of palm readings. They lubricated their machinations with so much warm flattery that no one could completely despise them.

They did a lot of business with the girls. But not one of them had succeeded in extracting more than a pittance from Eugénie, who was said to have arrived with at least twenty-five thousand francs in her basket. No matter how they went on about a Dream Lover, part Midas, part Prince Charming, Eugénie would laugh without being taken in, and never gave more than ten cents to the disappointed old crones.

"I will pray for you, my child."

The day came, however, when Eugénie felt the iron willpower that had guided her until then give way. This was at Absalon, in the hot springs there.

Elisa hoped to lose a few pounds in the baths. While they were soaking, they gossiped about this and that, about men and how fast youth flies.

"Work hard, my dear, make hay while the sun shines."

"That's just what I'm doing."

"So you are. You're a good girl. You don't give away your pennies to an Adolphe who couldn't care less about you. You tuck them away. You don't go out to dances, don't waste your money on clothes and trinkets. You're right. Gold and real jewels, that's what lasts. The rats can't eat them and they're there when you need them."

Yes, she was a good girl. She never went out, she had no friends, aside from the thick-lipped girl Adèle, who had been working at the house when she arrived, but hadn't resented it when she was thrust aside by Eugénie, and had to go to work next door, at the Lebels, as a laundress.

Now and then she came to see Eugénie and talked to her about her lover. She saw him every Sunday. He was a fine boy. They made plans together, would soon move in with an uncle, at Anses-d'Arlets, etc.

Adèle's confessions had always seemed to Eugénie like a ridiculous little joke, which she could not laugh at to her face (it was the best, after all, that the little broad-bottomed girl could hope for), but which she mocked inwardly.

And there, in the baths, next to Elisa who was saying how good the sulphur was for the complexion, how women should take care to have soft, supple, silky-warm skin, Eugénie suddenly thought about Adèle and did not feel like laughing.

Yes, it must be nice to have a lover, someone to lie down with, to relax with, to trust. Playing a part all one's life wasn't much fun. With a lover it wouldn't be money or sex that mattered (though there was no reason he shouldn't be a dashing, well-heeled fellow) but just the feeling of his gentle hand over mine, quivering.

Ah! If an old crone had come up just then to sing the praises of Tiburce the barrel maker, or François the mason, she would have had a receptive audience. But that night, with her heavy heart, Eugénie once again had to smile, to submit to men, without even the usual incentive of profit, merely languorous and weary.

It may be the effect of the warm baths, thought Elisa.

Eugénie's pace slackened for a whole week and this worried Elisa.

What could be the matter? Her smile is sad. She drags herself around. Hmm . . . I wonder how she's doing upstairs. Can I say anything to her, or do anything? She's as touchy as a one-eyed horse. What if I suggested . . . Of course, at her age my situation was different. Marcaton was about to set me up with an apartment. He was young and full of vigor. Which didn't prevent me from . . . But men don't mean a thing to Eugénie. Only money. What she needs is to get out more often. A little trip now and then with the officers. Maybe those very private little hotels near Case Navire, Bellefontaine. I'll talk to her about it. . . .

And so, one Saturday, Eugénie found herself with a brunette in red high heels and made up to kill, Georgette, and three navy officers, setting out together for Bellefontaine. The taxi driver was one of those unfortunate half-breeds with freckles, who had probably seen everything and paid no attention to the shrieks and giggles behind him. The officers were real gentlemen, just a bit dishevelled by punch parties since eleven that morning.

They had asked for a creole lunch and Elisa had prepared a *brandade* of cod and a pork ragout, heavily spiced and peppered in the native fashion.

They had done a valiant job, with tears in their eyes, moist nostrils, and burning palates.

"Why, we'd scuttle the ship before leaving anything on the platter!"

Three aged dry rums apiece had been necessary to quench the flaming throats. Now, with the wind in their hair, willing companions who bandied back puns and fended off roving hands, they found life bearable again.

"What's the matter with you, Armand, always trying to fathom Georgette?"

"Leave him alone. Can't you see that he is taking a sounding? Undulating mechanics, the Broglie theory . . ."

"Don't pay any attention to those nasty types, my sweet. You're mine, a magnetic mine. You magnetize and galvanize me. Don't leave me to sink into erotic depths. I'm afraid."

"Call him your magnetic pole. Watch him oscillate. You'll be swept away."

"What's come between us, you foul-mouthed rascal?"

"Eugénie's thigh . . ."

The sun was about to set. The road ahead, after a sharp curve, led away from the cliffs and down toward Bellefontaine in a series of loops. The taxi driver drew to a stop.

"Messieurs, 'dames, take a look at the sunset, if you like, or go on with your orgy. I'll be back in a minute."

The driver then got out of the car, walked around to the other side, turned his back, urinated, and went slowly back to his seat, all the while contemplating the red globe which was dropping (from sleep perhaps, after a hard day) into the sea.

"What did he say? What does he want?" The officers asked one another. Then when they saw the driver walk off to answer the call of nature, these bon vivants went quickly back to their witticisms, their salacious pranks. And so, when the driver climbed once again behind the wheel, they failed to notice Eugénie's momentary distraction, her brief, intense glance at the indifferent chauffeur.

The outrageous Georgette had designs on Captain Armand, to whom she promised, *"Chéri d'amour,* you'll have the first helping because you look like Sacha Guitry, the love of my life. . . ."

The other three-stripe officer and his two-stripe companion encouraged Georgette so heartily in her fond endearments that Armand was soon smothered in kisses, enraptured by the promises, half frantic with the teasing of the frenzied belle.

"A bit of decorum, my dear, come now, just a bit of decorum . . ." he gasped. "I believe in discipline, you know. . . . Come now . . ."

Skillful tickling soon put an end to his admonishments, and made the three conspirators laugh harder than ever.

At this moment, Eugénie asked the driver, "Monsieur, is your name Donatien?"

Donatien turned in his seat and looked the oddly hesitant girl straight in the eye. They had arrived and the others were getting out of the car. She lingered at the door. "Not very well broken in, this one," he thought. "Wants the job, but can't take the rum or the mauling."

"Yes, I'm Donatien. What of it?"

Eugénie, usually so self-assured, accustomed to the smiles and desire of men, their most gallant manners, felt herself on shaky ground. She was tongue-tied.

"What I'm doing isn't very nice, is that it?"

Donatien shrugged his shoulders. The girl must be dead drunk to be talking like this. Such a sexy little puss, too. . . .

"Nice or not nice, what do I care?"

He only reacts this way because he resents these snobbish officers with their fat wallets, thought Eugénie. Back in town, he'll go to bed without supper. He'll lie there thinking. . . . And me . . .

"Would you drive me back to town, Monsieur Donatien?"

"The return trip is paid for. Climb in."

"Well, girls, have you any advice?"

Anxiety, desperation, showed in deep wrinkles on Elisa's plump brow. She had tried gentleness with Eugénie, tenderly encouraging her to confess; she had scolded her jokingly, as a friend; she had given her a good shaking, as her elder, her mistress. But she had had no response whatsoever from these tight lips, this stubborn brow, this sad, languorous body.

"I just don't understand. A serious working girl like her, lively, flirtatious, full of fire. All of a sudden, she lets herself go, neglects her appearance, loses her charm, and just tries to get the job done as quickly as possible. For the men have complained, of course. 'What's happening to Eugénie? If she can't stand me, all she has to do is say so. There are plenty of others . . .' So I have to make up excuses: her little sister had a no-good lover, her godmother is dying, news from the front, from the occupied zone . . . I'm running out of ideas. She's been dragging around like this for two weeks. I keep asking her, 'What's the matter? Is it money? Is it this? Is it that?' Not a word! She just sits there with the same wretched look on her face. What do you think, Paulette?"

The ladies ruminated for a moment, then all began talking at once.

"It's black magic. A jealous rival must have bewitched her by pouring vinegar on her sanitary nap—"

"That's it. They gave her a "drive." Vinegar or a needle stuck in a photograph, it's deadly. . . ."

"Maybe she wants to reform . . ."

"Eugénie is in love."

Paulette was the last to speak, and in the silence that followed

all over his face. But she was there as an ambassadress and not as an outraged *patronne*.

"How do you do, my dear fellow. Monsieur Donatien, isn't that so?"

The driver, pleasant, polite, took off his hat and said in a warm, low tone of voice,

"At your service, Madame."

"I have a little matter to discuss with you. Is there anywhere we can talk?

Surprised, Donatien got out of his car, pointed to a quiet alleyway along the Savane.

"What can I do for you?"

"Oh, my dear man! You see before you a very unhappy woman. I'm getting on. Oh yes, don't try to deny it. My only joy in life, my one support in this evil world is my little niece. A sweet child, gentle, devoted, affectionate and happy. So happy, sir! She used to wake me up in the morning with her singing, like a little bird. She was so thoughtful, so solicitous. Why, she embroidered handkerchiefs for me, she pulled out my white hairs. Oh yes, I have them, no need to protest! I'm no spring chicken. Besides, I have a bad heart. It will catch up with me, one of these days, and I will go just like that. She will be all alone in the world.

"I'll leave her everything, of course; the house, jewels; but will that make her happy? Oh no! she's such a tender girl. What will become of her without me? She knows nothing of life. She's so young, so naïve. If she had a boy friend who was serious and reliable, I could go in peace. . . . But alas! Her little heart has spoken, and he turns a deaf ear. Is he married? Isn't she pretty enough? Hasn't she a good enough dowry? You know who I'm talking about, don't you?"

"Not that little tramp . . . uh . . . Eugénie . . ."

"Yes, Eugénie, but how dare you call her a tramp? . . ."

"You're kidding. . . ."

"I've never been more serious. . . ."

"Aren't you the madam at Number forty-six?"

"She's my niece."

"What a laugh! You mean Eugénie, the girl I took with all the sailors to Bellefontaine, who writes me little propositions?"

"Young man, have a heart! What do you mean, all the sailors?

She was going out with friends! And you make fun of her love letters!"

Donatien pretended to be blasé. Actually, he was just a man who refused to get involved, who was afraid of complications and strong feelings.

Eugénie, really and truly in love, he thought.

"Eugénie, the girl with the sailors . . . The day of the drive, she kept looking and looking at me. With the eyes of a drunk . . . She kissed me on the cheek. Just like that! And the letters . . . *my heart sighs . . . in your arms* . . . So she wasn't just pulling my leg; it wasn't a bet with the others."

"My poor young man, don't you understand what that means:—'in love'?"

Elisa had meanwhile slipped from French, which made the conversation stiff and formal, into a warm, colorful patois.

"My boy, this bit of a girl wants you. And you, working, driving, money is what you're after, and you don't care a damn where it comes from, right? Well then, tomorrow at about ten o'clock, stop by at the house. Eugénie will be downstairs. I'll be upstairs. You give her a nice little kiss. Not on the mouth, mind you, not a great clinch. A sedate little smack. She bursts with joy, repeats everything that was in those letters. You caress her cheek, that's all. Then you go away. Two days later, you bring her a red rose: passionate love in the language of flowers (so much baloney in my house). Are you catching on? You are the distinguished gentleman courting a young lady. You take it in easy steps. No sudden pounces. Because then you'll lose everything, the goose and the golden eggs."

Donatien ran his hairy fingers through his frizzy yellow mop, and finally suggested, "Well, sure, but now and then . . ."

"We'll discuss that later, my boy. Remember, you're not one of those fellows with only one thing on his mind, who doesn't care if he gets it standing up. No, you're a man of feeling, a sensitive soul, dreamy, absentminded. You're the man she must seduce, a man who deserves devotion, sacrifice. Are you with me? When she offers you a tie from Dominique's, or a ruby ring, take it with a superior sort of smile. 'Well, well, fancy that, Juliette remembered her Romeo.' Are you beginning to catch on, Donatien?"

"I get the idea, Madame, but still, there's this business about hands off . . ."

"Oh, come now. We'll see to that. Now and then you can give Eugénie a new zest for work. Just to recharge her batteries, shall we say. Once a month, perhaps? This way you'll keep three people happy."

"Three?"

"That's right. You yourself will be happy to have Eugénie under your thumb and to enjoy little presents, for friendship's sake, won't you?

"She'll be so happy to have someone to dote on, to cherish, a man who isn't like the rest, isn't that so?

"And what about me? Not only will my place be running smoothly again but I'll have the rare and touching spectacle of two innocent doves billing and cooing, one to another, in a bawdy house."

TRANSLATED BY MERLOYD LAWRENCE

Gilbert de Chambertrand

VACATION AT MONTE-BELLO

ALL those in Guadeloupe who can, abandon the stifling towns and low-lying parts of the island as soon as burning July opens wide the magnificent portals of summer. They move up the wooded hillsides to trim cottages or modest villas hidden among the mango trees. They go seeking the blessings of coolness in the shady mountains. So Guadeloupe is dotted from north to south with charming little nooks with names like Sofaia, La Roche Blanche, Monte-Bello, les Trois Rivières, Dolé, La Matouba.

The caprice of fashion brings sometimes one, sometimes another of these places into vogue. There are some which have fallen from their old position and are neglected today in favor of smarter rivals. Among those which are forsaken and which I prefer, Monte-Bello appeals to me especially.

A victim of mechanization, Monte-Bello has been deserted since the advent of the automobile. The road leading to it is of clay, and only the creaking country carts pulled by yoked oxen are not defeated by it. Formerly, the landowners of the region had carriages, and horses and mules could get a foothold in the soft earth. But since the automobile has replaced the landau and the cabriolet of yesteryear, the well-to-do build in other locations, reached by paved roads.

This solitude, peopled only by memories, holds for me the attraction of an enchanted life, and that is why the moment my vacation began, I closed my house in town, turned my back on everything modern, and in the serenity of the open country, far from the harsh bark of automobile horns and the roar of motors, I climbed onto the rustic cart. To the slow tread of the reddish-brown oxen, breathing in the good smell of moist earth and the myriad scents of vegetation, I ascended toward the cool and shady mountains, bluff by bluff, hillock by hillock, toward a free and tranquil life, toward the boundless peace of the forest.

By the next morning, the spell had taken possession of me. Tall trees grow a few yards from my door, age-old trees whose gnarled trunks convey a sense of strength, and whose branches, high overhead, entwined with tropical vines, barely let through the sun's rays. Enormous pear trees interlace their amazing roots on the surface of the ground, like the tentacles of an octopus, or gigantic snakes. They seem to crawl, to glide, to coil, to stretch. Between the knots of these reptilian roots, suddenly a palmetto appears, growing inexplicably in this spot. A dozen steps away a gigantic parasite, a wild apricot, wraps an ancient mango in its mortal embrace. Its thousand creepers, attached to the trunk like a thousand adders, each day tighten their strange clasp. Everywhere plant life is sumptuous, luxuriant, encroaching, imperious. Vegetation reigns supreme. A power, an ardor bursts forth from all directions. All species meet face to face in the general advance up toward light. There is an exuberance, a prodigious and confused orgy of shape, of mass, of line. Branches like beams support the majestic structure of dense foliage from which the trailing vines hang; tree trunks stand out like the shafts of columns with capitals of orchids; a mysterious chiaroscuro filters from the faraway clefts in the leaves, while the organ tones of the wind moan faintly, and the forest seems a strange, harmonious, sweet-smelling and spacious cathedral.

Beyond the forest all is different. From the edge of the road I discover a bright panorama to the east. The sea, blue in the morning, purple in the evening, and at the other side of the bay, the pale cliffs of Gosier and Ste. Anne. Venturing a few yards farther, I catch sight of Pointe-à-Pitre in the distance, brick-pink under the afternoon sun, behind its emerald necklace of islets.

The other evening, while crimson cirrus clouds slashed the jade sky, from my hammock under the mango branches I watched the steamer sail for France, a tiny wisp on the sapphire of the water. And I rejoiced that I had given no one my address. I shall receive no letters. I shall write none. It is an absolute rest. I have withdrawn from the world, I am making a true retreat here, between two stages of life.

Little by little around me, as the sky darkens, I hear the great insect concert beginning. In the same way each evening, from one end of Guadeloupe to the other, a brilliant nocturnal concert opens as millions of virtuosi sound off. Little croaking frogs, locusts, crickets, unknown small creatures, throbbing, singing, crying; in bushes, in ponds, on branches, each tunes up his pipe or strings. By starlight, by moonlight, in the countryside at peace, disturbed occasionally by the lowing of a cow, there is a symphony which lasts till dawn—the most fairy-like, the most curious, the most disquieting symphony dominated, depending on location and elevation, by the silvery-toned anvil of the *machauquet* or the deep-toned rasp of the *gratte-coui*.

When I awoke this morning the air was of an unusual clarity. In the woods the winged species were in full voice. Twitterings, songs, chatterings, cries, chirpings, whistles, trills, roulades succeeded each other, answered each other, rose to a pitch. The neighboring mountains, usually wrapped in cloud, were almost entirely free of them, and the least curve of their slopes was precisely outlined by blue shadow. The air was cool and thin; the sun radiant. To my eyes, "the universe smiled in its charming freshness."

I took advantage of this beautiful morning to go visiting. Monte-Bello, it is true, has fallen from its ancient splendor. But traces are easily found. Here stands the beautiful and spacious house whose structure has withstood perhaps fifty years of neglect. One recognizes in it the signs of a wealthy past. It is encircled by a broad veranda where one feels that the ghost of a finished era roams. Things are imbued with charm, and under the headdress of ruined slate which offers poor protection against the mountain storms, the old house seems like a gentle grandmother, rich in memories.

Down below there is a large abandoned garden, where the purple of the acalypha trees reveals the outline of the grand *allées* and where the rosebushes are choked by nettles. Farther away, there is a circular basin, its edges paved with mosaic, its bottom tiled in blue. No water has flowed here for a very long time, and the roots of the nearby trees have forced apart the ancient tilework and cracked the masonry.

Vestiges of a not so distant past, but how different from our time! It was hardly forty years ago, perhaps thirty, when all this was fresh, laughing, gay, alive. In these stately paths, overgrown now by brambles but resounding then to the joyful shouts of children, happy couples walked and smiled at life. Seated in her great rocking chair on that veranda, the mother listened for the familiar sound of a horse's hoofs on the road, signaling her husband's return. In this pool where mountain water murmured, young girls sported their golden bodies. A sense of everlasting security enveloped these creatures. The tranquil hours ran on and seemed destined to run on inexhaustibly; happiness dwelt under their roof.

How sweet it is, and how sad, in the midst of these ruins and this neglect to recall the shades of those who passed here and who attempted in the magnificence of beautiful days to mold and bring under control a too powerful nature. Each day set its own task. The effort was commensurate to the man and has not survived him.

A philosophical resignation arises from such things. In these hectic times, there is a singular eloquence in evoking the spirit of those not-so-distant days when our fathers still cultivated wisdom and were aware of the smile of the gods.

I have no bathroom. Not even a pool. There is one, actually, which belongs to the house. But it is no longer usable. The terrible roots have begun to destroy it, too, and soon it will be no more than a miserable ruin. At least until the road to Monte-Bello is paved. And it will be soon, they say, and the region will acquire a new fame at the same time that it encounters the sputtering of motors and the stink of gasoline.

In the meantime, I have the river.

A few hundred yards away, at the foot of an abrupt drop, there is a torrential brook, The Moustique, whose cool waters, well-stocked with crayfish, are both relaxing and bracing. Its banks are thick with guava trees, and nothing is pleasanter on coming out of the water than to gather the sweet-smelling fruit.

Access to the river is by way of a rough and winding path from which there is a view of the valley. The sugarcane plantations leave their mark as large green squares, contrasting with the brown squares of the tilled fields. One can pick out the farm laborers and their oxen, showing up as tiny dots, Lilliputian insects. In the distance, hills complete the picture, and one sees gliding above them the slow procession of clouds, beloved of the poet Moréas, the "showy hosts of clouds" of Jean Lorrain.

All day long the west wind pushed the snowy cumulus against

the mountain range. Frequently, too, at a great height, the light cirrus clouds come to a standstill and in the evening take on the colors of orange and vermilion.

But sometimes the ocean of the sky is traversed by tragic swells: squalls from the south, carrying in enormous nimbus clouds a deluge of showers, crash onto the forest and set torrential streams to roaring. Deep-toned storms full of sudden thunder spread bluish grays of all shades from one end of the horizon to the other, evoking images at once of a mouse's fur, the airy smoke of cigarettes, and the cold aspect of lead. Sometimes, too, cyclonic disturbances, which are turned aside by the mountains.

One of these, just a few days ago, upset the usual order of the winds and threw the docile flock of clouds into confusion. Torn cirrus, distorted nimbus fled one after the other toward all parts of the alarming sky. But the formidable pilgrim of the upper air did not stay with us long. It went off northward, a spinning top of a tornado, toward the great modern ships, which are floating palaces, toward the adventurous airplanes, heroic and fragile as birds.

Since then, the upper air has been well-behaved. The triumphal procession of cumulus sets its dazzling whiteness against the clear blue of the sky, and promises a long succession of beautiful days.

I shall not enjoy them again for a long time to come, alas. The vacation is drawing to a close. Like a house of cards, the days are tumbling after one another with ridiculous speed, and I see the final date approach relentlessly.

Serene days at Monte-Bello, peaceful hours lived far from the restlessness of men, the immensity of the past will soon absorb you. And all of you, friends and companions of my vacation, little green lizards who watched me with such curiosity and intelligence, swift hummingbirds who flashed ruby throats and emerald crests under my eyes, stealthy mongoose who created the illusion of carnivorous beasts in the underbrush, butterflies glistening like gems, enormous toads with their self-satisfied air, plaintive buntings, sugarbirds, and the familiar grosbeak—all of you, insect musicians, warbling birds, forgive me for breaking off so soon a relationship which gave me nothing but pleasure, and continue to be happy without me in your hospitable forest. I am only a man, and never has the remote curse of Eden weighed more heavily.

The cart has returned, that clumsy creaking cart hitched to red-brown oxen. I have unslung my hammock from the old mango. For the last time I have let my eyes wander over the magnificent scene, over the blue mountains, the forest, the delicate sky. In the branches of a sapodilla tree a bird is singing itself hoarse. All is peaceful, kind, serene. And I have closed the door.

Great docile oxen, you cannot move too slowly, carrying me back to the plain. May the ribbon of clay stretch out long beneath your feet!

But I shall not return again to the blue mountains, the deep woods. Through the leaves I can already make out the town at the far end of the bay. In a few hours the turning wheels of an active life will have drawn me into their cycle.

. . . Great red-brown oxen, quicken your pace. The mountain holiday is finished. Down there on the bare ground my brothers are at work. Like them, like you, I must bow to the yoke, I must stoop to the furrow, for the unending task.

TRANSLATED BY FRANCES WILLARD VON MALTITZ

Florette Morand

THE UMBRELLA LADY

In those days, to set out in an oxcart through the rough hill country, infested with highwaymen, was a very dangerous matter.
Therefore, the storekeeper of Petit-Canal, who provided the region
with rum, cod, rice, and lard, preferred to hire a dinghy when she
went for supplies in Pointe-à-Pitre.

It was a most sensible solution, a quick, easy trip, with few
risks, a credit to the intelligence of the Umbrella Lady, as she was
called in the village, behind her back.

She was a business woman in every sense of the word. Politicians came to her when they were out of power; she knew how to
mend broken marriages; and prepared the finest magic potions
with herbs known only to herself, which she picked in the dead of
night, alone on the road, stark naked beneath her black umbrella—or so the villagers claimed.

But the powers of this remarkable lady did not stop here, nor
did the list of her clients. She was also a sorceress! The awe that
she aroused was probably the reason for the mob of customers
who crushed one another at her counter, on paydays at Rougeol.

As soon as she decided to open her bazaar, all the other shops
of Petit-Canal folded for lack of customers.

Every two weeks, on Saturday, she omitted her usual séance,
and tended to her business affairs. (There is nothing like the eye of
the mistress.) In a loud voice, she went over her accounts, scolded
inefficient clerks, and found fault with clumsy employees, hired by
the day, who trembled at the very sight of her.

Alert, dynamic, full of stamina, she never missed a thing, in
spite of her age, nearly sixty, her physique, that of a whale, and
legs misshapen from filariasis, a disease which her medical lore
had overcome. Her bronzed face was still shiny and fresh, and
behind her eternal pince-nez, her little round eyes, alert and full of
evil glints, accustomed to penetrating the most tormented souls,
were somewhat frightening.

It was said in the village that since the death of her husband, a craftsman of very modest means, the "lady" had become "possessed." By what power? No one knew. But there were those who claimed that one dark and gloomy night, hearing the howl of the werewolf, she cried out joyfully, "He is one of ours!"

That was something to think about!

Of course, all these rumors were but whispered insinuations, for the Umbrella Lady never gave away any secrets!

One day, when her biweekly inspection was close at hand, she noticed that she would have to replenish her supply of cod and rice right away. Furious at her employees for their lack of foresight, she decided to make the trip the following day, a Friday. As usual, she embarked at about three o'clock in the morning in the hired dinghy, with her large black umbrella hooked over her arm.

The sea was smooth, but there was a gusty wind. The two sailors had hoisted the main jib; the skipper was steering the fragile craft, while taking fragrant puffs on his pipe. His men sang a sea chantey in low voices.

With her black umbrella under her arm, her leather bag on her knees, the lady sat quietly, thinking of the clients who would come to consult her in vain, of the errands she would do in town, of the heated discussions she would have with the dealers; for this "lady" was known to be closefisted and would bargain for hours on end.

The very thought of these negotiations made her clasp her bag lovingly to her bosom, a large pigskin bag containing both her fortune and her vast collection of jewels, which she kept with her at all times.

Dawn had risen over a violet sea; the sky grew radiant. Against the horizon loomed the green silhouette of the land around Pointe-à-Pitre.

The lady remained lost in thought and the sailors chatted rather drearily about various things. Their conversation was far more lively and salacious when they did not have such a venerable passenger on board.

The boat glided on and on, coming closer and closer to Pointe-à-Pitre. Nothing suggested that in a few minutes, due to the force of the elements, the Lady with the Umbrella would disembark in a most unexpected fashion. And yet, in less than a moment, a violent gust opened up her umbrella, and raised it on high, while the matronly passenger, offering no resistance, allowed herself to be swept away by the wind and the sea, then gently lowered onto the crest of a wave!

The men crossed themselves. Silent, calm, and quite unruffled, the lady moved slowly away, in great dignity beneath her black umbrella. The skipper claimed later that where her eyes had been, he had seen two gaping holes, the sight of which had made every hair of his shaggy beard stand on end.

After the first moment of shock, calling out in vain to the unconcerned lady, and reaching out to her with ropes and bamboo poles, the skipper, aware of his responsibility, lowered the sails, rolled his pants to the thigh, and jumped into the water.

An expert at the crawl, he soon reached the fugitive, who sat poised, in the same position as ever: aloof, dignified, her face like a mask beneath the black umbrella. But just as he held out his arm to grab her, a huge wave swept her away.

"Damn peculiar! Something evil is going on here; I thought I was holding the woman and when I closed my hand, guess what I had?"

The bewildered men said nothing.

"Foam."

"We're done for, skipper," whimpered one of the sailors. "We're through. We'll all be accused of having dumped her over to get her bag, and only God can prove we're innocent!"

"Instead of moaning and groaning, let's try . . ."

Five hundred yards away the fat matron sat beneath her umbrella, cradled between two waves.

"Start rowing, boys!"

But it was always the same. As soon as they reached the Umbrella Lady, she vanished, only to reappear again, an extraordinary distance away.

Though the men were courageous, the prey was elusive, the waves rugged, and the wind insane.

The ill-matched struggle with the elements kept on and on, from the waters of Ste.-Rose to those of Grippon, along the most dangerous shores, the most treacherous shoals.

Three fishing boats, intrigued by these peculiar maneuvers, had been following the dinghy for two hours when, weary of the struggle, the skipper decided to report the entire incident to the authorities in town.

The customs officers who listened to the story exchanged knowing looks and the skipper and his men were of course accused of having caused the disappearance of their passenger.

At about two in the afternoon, the prosecuting attorneys, the official divers, the customs men, newspapermen, and curious onlookers had embarked, some in hired fishing boats, some in dinghies, to "find the location where the deed took place and to recover the body of the unfortunate victim."

Various theories were expressed. Under custody in the official launch, our sailor boys agreed that they would never find a way out of this predicament. Merely for having reported what they had seen, the fishermen who had helped them in their search were held as possible accomplices, and kept under close scrutiny on deck.

The little fleet had just emerged from the yellow waters of the Rivière Salée, where the overpowering smell of the mangroves mingled with miasmas from neighboring swamps. When they reached the open ocean the accused showed them the way. On the other boats, people were already discussing the monstrousness of the crime, and the victim's son was railing bitterly against the thieves and murderers; the sheeplike crowd of spectators joined with him in the hue and cry.

"Hard labor! The guillotine!"

The boats left the cape to the north as they emerged from the fetid, murky waters of the Rivière Salée. They had been cruising about for some time when, to everyone's surprise, the following cry rang out, "Black spot to starboard!"

Everyone whipped about; necks were craned; eyes were peeled; binoculars were focused; voices were still; then a cry of doubt, of astonishment, of relief broke from every throat.

"Is it she?" asked the lady's son, stupefied.

"Yes it is!" gasped the customs men, unable to believe their eyes.

"Yes it is!" yelled the accused in triumph.

The wind was blowing the Umbrella Lady toward the boats at a wild clip.

"Mother!" wailed the son.

Local officials, judges, clerks, the prosecutor, the customs men all watched eagerly as ropes and floats were thrown toward her from a steamboat. The only person who still held doubts was a police officer, a florid Corsican who stood on the deck shouting as the lady came to a halt twenty yards away. Now surrounded by the boats, she floated calmly, without moving.

The Corsican decided this was the moment to dive into the sea after the cursed old crone, in order to be the first to show her what happens to those who play tricks on the authorities.

He reached her side, in spite of the choppy sea, but when he attempted to slip his arm around her voluminous waist he felt nothing but an enormous wave. It crashed over his head, and if he didn't reach bottom, it was thanks to the efforts of his devoted subordinates who hauled him out just as he was about to sink.

The mysterious Umbrella Lady floated away, her back to the wind.

Fascinated by this extraordinary flotilla, all the fishermen along the coast sailed out to swell the ranks, and to join in vain pursuit of the fugitive lady. Finally, as night fell, everyone came to the conclusion that "she who plays with fire must perish by fire."

And so, on the registry in the town of her birth, the facts regarding the Umbrella Lady were completed with the words, "Lost at sea."

Since then, on starless nights, fishermen out trawling now and then pass the silent Umbrella Lady, driven by the wind and the tide, without reprieve, a tireless, solitary pilgrim, wandering about the Caribbean in search of time ill spent. . . .

TRANSLATED BY MERLOYD LAWRENCE

Clément Richer

UP IN SMOKE

It all happened because of a seagull.

Of course it had no business being on the bridge of a Venezuelan freighter, even if we were bound for the Pacific with bales of cotton and spices from Cumaná, Coro, and Varinas, for places where people feel they need such things.

And naturally the seagull was exhausted when it landed on the *S.S. Marcella's* rear bridge, right in front of Koulie's eyes; he happened to be passing at that moment. The nearest shore was miles away, so it hadn't been able to pick its landing ground, but Koulie didn't give a damn about that.

He didn't like seagulls and after all he had a right not to like them. So much so that he pulled out his knife—a shiny thing he spent all his spare time joyfully sharpening—humming in a low voice as he made ready to cut up the seagull with as much care as any well-bred gentleman devotes to the same operation upon a roast chicken. With the difference that the seagull hadn't just emerged from the oven; instead it was kicking and struggling and uttering plaintive cries and shedding blood on Koulie's hands, which worried him not at all. There were few opportunities for distraction on the ship and he wasn't going to let this one get away. The previous month he'd been sorry to leave the village on the Caribbean isle where he'd first seen the light of the world, and had come with the aid of poverty and the dole to be a stoker on the *S.S. Marcella*. And he was inclined to blame a certain European country of which, strange as it may seem, his Caribbean isle was an integral part, for a state of affairs with which, needless to say, the seagull had had nothing to do. The fact that he had left a seductive young creature with amber skin waiting for him in his village did not help to mellow his character.

Yet had he suspected what that selfsame exhausted-looking seagull was capable of in a fit of bad temper, he would probably have thought twice before taking such liberties with it. And indeed there

184

was not a soul on the ship who wasn't aware of what one might expect from a seagull who had good reason to complain of a ship and its crew.

The truth of the matter is that everyone on board expected the worst when at the end of the morning the mate informed us there would be a little wind that evening and we were therefore to stoke the fires, as the captain was in a hurry to get to his destination—and that was Bundaberg on the far shores of Australia. The stokers were appalled, shook their heads and turned toward Koulie, looking him up and down and muttering. For every one of them took it for granted that if a storm did break, as the mate announced, it would be doing so on the deceased bird's wings. But Koulie knew nothing of such perverse winged creatures and their evil power. Furthermore, he had an excessive confidence in his knife, which prompted him to snicker insolently in the others' faces.

Since the approaching tempest (a high wind and a lot of salt-water whipped into waterspouts—the Pacific lacks imagination and knows no other kind of storm) would probably race over the sea faster than our cargo vessel could, we had better get to work without delay. All the more so as we soon noticed that it had suddenly become very hot in the stokehole, a place which at the best of times was hardly cool; and the men mopped their brows and cursed and flung evil looks at Koulie, whose thoughts were elsewhere.

The heat grew worse and soon after we heard a kind of stifled roar. The *Marcella* reared up out of the water and plunged heavily back on her stern with a crash that sent every shovel not solidly gripped flying up to the roof. Then there was a moment's silence while the wind parleyed with the sea as to the best way to worry the crew and soon set up such a din, rumbling and whistling, blowing and howling, that you could hear nothing else. I could see Manolo, a Santo Domingo man, moving his lips at my side. The waves were making too much of a row for me to catch what he said, but I knew he was talking about the seagull; about just why it had chosen the *Marcella*'s bridge to land on, when the freighter had been out on the open sea and far beyond the ordinary range of migrant birds; about the loving kindness we ought to have lavished on it at the time; and about the madness which had made that lout

Koulie (a black look at that impassive stoker) kill it without a thought for the way it would come back across our path again, sweeping every cyclone in the Pacific along with it!

We would never have to toil and strain in our lives again the way we had to just then. We couldn't build up any more steam, though we felt like making the boilers burst, and no one was watching the needle on the pressure gauge anymore; it had swung round to a point that wasn't usually safe. But the *Marcella* didn't make another half knot for all that. It wasn't her fault, we knew, since her screw wouldn't stay in the water more than three minutes running. And a ship without a screw is like a man without legs.

The *Marcella* was suffering, you may be sure, for she was a good ship, and we were sorry for her, and did all in our power to help, but getting her screw to stay in the water was a thing beyond our control. The thought occurred to me that the vessel was aware of that and was grateful to us; it was indeed trying hard to keep on to Bundaberg, where there was a fine sheltered port in which to moor safe and easy, while the crew went to see if the taste of gin in a few bars of their acquaintance had changed.

But they were far away, those bars, and so was the port so dear to their hearts. And for the moment it was sad to see the freighter grappling with water up to her funnel. The *Marcella* didn't know where to set her bows and the cursed squall plunged her down to the nadir of each hollow the waves left in their path; and it dragged her backward too, like a drowned man yanked out of the water, though not for long, for another gust blew in soon and sent the vessel back where it had been, or into another trough.

We only stopped ramming the boilers with coal to go rolling all together across the stokehold when a specially violent shock shook the freighter. Manolo had hit his head on something, and when the sheen of the open ovens lit up his face he looked like anything in the world but an inhabitant of it. No one spoke because it would have been a waste of time to try and make yourself understood in that cyclone and, as they say in New Guinea, when the wind tells the sea what the sea doesn't like, men should shut up and listen. We'd done nothing but that in the stokehole for hours: listen and stoke coal. As soon as you'd flung in a shovelful you had to kick the grid shut fast if you didn't want to go in along with the coal; hell wasn't hotter than those fires. I nearly went in bodily once or twice but Manolo stopped me, interposing an arm as my head was on the way in. He put his mouth to my ear and shouted that I was carrying my sense of duty too far: science had shown coal was a better fuel than human flesh, even frog-eating snail-chewing Martinique or French flesh, which made me laugh, though I'd never eaten a frog in my life of course, or a snail either, for that matter.

Manolo laughed too, his teeth shining out of a face caked with blood, then a jolt dragged us apart and another one flung us into each other's arms. Sometimes six or seven of us fell in a cluster all at once, because when the jolt came we each instinctively grabbed our neighbor and rolled all round the stokehole until we managed to get to our feet again. And we shot out our arms for the shovels which had followed us in our fall and gone bouncing about in our wake, a peril to life and limb. When one of us hurt himself and took his time getting up, Manolo hobbled over to him on all fours and asked after his health and if he thought he was in a first-class bunk.

Banzo, the oldest among us, used to say that rain right in the middle of a cyclone would diminish its violence. There'd been no lack of thunderclouds in the sky after sunset, but were they still in the same place? Or had the wind carried them away to the south? What was certain was that the seas were still high. The clock beside the gauge said 4 A.M. Day would dawn in a moment and we hadn't stopped stoking coal into the fires one instant, shovel on shovel, except for the time we'd spent rolling round the stokehold, separately or together, on our backs or bellies. Once Manolo thought he heard the strident call of a ship and cocked his ear, but there was nothing to be heard above the racket and he gave up. Yet he probably hadn't been mistaken and the siren may have belonged to a Danish freighter swallowed body and soul that night, as we heard later; we expected a similar fate ourselves.

The *Marcella* was crawling across the water as best she could, but it wasn't easy. No one in the stokehole had had a bite to eat since the previous morning, and the men couldn't take any more. You would have thought everyone else had gone overboard, because no one had shown the least interest in us since the storm began. To tell the truth, we weren't used to people taking much

notice of us even in normal times. Stokers aren't the most orna-
mental objects on a ship and they know it.

The only person we'd have really been happy to see was the
cook. Our tongues stuck to our palates and the incessantly flying
coal dust mingled with sweat gave our lips a bitter, salty taste. We
were hungry and thirsty, especially thirsty, so in the end we got the
idea of going to the cook ourselves, and Manolo made it clear I
should make the trip, pointing one after the other to his gullet, his
belly, and the stairway.

I staggered off with my head in such a spin I thought I'd never
get to the top. After that I can't remember how I kept going or
which way I went. When I got to the galley I found the cook
hanging onto the leg of an oven, which was bolted to the floor. He
was as white as his apron on washday, and since his mouth kept
opening and closing, I supposed he was moaning something or
other.

He had a broken leg and an arm in hardly better condition, as I
could see without closer inspection, but I hadn't the slightest desire
to help him at that point, and I began ferreting around the kitchen
for something to eat and drink. I opened the cupboards at random
and stuffed as many cans of food into my shirt as it would hold,
together with bottles of beer, which I wrapped in a napkin, knot-
ting the four corners together. And while I fumbled here and there
hanging on to anything which came my way with each new lurch of
the ship, the cook, still clinging to his oven, followed me everywhere with his eyes; and when I happened to turn my head toward
him, his look grew imploring and his lips moved. He was obviously
asking for help, but I wasn't the one to ask. All I wanted was
coffee. If it weren't for that I'd have been back in the stokehold
already, where the others were waiting for me with parched
throats. But my heart longed for hot coffee, and I knew the other
stokers were dying of the same longing, so nothing in the world
would have made me leave that galley without finding what I
wanted. I was determined to make some myself if I didn't locate
any, in spite of all the ship's wild tossing.

But the Holy Virgin came to my aid that day, and in the oven
that nincompoop of a cook was clutching with his one good arm I
found a large coffeepot fixed to the tray with hooks, and it was full
of good coffee whose smell leaped to my nostrils as soon as I
opened the door. Since I couldn't remove the coffeepot I set about

filling a flask I found lying around, and then I left, with a happy heart, taking no notice of the cook who went on bawling things no one could hear.

Going back was not an easy task and more than once I slipped and fell, but I did what I could, at the risk of breaking my limbs like the scullion, so that even when I fell the bottles of beer weren't the worse off.

But it was the flaskful of coffee that gave me the most trouble.

It slid out of my hands at the foot of the lower-deck stairway, and I soon saw that, as if it were a living thing, it didn't care to be caught again. Maybe it thought I ate snails for breakfast as Manolo had said the French did. Anyway, it was clearly doing all it could to avoid me, and I ten times as eagerly wanted it back, to keep until it had surrendered its contents. While I pursued and it retreated, I forgot the wind, the sea, and the predicament of the ship. If I was going to drown I wouldn't do so before I had drunk that coffee.

Finally I imagined that the flask, like an animal, was watching my least movement. I tried to pounce suddenly when it wasn't expecting the attack, but the wretched thing had eyes everywhere and slid away as soon as I put out my hand. So I began calling out, forgetting it couldn't hear me because of the sea's uproar; I said how worn out we all were and how we'd had nothing since the previous day and wouldn't be able to go on watching the pressure. I told it I had no designs on it at all, only on that coffee which was the sole thing I and my comrades wished for. I promised it would come to no harm. I called it my little darling, my sweet one, peg o' my heart and all the names a sailor uses to wheedle out of women what they usually refuse him at first.

Then, since flattery hadn't worked, I resorted to threats. I changed my language and tone, as a man will toward a girl too vainly chaste, saying what I thought of that slatternly bit of tin which, once I had drunk to the dregs what it now refused me, would be flung in the furnace. And while I was talking and cursing, I never ceased watching where it went, stopping when it stopped, jumping when it jumped.

At times that flask came to rest under my very nose, and the instant I shot out my arm with a chuckle of triumph, it slid suddenly away from me, only to bounce back a little ahead. I'd go dragging after it again, still on my belly, and it would flee for refuge to the other end of the landing, managing to give me the slip each time. But not for an empire would I have given up the chase!

In the end the *Marcella* herself took pity on my plight. Right in the middle of a rise she suddenly reared and yawed over to starboard, probably because some heavier wave had caught her off guard, so that the flask of its own accord flung itself foolishly into my arms, which I closed swiftly, holding it captive. And at this point I sat down on the landing and murmured lovingly to it (that coffee had a heady odor). Then I rose and went on my way to the stokehole, arriving without further mishap.

The stokers threw themselves at me and wrested away the cans of tuna and sardines and biscuits, all I'd found in the galley cupboards, and since they couldn't speak or I understand a word, they slapped me roundly on the back by way of thanks. They passed the flask round and round and when its fat belly was empty I remembered the vow I'd sworn on the landing below deck, and opening the furnace doors, I flung it in. At the risk of being flung in also, by the ship's pitching, I stayed there and watched it redden, lose shape, twist (in pain, it seemed), and I laughed so much that the others thought I'd gone out of my mind. They couldn't know, and I didn't tell them till later, when the storm had stopped howling louder than us, all the trouble that flask had given me on the landing.

We'd been so busy eating and drinking we'd almost forgotten our shovels and boilers, but now the day was dawning—a filthy day, with a funereal aspect and as stubbled with black as any of us—and as the sounds of whimpering and moaning came down to us from above we got back to work; stokers know their machinery well, and we could hear it running just as smoothly as before. If only the screw could have kept itself under water a little more regularly, the *Marcella* would have found harbor a fair while before. But the screw wasn't doing its job. I don't blame it. Manolo kept repeating that it was a good screw and you couldn't expect it to succeed when none of its peers would have done so either under the circumstances.

But, all the same, we felt it was out of position too often, spinning up in the air alone and gaining no advantage. The machinery held the same opinion, that was clear. The cylinders (pistons panting back and forth and suddenly accelerating, their heads in hot steam) were swearing at the erratic screw and its unevenness. The main bearing guiding the drive to that screw squealed three times as loud with three times as good reason, and the condenser sweated out its bad temper in transparent droplets which immediately evaporated as if to mark their disapproval.

The men spent all that afternoon, the second since the cyclone began, watching the way the *Marcella* behaved, and mentally calculating, given the force of the squall, how the ship would stand up to the sea's frenzy.

Night came soon, sooner than we had expected, and shortly after darkness had crept in, the freighter took on a list. Water had forced its way in and the holds had got their share. Maybe she'd sprung a leak? We thought our end had come. Everyone on board (as we learned later) had despaired of saving the steamer and had begun to think of putting the lifeboats into the water; given the state of the sea, this would have been sheer lunacy.

There was another remedy, and a far more fitting one, for saving the ship. Manolo was the first to realize it, and explained to us the idea, which we calmly carried out as soon as we judged the moment timely.

And, in fact, half an hour later Banzo, who had lived and voyaged more than any of us, suddenly stiffened, shovel in hand, and listened, listened, and all the wrinkles on his old face seemed to listen too. Finally he looked at us and laughed with an air of great contentment, and as we stared curiously at him he explained, with gestures, that the rain had come.

He had told us when it all began that rain usually did away with a cyclone's force. It wasn't always true, of course, but nevertheless it did happen that way very often. So the men stopped work and in turn cocked their ears, and indeed it seemed that there were drops of water spattering and ringing on the *Marcella*'s deck and hull, and that as they splashed onto the metal plates they weren't making quite the same kind of sound as spray from waves.

Manolo didn't dare open a porthole to make sure, for fear of the water pouring into the stokehole, because a stokehole's ovens can't stand flooding. However, after about an hour had passed one of the mechanics coughed, and every stoker, every coal-trimmer suddenly lifted his head, because they had *heard* him cough! And they all jumped around, shouting and singing:

> Let me kiss you darling, do,
> This one last time that I'll see you!

At the same time they made a show of kissing each other, the way the song said, and with their soot-blackened faces it made a comical scene. And they dealt each other great blows on the back, punctuating the song with the most appalling curses, competing to see who could shout the loudest and make the ugliest faces.

Manolo come over to me, and with a bow that would have made one of Isabella the Catholic's ladies-in-waiting pale with jealousy, he took my hand and forced me to bend my head so that I could duck low and pass under the crossed arms of all the other stokers, who had gathered in a circle. Then another stoker in his turn bowed to Manolo with the same low and expert bow and forced him to execute similar movements, all the way round till the last stoker forming the circle had been through the ritual. Some of them used their shovels like ceremonial batons, tapping their neighbor on the head to show everyone how happy they were, and for the sheer pleasure of hearing their own voices again and feeling themselves alive.

Then Manolo called for three cheers for the *Marcella* still steaming on its way with a list because the hold was half full of water. Now things were at the stage where we could tell from the freighter's movement that the intensity of the storm had waned, although we were still being vigorously shaken. We were hungry and thirsty of course, but we'd decided to wait a bit before making a fresh incursion into the kitchen, where I wasn't at all looking forward to facing the cook; and now that I could make myself heard, I lost no time in telling the others about him. They laughed at me and said you had to be a snail-eater to be so softhearted. They said I was as sentimental as a schoolgirl, the kind they saw in the towns with mauve ribbons round their waists and a governess at their heels.

The *Marcella* went sailing on as well as you could expect for the rest of the night, and its screw showed great good will and a clear desire to make up all the time it had lost while its propeller blades had been up in the air roaring at the storm. So that toward two o'clock in the morning old Banzo said that if we asked him, the freighter couldn't be far away from Bundaberg, where we'd have anchored two days before if it hadn't been for that cursed cyclone. The idea of walking on dry land again, which none of us had thought we would ever do, made all the men feel a mysterious stirring deep inside them.

Banzo hadn't been wrong, and just before dawn Manolo opened a porthole—the state of the sea permitted this by then—and the stokers saw lights in the distance.

We didn't start shouting or singing or bowing this time, but each stoker stood quietly and watched the lights around the port, lost in his own thoughts. Nothing in the world would have made him share these with his neighbor, for fear of being jeered at. And yet we were almost certainly all thinking the same thing, and there wasn't one of us who didn't have a tear rimming his eyelash and waiting to fall, if such had been permissible. But it wasn't permissible, because men—especially men in the stokehole—can't make an exhibition of themselves. Besides, everyone knows that only women cry in this world and that men are strong, brave, and resolute in all circumstances.

That evening, when the *Marcella* had been left rocking at anchor in the port, the stokers went ashore in groups and scattered out among the bars, where, between one gin and the next, they told the tale of the seagull, and the part—the catastrophic part—which Koulie had played in the whole affair.

One customer who had been listening to the story with particular interest wagged his head and asked, "And where is he now?"

At this we all began looking round about us, very surprised, as if we were expecting Koulie to rise up in our midst, although we'd all quite consciously helped to stuff into one of the raging furnaces the body of the stoker whose head Manolo, a little earlier, had smashed open with his shovel the instant the rolling ship had sent him sprawling on his belly across the stokehole.

There hadn't been any other way to avoid shipwreck and the principal thing had been to appease the wrath of the dead seagull (a vindictive breed) howling for vengeance with the voice of the cyclone it had driven furiously before it through the night. For us—and for the *Marcella*—it had been a matter of life or death, and Manolo hadn't had any difficulty convincing us of this. We had had to choose, and without delay, between our own lives and Koulie's. The choice was quickly made. It had been high time. With the freighter already listing heavily there'd not been a minute to lose. The best proof of this was that less than half an hour after Koulie had gone up the funnel in smoke, the rain had begun to come down and the cyclone suddenly calmed, which it wouldn't otherwise have done.

Of course, the official version was that a wave had washed one of the stokers overboard during the storm, and no one contradicted it.

But still, why did he have to kill that seagull?

TRANSLATED BY PATRICK BOWLES

Philippe Thoby-Marcelin

THE SUBMARINE

Sunset was fading over a dirty bronze-sequined sea, which, as the wind died down, suddenly fell flat between Port-au-Prince and the island of La Gonâve. Driven away from the neighboring huts and cabins where the lamps were being lit, the fetid night of La Saline spread out maternally, enveloping the ugliness of the outskirts—the mud, the poverty, and resignation.

Under Uncle Rémy's thatch-covered arbor, the ebony faces no longer shone; the old man's polished head alone held out, still reflecting the feeblest ray of light.

The bezique game was over. They had almost exhausted the news of the day, and the conversation was taking a languid turn. The bottle of rum was running dry. But, blessed by December's cool breath, gently sifting through the clothing and skin, a feeling of well-being and security filled the four men. Everything invited silence and peace of heart, and even the termites that constantly gnawed away at the dry palm of the arbor had become silent. Not far from there, however, to protect her ailing child from the mosquitoes or the evil spirits, a fisherman's wife was burning rubber and orange leaves.

Tired of pulling futilely on his terra-cotta *cachimbo,* Ti-Rouge suddenly raised his head, took the pipe from his toothless beak and aimed a great stream of blackish saliva at a good distance.

"Yes, my friends, I'm not lying to you. The situation of the country is not good," he said in his raucous alcoholic voice. "It is not good at all."

A self-styled pessimist (according to his cronies, his thirst caught hold of him as soon as he woke early in the morning), he would have thought himself slipping in the eyes of his companions had he not snatched them from the moment's invitation to leisure. An urgent need to gossip made his tongue itch.

"Nobody can tell you where the taxpayer's money has gone," he elaborated. "Maybe it went and hid in the hole of the crab that guards the Bois-de-Chêne riverhead."

Not knowing how to express his opinion, Absolam let out a little cackle, halfway between skepticism and pain, "Ho-ho-ho-hooo!"

Timothy cracked his knuckles, carefully stretched, yawned, and concluded in a plaintive tone, "At the present time, my friends, we are seeing things we never saw before, even during the American Occupation. People poking in garbage cans looking for a hunk of dirty bread or rotten fruit."

"And do you know what I bumped into yesterday evening?" asked Uncle Rémy. "A poor little woman crouched in front of a basket of filth eating pea pods. I looked at her a minute, then I shook my head, I just shook my head. Truly, my friends, I was struck dumb. . . . Finally, making an effort, I said to her, 'Poor devil, so you are that hungry!' She turned around and bared all her teeth like a dog that's been molested. And yet she was a human being, one of the good Lord's children, like you and me. But what upset me most of all, you may believe it or not, was that this unfortunate creature was a mulatto. Yes, gentlemen, a real one, with beautiful straight hair, pointed nose, green eyes—a white woman, you'd have thought."

"Hooo!" cackled Absolam again, with great pity this time, "ho-ho-hooo! That's all we lacked till now, the mulattoes are hungry too."

Ti-Rouge sneered, "You know as well as I do the saying, 'The stick that beats the black dog is also the one—' "

He stopped short as though he'd been caught red-handed and cast a furtive glance in the direction of the cabin. Haloed from head to foot like a picture of Our Lady of the Immaculate Conception, although she was black and shuffling along in her sandals, Mrs. Rémy was bringing in the light. She still looked young for her age since she was not stout. But by her gait—so heavy you would have thought of an emaciated tumble toy having the power of self-locomotion—you could tell her legs under her ample robe were deformed by elephantiasis.

She set the lantern on the table, picked up the cards and went out as she came in, without offering a word. She looked at no one and no one looked at her. And now (perhaps it was also a result of the light) the silence was becoming thick under the arbor, it was getting heavy.

Uncle Rémy was picking his ear with a spent match. He cocked his head to one side and was shaking it gently, his face alight with an indescribable joy, and Ti-Rouge thought that in this attitude, with his flaring nostrils, his moist lips and small eyes, he looked exactly like a young pig. The others also looked like animals— Absolam like a mouse and Timothy like an old burro. A wicked mania Ti-Rouge had, as he was envious and malicious, for comparing human beings with inferior species.

Shaking off the tension which held the group, his contempt reared its head like a serpent, ready to strike. He spat again.

"What you've been telling us is only petty details," he said scornfully. "As for those plucked mulattoes that seem to pull at your heart, all I can say is that there are still not enough of them. As long as all the bourgeois haven't tasted hunger, I'll say there is no justice in the world for the black Negro. But that's not the point. When I say that the situation is not good, I'm talking about business. You can cover the whole of downtown, looking to right and left, you won't find a single deal."

"You hear that!" sighed Timothy.

"Hooo," cackled Absolam sadly, "Ho-ho-hooo!"

Ti-Rouge puffed out his chest, "I go everywhere and ask where the country's money has gone and no one can answer, not even the big wheels in business."

"Ho-ho! Ho-ho! Ho-ho!" exclaimed Uncle Rémy in astonishment.

"No one!" emphasized Ti-Rouge.

"You hear that!" said Timothy again.

"No one, I tell you! And what's more, it's the same situation in the Treasury—not a centime. Then the President gets up, stamps his foot and says, 'The devil with it, if I don't do something, everyone will die of hunger!' And he assembles the ministers, the senators and deputies, the judges, those fine gentlemen of the Army, not to mention the government engineers, doctors, and agronomists. He has the fancy government cars brought out, piles everybody in, and takes them all on a little presidential tour in the North. When he arrives at Cap-Haïtien, he makes a long speech to the people, a broadcast as they say—in short, a real address, in pure French! And this is what he says: 'My friends, this country of yours, Haiti, is like a ship taking in water. All Haitians, rich and poor alike, must help me pump it out.' And when he has finished talking, he goes on a binge with his men. Then he comes back to Port-au-Prince. Now what do you suppose the Chief does to institute reforms? He publishes a special issue of *Le Moniteur* with his whole speech in it. And what else, will you tell me? A whole list of taxes that the poor people must pay: tax for this, tax for that! In fact, there isn't a thing the President forgets."

Ti-Rouge smiled modestly, scratching the nape of his neck, "That's when the people begin to understand what it means to pump."

Absolam did not particularly enjoy political discussions. Considering that stool pigeons were thick as rats in the whole republic, such chatter was always dangerous, even for an ordinary person. Imagine how much worse, then, for him, a messenger in the Department of Commerce. So he got up and left. Timothy, although he was unemployed, thought it a good idea to leave, too. And Ti-Rouge soon followed suit, having, he said, some business to attend to.

Uncle Rémy was not fooled by the bragging of the confidence man, but he was not in the mood to smile. He was preoccupied with the thought that his friends were leaving him earlier than usual and had the uneasy feeling of being unfairly deserted. It was as though the whole earth had become depopulated.

All around him, however, La Saline continued to live.

In the neighboring cabin, where rubber and orange leaves were still burning, the fisherman's child protested against his illness in an endless lament, made up of montonous inarticulate sounds which expressed his suffering more truly than words could have.

The mother had taken him in her arms, and gently patting his buttock, she cradled him with a wild desperate patience.

> *Maman-li allé lariviè*
> *Papa-li allé pêcher crabe.*
> *Dodo, ti titite maman-l'*
> *Dodo, ti titite maman-l'*
>
> *Si li pas vlé dodo,*
> *Crabe va manger li.*
> *Si li pas vlé dodo,*
> *Crabe va manger li.*

(His mother went to the river [to do the wash], his father went crabbing. Go to sleep, mother's little one. Go to sleep, mother's little one! If he doesn't go to sleep, the crab will eat him up. If he doesn't go to sleep, the crab will eat him up.)

Perhaps only at daybreak would the fisherman's wife come to the end of the lullaby:

> *Dodo, titite,*
> *Crabe la calalou!*
> *Dodo, titite,*
> *Crabe la calalou!*
> *Dodo, titite,*
> *Crabe lan calalou.*

(Sleep, little one, the crab is in the kettle! Sleep, little one, the crab is in the kettle! . . .)

Uncle Rémy heard neither the song nor the child's wailing. Long association with the poor had somewhat hardened him and he was only sensitive to misfortunes that were out of the ordinary.

Finding himself alone and not knowing too well what to do with his time, he was thinking, if one might call it that. Simple things—the woman, the shop, the nets and boats that he rented to the fishermen—all enmeshed in a vast and confused reverie. But these were, after all, serious matters, and he could certainly have a rest from them when the day was over. Doesn't the proverb say that when the road is long even a straw becomes heavy? Uncle Rémy was getting ready to draw a small advance on the sleep of the just, when suddenly he remembered Cius, the little servant boy, or rather, as they say, the *godchild* of the house. He opened his eyes.

Uncle Rémy had a pronounced weakness for discipline. Hence, for some two years, since Cius' parents had entrusted the boy to him, the old man's severity had rarely slackened. Moreover, the boy's father, with the harshness of mountain folk, had recommended that a close eye be kept on him.

"You must not spoil him," he had declared. "It's not that he's a bad sort; we can't say that, thank God. But he is not much for work. He's too fond of playing. Talk to him. If he does not listen to you, beat him. It will be for his good."

Every evening, therefore, after his friends had left, Uncle Rémy would seriously devote himself to the education of Cius. But this time his hand was itching more than usual for he had drunk plenty of rum in the course of the afternoon while he played cards.

He bellowed for the child with all his strength.

"Cius, hey, Cius, where are you? Don't you hear me calling you?"

"What did you say, godfather?"

"Come here, you little good-for-nothing!"

"I'm coming, godfather!"

"You always say you're coming but you never hurry to get here. But I advise you not to be slow this time."

"Here I am, godfather."

Uncle Rémy was startled. He had not seen the child who had approached noiselessly and was standing in the shadow at a prudent distance, though he knew the precaution to be futile.

"But . . . where were you, then?" asked the old man, in a sweet voice.

"In the courtyard, godfather."

"And what were you doing there, my child? Were you playing?"

"Yes, godfather."

"Ah, you were playing! That's just what I thought. But what did I tell you already?"

"That I mustn't ever play."

"Good! Then you know what you must do now?"

"Bring you the whip, godfather."

"Well, my son, what are you waiting for?"

"Nothing, godfather, here's the whip. I had already got it for you."

"So-o, my child, come closer so I can see you."

Cius took a step forward, then another. Two large tears started down his cheeks. Uncle Rémy seized him brutally by the ear and pulled him forward.

"Get down on your knees, you little scoundrel, and hold out your paws!"

Just as he was about to strike him, the old man turned apprehensively toward the gate of the courtyard. He saw nothing, for the darkness was thick, but he had a distinct feeling that someone was there.

"Who goes there?" he asked.

No one answered.

"I asked who goes there!" he shouted.

"It's me," said Absolam finally, near enough now to lower his voice.

The old man, reassured, sighed in relief. "Ho-ho, brother, so you came back. What good wind brings you here again?"

"It's nothing, Uncle Rémy. Only, Ti-Rouge . . . how can I tell you? It's not that I suspect him of being a *submarine,* heaven forbid! Only, I think he talks too much and that could be not exactly innocent. There, that's it!"

"Do you honestly believe, Absolam, that he's a spy . . . a *submarine?*"

"No, Uncle Rémy, I don't really believe it. I can't say that I do, not being in the habit of passing rash judgment on my neighbor. But this evening, I assure you, Ti-Rouge talked too much, and especially about politics. Anyway, you realize . . . As far as I'm concerned, I only want to put you on your guard. And your bezique games, I'd advise you to hold off for a while. In any case, caution is not cowardliness. I'm not coming here anymore."

Absolam instinctively looked around him. He noticed nothing unusual, but thought it wise, nevertheless, to steal away. As for Uncle Rémy, he was tormented by forebodings, by absurd and desperate ideas, and did not know what stand to take, what saint to turn to.

Overcome with anger, he turned on the child.

"Stretch out your paws," he cried. "Open them wide, and count to a hundred!"

TRANSLATED BY EVA THOBY-MARCELIN

Magloire-Saint-Aude

THE WAKE

to SIMONE A. GEORGES

THE dead girl was laid out on a narrow bed. Black and beautiful, she seemed to be asleep, relieved, as it were, of the sorrows of living.

It was out in Bel Air, at night, in an alley of dubious reputation.

Those in the room of the deceased seemed to be crushed under the weight of some mysterious affliction. On the porch, the neighbors had gathered together, and a whispered conversation continued between the mother and a woman whose job it was to wash corpses. The latter was smoking a cheap cigar, and spitting; she reeked of garlic.

Rumor had it that the girl had not succumbed to an illness, and that she had drawn her last breath without pain.

It was no natural death, people were saying.

Since drinks were being served in the gallery, I left Thérèse's chamber (Thérèse was her name) and went to sit, at the insistence of "la madre," between her and the washer of corpses, who thereupon demanded that I light her cigar. I struck a match and, as I raised it to her face, saw that she had owl-like eyes (the eyes of a sorceress), sharp animal teeth, and horribly calloused hands. Our eyes, sharp as lightning, met, before I turned toward the serving woman who was offering me cinnamon tea. This I drank, then a glass of rum and a cup of coffee. I knocked the ashes out of my pipe and filled it, at my ease, with Splendid tobacco, known for its aftertaste of chocolate.

At midnight, a furious man sprang out of the alley which adjoined the dead girl's house. A mulatto, with a paunch like a pregnant woman's, he whipped on before him a beautiful young girl in a transparent nightgown, with skin veined like marble and the look of an angel. The blows which tore at her flesh she did not feel. Blood stained the shoulder of her nightgown; far off in the darkness a dog howled eerily at death; then of a sudden a milk-white mongrel burst into the alley and began licking the young girl's feet.

My friends, Laurent P. and Gaston F., summoned me to drink a bottle of Barbancourt with them. Regretfully excusing myself, I left the mother and the washer of corpses to their gossip, and went to join the drinkers.

Then there I was in an armchair in a sort of open corridor leading to the dead girl's room, seated at the very door, face to face with the deceased.

Wearing a white dress, as for a first communion, ornamented at the neck with lace ruffles, Thérèse, in her eternal stillness, was not a mournful sight. There was no band around her chin, not a wrinkle in her straight bell-shaped skirt. On her lips, barely perceptible, was a mischievous smile, and her jet-black hair fell loosely over her forehead.

As I studied her face (I had only to stretch out my arm to touch the body), one thing in particular made me shudder. Her eyes were not tightly shut, and from beneath the lids she seemed to be looking at me—was indeed looking at me—with a stare that brought me close to panic. I tried to move, but my limbs were paralyzed with cramp; I wanted to speak, but I had no voice.

Thérèse continued to stare fixedly at me.

At me alone.

My own glance, as if magnetized, could not pull itself away from those eyes of hers, which belonged now to another world.

I managed, nevertheless, to swallow a drink which Laurent poured down my throat. Afterward I had hiccoughs, and Gaston brought me water with a few drops of lemon juice, which I gulped down at intervals, gasping for breath.

My hiccoughs continued, like a death rattle. They gave me aspirin as a sedative, but my discomfort did not end. I was in a cold sweat, and the dead girl kept on looking at me, her eyes now more than half-open, as if she were alive, so that I could see the hallucinated pupils.

Candles had been placed at her bedside. Of a sudden one of them flickered, as if the breath of some occult presence were blowing upon it, then went out.

The other candles, as if at a signal, followed suit.

In the ensuing twilight, Thérèse opened her eyes wide—eyes that were strangely beautiful—with a sensual and unseemly joy that verged on cruelty.

I forced myself to stand up, like a robot, and closed the dead girl's eyes. Terror froze my blood, and a wisp of smoke escaped from my jacket.

Suddenly, as I lifted my pipe to my lips, an indescribable feeling of peace pervaded my heart.

The guests had all departed.

For half an hour the cathedral bell had been ringing the Angelus.

In the eastern sky, the stars were growing pale.

TRANSLATED BY FRANCES FRENAYE

Joseph Zobel

THE GIFT

Of course there were sorcerers. Real ones. So many things happened which the old women and the old men blamed on sorcery, and not just to scare the children! But I didn't know any. Perhaps I didn't know where to look. In any case, I had never come across any proof that a particular person was endowed with supernatural powers. No matter how often people reminded me that, by day, sorcerers seemed like anyone else, that their evil activities blossomed forth only by night or in secret hideaways, I was still not convinced. I saw no one whose appearance or behavior seemed to fit the image I had formed from tales we children heard during the vigils for the dead or from the many ghost stories passed from person to person throughout the countryside and in which we loved to steep our imaginations.

No one, that is to say, until I discovered Monsieur Atis. Perhaps "discovered" is not the right word. Monsieur Atis was someone I had known as long as I can remember, who was there as soon as I began exploring the world around me and recognizing what I saw: grown-ups, things, trees; Monsieur Walter who made the bread, Madame Walter who ran the bakery shop; Mademoiselle Choutte who made coconut macaroons on Saturday night and Sunday afternoon; the wheelwright and his apprentice who, both armed with long tongs, placed a huge, red-hot hoop of iron around a wooden wheel, not quite so large, and then splashed it with cold water so that it tightened fast about the wood, and the whole thing became a beautiful wagon wheel, which I would have liked to roll about until the carter came to fetch it. And the carpenter who seemed to enjoy making corkscrew shavings, blonde or mahogany, like the hair on little girls in books. And the mango trees! Those on town property whose fruit we could gather from the ground or even pick whenever we liked, and those which belonged to Monsieur Tertulien or Madame Zizine, whose fruit had to be gathered on the run when it was ripe enough to be blown down by the wind.

And then there were the animals, the insects, and also the plants, those which were sweet to chew on, and those which were poison. And the tasty wild fruit.

All those things, all those rules of living, all that knowledge which we acquired so effortlessly, day by day.

It was just this way that I came to know Monsieur Atis. His trade was the most solitary of all. Even more solitary than that of the shoemaker, who, while beating the leather on the bottom of an old clothes iron laid on his knee, or while tugging on the greased thread, liked to laugh and chat with those who came to sit in his shop.

But Monsieur Atis could neither talk nor even look up from his task. In addition, he had one eye riveted, so to speak, to his work by means of a strange black device with a glass lens, which he wore like a monocle. With delicate tweezers, leaning over a stand covered with small instruments, he adjusted the dainty spoked wheels of the clocks which no longer ticked until he had brought them back to life. No one else in town had this power, this magic skill, but there was no need for him to hide, to live under cover of darkness. He worked in broad daylight, in sight of passersby, of anyone, or all alone. That was what delighted me about him. To me, Monsieur Atis himself did not seem to belong to exactly the same race as the others in town—and yet he had been born here like anyone else, like the trees which grew here, and had never been away.

He did not have fancy clothes, but was always clean-shaven. (One could even watch him shave every morning in front of a little mirror, the kind the Syrian peddlers sell, hooked onto his half-open door.) He fixed his woolly hair by applying a great deal of vaseline and parting it down the middle with determined brush strokes. He always wore a clean shirt and hemp sandals on his feet.

He certainly wasn't rich; his wife bought bread, gasoline, rice, lard, and salt cod on credit, like all the "unfortunates" of the town; and though the house he lived in belonged to him, it was actually no more than a wooden shack, like all the others that clustered humbly at the bottom of the village and whose courtyards lay next to the cane fields which dominated our lives.

So he was not rich, but he enjoyed as much prestige as those who had two-story houses at the top of the town: Monsieur

Aristide, for instance, a mulatto who owned a huge estate at Morne Régal and ran a café right opposite the church where the plantation managers came to play pool, along with the tax collector, my schoolmaster, and the foremen at the factory. Even the white plantation owners brought Monsieur Atis their watches to repair.

No, certainly not rich, but the watches of every size, of every description, which adorned the wall behind his workbench, and the alarm clocks lined up on the shelves above created a marvelous world in which he was master, and into which I had managed to penetrate.

Since then, I have lived in constant awe of Monsieur Atis. His craft seemed to me a calm, honest, and unpretentious form of magic of the most authentic and convincing sort. And because I have never been able to love anything whatever without showing it, he became aware of my devotion and, in return, considered me one of the most polite, helpful, and perhaps most intelligent children in town.

I was the only one whom he entrusted occasionally with a watch, nicely packed in a small box, to deliver to a client who had forgotten to fetch it Saturday night or Sunday after Mass.

"Make sure he sees the bill right on top, and wait."

Sometimes I collected money, but more often I was told, "Thank Monsieur Atis for me and say that I'll be around tomorrow to settle up with him."

Then I would suffer the humiliating sensation of having failed in my mission.

When I began, he would remind me again and again, "Whatever you do, don't drop it."

After hearing this so often, I soon understood that a watch is like a fresh egg, with one difference: if it falls, the case may not break, but everything inside will die quietly, instead of splashing dramatically over the ground like the yolk and white of an egg.

I could feel the watch ticking in my hand, through its wrappings, like the heart of a frightened little bird captured or rescued on a windy day. I had learned to make my own heart beat fall into rhythm with it. In the end, Monsieur Atis' apprehensions subsided, and when he gave me a watch to deliver, he reminded me instead to persuade the client that he was badly in need of money.

Eventually, too, my admiration for Monsieur Atis led to a taste,

a passion, for watches. A classic passion, nourished by the pain of
never possessing the desired object.

But how was it that given the special brand of ethics, defiant of
all morality and resistant to spankings, by which we children never
hesitated to appropriate anything that seemed necessary to our
games, our fancy—and that we dared not ask from the grown-ups
for fear of being rebuffed—how was it that I never felt tempted to
steal even a small watch from Monsieur Atis? Whether it was the
purity of my feelings for him, or a result of the magic powers
which I had conferred upon Monsieur Atis, the idea never crossed
my mind.

I think, on the contrary, that if by some miracle I had acquired
a watch, I would have entrusted it to him.

My greatest delight at that time was the catalogue he had given
me.

This catalogue had become for me a kind of imaginary world.
An enchanted world which I felt as though I had created myself. I
knew it by heart; I could describe every watch illustrated in it.
There were also alarm clocks, chimes, mantelpiece ornaments, and
barometers, but it was only the watches, pocket watches, wrist-
watches, and chronometers that interested me. To enter this enchanted world, all I had to do was open the catalogue. It was even
more intriguing to me than Monsieur Atis' workshop. I could re-
cite the contents with my eyes closed, pointing out that such and
such a model was in stainless steel, with ten rubies, a phosphores-
cent face, and a five-year guarantee, and that another was wafer
thin, with twelve rubies, and waterproof.

Of course I had my favorites.

I could have chosen a gold one, with a ten-year guarantee and a
case. Three or four of these were scattered through the catalogue,
but I had grouped them together into a kind of glittering constellation which did not tempt me the least bit. The one I had chosen,
and which to me was worth the whole catalogue, was a little silver
watch with a guilloche pattern (I did not know what this meant,
but felt it must be pretty) with a gold emblem, thirty-five milli-
meters in diameter, twelve rubies, a five-year guarantee, and a
silver chain. That was the one I intended to buy when I grew up,
and never had I desired anything so ardently, or with such conviction.

The picture of it in the catalogue so dominated my mind that the watch somehow reserved a place in the inevitable chain of events which the future held in store for me.

It was Monsieur Atis himself who put an end to this ambition— but in the most extraordinary way. The more I knew him, in fact, the more reasons I had for considering him a magician.

One day, for no particular reason—it was neither my birthday, nor Christmas, nor New Year's Day—Monsieur Atis gave me a watch.

"Here, this is for you. Do you like it?"

If at that very moment he had waved his hand and turned a toad to marble, I wouldn't have been more surprised.

I was seized with panic. With the watch clutched tightly in my fist, I ran off as though I had just committed a theft, or were being pursued by an evil spirit, and did not stop until I reached my mother's hut, where I quickly hid it in the rag stuffing of my mattress.

All day I kept the secret to myself, but that evening I went to meet my mother on her way home from work, far outside the town. As soon as I saw her with her big bamboo basket on her head, I ran up shouting, "I have a watch! Monsieur Atis gave me a watch!" I was out of breath and could say no more.

"What's the matter?" asked my mother, who hadn't understood any of my shouting.

"A watch! I have a watch! Monsieur Atis gave it to me."

My mother seemed to find my excitement extremely childish. At first she thought I had some kind of bad news.

But when I showed it to her, back in our hut, and she realized it was a beautiful watch, ticking away energetically and insistently, she exclaimed, "But it's a man's watch! It's a good one. And you want me to believe Monsieur Atis gave it to you?"

I couldn't possibly convince her. Without another word, she took the watch, grabbed me by the hand and marched off to Monsieur Atis' shop.

"Oh, yes," Monsieur Atis assured her, "I gave it to him. How else, after all . . . The child is so well behaved, so honest and thoughtful! It's a very old watch."

"Just what I thought," said my mother. "When he told me you gave it to him, I realized it must be an old watch that doesn't work any more."

"Oh, no! It works very well," said Monsieur Atis. "I gave him the key to wind it up. But you should buy him a chain for it. Just a little silver chain . . . The works are excellent, you know. Better than watches nowadays. Why, I don't expect to see the day it stops working!"

My mother seemed dumbfounded, both with surprise and delight. Monsieur Atis began to laugh.

"It works, don't worry, otherwise I would never have given it to him. It will go on working as long as I go on living."

To show her gratitude, my mother promised, "I'll hide it away. He won't have it until he's grown up. A watch like that isn't a toy!"

I was delighted that my mother shared my joy. I was grateful to her for appropriating the watch and hiding it for me. She did not even talk about it, for fear of arousing jealousy.

My catalogue immediately lost its magic; the photographs of watches lost their haunting effect upon me. Even the little silver watch with the guilloche pattern now left me cold. I no longer spent hours perusing the pictures.

Instead, my watch, hidden away where I could not find it, became an obsession with me, all the more powerful in that I had hardly looked at it or handled it when Monsieur Atis had given it to me. In my mind it was like a place or a person I had once known and would like to see again.

So one day, I started looking. It shouldn't be hard to find; our bare, cramped hut had few corners in which to hide things: the angles of the beams, the heap of crates and planks used as a frame for the bed, the army of little tin cans gathered here and there. The search was soon over.

Only the big basket was left, the wicker hamper which served both as a trunk and a strongbox, for linen, Sunday clothes, jewels, everything that must be cared for and treasured. The watch was there, simply tucked away beneath a lace petticoat which my mother wore with her mauve sateen dress for Mass on New Year's Day, for the funerals of local dignitaries, and (this had happened once) when she had to hold a friend's baby at its baptism.

It was in a cardboard box—a flat box which had once held medicine—its key tied on with a crude bit of string, among the religious medals, the offering card for the church, and a necklace of garnet-colored glass with a gilt fastener, no doubt my mother's most precious belongings. It was as though I saw it for the first time, and yet I recognized it. It was not very shiny, silver probably, worn to a smooth patina, with a locomotive engraved on the back, and on the front, its fascinating white enamel face with handsome blue numerals each set apart from the next by a gold dot. My first move was to take the key, open the case, and wind the movement, as I had seen Monsieur Atis do so many times. And the watch began to palpitate with a powerful, discreet rhythm, like a pulse which began in the very bowels of the earth. I handled it with a thousand loving gestures—a kind of adoration, of improvised worship. But at last I had to bring myself to put it away, exactly as I had found it, so as not to leave any traces of my intrusion.

The watch was no longer mentioned. Neither by Monsieur Atis, nor my mother. Nor by me, of course. But two or three times a week, I would slip into the hut, open the hamper, take out the watch, wind it, listen to it, put it in my pocket, look at the time. I would put it on the table and stare at the hands until they marked a new hour. I would have liked to polish it with lemon juice and ashes, as I had seen people do with rings, chains, and silver medals. Or better still, if only I had been able to obtain some of the liquid which Monsieur Atis used on a flannel rag! But it was better to avoid anything which might betray me.

After a while, I lost my scruples; the watch belonged to me, I was only looking at it, handling it gently, all alone, putting it carefully back in place, every time. I was doing no harm.

I would be lying, however, if I pretended that I never once wanted to take it out with me, to show it off. But I knew very well that to yield to the temptation was to give away my secret, to expose myself to a dreadful spanking, and to risk not seeing the watch again for a long time, since it would be hidden away more carefully than ever.

Soon the first Sunday of the local festival was at hand. For the occasion, my mother gave me two pennies. I was to pay my second annual visit to my godfather (the first took place on New Year's Day) and this would mean as much as ten pennies for me. In one way or another, and without asking—for I really was a well-brought-up child who did not ask grown-ups for anything, certainly not for money—in one way or another, I managed to collect about a franc to treat myself to a few of the amusements that were not free, especially a few rides on the merry-go-round.

This first Sunday of the festival was the occasion I had waited for. Just this once—still unbeknown to my mother—I would take my watch out with me. The truth was, this time the temptation had been so great that my scruples and fears gave way; I could not resist.

That Sunday I waited until my mother had returned from Mass and had put the scarf which she had worn that morning back in the hamper. I was then almost certain that she would not open the hamper again until the following Sunday. As soon as she had left to go to market, I pulled out the watch, wound it up, and put it in my pocket.

But disobedient children never get away with anything; they haven't a chance!

In the crowd near the merry-go-round, where the horses flashed by to the roar of drums and the clarinet, I took out my watch to look at the time, rather proud but pretending to be casual. Someone passing behind me jostled my elbow; the watch flew out of my hands and fell on the pavement. I picked it up so quickly that it might not have fallen at all. But it had stopped ticking. I shook it, pressed it again to my ear, looking at it as though it were a person who has lost consciousness but will revive at any moment. I moved away from the crowds, taking the watch off by itself the way one would isolate someone who suddenly felt faint; I opened it, wound it; the key turned and turned, but the watch remained still. What could I do?

I thought of putting it back where it came from. My mother would never notice. At least not for a long time. Yes, of course, but it was sadness much more than the fear of being discovered that hung over me now. There was only one solution: to take the watch to Monsieur Atis, to tell him that it had stopped working for no particular reason. Perhaps because it hadn't been used for a long time, one never knew. Then he would repair it; I would put it back in its hiding place and not touch it again. Since my mother never went to Monsieur Atis' shop, there was every chance that she would never find out.

Heartened by this thought, I set out resolutely to see Monsieur Atis.

In spite of my preoccupied state of mind, as soon as I came into town I noticed a certain commotion in the streets. People ahead of me were running. I even thought I heard shouts.

There was a crowd milling in front of Monsieur Atis' house. It was Madame Atis who was shouting. Neighbors were rushing into the house, clutching bouquets of those leaves whose odor is used to revive women when they succumb to heat prostration on Good Friday, following the Way of the Cross. Others brought vials of medicine. They came out of the house wearing the expressions of passengers who arrive at a bus stop just as the bus has left. Madame Atis' lamentations kept bringing more people to the scene.

Monsieur Atis was dead.

"His heart," said someone.

"All of a sudden," said someone else, "at about four o'clock."

I took out my watch.

Just as I thought: it had stopped at exactly four o'clock.

TRANSLATED BY MERLOYD LAWRENCE

Raphaël Tardon

CALDERON'S REVOLT

THE Sertão at eleven o'clock in the morning is a white furnace. Flames like molten tin tremble above the overheated earth. About twenty *vaqueiros*—cowherds of the Sertão—had gathered in the shade of a roof made of carnauba palm leaves; the sides of the structure were left open. They squatted back on their heels in characteristic posture, gossiping and chewing wads of *rolo de fumos,* their thick black tobacco, while waiting for their wealthy boss, the *fazendeiro* Aldo Duverly, who had gone over to the neighboring village of Campina Grande.

"Look at those chameleons!" Manuel le Caboclo's voice rang out. "You could sit here ten years and not notice them, eh, fellows?"

And indeed, as their movement is very slow, the reptiles might have been there quite some time. Now an extraordinary drama was in progress. The creatures faced each other a yard apart, crests erect, great round eyes starting from their orbits, the slightly lifted tails stiff. Their bodies teetered from front to rear, all four feet, like little clawed hands, placed flat on the ground. Forming the apex of this prehistoric triangle, a female waited, immobile, one eye on each suitor.

Moving his paws forward in slow motion, the younger chameleon advanced a step. The fat one followed suit. The female turned away, as if bored by a ritual that had already gone on too long.

Each then warily cast a bulbous glare at his adversary; then, lowering his sagittal crest, rolled a fragile pearly glance at his lady love. Sensible of this homage, she forgave them their lack of combativeness and turned toward them. Alas! The fiery youngster resorted to a trick his elders would have called dirty fighting. Of a sudden, he reared up on his belly and, nearly vertical, his crest splayed out like a fan, rushed at his rival. Rear paws paddling, tail sculling frantically, he seized him by the throat.

The big chameleon was flung onto his back. Half-strangled, he beat the air with his claws in an attempt to lacerate his enemy's

214

stomach, then swung his younger foe violently from right to left, back and forth, twisting and jolting that animal embedded in his throat.

Winded, feeling his life's blood slipping away, he paused for breath, then beat the ground with great blows of his switchlike tail, spitting out red clots. All at once, making a prodigious effort, he reared up so violently the other lost his footing. But then the big one fell again while seeking for purchase with his hind paws, and as he hit the ground he flicked them out and down. No use! The younger instantly shifted his body, and instead his opponent tore his tail into two equal thongs, equally alive. This pain made him reckless; he tensed back and drove his hind claws into the dying reptile's belly. The loser stiffened at last in a puddle of muddy blood, four paws spread out, curved nails half retracted.

With his round left eye the victor sought the female. There was no need to summon her. She came frisking across, a miniature monster who licked first his throat and chest with little dabs of her long blackish cordlike tongue, split at the end, and then his eyes. He accepted this tribute of love, then culminated his triumph: climbing onto his enemy's corpse, he defiled it in short spurts.

The men watching the fray were startled by a harsh whistle. So preoccupied had they been with the chameleons no one had heard the engine of Duverly's jeep. Hastily mounting their horses, they assembled around their boss.

"What's new since I left?" he demanded.

A thin cowherd with sun-parched face spoke up, "Since you left, three babies have died every day. No baby's had a first birthday in Guadalcanor now for two years. The doctors call it undernourishment, hydrophobia, dropsy, pellagra, dehydration—I don't understand all that. I told them to write it down for you. Here."

Aldo stuffed the scrap of paper in his pocket. "I'll see about it. What else?"

The cowherd made no answer. His comrades sat stiff in their saddles, looking variously at their harness, their horses' ears, their own fingernails.

"I said, *what else?* Come on, you bunch of *bougres!* What are you hiding?"

The man decided to speak out; in any case, if he didn't soon get back to the *fazenda* he'd die of sunstroke.

"Your favorite heifer's dead, senhor. The one you called Europa.

The best of the lot, she was, with her sleek coat and that black star on her forehead. A beauty."

Bareheaded under the terrible sun, the *fazendeiro* got down from his jeep. Imperturbable, the thin cowherd continued, "You want to know what happened? It's simple. Your heifer was looking for a shady spot, and blundered into a cave full of those wild wasps' nests, the *marimbondos*. They fell on her like furies. Oh, Mother of God! you should have seen it. She was stung as many times as there are stars in the sky above São José, and she took fright with the pain and fled. Just put yourself in her place. . . ."

"And what then?" Duverly roared.

"What then? Don't you understand? She ran off . . . and Calderon rode after her, at the risk of breaking his neck a hundred times over."

"I don't give a damn about that, do you hear? Calderon could have killed himself a thousand times, and I'd fling him away like my first *cruzeiro*. You should have saved the heifer, you eunuchs! What happened to her? Come on, speak up!"

"It's my painful duty to tell you your heifer's dead. She went over the Allegro precipice. And we couldn't bring back the remains either; Pizon had already broken both legs trying to get down into the canyon. So we gave up."

Flecks of foam gathered on Duverly's lips. He howled with rage, "Was Calderon on guard?"

A heavy silence fell on the group. Then a cowherd around thirty years old detached his horse from the rest; from under his three-cornered leather cap, gray eyes gazed out at the *fazendeiro,* his blank face betraying neither fear nor bravado.

"Get off your horse," Duverly ordered. "And get ready to die!"

The man dismounted. He was a good head taller than Aldo.

"Were you on guard?"

The cowherd nodded. "I did the impossible, senhor."

"So, you did the impossible and you're still alive?"

"It's not my fault I didn't die, and my horse with me, senhor."

The *fazendeiro* threw a scornful glance at Calderon's mount.

"That, a horse? That carcass? Is that what you have the impertinence to guard two hundred of my cattle with—that broomstick? I'll . . ."

And with a powerful left hook he tore open the right side of the man's jaw. In that raging heat the blood surged out like juice from a ripe tomato crushed on a wall. Aldo paused to consider the huge emerald set in platinum on his ring finger.

Calderon did not flinch, nor did he raise his hand to his cheek; he didn't even glance at the *fazendeiro*. With folded arms and eyes half-closed he seemed lost in contemplation of the horizon, where the fires were dancing as if at the door of a colossal oven.

Aldo's face turned vermilion. Fists clenched, he yelled, "Bastard! I'll teach you to let my heifers die! I'll mark your other side for you; then you'll remember Europa, you'll remember me. Just you wait!"

He drew back a step, then all of a sudden gasped, seeming to suffocate, and fainted without a sound. The horsemen breathed a long sigh. Unhurried, they removed a hammock from the back of the jeep, laid their chief in it and, with a cowherd holding each end of this makeshift stretcher, galloped off to the *fazenda*.

Two doctors examined Senhor Duverly. Heads bound in damp towels, each carried a parasol to walk the few yards separating them from the *fazendeiro*'s dwelling. They agreed on the diagnosis: sunstroke. The treatment was simple: wrap the sick man in damp sheets and make him drink as much water as he could hold without vomiting.

Squatting next morning on the beaten earth floor of his hut, after the usual fashion of *vaqueiros* resting, Calderon offered up his swollen cheek to the questionable ministrations of his wife Theresa, one of the *catimbòzeiro's*—the local sorcerer's—regular customers. Theresa la Bahianaise, a fleshily beautiful dark-skinned creature, sat on a box and dipped a dirty rag into some liquid she kept in an old guava tin. In the atrocious heat the wound already looked nasty. A yellow growth of pus lined its edges. Theresa concluded her treatment with an indescribable unguent. Then she poured coffee into the two halves of a coconut, a kind of bowl which in the Sertão is known as *quimbo,* and watched her husband while she sipped the hot drink. Still asquat, arms hugging his knees, Calderon brooded over his bowl. Theresa wiped her lips with the back of her hand.

"Does it hurt much, boy? No strength to chew this morning, eh? Don't you want anything at all?"

He didn't answer, but she wasn't put off.

"Here, there's still a piece of brown sugar left. Shall I break it into your cup? It's Saturday, not Sunday, but we can look forward a bit, can't we?"

Still no answer. After a pause, she went on. "I know what's wrong with you. It's not so much what he did to your cheek as the fact you can't kick him in the arse for it. Isn't that right?"

For the first time, Calderon looked at his wife and cast her a thin smile, at once tender and sad.

"You'll hurt yourself, boy. Don't move. Well, I guessed it. And you do need a new horse; that old hunk of meat's been going ten years in the Sertão and has lived through two *secas*. . . . Get another. There's no cowman can work without a proper horse, boy."

She smiled and drew back a lock of her jet-black hair. Calderon pulled his knife from its sheath and broke off a piece of sugar, which he offered his wife. "If you won't take some, I won't either," he declared as she hesitated.

"All right, my dear, if it pleases you."

They sugared their coffee in silence, stirring it slowly in the coconut shells; she with a little tin spoon, he with his knife blade. A shadow fell on the floor of the hut and they looked up at a young man whose arrogant face was ravaged by acne; he wore a wide leather belt with copper studs and a dagger on each hip.

"Still here, good-for-nothing? What's keeping you from work? The boss wants you, pronto!"

The blood drained from Calderon's face. He shut his eyes and clenched his teeth. Theresa cut in quickly. "Think of the horse, boy, and dont get worked up! Think of this land we've worked with our guts. Get a grip on yourself and go see him. You've got to. Remember what Julião said the other day?"

Without finishing his coffee, he rose and went out. Theresa ran to the door.

"Calderon! Do you remember what he said?"

He turned. "Do you expect me to forget? 'With fire and sword!'"

No. That wasn't at all what she had expected. As he went off with the rangy walk of the *vaqueiro,* she called after him, "Think of the horse, boy."

The doctors were in Senhor Duverly's room when the servant announced that Calderon was waiting.

"Bring him right in," the *fazendeiro* ordered. "You're not in the way," he told the medical men. "Don't go."

Calderon entered, cap in hand. He was in working clothes, sheathed in leather to keep off the cactus and brambles of the *caatinga*.

"Good morning, senhor. God grant you long life. Did you call for me?"

"Morning, Calderon," his boss answered in a friendly tone. "Aren't you going to ask after my health? But I understand how you feel. And you? How's your cheek? Mother of God! Turn round and let me see!"

Calderon, bewildered, did as he was told.

"It's a nasty wound," Aldo acknowledged. "My dear Cavalcanti, take this lad as soon as I've done with him, and go straight to the dispensary. Is that understood?" And suddenly furious, "That's dung he's smeared on his face! He or his wife has been to that witch doctor." He sighed. "Calderon, listen to me. It's not that I'm sorry for what I did to your good looks after you lost my best heifer. No, it's not that. But last night my mother came to me in a dream and told me I should get rid of the stone that did you all the damage; she said it would bring me bad luck. On the other hand, it might make someone else happy: it's worth forty-five thousand dollars! Now, it's yours. I wanted to give you this emerald in the presence of my doctors, who could bear witness, if need be, that it really is a gift. Well, what are you waiting for, you idiot?"

Calderon gazed at the jewel with the same faraway look he had bent on his bowl of coffee; there was also something obstinate in his face. The huge sum represented by this green pebble had no clear meaning for him. True, he imagined that it would purchase several of those little Sertão horses so invaluable for herding cattle and so resistant to the heat and other perils of the *caatinga*. This he knew. But something in his mind forbade acceptance. Then again he heard Theresa's voice in his ear: "Think of the horse, boy. At ten thousand *cruzeiros* each you could buy fory-five hundred horses; though there'd be no sense to *that*. At any rate, we could get away from the Sertão, go down South, buy a fine house with a garden, servants, land, a car . . . be free, rich, happy . . . water running from a pipe day and night. Take it, please, Calderon; take that fabulous stone!" But he could hear another voice also, which said, "You'll abandon your friends. All those who've been born to live, suffer, and die in poverty in the Sertão, under the devilish sun that goes on for hours, days, weeks, months, life, an eternity—the *seca* sun that kills trees, birds, animals, the cascading rivers, children, the land. Can you leave them to the fate you've shared until now, Calderon?"

The voice of the *fazendeiro* struck out so angrily that even the wound on his face seemed to draw back.

"If you refuse, I'll throw you out, you and your wife, within the hour; and have your cabin burned. This cowboy's got the nerve to hesitate over accepting a gift fit for a king! Do you realize the Queen of England herself would gladly kneel and pick it up in her teeth? Yet this son of a whore . . ."

Taking a painful breath, leaning back against the bedstead, a thought struck him. "You wouldn't by any chance belong to that band of hyenas which listens to the ravings of that carrion Julião?"

Theresa's imploring voice echoed once again in Calderon's ear.

"Think of the horse, boy." And then in a low whisper, "think of your wife, darling." In spite of himself, a tender smile formed on his lips.

Duverly roared, "Well, have you managed to make up your mind, vermin? Go on, now, take this stone and show yourself off!"

"You're very kind, senhor—my feelings got the better of me . . . happiness . . . you're very kind. God bless you." (Think of the horse!) "Too kind, if I may say so . . ." He backed away. "If happiness could kill . . ." (Think of your wife.) " . . . I'd be dead already. That's a fact, senhor." He was near the door. "Like the magician who turns everything he touches to gold . . ." (Think of the horse.) "The magician, the fairy of freedom, yes . . ." (Think of your wife, you fool.) "Freedom, that's when you're never hungry and never envy anyone, eh, senhor?" He turned the knob. "When you choose your own work . . . and your boss . . . and what you do in your spare time . . ."

"What the devil is he talking about?" Aldo inquired.

But Calderon added quickly, "You're the soul of generosity, senhor." The door shut behind him.

Outside he was met by the blast of total sunlight from a white sky. Dr. Cavalcanti, adjusting his great sisal hat on his head, followed. What heat! But where had that cursed cowherd gone? Maybe one could buy the emerald from him right away for the price of just one horse. Where was he? Ah, over there. . . .

Ten yards from the house, surrounded by a gang of children (just his mental age!), the cowherd was playing some kind of game. In three strides Dr. Cavalcanti caught up with them; then his hair stood on end and his tongue cleaved to his palate. Calderon had borrowed a slingshot from one of the urchins and, as if it were no more than a chunk of coral, placed the huge emerald in its sling. By the time the doctor managed to free his tongue, the slingshot was drawn taut. "Calderon!"

Calderon looked around at him and winked.

"Are you mad? Oh, no, you cannot do it! It's a fortune, Calderon! Riches, happiness, the world! Think of your wife!"

The smile in the *vaqueiro's* eyes vanished.

"I *am* thinking of her," he growled, and shot the stone so far into the sky it was never again seen upon this earth.

TRANSLATED BY PATRICK BOWLES

Aimé Césaire

MEMORANDUM ON MY MARTINIQUE

AND my original geography also; the map of the
world made for my use, not painted the arbitrary
colors of scientists, but with the geometry of my
shed blood

and the determination of my biology no longer
imprisoned by a facial angle, by the texture of
hair, by a nose sufficiently flat, by a sufficiently
melanian tint, and the niggerness no longer a
cephalic index, or a plasma, or a soma, but measured
with the compass of suffering

and the nigger each day more base, more cowardly,
more sterile, less profound, more exteriorized,
more separated from himself, more shrewd
with himself, less immediate with himself

I accept, I accept all that

and far from the sea which breaks under the
suppurating syzygy of blisters, the body of my
country marvelously bent in the despair of my
arms, its bones shaken and in the veins the blood
hesitating like a drop of milk at the wounded point
of the bulb . . . and now suddenly that force and
life assail me like a bull, repeat the act of ONAN
again who committed his sperm to the fecund
earth, and the wave of life encircles the papilla
of the hill, and all the arteries and veins move
with new blood, and the enormous lung of breathing cyclones, and the hoarded fire of volcanos
and the gigantic seismic pulse, which beats the
measure of a living body in my firm embrace.

And we are standing now, my country and I,
hair in the wind, my little hand now in its enormous fist, and force is not in us, but above us, in a
voice which pierces the night and the audience like
the sting of an apocalyptic hornet.

And the voice declares that for centuries Europe
has stuffed us with lies and bloated us with pesti-
lence,

> for it is not true that the work of man is finished
> that we have nothing to do in the world
> that we are parasites in the world
> that we have only to accept the way of the world

but the work of man has only begun.

and it remains for man to conquer all prohibitions immobilized in the corners of his fervor

and no race has a monopoly of beauty, intelligence, strength

and there is room for all in the rendezvous of
conquest and we know that the sun turns around
our earth lighting only the portion that our single
will has fixed and that every star falls from sky
to earth at our limitless command.

TRANSLATED BY LIONEL ABEL

Spanish Section

INTRODUCTION

THE larger islands of the Greater Antilles—Cuba, Puerto Rico, and the Dominican Republic (which occupies the eastern two-thirds of Hispaniola) have all been, though colonized by Spain, the objects of unending tug-of-war between the Hispanic influence and that of the United States. Each has undergone some sort of direct intervention or control by this country, although each again is far more closely connected by language and tradition with Latin America, and with its stratified and paternalistic social system.

In 1917, the Mexican philosopher José Vasconcelos made a trip to that "Enchanted Garden," Jamaica, and, in writing of it, sharply attacked British colonialism as merely economic in character, a criticism which is now constantly being turned upon the U.S. "It was a misfortune," he concluded, "for Jamaica to have fallen into British hands, for if it had remained Spanish it would be a nation like Cuba, Santo Domingo, or Mexico. It became English and was turned into a trading post, a factory without character, culture, or self-respect." These are harsh words, and made less exact with time, but they are not without meaning for ourselves in 1966; we are open to criticism on the same score.

Something will have to be done to reconcile more nearly the differing social points of view of this country and of Latin America, if a better adjustment is to prevail; but something also, as Dr. Frank Tannenbaum points out in *Ten Keys to Latin America* (Knopf, 1963), *is* being done, whether or not we realize it. Speaking from the frame of reference of economics, he writes: "We still fail to recognize that the 'American Way of Life,' the American presence, is incompatible with a socially and politically stratified world. A mass market requires an egalitarian society based upon the mass. We have remained unaware that the changes we are pressing upon the world are, in effect, political and social." An object—a light bulb, a girdle, an automobile—that is mass produced, cannot in the future be the property only of an upper class. Whatever the have-nots do not yet have, they do have a knowledge

227

of and desire for an increasing share in the tangible goods of this world. As Dr. Tannenbaum says, noting the increasing migration to the city of the rural population: "The city seems to contain all the things the poor desire but have no way of getting. The city is the visible embodiment of the twentieth century while the place these people came from is back in the thirteenth. That is why they can never go back. Places like Guatemala City, Port-au-Prince . . ." or San Juan, or Havana ". . . are of this world while most of the rest of the land belongs to a society which ceased to exist in Europe centuries ago."

The writer in the Spanish-speaking islands faces a complex situation. On the one hand, all the social and economic problems are there, clearly outlined; on the other, although there exists a vital poetic and literary tradition, with resulting prestige, it is impossible to make a living from writing alone. Though generally the gifted writers of Spanish America are known to each other, and to that intellectual society which exists without concern for boundaries, the massive social problems seem beyond their power to mitigate.

In stories from these islands, or from South America, that I have read there is usually some theme of struggle involved, some element of great effort: the prevailing Catholicism is matched by a strong anti-clerical tradition; man is pitted against nature, or against society; the wealthy landowner orders those on his plantation about as his grandfather did before him, while his workers plot his undoing; race works against race; parents work against hunger and privation in their search for a livelihood; the great impetus toward mass-education is more than matched, a cruel paradox, by the population explosion. Here then is surely the place for the writer, for he can point out the reality of the present scene; he can make clear—imaginatively, sharply clear—for instance, that less food per capita is now produced than was the case twenty years ago; he can judge the values of city and countryside and show what must be retained. One genre of writing that is not usually found, curiously enough, is the humorous. The ghost of Cervantes does not walk abroad in Cuba or Puerto Rico, more's the pity. When all is said, though, the Latin American writer—for intellectuals from all these various countries belong to one world—has open to him a place of unique importance in a better society, in the resolving of conflicts between cultures, and in the forging of that "Cosmic Race" foreshadowed by José Vasconcelos a generation ago.

Nicolas Guillén

WAKE FOR PAPA MONTERO

to VINCENT MARTINEZ

You burned the dawn
with the flame of your guitar,
juice of the sweet cane in the gourd
of your dusky quick flesh
beneath a dead, white moon!

Music poured from you
as round and mulatto as a plum.

Drinker of tall drinks,
gullet of tin,
boat cut loose in a sea of rum,
horseman of the wild party:
what will you do with the night
now that you can no longer drink it,
and what vein will give you back
the blood you've lost,
gone down the black
drain of a knife wound?

They certainly got you this time,
Papa Montero!

They were waiting for you in the tenement,
but they brought you home dead;
it was a drunken brawl,
but they brought you home dead;
they say he was your pal,
but they brought you home dead . . .
nobody could find the knife,

but they brought you home dead . . .
Baldomero's done for—
Attaboy, you old dancing devil!

Only two candles are
burning a little of the shadow;
for your humble death
two candles are too many.
But brighter than the candles
is the red shirt
that lighted your songs,
the dark salt of your music,
your glossy straightened hair!

They certainly got you this time,
Papa Montero!

Today the moon dawned
in the courtyard of my house;
it fell blade-wise to earth,
and there it stuck.
The kids picked it up
and washed its face,
so I bring it tonight
to be your pillow!

TRANSLATED BY LANGSTON HUGHES

Juan Bosch

THE BEAUTIFUL SOUL OF DON DAMIÁN

DON DAMIÁN lapsed quickly into a coma as his temperature rose to over 104. His soul felt very uncomfortable, almost on the verge of being consumed by the heat, and for that reason it began to retire, gather itself into the heart. The soul had an infinite number of tentacles, like a squid with countless feet, each thrust into a vein and some of the slenderest into capillaries. Little by little it withdrew these feet, and as it did this Don Damián's body heat dropped and he grew pale. First his hands turned cold, then his legs and arms; his face began to grow dreadfully pale, as those gathered about his sumptuous bed noticed. The nurse herself became frightened and said it was time to send for the doctor. The soul heard her words and thought: I must hurry, or that man will come and make me stay here until the fever consumes me.

It was growing light. Through the windowpanes came a wan light which announced the dawning day. Peering out of Don Damián's mouth—which was parted to let a little air in—the soul could see the light and told itself that if it did not act promptly it would not be able to do so later, inasmuch as people would see it leave and would prevent it from abandoning the body of its master. Don Damián's soul was ignorant of certain things; for example, it was unaware that once free it would be completely invisible.

There was a prolonged rustle of skirts around the rich bed where the sick man lay, and the sound of hurried words which the soul could not quite make out, engrossed as it was in escaping from its prison. The nurse came in with a hypodermic syringe in her hand.

"Please God it is not too late," clamored the voice of the old servant.

But it was too late. At the very moment the needle entered Don Damián's forearm, the soul withdrew the last of its tentacles from the dying man's mouth. It seemed to the soul that the injection had

231

been an unnecessary expense. In a second, cries were heard and hurried footsteps, and while someone—undoubtedly the servant, for it could not possibly have been Don Damián's mother-in-law or wife—threw herself sobbing upon the bed, the soul took off into space, straight toward the superb chandelier of Bohemian crystal that hung from the middle of the ceiling. There it clung with all its strength and looked below: Don Damián was already a yellow shell, his features almost transparent and as brittle as the crystal; the bones of his face seemed to have become more prominent and the skin had taken on a repulsive luster. Around him his mother-in-law, his wife, and the nurse were milling; with her head buried in the bedclothes the old servant sobbed. The soul was completely cognizant of what each one was feeling and thinking, but it did not want to waste time watching them. The room was growing lighter by the minute, and it was afraid it might be noticed there where it hung, clinging to the lamp with a fear beyond words. Suddenly it saw Don Damián's mother-in-law take her daughter by the arm and lead her into the hall, where she spoke to her in an almost inaudible voice. These are the words the soul overheard: "You are not to behave as though you had no rearing. You must show grief."

"When the people get here, Mama," whispered the daughter.

"No, right now. Remember that the nurse may talk afterward."

Whereupon the newly minted widow ran toward the bed as though beside herself, screaming, "Damián, my Damián, oh, my Damián! How am I going to live without you, my beloved Damián?"

Another soul, less wise in the ways of the world, would have been astounded, but Don Damián's, from its vantage point on the chandelier, was admiring the fine performance. Don Damián himself employed the same tactics on certain occasions, especially when it was a question of what he called "protecting his interests." The widow was fairly young, and attractive, whereas Don Damián was over sixty. She had had a sweetheart when Don Damián began courting her, and the soul had suffered unpleasant moments because of its ex-master's jealousy. It recalled one scene in particular which had taken place only a few months before in which the wife had said, "You can't forbid me to talk to him. You know perfectly well that I married you for your money."

To which Don Damián replied that with that money he had bought the right not to be made a fool of. The scene was extremely disagreeable, with the mother-in-law putting in her oar and threats of divorce. In a word, a bad moment, made even worse by the fact that the discussion was cut short because of the arrival of some very distingushed visitors whom both husband and wife received with charming smiles and delightful manners that only it, the soul of Don Damián, could assess at their real value.

The soul was still there, on the chandelier, recollecting these things, when a priest arrived in great haste. Nobody knew why he had showed up so opportunely, inasmuch as the sun wasn't quite up yet, and the priest had been with the patient during the night.

"I came because I had a foreboding; I came because I was afraid Don Damián might yield up his soul without making confession," he tried to explain.

To which the deceased's mother-in-law suspiciously replied, "Why didn't he confess last night, Father?"

She was referring to the fact that for nearly an hour the minister of the Lord had been alone behind closed doors with Don Damián, and everybody had believed that the sick man had made confession. But this had not been the case. Perched up on the chandelier the soul knew he had not, and it also knew why the priest had shown up. That long private interview had had as its subject a somewhat arid matter; for the priest had proposed to Don Damián that he leave in his will a considerable sum for the new church that was being built in the city, and Don Damián wanted to leave even more money than was requested, but to a hospital. They could not reach an agreement and when the priest got home he noticed that he did not have his watch. What was happening to the soul, once it was free, was nothing short of miraculous, this business of being able to know things that had not happened in its presence as well as to divine what people were thinking and going to do. The soul recalled that the priest had said to himself, "I remember that I took out my watch when I was at Don Damián's house to see what time it was; I must have left it there." So this visit at such an unusual hour had nothing to do with the kingdom of God.

"No, he did not confess," explained the priest, looking Don Damián's mother-in-law in the eye. "He did not get around to it last night, and we agreed that I would come first thing this morning to hear his confession and give him communion. I have come too late, and it is a great pity," he said, as he turned his head toward the different corners and the gilt tables, without doubt hoping to see his watch on one of them.

The old servant, who had been waiting on Don Damián for more than forty years, raised her face with its tear-reddened eyes. "After all, it was not necessary," she asseverated, "and may God forgive me. He did not need to confess because he had a beautiful soul, a very beautiful soul had Don Damián."

The devil, now this was interesting! Don Damián's soul had never envisaged itself as beautiful. Its master did certain strange things, and as he was an outstanding example of a rich man who dressed in the height of fashion, and managed his bank account with great dexterity, the soul had not had time to give thought to certain aspects that might bear upon its own beauty or possible ugliness. For instance, it recalled how its master had instructed it to feel good when after prolonged interviews with his lawyer Don Damián found a way of foreclosing his claim to the house of some debtor—who afterward often had no place to live—or when with the persuasion of jewels and cash in hand—for her studies, or because of her ailing mother's health—a pretty young thing from the working-class quarter agreed to visit a luxurious apartment Don Damián kept. Was it beautiful or ugly, the soul asked itself?

From the time it had managed to escape from the veins of its master until it became the object of this remark by the servant, very little time had elapsed by the soul's calculations, and probably even less than it thought. Everything was happening very quickly and, besides, with great confusion. It had felt as though it were boiling in the sick man's body and realized that it was the temperature that was going up. Before it had withdrawn, long before midnight, the doctor had warned that this might happen.

He had said, "Possibly the fever will rise toward morning; if that happens you must be on the alert. If he gets worse, call me."

Was the soul going to stand by and let itself be roasted? Its vital center, so to speak, was close to Don Damián's bowels, which gave off flames. It was going to die like an animal in an oven, and that did not appeal to it. But, as a matter of fact, how much time had elapsed since it left Don Damián's body? Very little, in view of the fact that it was still suffering from the heat in spite of the slight coolness the dawning day was spreading which reached the chandelier where it clung. It thought that the change of climate between the bowels of its sometime master and the glass of the chandelier had not been too sharp, thanks to which it had not caught cold. But with or without a sharp change, what about the servant's remark? "Beautiful" was the word the old woman had used, and she was a truthful person who had loved her master simply because she loved him, not because of his distinguished appearance or because of the gifts he gave her. In the words that followed, the soul did not feel the same ring of sincerity.

"Of course, his was a beautiful soul," agreed the priest.

"Beautiful is putting it mildly," affirmed the mother-in-law.

The soul took another look at her and observed how, as she spoke, she kept her eyes fixed on her daughter. Those eyes seemed to be ordering and pleading at one and the same time. It was as if they were saying: "Start crying this very minute, you imbecile, before the priest realizes that the death of this wretch has made you happy."

The daughter instantly understood that silent and angry language, for she at once broke into woeful lamentation. "Never, never was there a more beautiful soul than his. Oh, my Damián, my Damián, light of my life."

The soul could stand no more; it was torn between curiosity and disgust; it wanted to assure itself that it was beautiful and to get away from that place where everybody was trying to pull the wool over everybody else's eyes. So, curious and disgusted, it took off from the chandelier in the direction of the bathroom, whose walls were covered with huge mirrors. It calculated the distance carefully so as to fall on the carpet without making a noise. In addition to being unaware of the fact that people could not see it, it was equally unaware of the fact that it was weightless. It felt a great relief when it saw that it passed unnoticed and ran breathless to look at itself in the mirrors.

But, good Heavens, what was happening? In the first place, it had grown accustomed during more than sixty years to seeing through the eyes of Don Damián; and those eyes were high, almost five feet ten inches from the ground; it was, moreover, accustomed to the lively face of its master, his light eyes, his gleaming hair that was turning silver, to the proud bearing of his shoulders and head, to the fine clothes he wore. And what it now saw was nothing of all this, but instead a strange figure barely a foot tall, soft, colorless, without clear contours. In the first place, it resembled nothing it had ever seen before. For instead of what should have been two feet and legs as was always the case when it inhabited the body of Don Damián, there was a monstrous, and at the same time small, cluster of tentacles, like those of a squid, but devoid of any order, some shorter than the others, some thinner, and all as though made of dirty smoke, of some nondescript, intangible mud, seeming transparent without being so, flabby, limp, which buckled with repulsive ugliness. Don Damián's soul felt itself lost. Nevertheless it mustered courage enough to look up. It had no waistline. The fact is that it had neither body nor neck nor anything, except that where the tentacles came together a kind of drooping ear emerged on one side, something like a wrinkled, suppurating crust, and on the other a tuft of colorless hair, coarse, some twisted, others straight. But that was not the worst, nor even the strange grayish, yellowish light that enveloped it; the mouth was a formless hole, a cross between that of a mouse and the gaping cavity in a rotten fruit, horrible, nauseating, truly revolting, and in the depth of this cavity glittered an eye, a single eye, holding dark reflections and an expression of terror and perfidiousness. How was it possible that those women and the priest could go on insisting in the adjacent room, beside the bed where Don Damián lay, that his had been a beautiful soul?

"Go out, me go out in the street looking like this, for people to see me?" it asked itself, in what it believed its loudest voice, still unaware of the fact that it was invisible and inaudible, lost in a black tunnel of confusion.

What was it to do, what future awaited it? The bell rang. In a moment the nurse was saying, "It is the doctor, madame. I'll go to the door."

On hearing this Don Damián's wife began to howl again, calling upon her dead husband and bemoaning the loneliness in which he had left her.

Paralyzed before its own image, the soul realized that it was lost. It had become accustomed to its refuge, to the tall body of Don Damián; it had even become accustomed to the unbearable smell of his bowels, to his heartburn, to the annoyance of his colds. Its thoughts were interrupted by the doctor's greeting and the voice of the mother-in-law declaiming, "Oh, doctor, what a misfortune, doctor, what a misfortune!"

"Calm yourself, madame, calm yourself," replied the doctor.

The soul peeped into the death chamber. There around the bed the women were gathered; standing at the foot, with an open book, the priest began to pray. The soul measured the distance and gave a leap. It was easier than it had believed, as though it were of air or were some strange animal that could move without being heard or seen. Don Damián's mouth was still slightly open. It was as cold as ice, but that did not matter. The soul slipped swiftly through it and instantly slid down the larynx and began to thrust its tenacles into the body, penetrating the inner walls without the least difficulty. It was settling itself in place when it heard the doctor speak.

"Just a moment, madame, if you please."

The soul could see the doctor, though very vaguely. He approached the body of Don Damián, picked up his wrist, seemed perplexed, laid his cheek against the dead man's chest and rested it there for a moment. Then, slowly, he opened his bag and took out a stethoscope; carefully he put the two discs in his ears and held the other end of the tube over the place where the heart must be. His expression once more became puzzled; he hunted about in his bag and took from it a hypodermic syringe. With the air of a sleight-of-hand artist making preparations for a sensational act, he told the nurse to fill the syringe while he began tying a slender rubber tube around Don Damián's elbow. Apparently, all these preparations alarmed the old servant.

"But why are you doing that to him when the poor thing is already dead?" she asked.

The doctor looked her in the eye with the air of a superior being, and this was what he said, though not so much for her to hear as for the wife and the mother-in-law of Don Damián, "Madame, science is science, and it is my duty to do everything in my power to bring Don Damián back to life. Souls as beautiful as his are not seen every day, and we cannot let him die without exploring every possibility."

This brief speech, spoken with august calm, alarmed the wife. It was easy to note a hard glitter in her eyes, and a strange tremor in her voice.

"But isn't he dead?" she asked.

The soul was now all back in place and only three tentacles were still feeling about for the old veins where they had been for years and years. The attention it was giving to getting those tentacles where they belonged did not, however, prevent it from noticing the puzzled accent in her question.

The doctor did not answer. He took Don Damián's forearm and began to rub it with his hand. It was at this point that the soul began to feel the warmth of life enveloping it, penetrating it, filling the old arteries which it had fled to avoid being consumed in the fire. Then, almost simultaneously with the beginning of this warmth, the doctor sank the needle into the vein of the arm, untied the ligature above the elbow and began to push down the plunger of the syringe. Little by little the warmth of life rose to Don Damián's skin.

"A miracle, Lord, a miracle," muttered the priest.

Suddenly, as he witnessed that resurrection, the priest turned pale and gave his imagination free rein. The donation for the church could be counted on, for how could Don Damián refuse his help once he told him, during the days of his convalescence, how he had seen him brought back to life seconds after he had prayed for such a miracle? "The Lord heeded my pleas and brought you back from the tomb, Don Damián," he would say.

Suddenly the wife, too, felt that her mind was a blank. She looked anxiously at her husband's face and turned toward her mother. Both of them were disconcerted, silent, almost terrified.

But the doctor smiled. He was pleased beyond words, though he tried to conceal it.

"Ah, but he has been saved, thanks to God and to you," the servant cried out, weeping tears of joy, and taking the doctor's hands in hers. "He has been saved, he is coming back to life. Ah, Don Damián will know how to repay you, sir," she assured him.

That was just what the doctor was thinking, that Don Damián had plenty with which to pay him. But he said something different. He said, "Even though he were unable to pay me, I would have done what I did, for it was my duty to save for society such a beautiful soul as his."

He was answering the servant, but he was really speaking for the others to hear; above all, so they would repeat his words to the patient, some days later, when he was able to sign.

Wearied with all the lies it had heard, Don Damián's soul decided to go to sleep. A second later Don Damián moaned, though very weakly, and moved his head on the pillow.

"Now he will sleep for several hours," explained the doctor, "and nobody should disturb him."

Saying this he set the example and left the room on tiptoe.

TRANSLATED BY HARRIET DE ONÍS

Eliseo Diego

SOMETHING TO EVERYONE

A MAN, blind from birth, chanced to own a certain object that came to be his sole possession on earth. He could never know fully what that thing was, yet he was content to let his fingers touch it at some point, and with that as a beginning, to move on, tracing the forms as they were born one after another in a succession of gifts of incredible grace. But that did not satisfy him completely, because what he knew of it could only arouse a thirst for what was lost, and realizing that he could never come to possess it entirely, he gave it to a deaf man, a friend of his from childhood, who happened to be visiting him one afternoon.

"What beautiful girls!" the deaf man exclaimed. "What girls?" cried the blind man. "These!" shouted the deaf man, pointing to the object. Finally he reminded himself that they would never reach accord with each other by that method, and he placed the object in the blind man's hands. The blind man ran his fingers over the familiar weight of the forms. "Ah, yes, the girls," he murmured and gave them to the deaf man.

The deaf man carried them home. They were three girls with hands clasped. The lines of their hair, their arms, and their draperies met and mingled with a delicate and infinite grace. They were of an almost transparent marble. Shafts of light passed through them from within. The deaf man, whose eyes were like an eagle's, discovered a spring in the base. When he pressed it, the maidens began to dance. But the deaf man realized then that he would never come to possess them entirely and he gave the three dancing girls to a friend who came to call on him.

"What charming music," the man said, pointing to the maidens. "What's that?" the deaf man said. "The music of the dance," the man explained. "Yes," the deaf man said, "I knew there must be music, but I did not know what it was like." And he gave the man the three dancing figures.

The man took them home. The music was like the soughing of

the wind through cane stalks; it was born and died of itself, and its configurations were shaped to the three dancers. The man contemplated with wonder the perfect unity of the figures, the music, and the dance. But in the end he realized that he could never possess them wholly and he gave them to a wise man who came to visit him.

"The Three Graces!" the scholar exclaimed. "Do you know what you have here? They are the Three Graces that Balduinus made for the daughter of the Duke of Burgundy!" The man understood then that their names explained the mysterious aloofness on the faces of the dancers. "You think about them," he declared, pointing to them. And the wise man took the Three Graces home with him.

Enclosed in his study there, he made them dance and thought about them aloud, about their real names, the secret relationships of their bodies in the dance and of the dance itself and the music, the magical birth of their bodies, the offspring alike of divinity and the craftsman's love. But before long the wise man died, taking with him the uneasy feeling that never, as long as he lived, could he have possessed them completely.

His ignorant family sold the Three Graces to an antique dealer no less ignorant than they. He consigned the maidens to a show window where he displayed his toys. One night a little boy saw them there. He stood looking at them a long time with his nose pressed against the glass, bitterly regretting that he would never own them. That was indeed the case, for not long after the boy had gone home a fire destroyed the shop, and the Three Graces inside the shop.

That night the child dreamed of them. And in his dream they were his, completely his, eternally his.

TRANSLATED BY JOAN MACLEAN

Eliseo Diego

HOW HIS EXCELLENCY
SPENT THE TIME

"... and the proper time is never found ..."

(*Book of Patronio* by Don Juan Manuel)

ALL afternoon His Excellency had been traveling over the entire countryside, along rough trails full of enormous thorns. He was tired, sweaty, dusty; he wanted to sit down somewhere, to have a drink of something that would cool his burning throat. He stopped for a moment at the edge of the highway and mopped his temples with a fine linen handkerchief. Sheltered between two slopes, among almond trees, he saw before him an inn with red roof tiles and clean whitewashed walls. With a sigh, His Excellency walked slowly toward it.

Now he sits down at a rustic table, beneath a bower that casts its cool shade over the red tiles. From the orchard soft scents come to him, he hears the distant barking of a dog, the cacophonous crowing of a cock, in short, the gentle pulsation of the living countryside. His Excellency lays aside his cloak, which overflows the bench in heavy, dark folds, and takes off his hat with a sigh. Only then does he realize that the innkeeper has been observing him for some time from the black background of the doorway.

The innkeeper was standing motionless, his smooth arms hanging loosely, staring at him with his head bent downward a little. Instantly he moves; he approaches with a smile. "What does His Excellency wish?" he asks, wiping a table with a cloth in the age-old gesture of innkeepers. His Excellency smiles. "Have you a good wine?" "It's very good indeed! And some olives . . ." Whereupon the innkeeper vanishes, only to reappear immediately and set on the table an earthenware jug, a glass, and a plateful of delicious olives. Oddly enough, the innkeeper sits down at the table, too.

"I have a dog," the innkeeper begins.

"Good," His Excellency remarks, sipping his wine.

242

"I keep him out there," the innkeeper goes on, pointing with an enormous hand at the red knoll among the almond trees. "He's minding the goats. My dog is very smart. He lets me know when Juanón is stealing wine from us by taking hold of my hand."

"Ah," His Excellency comments. The wine is like a benediction in his throat, the spot is cool; he has worked very hard that afternoon and he does not want to be reminded of anything. He is beginning to suspect that the rustic knows. "And how many cows do you have?"

"My dog knows a lot," the innkeeper stubbornly goes on. "He can all but talk. Maybe he'll start talking quite soon. Sooner than you'd think."

In the pause that ensues, the leaves of the almond trees speak to one another and answer softly.

"If Your Excellency could grant me one favor, just one."

Ah, here it comes! His Excellency thinks as he sips the cool wine. And aloud he says good-humoredly, "I'll grant it. What is it, my friend?"

"Not to take me away until the dog can talk," the countryman says with a bow.

"It's already granted," His Excellency assures him with a friendly sweep of the hand. He would not have to make even a move. "And how did you know who I am, my friend?" Outlined against the red sky of evening, the silhouette of a huge shepherd dog looms.

The innkeeper smiles foxily. "When I saw you sitting here my chilblains started to hurt like anything." The mournful howling of a dog arose, hoarse and long-drawn. His Excellency chokes, spits out the wine, and rises, overturning the bench. "The dog has talked," he says. "Let's go."

TRANSLATED BY JOAN MACLEAN

Lino Novás Calvo

"ALLIES" AND "GERMANS"

KNEE-HIGH to a grasshopper though I was, I was already an "Ally." My father called me Tomtit. But at the time I did not believe that man was my father. He had happened by the sugar plantation in Georgina one day, and then left. I was born and grew and for many years I did not even hear his name until he was a "German" and I an "Ally." By that time I was alone, and in Havana, with nobody but old Pedralves, a cabby of Havana, and the drivers of his stand, already known as "Allies." A little while before, a kind of huffing coffeepot, spouting smoke from all sides, had been turned loose in the streets, scaring the horses, and they were called "Germans." Instantly two factions sprang up, for the cabdrivers lowered their fare to ten cents, while the flivvers charged twenty. The drivers of the tin lizzies called the others "Allies" and headed their cars at the horses.

My father showed up one day at the wheel of one of those tin beasts, calling the cabdrivers names like tramp steamers, old fogies, holdovers from the days of Spain. That father of mine, Marcos "Tilburi," would stop his Ford at the corner of Subirana, order a cigar and a shot of cheap gin, make unflattering remarks about the grocer's mother and wife, and go off laughing. I hung around the grocery store of the one-eyed man and listened. Tilburi did not know that I was his son, or I that Tilburi was my father. I was called Pedralves like the old cabdriver, and his "Allies" took me to eat at the Guajiro's tavern, and prophesied that with time I would be something special. Tilburi came to the tavern, calling everybody a son-of-a-bitch, and laughing behind his close-clipped mustache. Pedralves said Tilburi was a no-good and never told me that he was my father. I knew that the Ford driver lived in the third room front with a Negro woman. Only Pedralves knew that Tilburi was my father, for he himself had formerly been the overseer on that plantation of Martinón, and when my mother threw herself into the boiling sugar cauldron, he brought me to

Havana, had me baptized, and entered on the birth register as his son. Nobody argued with him about this. So I was called Pedralves, but the old fellow knew that Tilburi "was the man." The latter saw me around, scared me, and called me Tomtit. "How could Pedralves have had such a shrimp of a son?" asked Tilburi.

Pedralves was a tall old man, stooped, and with a long white mustache. It was at the Guajiro's tavern that all the "Allies" of the neighborhood hung out. Tilburi went there because he lived in Subirana, and perhaps to laugh at the cabdrivers. These in turn joshed about the tin lizzies until they realized that it was no laughing matter, and this got their hackles up. About that time there began to be plenty of money around, and the "Germans" always had fares, even charging a quarter. Before our eyes the horses began to grow gaunt, and the cabdrivers had an air of sadness and talked together in small groups in low muffled voices, like conspirators, at the cabstand, in the tavern, at the grocery store. The object of their hatred was the Fords. Pedralves himself watched them go by with a malevolent gaze, as though they were wild pigs that had sneaked into the yucca patch, making him feel like whipping out his machete and going after them.

For that reason Tilburi's jokes were no longer amusing. Before, they had tolerated and even liked him. Pedralves knew his past, but held his tongue, and even acted as though he found his antics funny. Tilburi had once been a cabdriver himself, before the Fords spawned their multiple offspring. Whereupon he sold his cab for what he could get, gave the horses to a brother of his wife, and bought himself a flivver. It was then that all the cabdrivers stopped laughing when Tilburi came in shooting off his mouth about everybody. He paid no attention. Those old men were behind the times and did not know how to keep abreast of things. Pedralves was the Kaiser, and there was a little sawed-off fellow he called the Mikado. At the time it was still a joke and nobody took it amiss. But then things changed. The drivers of old cabs and horses whose ribs you could count were ruined, and the worse off they were, the less call there was for their services. Mariana began to cry.

Mariana, Pedralves's wife, was a small, roly-poly little woman, the same age as he. People thought I was her son, and said that I took after her because I was small like her and had light eyes. The three of us lived in a room that was small, too, around the corner from Subirana, which opened onto a vacant lot. Today this has changed. Somebody drained the swamp, then some more houses were built, and in what was left of the lot boys play ball. The tenement itself, which was of wood and pieces of tin, disappeared, and in the end nothing will be left of all this but my story. For that reason I decided to write it. Not for myself, but for Pedralves, and the swamp, and Tilburi, my father. Nobody would have said that Tilburi, with his broad shoulders and hairy arms, could have had a son so skinny and blond and full of notions. But that was the way it was; Pedralves was sure of it, and I believe whatever Pedralves may have said his whole life long.

As I said, Mariana cried. The old man could not afford to paint his cab, and the nag got nothing to eat but cornstalks. "It hurts me because of the child," said Mariana. "He's going to be left alone in the world with no one to bring him up, and he'll come to a bad end." Even she was ignorant of the fact that I had a father so near at hand. By this time Mariana was too old to wash clothes, or do anything, and she talked to herself. I fled from that tenement crawling with big-bellied pickaninnies and washtroughs foaming with suds, and women with big behinds and black heads tied up in bandannas that ended in bright red horns. I preferred to go to the cabstand, and feel myself a driver like old Pedralves. A fight began inside me like that of enraged cats. One of the cats was what I felt for Pedralves and the other was my attraction to the tin lizzies. These had slid into my soul and in the end it would be useless to try to drive them out and remain loyal to Pedralves. I could not hate the Fords the way he did, and even Tilburi seemed to me haloed in a kind of nobility. I already adored him, because he was the man who knew how to drive the car, which was a god. I dreamed about it, and walked around and around any that was standing idle, and would have given my life to drive one of those metal animals for an hour. At that time they did not seem as ridiculous to us as they do now when we come across pictures of them in old newspapers. Perhaps for that very reason the cab-drivers closed ranks against them. They saw that people's eyes yearned toward the motor vehicles and that in a little while nobody would want to ride in the others. Mariana cried and talked to herself.

This was how the drama began: Pedralves was a former anar-chist and he must have been the one who thought up the idea of forming a terrorist group. He had once emigrated, had been in Peru, and had read Bakunin and González Prada. He had known the latter personally and cherished an autographed photograph he had given him. But now he was no longer an anarchist. At least, he did not think of destroying the established order, but rather of destroying the new order, the Fords which were ruining all the cabdrivers. Now I can imagine what that meeting must have been like. Some twenty drivers, those he could absolutely depend on, gathering at night beside the swamp, and drawing lots. Out of this drawing would come the group of three or four whose mission it was to puncture the tires of the Fords and, in some way, paralyze their motors. The latter was a more difficult problem. None of them knew how the engine worked, nor what had to be done to throttle its pulsations. One of them suggested putting charges of dynamite under them, but Pedralves, who was the director of the group, vetoed the idea. "Everything we do must be done without running any risk," he said, "We can't behave toward these people like gentlemen; we have to be rascals like they are. Bombs are out."

At the time I knew nothing. I noticed that Pedralves was sharpening an awl, and one night he knocked his wife down because the old woman started to open a package he had brought home. Mariana thought it was something to eat. I think it was some kind of powder intended to put the Fords out of commission. Quicklime, perhaps. A few days later Tilburi came into the tavern saying that the time had come to make a clean sweep of all the cabdrivers, of all the "Allies," for they had poured quicklime into the tank of one Ford and had punctured the tires of two or three others. The police showed up and checked the rooms in the tenement, but found nothing. Days later it was said that there had been more punctured tires, and that instead of quicklime, sugar had been put into the gas tanks. Someone must have enlightened Pedralves about how to do these things, and he in turn had passed the information along to another. The police could make no arrest at the time, but a little while afterward they surprised Pedralves himself fiddling with the carburetor of Tilburi's Ford and took him into custody. At first Mariana did not know what had happened. She spent four days in the house, eating nothing but garlic soup, and talking to herself. She thought the old man might have found a passenger who wanted to go out to the country, and then when he came back he would bring a roll of bills. She sent me to the tavern so someone would invite me to eat. Tilburi did, but the eyes of Pedralves's friends formed a hostile circle around me, and I ran away and spent the afternoon in the empty lot, crying. I didn't know where Pedralves was and I prayed to God that he would never come back, that his horse had stumbled and that someone had pulled him out from under the overturned cab dead. Tilburi said nothing. Now when he came in he was less jocose and he looked at the cabdrivers with a mixture of anger and sadness.

Finally the whole thing came out. It was Tilburi himself who told it at the tavern. He had been to jail to see Pedralves and to offer him help. The old man listened to the Ford driver with head high, and when the other finished what he had to say, he spat in his eye. That was his only answer. Tilburi came back to the neighborhood and laid the facts before his tavern audience.

"I'm sorry," he said. "The crazy old fool! He's going to let his wife and child starve to death."

The other cabdrivers heard him out in silence. Tilburi got into his Ford and left, jouncing over the ruts in the street. The drivers followed him with their eyes, silent to a man, motionless, like old piles driven in a swamp. Even the dishwasher stood with his dirty napkin in his hand, and the wife of the tavernkeeper, who waited on table, raised her distended belly and stood half bent back on herself, watching the Ford driver disappear.

Pedralves did not come back for several days. I slept in the old man's bed alongside Mariana's. One night I woke up dreaming that I saw the old woman floating above the floor, trying to get out through the transom, and then through a crack in the door, mewing like a cat that had been shut in. The tenement was in dead silence, and the moonlight filtered through the cracks of the door, faintly illuminating the room. I leaped out of the bed—the cot— and rushed naked into the yard. I had seen nothing, but I was terribly frightened. Some of the neighbor women came out into the yard and went to turn on the glaring light of our room. Now I think there must be something. Naturally, I don't believe in anything, but there must be something. Otherwise, I would not have awakened at that moment when Mariana was gasping out her last breath. Nothing could save her. And anyway, the neighbors would not have done anything for her. We were the only white people there. For some reason they had got the idea into their heads that the Pedralveses had the evil eye and worked white folks' magic. Ever since they had come there, all the children had died. Not that the neighbors regretted this too much, of course. There were too many children, always crying and asking for food. This coincided with the appearance of the Fords and the hard times for the cab-drivers. Most of the men in that tenement earned their living from the cabs: repairing them, curing the horses, making harnesses. So the children died. The adjacent swamp was full of miasmas, and the children went there to play in the mud. In one month six children had died, and someone said Pedralves and his wife were responsible.

But when Mariana died the whole neighborhood lighted candles in the room and the women took turns sitting up with her. I was sleeping in the yard then, under the moon. Someone carried word to Pedralves in jail; nobody had money for the funeral. But Pedralves's sentence was not yet up, so someone notified Tilburi. He brought the money, and he himself kept vigil beside the corpse. Nobody thought that Pedralves would show up. The old man appeared in the doorway like a ghost: tall, more stooped than ever, his face hidden in his white beard, and with a gleam of fire in his eyes. It was that look I saw, and nothing more, when he appeared in the doorway. Tilburi stepped aside, and then left without saying a word.

"Everybody get out of here," Pedralves ordered.

They all obeyed. The women clustered in the yard, in the moonlight, talking in hurried voices. The old man closed the door and knelt in front of the corpse and, without speaking a word, kept his eyes fixed on the drawn face until the dawn. From the floor I watched him, without saying anything either. That whole night the women stayed in the yard, around a big Negro who was new there. This man had known Pedralves in the country. People said he had something against Tilburi because of the latter's wife, but I don't know about that. Simón had been living in a room in the tenement, alone; nobody knew what he worked at. I think now that the man had spent years in jail, and that Tilburi's wife was really his. An old chauffeur told me that not long ago. But nobody there knew it. Simón talked about having known Pedralves and that he was an evil spirit. This was to throw people off the scent. His secret hate was against Tilburi, not Pedralves. Pedralves got up the next morning and followed his wife's body to the Colón cemetery. It seemed that the old man did not remember Simón. When he saw him afterward, when he came home, he did not greet him. Pedralves went in and out of the house now without speaking to anybody, and he did not talk to anyone in the tavern, either. He had gone back to his cabdriving. For several weeks there was no mention of punctured tires or of sugar in the gas tanks.

But the members of the group had not given up. The drawing of lots had given them a mission, and they had to carry it out. Pedralves himself was arrested again, but there was no evidence against him, so they released him. It was then that the strange thing happened.

Simón showed up one day with a white woman. She was a servant girl, with sweet, light eyes in which a constant fear fluttered. Today I can understand many things. Someone said that Simón had got hold of her through fear, indirectly. I don't know. This is a tricky subject and, in the last analysis, it doesn't matter. The fact is that Simón brought the servant girl, who had been working for a well-to-do family, and stuck her away in that room. The woman imitated everything the others did and tried to become one of them, but her words came out with a counterfeit ring, and the other women laughed at her. That was all. Nothing happened as far as Manuela was concerned until people began to say that she was crazy and bewitched. Maybe there was something in this, but it does not matter. Simón was seen somewhere with the terrorist group. The tenement went on saying, through Manuela's lips, that Pedralves was responsible for the death of the children.

"He's going to kill off all your children, girls," Manuela said to them. "He's a white man who's up to no good, believe me, girls," the blond woman kept repeating.

The others no longer laughed. They even forgot that Manuela was a stranger among them, and they hated the old man more every day. They even egged on the older or stronger boys to hit me. Well, I defended myself. It's the least you can do in this world. This business of turning the other cheek is not to my way of thinking. It has got me into trouble at times, but I don't regret it. One of the two is bound to come to the ground, and I won't say that I haven't often been the one who has taken the punishment. But at least I didn't take it lying down.

Pedralves was not aware of what was going on. He seemed to be living in a dream. He didn't hear what was being said around him, and he came to the room only to sleep for a few hours. The cabdriver "Almamía" was now his closest friend. He may have been the link between the different groups. For several weeks longer the alarm over sabotage to the Fords died down, and then suddenly another wave broke out, and this time they did employ the method of gentlemen: Tilburi's Ford was blown sky high. A charge of dynamite had exploded in the engine. Tilburi had just turned his back on it, going into the tavern. Nobody had seen anything, but when the smoke settled, Tilburi's wife appeared and whispered something in his ear. Nobody knows what she told him, but I can imagine. She must have had word about who had blown up the car. "It was my husband Simón," she must have said to him. She had found it out from somebody. Tilburi stood there thoughtfully, looking at the wreck of his Ford. I had just come out of the tavern, and I, too, stood gazing at the ruins. For a time I lived among them, examining each broken piece, caressing it as though it were a relic. As though that were a shrine, a holy sepulcher, destroyed by the barbarians. Except that I adored the sepulcher of a god of the future, not a god of the past.

For the time being, Tilburi said nothing. Pedralves was arrested again, but he had an alibi.

"I didn't do it," he said to the policeman, "but in my opinion the one who did it performed an act of justice. The cars are ruining us all."

He stroked his mustache and left the police station with head high. I had been at the stand with him when they arrested him, and I went along with him. It was the first time I had seen the inside of a police station. I'll never forget it. They let him go, as there was no evidence against him, but they arrested another man. Tilburi kept mum. He told the police he knew nothing.

"It was old Pedralves, girls," said Manuela, in the tenement. "It was him, never doubt it, with his evil heart. You don't know him."

All of a sudden Tilburi disappeared. He did not have the money now to buy another car. Or perhaps it was that he was waiting to do something before he went back to work.

Manuela intercepted the old man one afternoon and she accused him, shouting in the middle of the yard, "You're to blame, you devil. You have brought misfortune to this house. I know. You are a white devil, a man who casts the evil eye, who goes around blowing up Fords."

Pedralves cleared her out of his way with a shove of his hand, and Simón rushed out like a firecracker and caught the old man by one of his long arms. Pedralves stood up to him, looking him in the eye with that air of a madman which had been coming over him. Simón pushed him toward his room and led Manuela toward his. The blonde then embraced her man, letting out hysterical screams. That was when they began to say that she was crazy, afraid that she would set fire to the babies' cribs. Simón shut himself in with her. For over an hour she could be heard moaning and crying. For that reason the people in the tenement later suspected Pedralves when Simón was found dead.

The thing happened like this. I was still being fed at the Guajiro's tavern. I didn't lay eyes on the old man all day long. He would come home late at night, and ask me if I had eaten. Sometimes he gave me a few cents for candy or brought me a pair of pants. That Christmas Eve of 1915 he brought me a pound of nougat, and then on Twelfth Night he made me a gift of a pair of shoes. They were the first I had ever had, but he would not be able to give me any more. He had sold his cab and was driving a hired one from the stable of "Almamía," who was the last survivor.

And it was around Twelfth Night, too, that the business came to a head. Tilburi had returned for an occasional meal at the tavern. People wondered what he lived on. Someone said his wife loved him very much, and she found the money for him to eat. Naturally, they did not say this to his face. All the jokes and wisecracks had emanated from that grocery-store corner and the other where the tavern stood. People never saw Tilburi without the blowing up of his Ford coming to mind, and they suspected that in some way he was preparing his revenge.

"I wouldn't trust that guy," said the grocery-store owner. "Before, he was full of the Old Nick, but now there's death in his eyes. I wouldn't trust men who change like that. If you ask me, he's doing his own detective work. Just you wait. Someone is going to get bumped off in this neighborhood."

And so it happened. Somebody did get bumped off. Simón's visits to the tenement grew more infrequent, and Manuela was

clearly crazy. At least, she was beginning to be. The other women saw it, and they took their little ones to the washtroughs with them while they washed. Nearly everybody had forgotten about Tilburi. Manuela and Pedralves were enemies, and the whole tenement now hated both of them. Sometimes Simón came late at night and left around noon, wearing a pair of wide blue pants, a pleated shirt, and a red handkerchief at his neck. As he went by, the women opened their eyes. Some of them leaned against the frame of the door. That night somebody was waiting outside for Simón. The latter opened the door, took a few steps across the yard, and left. It was still early, and there was no moon. Perhaps that was what Tilburi was waiting for. He had not been seen in the neighborhood except when he went into or left his room. People had forgotten about him.

Old Pedralves had just shut the door of our room when he saw something through the crack.

"I'm going down there," he said to me. "I'll be right back. Put out the light."

I followed him to the door. The women in the yard watched us. And this is what they recalled later: Simón had come out suddenly and old Pedralves had followed him. That's what they told the police. Simón had disappeared from sight, but the old man followed down the street toward the vacant lot. Nothing more was heard. Then I ran in the same direction. Just as when Mariana had died, I had a presentiment. This often happened to me. One doesn't know just what is up. You fear nothing specific and suspect nothing clearly. It's as if a hand had clutched your heart, while several other smaller hands tug at your nerves, and many successive mouths dim your eyes with their breath. I followed, as I say, in the old man's steps, as though drawn or pushed by some mysterious but undeniable force. At the edge of the lot I stopped. There I began to ask myself where I was going. The air seemed to have thickened, as though the warmth had congealed. It was hot and the silence filled everything. Out of that silence there rose, from time to time, the faint croaking of a frog. I was going to start out again when I heard a stifled noise, like the breathing of a galloping horse, but without the sound of hoofbeats. It drew nearer and nearer, and in a little while the shadowy figures of two men took definite

shape, coming toward me across the lot. When they came abreast of me they stopped.

"There you have him," said Pedralves, pointing toward me. "When it gets light, take a good look at him. He is your son. He's yours. I am the only one who can guarantee it. But if you have any doubts, go back to the sugar plantation. There'll be someone there who will bear me out."

It was Pedralves and Tilburi. The latter was still carrying a short machete in his hand.

"Give me that machete," Pedralves went on. "You have to look after the kid. This is going to be found out. Nobody will suspect you. You can buy another Ford and raise the boy. I no longer have a cab, and, anyway, the time for buying cabs is past. I've got nothing more to do in these streets. My place is in the Principe jail."

Tilburi, with his legs wide apart, the machete in his hand, kept his eyes on the ground. He had trouble breathing. For over half an hour he stood like that. He did not seem to hear the old man's words. These were now deep, serene, firm, with no trace of irritation.

"You're still young," he went on. "There you have a son. I can't bring him up. Try to understand that. But even if you object, it won't matter. Nobody will believe that it was you who killed Simón. I'll say I did it, and everybody in the tenement will back me up, gladly."

Can you imagine it? What I felt at the time must have been a complete muddle. I don't remember it. At any rate, I wouldn't know how to give it form with the imagination or the senses. Something strange, confused, contradictory. I am not even sure I understood clearly what was happening. But one thing I did know: Tilburi had killed Simón and his body would be lying somewhere in the lot. But what I could not understand too well was the attitude of the old man. Now he was talking to his enemy the way a saint might talk to a repentant sinner. Tilburi did not answer; he just stood there, without moving, his arms away from his body, like a giant ape. But what was the old man talking about? What did he mean by "he's yours" and "this is your son"?

It took me awhile to understand it. But I was sure of one thing: I would have liked to be the son of Tilburi, the man who knew how

to drive a car. He did not move from the spot. The old man took the machete out of his hand; Tilburi released it little by little. What was going on in his mind? It is useless to ask. Nobody will ever know what goes on in a man's mind under those circumstances. Not even he himself. I never asked him, either. I understood that there are things that should never be stirred up. It would be like digging in a grave or draining a swamp. Or perhaps plucking a flower to bits.

The old man took the machete and said to me, "Let's go home. He'll come for you. I am sure of it."

What was he talking about? I didn't ask him, either. I followed him in silence, turning my head until Tilburi was lost from sight. He did not move from where he was standing as long as I could see him. He must have stayed there all night. But the next morning he wasn't there anymore. Pedralves came up to the tenement with the machete in his hand, and threw it into the middle of the yard. There were still three or four people up, and in a minute everybody had rushed out.

Pedralves drew himself up in the middle of them and said, "I killed Simón. You can go and report it to the police. I killed him because he was the one who blew up the Ford and punctured the tires of the others. On his account I had to go to jail and because of him my wife died, deserted by everyone. There you have the explanation, in case you are interested."

It was the same story he told to the police and the judge. The whole tenement, with the exception of Manuela, backed up his words. Manuela remained strangely silent, talking and laughing to herself. I never knew any more about her. Putting two and two together, I realize that old Pedralves had lied. Without doubt, Simón had blown up the Ford, but it was Pedralves and his men who punctured the tires and poured sugar in the gas tanks. Afterward he had been sorry. Some change had been going on in him since his wife's death.

When they led him off to his cell the next day, he put his arms around me, saying, "You stay here. Someone will come for you. You go with him and do as he tells you. He's your father."

It seemed to me as though he was still talking in his sleep. Who was my father? Tilburi? That whole day I sat in the place where they had blown up the Ford, thinking. I would never see the old

man again until his trial. Then they would take me there and ask
me what I knew. What should I say? Tilburi had not come back to
the tavern or the store. I was still living in the room in the tenement and I ate what Pedralves' friends gave me in the tavern.
They, too, believed that the old man had killed Simón. I, I told the
judge, had seen nothing. I had followed the old man and had
overtaken him in the street with the machete in his hand. That was
all I knew. Why didn't I tell the truth? I don't know. Perhaps
because of the car. The car meant more to me than all the rest.
Even more than old Pedralves. In some obscure way I wanted to
save Tilburi because he was the man who drove the car. For no
other reason.

That is all. But the old man must have had other reasons. Men
are very different one from the other. The old man had been
moved by sentiments all his life, and sentiments are strange mix-
tures. Anyway, his were. I saw him that day in the prisoner's chair,
looking straight ahead of him. When he stood up, he talked with a
strong, cold voice such as I had never heard in him before. It did
not seem to come from his breast but from his head. And undoubtedly it did. I never saw him again. He did not give me more than a
couple of glances. How was it he did not fear that I might tell the
truth? Another mystery.

But that's the way it was. My story is not a story. In a few days
Tilburi showed up and asked me, as though it didn't matter to him
one way or the other, if I wanted to go and live with him. Then
Tomasa, his wife, came and took me with her, and fed me, and
asked me if I wouldn't like to be a chauffeur like Tilburi. I told her
I would and threw my arms around her, crying for happiness. And
that was all that happened. From then on I did not go back to the
tenement, nor did I ever know anything more about Manuela.
Tilburi had got himself a new car and he let me ride with him in
the driver's seat. That was how I left off being an "Ally" and
became a "German." But I did not know what was going on
between the real Allies and Germans across the sea. Only much
later . . . but what does that have to do with our "Allies" and our
"Germans"?

TRANSLATED BY HARRIET DE ONÍS

Abelardo Díaz Alfaro

JOSCO

INDELIBLE shadow of Josco on the hill that dominates the valley of the Toa. Head lifted high, razor-sharp horns thrust against the bloody cape of a brilliant sunset. Pointed, tawny, the crown in shadow, his walk slow and rhythmic. A gelatinous foam fell from his black, spongy lips, leaving behind a stellar silver on the jeweled green, like the winding track of a snail. Chocolate as to color, as to character withdrawn, he was an indefatigable fighter. When the stars had pinned their darts of light high above the black crest of Farallón Hill, we would see him descend from the heights, majestic, arching his thick neck, and shaking the air over that virgin earth with his male bull's snort; then hurl a long and powerful bellow toward the gullies of San Lorenzo.

"A real bull, a sire like that one, none like him; wasn't born to the yoke," Jincho Marcelo told me; one sullen black night he had watched over his birth by the trembling light of pitch flame. He had reared him and loved him like a son; his only son.

A solitary man, born one tumultuous morning, Jincho saw in that bull the incarnation of his own manliness, his own restlessness, of his tough and primitive spirit. And bull and man became fused into one landscape, one sorrow.

There wasn't a bull crossing the boundary from neighboring estates on whose flank Josco wouldn't engrave, with a sure horn, his male inscription.

As the silver tip of the moon marked the curtain of night, I heard old Leopo say to Jincho, "Marcelo, tomorrow go get me the American bull I bought from the Velillas; I want to use him for breeding; we must better our stock."

I watched as Jincho's narrow mind, strong and primitive, struggled with an idea too bloody, too painful to be realized. After a short pause, he muttered, his voice breaking, "Don Leopo, what will we do with Josco?"

"Well, we'll yoke him for the hauling of sugarcane; it's tough, and the bull is strong and sturdy."

"Forgive me, Don Leopo, but that bull has sired a whole nation; he's proud, he's not suited to the yoke." And he descended the spiral staircase and passed along the moonlit path until he disappeared into the sea of shadows that was the cane plantation; bleeding, as if they had stabbed him to the heart with a rapier.

The next day I saw Jincho come through the gate from the next property, leading an enormous white bull by a rope; his horns short, his powerful forehead sepia-colored; the dilated nostrils drilled through by an iron ring. Jincho came slowly along the *guayabal* path as if he were being pushed, not at all anxious to get there.

Suddenly a powerful bellow rang out over the *mayú* plantations of Los Cocos, resounding in the San Lorenzo gullies and on the jagged peaks of Farallón. A flash of joy lit Jincho's drawn face.

It was Josco's war cry, his challenge to contest, with daggers of horn, the supremacy of the herd. His head swung up and down, and he jabbed viciously at the ground, bringing up sod and grass on his horns; blindly he lunged at the air, as if fighting with shadows.

Jincho, on the hilltop near the house, held back the white bull. Josco, striding lightly forward, came out on the path. For a moment he halted, then whirled around, agile, and began to lance the small guava trees that bordered the path, his crowned head garlanded with branches, wild flowers and rattans. On he came slowly, cautiously, with a repeated and monotonous bellow. Stretching his neck, the sound culminated in a long trumpeting roar. He raked the earth with his hoofs until clouds of golden dust rose skyward. He advanced, then stopped, immobile, hieratic, tense. On his dark spongy lips the foam erupted in bubbles of silver. For a short time he stayed thus. His neck arched, his muzzle close to the ground, he snorted violently, as if tracking some mysterious scent.

At the homestead, people began appearing on the balcony. The crowd gathered from their mud huts. Urchins with swollen bellies perforated the air with shrill cries: "Josco is fighting with the Velillas' American." Their voices echoed in the surrounding hills. The children shouted at Josco, "Give it to him, Josco; you can . . ."

Josco continued to advance, head lowered, his walk slow and stately. And Jincho, unable to control himself, let loose the white bull. Suspicious, he squared off and began digging into the earth with his broad hoofs and emitted a hoarse bellow.

"Hey . . . hey . . . What say . . . Josco," shouted the multitude.

"Go to it, my Josco," Jincho shouted.

And the dry and violent crash of horns rang out. The peons' shouts became deafening: "Give it to him . . . Hey . . . Josco!"

Heads glued together, eyes black and brilliant, blood-flecked, nostrils dilated, hoofs dug firmly into the ground, hind legs spread, lion tails erect, their contact governed by muscles undulating over firm flesh.

A collision of forces that by its very potency immobilized them both. Neither slackened; they seemed as if stamped upon the colorful landscape.

The foam thickened. The arduous grunts pulsed like bellows. Suddenly they separated horns and made lateral stabs, trying to lacerate each other's foreheads. Their horns resounded like the clacking of castanets. And again they joined horns, heads blossoming with daggers.

One group exclaimed, "The white is bigger and carries more weight."

Jincho responded angrily, "But Josco is smarter and better bred."

Making a supreme effort, the white bull drew back a little, then proudly advanced, imposing on the sculpture of his body all the strength of his weight. Josco recoiled, swept back by the force of this avalanche.

"Hold fast, my Josco," shouted Jincho in desperation. "Don't run. You've got the blood."

Josco sank his hind legs in the ground, seeking a foothold in order to resist, but the white one was forcing him back. Bending his hocks, he tried to arrest the push, then straightened out anew and retreated rapidly, tempering the white one's attack.

"You see, he's bigger," added one of the onlookers sadly.

"But he doesn't run," spat Jincho.

Josco's hind legs hit an irregularity in the terrain which served as a stand. Now taut, he leaned to one side, moving his body out of the line of the white one's onslaught, which had lost its momentum. With the latter off balance, Josco, taking advantage of his opponent's difficulty, whirled rapidly and aimed a sure stab at him, tracing a bloody gash on the white flank. The wounded bull bellowed in sudden pain and fled, terrified, amidst the shouts of the jubilant peasants.

Jincho, quivering with emotion, cried out huskily, "Mighty bull, cunning bull, noble bull!"

And Josco stretched his classic body, lifted his triumphant head, and pointed golden horns at the sun, stabbing the blue cape of a cloudless sky.

The white one stayed on as sire. Pompous, he paced up and down the fence enclosing the cows.

They tried yoking Josco with an old ox to tame him, but he reverted to violence, endangering the peasants.

He became fretful, intractable, and could be heard bellowing plaintively, as if oppressed by an unbearable sorrow.

He kicked viciously at the oxen's corral—those beasts of burden whose necks were hairless and whose grazing was peaceful. Lifting his head above the barbed wire, he lowed sadly. He was now docked, a maimed ox, a castrated ox. That sundown I contemplated him in the afterlight of a dusk tinted the red of bulls' blood, on the green hillock that dominates the Toa valley. No longer did he have his former arrogance, no longer did he lift gracefully his crowned head; I saw him falter, as if crushed by an infinite grief. He slavered, stretched his neck, and brayed weakly, then descended the hill; his shadow melted into the mystery of the night.

The next day Josco didn't appear. He was hunted throughout the district. It was impossible for him to have wandered off into the other plantations, for there were no gaps in the *mayú* hedges, nor in the wire fences along the boundaries. Jincho went back and forth, desperate.

Tío Leopo pointed out, "Perhaps he took the Farallón path toward the stand of corn by the river." Jincho went there. He returned, discouraged. Then he headed toward a tree-lined ravine near Los Cocos, where Josco frequently drowsed.

We saw him raise his hands, and in an anguished voice he shouted, "Don Leopo, Josco is here!" We ran toward Jincho; he stood with his head bowed, eyes blurred with tears, and pointed to a slope among some roots, reeds, and wild flowers. And we saw an inert Josco, his hind legs spread stiffly apart, his head buried beneath the weight of that muscular body.

His voice trembling with emotion, Jincho exclaimed, "My poor Josco, he has broken his own neck from rage. . . . Don Leopo, I told you. That bull was sire of a nation; he wasn't born for the yoke."

TRANSLATED BY NICK VANDEMOER

Pedro Juan Soto

THE INNOCENTS

to climb up to the sun on that cloud with the pigeons without
horses without women and not to have to smell the junk burning
in the lot with no one to make fun of me

Dressed in a suit that had been made and sold to contain some
other man, he could see from the window the pigeons fluttering
about the eaves of the house opposite.

or with doors and windows always open to have wings

He began to flap his hands and coo like the pigeons when he
heard a voice behind him.

"Baby, baby."

The woman, dried up by age, was seated at the table, under-
neath which stood the flimsy suitcase, a rope its only lock; she
looked at him with her bright eyes, spread out over the chair like a
hungry, abandoned cat.

"Bread," he said.

Her hands on the table, the woman pushed back her chair and
went to the cupboard. She took out some bread that was lying
unwrapped upon boxes of rice and gave it to the man, who was
still gesticulating and mouthing sounds.

to be a pigeon

"Stop your noise, Pipe."

He crumbled the piece of bread on the windowsill, paying no
attention to her.

"Stop your noise, baby."

Some men playing dominoes under the awning of the grocery
store stared up at them.

He left off moving his tongue from side to side in his mouth.

with no one to make fun of me

"Walk in the square," he said.

"All right, Hortensia is coming now to take you for a walk."

"In the square."

"No, not in the square. They took it away. It flew away."

262

He pouted. His attention shifted again to the fluttering pigeons.

no more square

"It wasn't the pigeons," she said. "It was the evil one, the devil."

"Oh."

"Must ask Papa God to bring back the square."

"Papa God," he said, gazing upward, "bring back the square and the river . . ."

"No, no. Without opening your mouth," she said. "Kneel down and talk to Papa God without opening your mouth."

He knelt by the windowsill, joined his hands and stared out over the flat roofs.

I want to be a pigeon

She looked down at the men's Saturday morning idleness and the bustle of the women going to and from market.

Slowly, heavily, but erect, as if balancing a bundle on her head, she went into the room where, in front of the mirror, her daughter was removing hairpins from her hair and piling them on the dresser.

"Don't take him today, Hortensia."

The younger woman glanced at her out of the corner of her eye.

"Don't start that again, Mama. Nothing'll happen to him. They'll take good care of him and it won't cost us a cent."

Freed of its pins, her hair formed a black mass about her ears.

"But I know how to take care of him. He's my son. Who knows better than I?"

Hortensia, in the mirror, studied the small, lean figure.

"You're old, Mama."

In the mirror, one fleshless hand was raised.

"I'm not dead yet. I can still look after him."

"That's not the point."

The curls remained stubbornly tight, in spite of her efforts to loosen them with a comb.

"Pipe is innocent," the mother said, her words drawn from a sea of pity. "He's a baby."

Hortensia threw down the comb. She took a pencil from the

purse that lay open on the dresser and began to darken her scanty eyebrows.

"There's no cure for that," she said to the mirror. "You know it. So the best thing . . ."

"In Puerto Rico this wouldn't have happened."

"In Puerto Rico things were different," said Hortensia over her shoulder. "People knew him. He could go out because people knew him. But in New York people can't be bothered and they don't know their neighbors. Life is hard. The years go by while I sew my life away and I'm still not married."

As she looked for her lipstick, she saw in the mirror her mother's despondent face.

"But that's not the reason either. He'll be better taken care of there."

"That's what you say," her mother replied.

Hortensia tossed eyebrow pencil, lipstick, and comb into her purse and snapped it shut. She turned around—a thin blouse, greasy lips, blackened eyebrows, tight curls.

"After a year here, we deserve something better."

"He's not to blame for what happens to us."

"But if he stays here he will be. Take it from me."

She darted to her mother, grasped her arm, and pushed up her sleeve to the elbow. On the thin corded flesh was a purple bruise.

"He's already raised a hand to you, and I'm never easy in my mind at the factory thinking what might be happening to you and to him. And if this has already happened . . ."

"He didn't mean to," the mother said, pulling down her sleeve and staring at the floor, at the same time twisting her arm to make Hortensia let go.

"He didn't mean to when he had you by the neck? If I hadn't grabbed the bottle, God knows what would have happened. There's no man here to stand up to him, and I'm worn out, Mama, and you're scared to death of him."

"He's a baby," the mother said in her gentle voice, withdrawing into herself like a snail.

Hortensia half-closed her eyes.

"Don't give me that. I'm young and I have my life before me, but he hasn't. You are worn out and if he went away you could live out the rest of your days in peace and you know it but you don't dare admit it because you think it's wrong but I'll say it for you *you're worn out* and that's why you signed the papers because you know they'll take better care of him in that place and then you can sit down and watch the people go by in the street and whenever you take the notion you can get up and go out and walk around like the rest but you'd rather think it's a crime and *I'm* the criminal so you can go on being the long-suffering mother and *you have been a long-suffering mother* no one can take that away from you but you've got to think of yourself and of me. What if the horse knocked him down when he was ten years old . . ."

The mother walked rapidly away, as if she were being pushed, as if the room itself were blowing her out, while Hortensia went on, ". . . and for the other twenty he's lived knocked down like that . . ."

And she turned to watch her mother go, not following, leaning her weight on the dresser upon which her fists beat out a rhythm for what was almost a scream: ". . . we've had to live all those years with him."

And in the mirror she could see the hysterical carnival mask that was her face.

and there's no roosters and there's no dogs and there's no bells and there's no wind off the river and there's no buzzer from the movie house and the sun doesn't come in here and I don't like it

"All right," the mother said, bending over to brush the crumbs off the windowsill. Below in the street, the boys were hitting a rubber ball and chasing it.

and the cold sleeps sits walks with you in here and I don't like it

"All right, baby, all right. Say amen."

"Amen."

She helped him to his feet and put his hat in his hand, for she saw that Hortensia was coming toward them, serious, her eyes red.

"Let's go, Pipe. Give Mama a kiss."

She put her purse on the table and bent over to pick up the suitcase. The mother threw herself around his neck—her hands like pincers—and kissed his burned hazelnut of a face, running her fingers over the skin she had shaved that morning.

"Let's go," Hortensia said, picking up purse and suitcase.

He pulled away from his mother's arms and walked toward the door, swinging the hand that carried his hat.

"Baby, put your hat on," his mother said, and blinked lest he see her tears.

Turning, he placed on his vaseline-coated hair that which on account of its smallness looked like a toy trying to compensate for the waste of cloth in the suit.

"No, he better leave it here," Hortensia said.

Pipe pouted. The mother kept her eyes fixed on Hortensia, her jaw trembling.

"All right," Hortensia said. "Carry it in your hand."

Again he walked toward the door, the mother following, barely restraining herself from reaching out to him.

Hortensia barred the way. "Mama, they'll take care of him."

"Don't let them mistreat . . ."

"No. There are doctors. And you . . . every two weeks. I'll take you."

They were both making an effort to keep their voices steady.

"Go lie down, Mama."

"Tell him to stay . . . not to make any noise and to eat everything."

"Yes."

Hortensia opened the door and looked out to see if Pipe had waited on the landing. He was amusing himself by spitting over the stair rail and watching his saliva fall.

"I'll be back early, Mama."

The mother stood by the chair that was now one too many, trying to catch a glimpse of her son through the body that blocked the doorway.

"Go lie down, Mama."

Not answering, her hands clasped, she stayed rigid till chest and shoulders were shaken by a spasm, and, hiccuping, she began softly to weep.

Slamming the door, Hortensia ran downstairs with Pipe as fast as she could. Faced with the immense clarity of a June midday, she longed for hurricanes, eclipses, blizzards.

TRANSLATED IN COLLABORATION WITH THE AUTHOR

Carlos Montenegro

TWELVE CORALS

Plácido dozed. The horse was old and tame enough for him to take a nap and thus shorten the trip to the village. From there on, while the danger lasted, he would feign sleep. Dogs had taught him that: they would pass through familiar places without a care, their tails neither raised nor lowered, sniffing everything, blessing the corners, the posts, even the doorways. But when going through an unfamiliar district, they steered clear of the houses, head and tail drooping, even limping a bit.

Plácido, imitating them, pretended to sleep, slackening the reins that the rawboned horse might go at a slower pace. Thus, inoffensive, he would pass through the village and on along the road till he lost sight of Don Cipriano's store, around the angle of La Pastora. After this point, however, man and beast were different. All was motion. Plácido, leaning slightly to one side, spurring the trotter's flank, straightened his sombrero of *yarey* which until now had hidden his face. He carried saddlebags full of salt for the rebels located in the hills—a hundred and twenty-five pounds at least.

Sometimes, in the very bottom, was a little gauze and quinine, though not always, for it was the salt that was important. Now, something pricking like a nail began to worry him: the trouble was the *yarey*. Don Cipriano's nephew, as Plácido was relaxing one morning, had said with obvious purpose, "They're looking for someone who went by with a new *yarey* and returned bareheaded."

The boy spoke while rinsing out a glass. He looked sly, but Plácido did not give himself away, though his face went pale. . . .

"And that's a crime?"

"Don't know. I think they suspect he's mixed up with the rebels, and that the sombrero stayed with them. . . . You know how the sergeant is; he says he'll hang him if he's caught."

So along went Plácido, his eyes now wide open. He settled himself in the saddle, and since the crossroad neared, slumped for-

ward, bending his head as if asleep; though how wide-awake he
really was!

With eyes closed the images became more precise—above all,
that of the sergeant. A thickset brute. More thickset and brutal
when the rebels or their friends were concerned. Those who were
brought before him entered his presence shivering, and did not
come out the same, if they came out at all.

The sergeant weighed heavily on Plácido's mind, as did the
pounds of salt in the saddlebags and the *yarey* he'd left in the hills.
He thought also of the cockfight pit. The Sunday before he had lost
a "cinnamon" that was "like a tiger," just when he was about to
win a doubloon on him. He heard again the sergeant's voice: "I
bet a doubloon! A doubloon on him!" The bleeding cinnamon
heard the sergeant's shout: "Come on, red, you're high class!" But
the cinnamon could strike no longer; he lowered his head, dragged
his tail and awaited the finish, while his adversary, encouraged,
slashed him with lightning spurs, again and again. Blinded, he
leaped up once more, in one last effort, but quickly fell back
again.

"Pick him up, Plácido," someone called out. "Keep him for
breeding."

Plácido, intent on the fight until that moment, smiled. No. Not
for breeding! Quality is one thing, the "law of the underdog" another. To let himself be killed like this, not lifting a foot from the
ground!

A stumble of the horse shook him. Would it be his fate also, this
"law of the underdog"? Better to head for the hills at once. What if
the sergeant were to catch him now! He would not be brave. But
each man is what he is. Like the cocks. He could exist in the
village like the *majá,* the snake that slips out among the enemy;
not on one side or the other—on both. . . . At times he thought of
himself as a cock loose in the center of the ring, without spurs,
facing a terrible enemy. Today the salt, tomorrow the mail, even
the new *yarey.*

One day the storekeeper had said, "Hey, Plácido, you've bought
half a dozen sombreros this month."

"Yes, they get lost, two were for Nicasio," he replied, grinning
unhappily.

Always in danger, wary of disaster. With no improvement in
sight. The soldiers in the thickets had gain of a sort. An assault, a

surprise attack. They would rush out at a gallop, machetes in hand. Then came the climax: the struggle, hoarse shouts, death. There would be a moment of fierce attack. The horses now wild, bodies rigid. . . . Man was then like a triumphant animal, like a fine cock. The last like the first, all equal. . . . Plácido's situation was different, always slippery, always in disguise. *Majá.* Smiling unhappily in the store while buying salt, or a machete, or a new *yarey.* . . .

"So much salt, Plácido!"

"Those fellows killed another of my cows yesterday; I have to salt the hide. . . ."

The fighting pit barely paid off. There was the sergeant shouting, boasting of his money on the "red." As if there were red cocks!

But there are men for every job, just as there are cocks of all sorts. And Plácido, too, was what he was. It would have suited him better to stay in the thickets rather than carry salt to the revolutionaries. He had a good horse, just as he had a fierce expression. And here he was, mounted on this old rawboned animal, smiling at everyone. . . . At the rebels, too. What a mess! Not everyone realized what he had to do each day, in the shadow of the gallows. But he smiled anyway, as an unhappy man would. And he carried a new *yarey* to whoever wanted it. He had one in his saddlebags at the moment.

Not once had he said: "It's too dangerous." That was left for him to think, as now when entering the town. Trembling slightly, he heard someone call out.

"Hey, *paisano, paisano!*"

For a moment Plácido considered jumping off his mustang; he went stiff.

"Hey!"

But he pretended not to hear, as if dozing, and let the animal amble along.

"Hey!"

At last he turned around. A soldier was coming toward him, his musket cradled in his arms.

"Come on; the sergeant wants to see you. . . ."

"The sergeant?"

The soldier seemed to jeer. It was the war. Ambush and killing had augmented the hatred until it was dense enough to touch. Suddenly a shot is heard, a man falls with a bullet in his chest. But

there's nothing to be seen. The shot, and nothing more. Again the road would be terribly difficult, the heat suffocating, and the thick woods they went through; fever. The marshy waters were poisonous. And you had to march through swamps or across plains like deserts. The hatred grew. At times of greatest misfortune, perhaps not; rather, one thought: "What are we doing here?" And some soldiers, too, had taken to the hills. Then at other times, when a man was at his weariest, the tumult would start all over. It surged suddenly down from the hilltop, or out of a ravine. Galloping horses and a brilliant avalanche of steel blades. There was only time left to die. To cover your face with your arm and die, the last thought broken off. . . .

Plácido did not think of escape; he withdrew into himself and settled down unhappily on his horse, squeezing the saddlebags as if to make them smaller.

"The sergeant wants me?"

"He's called for you; he'll tell you soon enough. . . ."

Again he thought of the pit, of his cock, the cinnamon, head and tail drooping, allowing himself to be killed. Already he felt the sergeant's fists, like the kick of a horse, resounding in his skull; though his face was pale, a vestige of that characteristic smile remained on his lips. He thought not only of his cinnamon but also of another he had owned, an Evil Eye cock called La Serpiente. It crouched, it slithered aside, while the blows of its opponent slashed only air. Those who knew it bet against it. "It's got better sense than to be perfect," they would say. But La Serpiente would always escape, until one day it ran away without a scratch on it. When it was brought back to the pit, a mouse killed it.

No, Plácido's law was not that of the underdog. If he accompanied the soldier without resisting, it was because that was his job, that was his fate. He had to look miserable from his head to his horse's hooves, not being mounted on his dappled pony, which would be difficult to catch.

Keeping an eye on the fellow, he threw a handful of salt to the ground. Feigning an indifference that indeed compromised him more, he made no more effort to ask questions.

Well, it looked as though his hour had come. The damn *yarey!* Maybe they'd hang him. . . .

He threw out another handful. Then two more. Ah, and the

yarey he had with him? How would he explain everything? The others at the store would turn against him too. But, above all the salt. . . . That salt!

Since the soldier glanced at him as he was about to throw more away, he tried to smile, but it came out twisted. It didn't matter to the soldier, who didn't even notice Plácido's pallor. He was probably used to having everyone he conducted to the sergeant turn pale.

Plácido shifted about in his seat, overplaying it, while he threw several more fistfuls to the ground; already the bag on the soldier's side felt heavier.

"What are you doing?" the latter asked, yawning.

"The beast is thin; you can feel his bones through the saddle."

"He probably says the same thing about you."

"Ha, ha. You're very funny."

Bored, the man looked up at him. "The sergeant said, 'Bring me that cockfighter who lives down beyond La Pastora.' I was headed there when I saw you. 'Bring him to me at once,' he said. If he sent for you, you must know what he wants."

"No, I don't, but I'm at his service. I'm a peaceful man, as everyone knows."

By the time they arrived at the barracks, Plácido had been able to get rid of only a few more handfuls.

"Bring along the horse, it might be a long stay."

No, it wouldn't take long. There was the sergeant with his brutal appearance, his body so unlike Plácido's own. He, tall, thin, bent. The other short, square, red and aggressive. On the table, within reach, a pen and the lash.

"Ah, it's you!"

Everything had changed; the brute was now made of silk.

The sergeant regarded Plácido as if he had nothing against him, then ordered, "Bring coffee for my friend." Thus did peasants operate when he visited them; before anything, a little coffee.

Plácido began to recover; this wasn't so bad . . . but . . . the salt, the *yarey* in his saddlebags . . . he almost wanted to turn himself over to his fate.

The other let fall an easy hand on his shoulder, saying cordially, "Come with me. I want you to see something."

Plácido couldn't help getting cold feet. Following the sergeant, he entered a patio lined with chicken coops.

"Look! What do you think of them? Have you ever seen their equal?"

Plácido was all one could ask for in a man; he lived close to death. But he was also a cockfighter. Perhaps before all else he was a cockfighter. Not for himself alone, but for everyone. He wasn't then the old man he is today. One could say of any of his roosters that "Plácido raised him." If he had joined the rebels, the reason was that he was born a Cuban. Now mute with astonishment, he went from one cage to another, all else forgotten, showing his admiration by exclaiming and clapping his hands.

On coming to the last cage, he turned to the sergeant and burst out, "Twelve Corals! They're twelve corals!"

Full of pride, the other laughed aloud.

"What did you say? What's that?"

"Twelve corals!"

He had never heard this expression, but he liked it. And offered by Plácido, it meant something superlative.

"Then, are they good?"

"Oh! *Good?*"

Plácido took up one of the roosters to calm it, passed it from hand to hand, his agile fingers arranging the feathers, and after weighing it, lifted the cock high, examining its profile.

"A real bird!" he exclaimed.

The sergeant was convulsed with joy. True, it was true. Why had he not noticed it before? They *were* like corals. The coffee had just been served, and while they drank they laughed happily.

Then it occurred.

To reach the patio they had followed a corridor from the sergeant's office. . . . And Plácido had just seen that his saddlebags full of salt, and the *yarey* that had been hidden, were placed on the office desk.

When he saw this, he had been laughing. The sergeant was saying, "One is for you. You'll cut and trim the feathers for me. Now, to those corals!"

Plácido no longer heard; he paled, seeing the soldier advance down the passage.

"Is something wrong?" inquired the sergeant, solicitous.

Plácido shook his head, his smile fading. The other insisted. It had been some time since he had been so happy. His habitual cruelty was acquired, almost professional; this joy was now his own. What was the matter?

The soldier waited a few paces away, impatient but respectful. The sergeant noted his presence with ill humor.

"What do you want? Leave me alone."

The man's insistence struck him as strange.

"Sergeant . . ." But the sergeant's full attention was for his friend. And besides, Plácido had just placed a hand on his shoulder.

"Strange. I thought something was wrong with you. It's nothing? Wait, then."

Satisfied now about Plácido, he would solve whatever problem there was and return in peace to his treasure.

Plácido watched him go toward his office, then glanced at the high mud walls surrounding him; there was no escape. Just as he thought he had the solution everything changed. Maybe there was still time. . . . He thought again of La Serpiente, crouching, sly, slippery as a *maja*. He must be no less.

The sergeant reappeared, raging. "Imbeciles! All imbeciles!" he had shouted. For the first time, he was furious that he must hurt an enemy. Why did it have to happen just then? He had been so happy! But now he would crush the traitor with one blow. So, twelve corals?

The two came face to face, the sergeant furious, but with some small hope left; Plácido smiled, appearing moved.

"You noticed something was going on?" he asked. "You know, one is what one is. One knows one's business and does well to hide it when all the others do is watch. If one tells what one knows, one loses out."

Ah! What line was this miserable man taking, who should be denying everything? Encouraged, Plácido continued, as if La Serpiente were present.

"I've told no one my secret. With you it's different, and if you promise to tell no one. . . ."

The sergeant was calming down. But didn't this fool realize he knew all? That even the storekeeper had accused him?

Moving his head from side to side, Plácido put his hand on the other's arm, then, looking about him, said in his ear, "When do you want to fight them? No, wait. Before trimming. . . . Wait, I'll show you. Not a word, eh?"

He came closer and whispered, "Without their noticing, bring me a fistful of coarse salt; there's plenty in my saddlebags."

The sergeant's face was transfigured. Never had he so waited on every word, never had his happiness been so well substantiated.

Plácido came even closer and added, "Some fools give them pepper to fire the blood. That they have to excess when they're really fine. Salt! They must have salt to chill their blood, so that they have the advantage."

The other's laughter broke against the patio walls. He shouted, "That's what I told them. Imbeciles! Ha, ha, ha." He roared with delight, grasping with both hands the trembling Plácido.

A doubt crossed his mind. Lowering his voice, afraid of ruining everything, he asked, "But . . . the sombreros?"

Plácido pretended not to hear. "Bring the salt; come on, man. Ah! One is for me? Then. . . . bring me the *yarey* I have in one of the saddlebags. It's the best thing for transporting a fine rooster. I always use them."

The barracks filled with the sergeant's roar. He went down the passageway bent over with laughter, pushing off those in his way.

"Out! Imbeciles. So it was salt and sombreros for the rebels! What cowards you are!"

Plácido spent all day trimming the birds. When finished, he put in his *yarey* the one whose wings were bound with wire; the sergeant, laughter splitting his sides, was completely happy.

It was late, and they were lowering the flag, when Plácido again mounted his mustang. Leaning toward the sergeant he recommended once more, "You know now. Every morning a few grains. . . ."

Already on his way, he turned back to tell him, "Oh, and don't ever call a cock 'red.' The one that lost on Sunday was cinnamon."

TRANSLATED BY NICK VANDEMOER

Lydia Cabrera

TURTLE'S HORSE

TURTLE was reading *The Illustrated Havana* on the bank of a stream where Goodman White Horse came to drink twice daily.

"Good morning, Dame Turtle," Horse said.

Turtle looked at him fixedly over her spectacles and answered with disdain, letting the words fall slowly, "Horse is my horse."

Goodman Horse stood stock-still, not knowing what to reply. Nothing occurred to him. But when he returned to the stream that evening, he shouted at the Goodwife, his words also falling slowly, "Turtle—hasn't—got—a—horse."

Shortly after this, Turtle went to Court and said to the King, "Horse is my horse" (which gave rise to a good deal of talk).

The King sent for Horse and said to him, "So you're Turtle's horse?" Horse didn't know what to reply. Nothing occurred to him. After thinking it over, he went to Turtle's house, and said, "Let's go and see the King. You owe me an explanation."

"Alas," whined Turtle, "today I'm as good as dead! Indeed, Goodman Horse, I cannot even walk!"

"If you can't walk, I'll carry you."

"With these aches and pains, Goodman Horse?"

"Get up on my back."

"I'll fall off, Goodman Horse, I'll fall off." Making a supreme effort, she climbed onto his back; then at once, like a hard round stone, she rolled to the ground.

"Wait, I'll throw on a blanket. You'll be more comfortable." But at the slightest movement, Turtle, racked with pain, would go tumbling off onto the earth.

"Wait, I'll get my saddle."

"And how shall I hold on?"

"I'll fetch my bit and reins."

"And supposing we are attacked by dogs on the way?"

Goodman Horse gave her a whip. "You can frighten them off by cracking this."

"May everything go according to the love of God, Goodman Horse! If you trot too fast, it'll be the death of me."

And they began their journey.

Gongorín—Kinyón—Kinyón—Kiyon
Gorín—gogorín—gogorín,
Kinyón, Kinyón, Kiyon.

The trees laughed through their leaves as they watched them pass.

"Get down, now, Dame Turtle, in case one of the courtiers sees me like this."

"No, Goodman Horse, certainly not!" And she cracked the whip.

"Get down, Goodwife Turtle, get down!" And so they argued, but from an upstairs gallery the King had seen Turtle firmly ensconced on "her" horse; a little later he came out to meet them, shouting, "Oh ho, you are Turtle's horse, no doubt about it!"

Then Goodman Horse reared up on his hind legs and dashed away across country as though spurs of red-hot iron pressed into his flanks. Clutching his mane, Turtle hung on for dear life; but, just as they were crossing a stream, "Thanks," called out the Goodwife, and dropped off into the water.

Goodman White Horse, bereft of reason, fled from this world. He went running, running, running until he fell over the edge and rolled down into an abyss, to the bottomless solitudes of night, through the empty sleep of the stars.

And in death the white horse is fleeing still.

TRANSLATED FROM THE SPANISH

Lydia Cabrera

WALO-WILA

THERE were once two sisters, Walo-Wila and Ayere Kénde—or Kénde Ayere. Walo-Wila never went outdoors. No one had ever seen her.

Ayere Kénde leaned over the balcony. With her elbows on the railing, Ayere Kénde was enjoying the evening coolness which came up from the sea.

A wooden horse with music went by. He said, "A little water, please."

Ayere Kénde had a golden goblet. She filled it with water and gave it him to drink.

Said the horse, "What a handsome goblet, Ayere Kénde. I've never seen anything to equal it in all my life!"

"Oh, fairer, far fairer, is my sister... !"

"Then I want to see her, Ayere Kénde. Let me in."

"If you marry her you'll see her, brother," said Ayere Kénde.

Walo-Wila lived and died behind the closed shutters. Died and lived.

Kénde Ayere sang:

> "Walo-Wila, Walo Kénde,
>   Ayere Kénde,
> Here is a visitor, Kénde Ayere!"

Walo-Wila asked:

> "Walo-Wila, Walo Kénde,
>   Ayere Kénde,
> Who is the visitor, Kénde Ayere?"

> "Walo-Wila, Walo Kénde,
>   Ayere Kénde,
> Brother Horse, Kénde Ayere."

> "Walo-Wila, Walo Kénde,
>   Ayere Kénde,
> What does Brother Horse want, Kénde Ayere?"

277

"Walo-Wila, Walo Kénde,
    Ayere Kénde,
What but marriage, Kénde Ayere."

"Walo-Wila, Walo Kénde,
    Ayere Kénde,
Tell Brother Horse that I am ugly, Kénde Ayere.

Walo-Wila, Walo Kénde,
    Ayere Kénde,
That I am one-eyed, Kénde Ayere.

Walo-Wila, Walo Kénde,
    Ayere Kénde,
That I have boils, Kénde Ayere.

Walo-Wila, Walo Kénde,
    Ayere Kénde,
That I am putrid, Kénde Ayere!"

"Farewell, farewell!" said the horse.

Ayere Kénde was on her balcony. The Goat-Man passed, the Bull-Man, and the Water-Tortoise-Man.

The Tiger-Man passed, the Elephant-Man and the Lion-Man. Each of them was thirsty. When Ayere Kénde offered them her goblet of fine gold, they all praised the goblet, and she would say, "Fairer, far fairer, is my invisible sister."

And they all wanted to see her, but Walo-Wila sang, like a shadow singing behind the shutters:

"Alas, for I am ugly,
    For I am one-eyed,
    For I am bandy-legged,
    For I have scurvy!"

And they went away in disgust.

Stag, the son of the Honeysuckle, had not yet drunk from the golden goblet.

Ayere Kénde was enjoying the coolness of evening on her balcony; she was rocking in the rocker while the breeze rocked the balcony. (With far-off dreams in her eyes.)

Stag approached. He said, "Ayere Kénde, give me a drink in your golden goblet."

Ayere Kénde offered him the full goblet.

Said Stag, "I have never seen anything fairer."

"Oh, fairer, far fairer, is my sister whom no one has seen!"

"Show her to me, Ayere Kénde. I shall know the right way to look at her."

"Your eyes are gentle. If you marry her you'll see her, brother: you may not touch her. Wait, wait."

> "Walo-Wila, Walo Kénde,
>   Ayere Kénde,
>   Here is a visitor, Kénde Ayere."

And Walo-Wila replied, sad as nightfall at the window:

> "Tell him that I am ugly,
> That I am a cripple,
> That I am one-eyed,
> That I have boils . . ."

"I'll marry her," promised Stag.

Then said Walo-Wila, "My sister's mother lives at the bottom of the sea. My sister's mother is called Kariempembe."

At midnight Walo-Wila gave Ayere Kénde a pumpkin filled with pearls.

At midnight Kénde Ayere spilled out the pearls. She called Stag and handed him the pumpkin, now empty.

"Go down to the bottom of the sea."

Stag ran to the shore. The whole shore was saying, "Walo-Wila, Walo-Wila, Walo-Wila, Walo-Wila."

And he went in, between the moon-sharpened waves.

Ayere Kénde kept vigil all night on her balcony. At dawn Stag returned. He brought the pumpkin brimming with blue water from the sapphire depths of Olokun . . .

Said Ayere Kénde, "Go into my sister's chamber."

And Walo-Wila was fairer, far fairer than the goblet of Ayere Kénde.

When the moon kisses the sea . . .

TRANSLATED FROM THE SPANISH

Emilio S. Belaval

THE PURPLE CHILD

IN the morning, Monsona Quintana said to her husband, Anacleto Quintana, "Last night another was born to us. I didn't want to wake you. I managed alone as best I could."

The father was not much moved, shall we say, by the new infant's birth. There were sixteen hungry mouths beneath his roof already, and one's children aren't fed with cundeamor seed.

"Something must be bought, I suppose," he inquired suspiciously.

"I've already mended the hammock and made some smocks for clothes. Don't worry."

"I'll see it later," the father answered, somewhat relieved, as he left for his fields.

Monsona Quintana was hurt more by her husband's indifference than by the birth: That son of a bitch isn't going to love my *guimbo*—my little mite. Leaving without even looking at him! She was trying to finish the morning coffee in order to cast a look three yards long at her precious infant. The hungry beaks in the house were all crowded around the hammock, gazing in wonder at the new baby.

"But how little he is!"

"He hasn't stretched out his foot yet."

"When will he open his eyes, Ma?"

Hearing their chirping, Monsona Quintana felt frantic at not being able to give her *guimbo* that first glance when a mother sees with what threads of light her child is embroidered. But not even that pleasure is allowed an Indian from my country when she delivers at dawn. She shook the fire shovel under the coffee so that the wretched thing would heat up, her eyes more on the hammock than on the grate, more curiosity in her face than afterpains in her body. At last she could serve the coffee, cart in her tin of water, put out the fire and, her heart in flames, go look at her *guimbo*.

Monsona Quintana's child was one of those purple ones of our

280

mountain regions, a poor copy in scrofulous wax, a sad little canvas bordered by tuberculosis; never to know any color but death's. Monsona Quintana's heart braced itself as she looked at that bit of human skin.

"Beautiful little mite; more than beautiful, precious; more than precious, divine!" she continued as she took up her purple bundle.

She was a worn, bent Indian woman from my country who had borne seventeen children; her belly was so swollen that her husband no longer knew when she was pregnant. Motherhood had devoured the youth of one who had once had the colors of a rosary and the breasts of a sleeping dove. Now only the ghost of a mother was left, exhausted from carrying brook water to her hut, without embellishment except for the small hangers-on of her soul—thus was that Indian *jíbara* of my land. This time, heaven had posted a warning in Monsona Quintana's heart; her latest child was so emaciated he could hardly be called the shadow of a son.

"If only I had enough milk for him," she sighed, touching her breasts.

The baby stretched out a small foot, and the mother forgot all her troubles. His daring to move in that pile of rags set the mother going.

"Look at his pretty little foot," she cried. "He has the color of an Indian, the angel."

She went to prepare the *tautúa* water to loosen his bowels. From her dress she drew a bottle and a new nipple, bought by saving a few grains here and there, without her husband's suspecting that the bread was short.

The infant drank without sucking and fell asleep in a spiral of dreams, the sleep of a purple child, the sleep which resembles death but that to Monsona Quintana was the repose of an angel healing his wing. "Why have I become so fond of this *guimbo?*" she asked herself, feeling a deep joy; she, to whom motherhood could no longer bring joy; one to whom the cycle of the womb brought only trouble, year after year.

When the women of the neighborhood came in, Monsona Quintana showed them the purple child with all the arrogance of one who has given birth to the finest baby in the district. One of the potbellied girls lifted him up and gushed; "Look how cute he is, Monsona. . . . I hope mine turns out as well."

"He looks a little purple to me. Is he cold?" inquired another.

"You'll have to raise him on soured milk. It seems to me this one's a little delicate," another warned, swallowing the repugnance she felt.

Monsona Quintana grabbed her bundle hastily, to counteract the ill omen. Bah! What crabs pregnant women are! Her *guimbo* a little purple? That was just his Indian color, like one of the local roosters. If he was cold, she would warm him with her maternal warmth, this little one squeezed against her fat abdomen. This child from heaven, with the beak of a dove, would grow up to be commissioner and care for his invalid mother.

But the women's idle talk cut Monsona Quintana to the heart; one of them hardly dared look at the child, fearing that her own unborn one would somehow contract a disease. Was the *guimbo* really sick? Was he really cold? He had arrived on time, and came with only one pain; she had suffered little. The baby then drove away his mother's fears, bleating out his first cry. She leaped up, more agile than a goat, to satisfy his hunger. Soon the midwife came, with old eyes and dirty hands, to look at the navel of the purple child.

"They tell me things went easily last night."

"Almost without pain. I didn't have to wake Anacleto. Tell me, do you see anything wrong with my baby?"

"I don't see anything the matter with him. It's true, his color isn't healthy. I've told you before, you shouldn't carry so much water when you're in that condition. It's bad for you."

"But have you seen others like him?"

"Yes, woman. Only they grow up thin and give a lot of trouble. I'll bring you something for him."

Any fatigue brought on by the new baby didn't bother Monsona Quintana. She was willing to suffer for her *guimbo* from morning till the following dawn. She would show these busybodies what a mother could do to warm her sickly child! Tax herself to the limit, she would, to save him. She took off her new petticoats to make him some good diapers, then, her eyes on the hammock, she offered up prayers to Saint Risa, patron saint of Indian children. Two or three days later, she said to her husband, "Bring me one of our nieces to look after the house. From now on I want only to tend to my baby."

"Is he sick?"

"That's what they tell me. Do you want to see him? After all, you're his father."

Anacleto Quintana went over to the hammock and scrutinized the child from head to toe. He was puzzled, for it was the first time he had seen his woman with this feverish look in her eyes, a look that didn't go with her usual vigor.

"I don't see anything wrong with him. A little thin, yes."

"Do you think he's sick?"

"Njú! His color is like any small child's. Some die as soon as they're born."

The truth would not penetrate Monsona Quintana's head. Though her baby was a bit skinny, her heart still drew the breath of hope. What he needed was her warmth so that he would grow more beautiful than a purple rooster, and there she was, coarser than a calf's hide but fiercer than an overseer, prepared never to sleep if that would heal her *guimbo*.

Anacleto Quintana had to bring her a niece to take care of the house and cook. Monsona Quintana braced herself for the struggle with death over her child. Her husband stared at her, worried more by her frenzied energy than by the baby's color.

"You're killing yourself, Monsona. Lie down a bit . . ."

"Death can't take him while I have an eye on him," murmured the *jíbara,* shaking off her fatigue.

The *guimbo* had buried himself in Monsona Quintana's belly as if he wanted to return to the womb. There was no way of separating them, each looking into the other's eyes—he, purple, in spite of the starchy whiteness of *marunguey* with which his skin was powdered, and she, yellowed by one night of sleeplessness after another.

Heaven, taking pity on those swollen eyes, on those feet carrying them both back and forth, back and forth, decided to loose the *guimbo* from that fat belly. He was ravaged by fever, and one knew he was alive only by his metallic panting. Monsona Quintana fixed her eyes on the heavens with an arrogance such as would cause the guardian angel himself to descend, fearing some blasphemy. Anacleto protested, convinced that nothing could be done about that color which, in the *jíbaro* children of my country, is the tinge of death.

"You're going to get sick if you continue like this, woman."

"Death can't take him while I have my eye on him," she insisted, hoping for a miracle, impassive before the suffering she had spawned.

Night after night, ashes were put out in the evening dew and a pinch taken for the *guimbo's* milk; day after day, a new herb failed, one that had been infallible in curing babies of shortness of breath; hour after hour, the lines of agony deepened around her eyes. Monsona Quintana was no longer the fanciful *jíbara,* with gay ribbons hanging from her heart; she was a terrible mother, not giving up before the ambush of death, a pain-deadening lloroza leaf stretched across her swollen belly, her lips ceaselessly praying heaven not to forget her.

Monsona Quintana's martyrdom was not to end in one month, nor in two, nor in three. The *guimbo* was dying slowly, sewn still to the *jíbara's* womb, as if wishing to take his mother with him that they might sleep together in a dream of song, beneath purple sheets. She, the unfortunate *jíbara* of my country, that wasted mother whose exhaused breasts had failed her, whose prayers met only the inflexible will of heaven, and the misery of whose hut constituted her only solace on earth!

There came a time when her *guimbo* whimpered with the whimper of a purple child, whom death has been pulling forth little by little from the protective womb. There was no warm cactus fig that could overcome the chill hardening his skin; no scented bath that could allay the fever that melted him like wax. Fearfully, yet in a fury of passion, the mother walked up and down with him, her faith ignored by an inscrutable heaven, to which sometimes a *jíbara's* prayers do not reach. The medicine woman did not know how to stop the crying that now even Monsona Quintana felt as coming from her own bleeding womb.

Grimly, Anacleto awaited a double funeral; the children were mute for fear their laughter would disturb the dying child, and the mother's monotonous lament continued to be heard.

"Don't die, my precious *guimbo,* don't die; if you die, your Mother will be left all alone," she implored, appealing to any breath of consciousness remaining in the convulsed body, repeating each word as if it were part of a tragic lullaby, surrounding the dying child with a sweetness as of twenty calyxes.

But the *guimbo* died; he fled from his mother's arms as she was stiff with bitterness and fatigue. Death had reclaimed that rind of love which was little more than an aberration. Nobody dared to laugh or sing during the wake for the purple child; the whole community feared the mother's blasphemous heavenward glare.

I witnessed the burial of Monsona Quintana's purple child. I came across it as I was driving a government car one afternoon, trying to sell the lavish panorama that is our landscape to some North Americans. Anacleto and his friends were taking him to be buried in a small white box, with three wreaths of paper flowers carried by sniffling children covered with lice and tears; a sad retinue of barefooted angels who dared not look toward heaven.

In my country, friends, she who gives birth does indeed care for her young, even though many a tubercular *guimbo* is lost from her arms.

TRANSLATED BY NICK VANDEMOER

Alejo Carpentier

RETURN TO THE SEED

"What do you want, old man?"

The question fell from the scaffolding, over and over again. But the old man did not answer. He just kept going from place to place, prying, drawing from his throat a long monologue of incomprehensible phrases. The roof tiles had already fallen, covering the stone debris with their mosaic of fired clay. Up at the top, picks pried masonry stones loose, making them roll down a wooden canal, raising a cloud of lime and plaster dust. And through the embrasures—empty spaces like pulled teeth in the wall—were thrown, shedding their secrets, oval and square flat ceilings, cornices, garlands, dentils, astragals; and gummy paper hung from the façades like the molted skin of a serpent. A statue of Ceres with a broken nose and a graceless peplum, her headdress of ripe wheat streaked with black, was witnessing the demolition. Ceres stood erect in the back courtyard, on a fountain of grotesque blurred masks. When brightened by the sun at the hour of shadows, the fountain's gray fish yawned in tepid, mossy water, as with their round eyes they watched the workmen, black against the clear sky, reduce the secular height of the house. The old man had sat down at the foot of the statue, his chin resting on his shepherd's crook. He watched the up-and-down movement of the buckets in which valuable remains traveled. The muted street noises could be heard, while overhead the pulleys, harmonizing with the rhythm of iron striking stone, warbled like unpleasant and brazen birds.

Five o'clock struck. The cornices and scaffolding were deserted. Only stepladders were left behind, in preparation for the attack on the following day. The air turned cooler, freed of sweat, of blasphemies, of the screeching of ropes, of axles calling for the oil can, and of slaps on greasy backs. Dusk came more quickly for the pruned house. It was now draped in shadows at an hour when its fallen balustrade used to shed some glow from the sun on the façade. Ceres pressed her lips tightly. For the first time, the rooms would sleep without shutters, wide open on a scene of rubble.

286

Contrary to their wishes, several capitals lay among the weeds. The acanthus leaves uncovered their vegetable nature. A vine dared to advance its tentacles toward the Ionic volute, attracted by a certain familiar air. When night fell, the house was closer to the ground. Up high, a door frame still stood upright, shadow boards hanging from its disarranged hinges.

Then the old Negro man, who had not moved, made some strange grimaces, raking his staff over the flagstone cemetery.

The marble squares, white and black, flew up to the floors, covering the ground. The stones leaped accurately back into the holes in the walls. Walnut doors, together with all their nails, fitted themselves back into their door frames, while the screws of the hinges sank once more into their holes with swift rotating motion. In the dead quarry, lifted by the efforts of the flowers, the roof tiles gathered together their fragments, raising a sonorous clay whirlwind, only to fall in a shower over the frame of the roof. The house rose, brought back once more to its habitual proportions, modest and well groomed. Ceres became less gray. There were plenty of fish in the fountain once more. The murmur of its waters called back forgotten begonias.

The old man placed a key in the lock of the main door, and began to open the windows. His footsteps sounded hollow. When he lit the brass lamps, a yellow shiver ran over the oil portraits of the family, and people dressed in black whispered in every room, to the beat of spoons stirred in cups of chocolate.

Don Marcial, Marquis of Capellanias, lay on his deathbed, his breast covered with medals, and escorted by four tapers with long beards of melted wax.

The tapers slowly grew taller, sweating less. When they attained their natural size, a nun put them out, first getting a light. The wicks grew white, casting off snuff. The house was emptied of visitors, and carriages departed into the night. Don Marcial fingered an invisible keyboard, and opened his eyes.

Unclear and jumbled, the beams on the ceiling fell into place. The medicine bottles, the silk tassels, the scapulary at the head of the bed, the daguerreotypes, the shutters—all came out of the fog. When the doctor shook his head disconsolately, professionally, the patient felt better. He slept a few hours and awoke under the black and bushy-browed gaze of Father Anastasio. Once frank, detailed, laden with sins, his confession now became reticent, ashamed, full of concealment. And just what right, when all is said and done, did that Carmelite monk have to intrude into his life? Don Marcial found himself, suddenly, fallen on the floor in the middle of the room. Freed from a certain pressure at the temples, he arose with surprising speed. The naked woman, waking up on the brocade of the bed, sought skirts and waists, taking away with her, shortly thereafter, the rustle of her crushed silks and her perfume. Downstairs, in the closed carriage, hiding the tacks of the seat, lay an envelope containing gold coins.

Don Marcial did not feel well. As he straightened his tie in front of the dresser mirror, he seemed flushed. He went downstairs to his study where men of the law, lawyers and scribes, awaited him in order to proceed with the public auction of the house. Every effort had been useless. His possessions would go to the highest bidder, to the beat of a gavel striking a board. He greeted the men, and they left him alone. He was thinking of the mysteries of the written word, those black threads looped together and broken apart on broad sheets of paper, filigreed with sums, making and breaking agreements, sworn statements, alliances, testimonies, declarations, surnames, titles, dates, lands, trees, and stones; balls of string pulled from the inkwell and entwining themselves about a man's feet, forbidding him ways outside the law; a noose at one's throat, which pressed hard on the sordine on hearing the feared sound of words set free. His signature had betrayed him, complicating itself into knots and entangled in lawyers' affairs. Tied up by it, the man of flesh was becoming a man of paper.

It was dawn. The clock in the dining room had just struck six in the afternoon.

Months of mourning went by, darkened by ever increasing remorse. At first, the idea of bringing a woman into that room had seemed almost preposterous. But, little by little, his appetite for another body was displaced by growing scruples that ended in flagellation. One night, Don Marcial made his flesh bleed by beating himself with a belt; afterward, he felt an even stronger desire, but only of short duration. It was then that the Marquise returned, one evening, from her outing to the shores of the Almendares River. The horses of her carriage were wet only with their own sweat. But during the entire remainder of the day, they pounded the stable door with their hoofs, irritated, it seemed, by the immobility of some low clouds.

At sunset, a jug full of water broke in the Marquise's bath. Later, the May rains overflowed the pool. And that old black woman, somewhat wild but gentle as a dove, went about the yard murmuring, "Distrust the rivers, madam; distrust whatever is green and flows!" Not a day passed that the presence of running water was not revealed. But such a presence, finally, was but a cup of water spilled on a gown brought from Paris, the night they returned from the anniversary ball given by the captain general of the colony.

Many relatives appeared once more. Many friends came back. The chandeliers in the salon glowed bright and clear. The cracks in the walls mended. The piano turned into a clavichord. The palm trees lost several rings. The vines dropped from the first capitals of the pillars. Ceres' shadows disappeared, and the capitals seemed recently carved. More ardent, Marcial often spent entire evenings embracing the Marquise. Crow's feet, wrinkles, and double chins disappeared and the flesh became as firm as before. One day, a smell of fresh paint filled the house.

The blushing was sincere. Each night the panels of the screen were spread out further; skirts fell into darker corners, and there were new lace barriers. Finally, the Marquise blew out the candle. Only Marcial spoke in the darkness.

The couple left for the country in a large caravan of carriages— gleaming sorrel rumps, with silver bits and patent leather shining in the sun. But in the shade of the Easter flowers which reddened the interior portico of the house, they noticed that they had scarcely met. Marcial authorized the playing of national tunes and dances, to amuse himself a little during those days redolent with eau de Cologne, perfumes, benzoin baths, flowing hair, and sheets taken from wardrobes that shed bunches of vetiver roots when opened. There was a breath of fermented cane liquor floating on the breeze at nightfall. Flying low, the turkey buzzards announced the coming of reticent showers whose first drops, large and sonorous, were drunk by roof tiles so dry they had the ring of copper. After a certain particular dawn, prolonged by an ineffectual embrace, relieved of disagreements, and the wound having healed, both of them returned to the city. The Marquise changed her traveling suit for a bridal gown, and, as was the custom, the couple went to church to regain their freedom. Presents were returned to relatives and friends, and with a flourish of bronzes and a display of ornaments, each person took the road home. Marcial continued to visit Maria de las Mercedes for some time, until the day their rings were taken to the jeweler's to have the engraving removed. A new life was beginning for Marcial. In the house with the tall gates, Ceres was replaced by an Italian Venus, and the masks on the fountain raised their relief, almost imperceptibly, on seeing the brass lamps still burning when dawn had already arrived.

One night, after drinking heavily and growing dizzy with the smell of the cold tobacco left by his friends, Marcial had the strange feeling that the clocks in the house were striking five, then four-thirty, then four, then three-thirty . . . It was like remotely perceiving other possibilities. Like thinking, when one is enervated by sleeplessness, that one can walk on the ceiling with the floor for a ceiling, among furniture firmly fixed between the beams. It was a fleeting impression which did not leave the slightest trace in his soul since he was hardly given to meditating at that time.

And the day he reached his minority, a big party was given in the music room. He was happy to think that his signature had ceased to have any legal value and that the scribes and lawyers, together with all their termites, were erased from his world. He had come to the point where the courts ceased to be feared by those whose flesh was not wanted by the law. After fortifying himself with generous wines, the young man took down from the wall a guitar studded with mother-of-pearl, a psaltery, and a horn. Someone wound the clock that played the "Tirolesa de las Vacas," and "La Balada de los Lagos de Escocia." Someone else put his mouth to a hunting horn that slept curled up in its copper rings, on top of the red felt of the cupboard, next to the transverse flute brought from Aranjuez. Marcial, who was daringly flattering Miss Campoflorido, joined the merrymakers, picking out on the piano the melody to Tripili-Trapala while playing false accompanying chords. And they all went up to the attic, suddenly, remembering that the clothes and livery of the House of Capellanias were kept there, under the beams that were recovering their mortar. The court costumes lay between sheets frosted with camphor; there was also an ambassador's short sword, several firearms wrapped in greased cloth, a mantle of some Prince of the Church, and some long full-dress coats with damask buttons and blurry damp areas around the creases. The shadows harmonized with amaranth ribbons, yellow trinkets, faded tunics, and velvet flowers. A blacksmith's costume with a mesh of little balls, created for some Carnival masking, caused much applause. Miss Campoflorido rounded her powdered shoulders under a blood-red shawl which had been worn by a certain grandmother on occasions of great family decisions in order to brighten the failing flame of some rich Order of St. Clare nuns.

Masquerading, the young people returned to the music room. Marcial, wearing a governor's tricornered hat, struck three blows on the floor with his cane, and thus gave the signal to start the waltzing, which the girls' mothers found horribly improper for young ladies, considering that they allowed their waists to be encircled by their partners, the men placing their hands on the stays of the corsets which all the girls had had made according to the recent model in *The Garden of Styles*. The doorways grew dark with the presence of domestics, stableboys, servants who came from their distant quarters and suffocating mezzanines, to watch that noisy party with admiration. Afterward, they played blindman's buff and hide-and-seek. Marcial, hiding with Miss Campoflorido behind a Chinese screen, planted a kiss on the nape of her neck, receiving in reply a perfumed handkerchief whose edges of Brussels lace had a certain body warmth. And when the young ladies left at dusk for their bulwarks and towers, painted gray-black above the sea, the young men went to the Dance Hall where a mulatto woman wearing large anklets swayed deliciously, and never lost—no matter how excited the clog dance—her high-heeled slippers. And since it was Carnival, next door, the people at the Cabildo Arara Tres Ojos raised a thunderous drumbeating behind the separating wall, in a patio planted with pomegranate trees. Climbing on tables and benches, Marcial and his friends praised the charms of a Negress with graying, kinky hair, who became beautiful again, almost desirable, when she glanced over her shoulder as she danced with a hearty, challenging gesture.

The visits of Don Abundio—the family lawyer and executor— became more frequent. He would sit down gravely at the head of Marcial's bed, letting his hardwood cane fall to the floor in order to wake him up ahead of time. As Marcial's eyes opened, they fell on a dandruff-covered alpaca frock coat whose shiny sleeves were collecting title deeds and income. Finally, there was only a reasonable pension left, so calculated as to put an end to all nonsense. It was then that Marcial had wanted to join the Royal Seminary of St. Charles.

After mediocre examinations, he frequented the cloisters, understanding less and less each time of the explanations given by the monks. His world of ideas became emptier and emptier. What at the beginning had been an ecumenical assembly of peplums, doublets, gullets, and wigs—controversial and sophistic—now took on the immobility of a wax museum. Marcial felt satisfied with a scholastic exposition of systems, accepting as good whatever was said to be good in any textbook. The words "Lion," "Ostrich," "Whale," "Jaguar," could be seen written over the pictures in the natural history book. In the same manner, "Aristotle," "St. Thomas," "Bacon," "Descartes," headed dark pages where boring interpretations of the universe were catalogued, at the margin of some thick chapter. Little by little, Marcial stopped studying these interpretations, finding himself relieved of a heavy weight. His mind became light and gay, admitting but one, instinctive concept of things. Why think about a prism when winter's clear light lent greater detail to the fortress of the port? An apple that falls from the tree is incitement only for one's teeth. A foot in a tub of water is but a foot in a tub of water. The day he left the seminary he forgot all books. A gnome became a ghost once more; a specter became synonymous with phantom; an iguana was a creature with a hard shell and spikes down his back.

Several times, walking rapidly, his heart pounding, he had gone to see the women who gossip behind blue doors at the foot of the city wall. The memory of the one wearing embroidered slippers and sweet basil leaves behind her ears pursued him, on hot afternoons, like a toothache. But one day, the anger and the threats of a certain father confessor made him cry with fright. He had fallen for the last time into the sheets of hell, he renounced forever wanderings in little-frequented streets, his last-minute cowardices which made him return home furious after leaving behind him a certain cracked sidewalk—a sign, as he walked with his eyes on the ground, that he should turn back in order to trample on that perfumed threshold.

Now he was living through his mystical crisis, full of prohibitions, Pascal lambs, porcelain doves, Virgins with celestial blue mantles, gold paper stars, Magi, angels with wings of swans, a donkey, an ox, and a terrible St. Dionisius who appeared to him in his dreams with a hollow space between his shoulders, and the vacillating walk of someone searching for something lost. The saint would bump into his bed and Marcial would awaken, frightened, reaching for his rosary of deaf beads. The wicks, in their little pools of oil, shed a sad light on images that were recovering their original color.

The furniture grew taller. It became increasingly more difficult for Marcial to hold his forearms on the edge of the dining table. The armoires with ornate cornices, broadened their fronts. Stretching their torsos, the Moors on the staircase held their torches closer to the balustrade of the landing. The chairs became deeper and the rocking chairs had a tendency to go over backward. No longer did he need to fold his legs when he reclined in the bathtub with marble curtain rings.

One morning, as he was reading a licentious book, Marcial suddenly felt like playing with his lead soldiers asleep in their wooden boxes. He hid the volume once more, under the bowl of the washbasin, and opened a closet sealed by cobwebs. His study table was too small to hold so many people. Therefore, Marcial sat down on the floor. He arranged the grenadiers in lines of eight. Behind them, the artillery soldiers with their cannons, swabs, and linstocks. Closing the ranks were the fifers and kettledrummers, with an escort of drummers. The mortars had a spring that allowed them to fling a grass ball more than a yard away.

"Pum! . . . Pum! . . . Pum! . . ."

Horses, flagbearers, drummers would fall. He had to be called three times by the colored boy, Eligio, before making up his mind to go wash his hands and go downstairs to the dining room.

From that day on, Marcial kept the habit of sitting on the floor. When he realized the advantages of such a habit he was surprised not to have thought of it sooner. Pressed against the velvet of the cushions, the grown-ups perspired a great deal. Some of them smelled of notaries—like Don Abundio—because they ignored what it was like to stretch out on the cool marble floor. Only from the floor can one encompass completely the angles and perspectives of a room. There is beauty in the wood, mystery in the paths of insects, shaded corners that are ignored from a man's height. When it rained, Marcial would hide under the clavichord. Each clap of thunder made the resonant box tremble, setting all its notes singing. From the heavens, lightning fell to build a dome of pauses: organ, pine grove in the wind, cricket mandolins.

That morning they locked him in his room. He could hear whispering throughout the house, and the dinner they served him was much too rich for an ordinary day. There were six pies from the Alameda pastry shop—when ordinarily, he was allowed to eat only two, on Sundays, after Mass. He amused himself looking at travel scenes until the ever-increasing buzzing made him peek through the blinds. Men dressed in black were arriving, carrying a box with bronze handles. He felt like crying, but at that moment the coachman, Melchior, appeared, showing a broad smile above his noisy boots. They began to play chess. Melchior was a knight. He was a king. Using the tiles of the floor for a board he could advance one at a time while Melchior could jump one ahead and two to the side, or vice versa. The game continued until after sunset, when the Commercial Firemen passed by.

When he got up, he went to kiss his father's hand as he lay on his sickbed. The Marquis was feeling better and spoke to his son in his usual manner and with the usual examples; the "yes, father," and "no, father," fitted the beads of his rosary of questions like the altar boys' replies at the service of the Mass. Marcial respected the Marquis but for a reason no one could have supposed. He respected him because he was tall, and went to balls with his chest resplendent with decorations; because he envied him his saber and the bullion embroidery of his militia officer's uniform; because at Christmas he had eaten a whole turkey stuffed with almonds and raisins, to win a bet; because on a certain occasion, probably intending to beat her, he had carried off to his bedroom one of the mulatto women, who was sweeping the rotunda. Marcial, hidden behind a curtain, saw her emerge later, weeping and unbuttoned, happy with her punishment, for she was the one who usually got to empty the compote bowls that were returned to the pantry.

His father was a terrible and magnanimous person whom one must love after God. For Marcial, he was more God than God himself, because his gifts were daily and tangible. But he preferred the God in Heaven because He bothered him less.

When the furniture had grown a little taller, and Marcial knew as no one else what was under the beds, armoires, and escritoires, he hid a great secret from everybody: life had no charm outside the company of the coachman Melchior. Neither God, nor his father, nor the gilded Bishop of the Corpus procession, were as important as Melchior.

Melchior came from far away. He was the grandson of vanquished princes. In his kingdom there were elephants, hippopotamuses, tigers, and giraffes. There, men did not work as Don Abundio did, inside dark rooms stuffed with papers. They lived by being more cunning than the animals. One of them had taken a great crocodile from the blue lake by piercing it with a spear hidden in the tightly pressed bodies of twelve roasted geese. Melchior knew songs that were easy to learn, because the words had no meaning and were repeated often. Melchior stole candy from the kitchens; he escaped at night through the stable door, and once he stoned the Civil Guards, disappearing presently into the shadows of the Street of Woe.

On rainy days Melchior's boots were set out to dry in front of the kitchen fire. Marcial would have liked to have had feet large enough to fill such boots. The right one was called Calambin. The left one, Calamban. That man who subdued wild horses by merely sticking two fingers in their thick underlip; that man made of velvet and spurs who wore such tall silk hats, also knew how cool the marble floor could be in summer, and he would hide under the furniture pieces of fruit or pies snatched from the trays intended for the grand salon. Marcial and Melchior held in common a secret cache of bonbons and almonds which they called the "Uri, uri, urah," with prolonged peals of laughter. Both of them had explored the house from top to bottom, and they were the only ones who knew there was a small cellar under the hall, and that in a useless attic over the servants' quarters, twelve dusty butterflies had just lost their wings in a box of broken crystalware.

When Marcial acquired the habit of breaking things, he forgot about Melchior; he got closer to the dogs. There were several in the house. The large tiger-like one; the hound that dragged her teats; the greyhound, too old to play with; and the woolly one the other dogs chased at certain particular times and the maids had to lock up.

Marcial preferred Canelo because he dragged shoes out of the bedrooms and dug up the rosebushes in the yard. Always black with coal or covered with red clay, Canelo devoured everybody else's food, squealed without cause, and hid stolen bones at the foot of the fountain. From time to time, he also sucked recently laid eggs, knocking the hen into the air with a brusque blow with his snout. Everyone aimed kicks at Canelo. But Marcial would get sick whenever they took him away. And the dog would return triumphant, wagging his tail, after having been abandoned beyond the poorhouse, to regain a position which the others in spite of their special capabilities in the hunt or as vigilant guardians never did achieve.

Canelo and Marcial urinated together. Sometimes they chose the Persian rug in the living room, making designs in its wool like clouds that spread slowly. That cost them a beating with a belt. But the lashes of the belt did not hurt as much as some grown-ups thought. They turned out, on the other hand, to be admirable pretexts for setting up a howling concert, and to provoke compassion in the neighbors. When the cross-eyed woman out in the shed called his father "a barbarian," Marcial would look at Canelo, and smile with his eyes. They would cry a little more, in order to earn a cookie, and then everything would be forgotten. They both ate dirt, they rolled over in the sun, drank from the fishpond, looked for shade and perfume at the foot of the sweet basil bush. When it was hot, the damp stones would become densely peopled. There would be the gray goose, with a bag hanging between her knock-kneed legs; the old rooster with a raw behind; the lizard that said "uri, urah," as he pulled from his throat a pink tie; the sab juba born in a city without women; the rat that blocked his hole with a tortoise shell. One day, they pointed out the dog to Marcial.

"Bow-wow, wow!" he said.

He spoke his own language. He had achieved supreme freedom. Now he tried to reach with his hand objects that were beyond the reach of his hands.

Hunger, thirst, heat, pain, cold. As soon as Marcial reduced his perceptions to these essential realities, he renounced light, already an accessory. He did not know his name. Baptism with its disagreeable salt, now removed, he no longer wanted the sense of smell, or hearing, or even of sight. His hands brushed pleasant forms. He was a completely tactile and sensitive being. The universe came in through his pores. Then he closed his eyes that could only make out nebulous giants, and penetrated a warm body, wet, full of darkness, dying. The body feeling him curled up inside its own substance, slipped toward life.

But now time ran more quickly, drawing out his last hours. The minutes sounded like cards slipping under the thumb of a player.

Birds returned to the egg in a whirl of feathers. Fishes covered the roe leaving a flaking of scales at the bottom of the pond. Palm trees folded their palms, disappearing into the earth like closed fans. The trunks absorbed the leaves, and the ground pulled at everything that belonged to it. Thunder resounded in the corridors. Hair grew back on the skin of the gloves. Wool blankets unraveled, filling out the fleece of distant lambs. Armoires, escritoires, beds, crucifixes, tables, blinds, flew into the night searching for their ancient roots at the edge of the jungle. Everything that was nailed down fell apart. A brigantine anchored no one knows where hastily took back to Italy the marble of the floor and fountain. The arms collection, the hardware, the keys, the copper pots, the horses' bits, all melted away swelling a river of metal which roofless galleries channeled toward earth. Everything was metamorphosed, returned to its origin. Clay returned to clay leaving a wilderness instead of a house.

When the workmen returned the following day to continue the demolition, they found the work already done. Someone had carried off the statue of Ceres, sold the previous day to an antique dealer. After complaining to the syndicate, the men sat down on the benches in a municipal park. One of them recalled the widespread story of a certain Marquise de Capellanias, drowned one May afternoon, among the arrowroot of the Almendares River. But no one paid attention to the story because the sun traveled from east to west, and the hours that grow to the right of the clock should be stretched, lazily, since they are the ones that most assuredly lead to death.

TRANSLATED BY ZOILA NELKEN

Tomás Blanco

THE CHILD'S GIFTS:
A Twelfth Night Tale

THIS is the story of three men of good will who lived in a faraway time, many long centuries ago.

Each of them dwelt in a different region of the Earth. And each, by reason of his uprightness, his wisdom, and his benevolence, was prince of princes in that remote corner of the world where he dwelt.

One was a man ripe in years, strong and well-knit, tall and spare, with firm red lips, rosy skin, and flowing snowy beard. He had eyes the color of emerald, with a gleam of polished steel in their depths. And, as his country lay in the pathway of the setting sun—beyond the western horizon—he was known to all as Monarch of the West. But his name, his true name, was no more—and no less—than Balthasar.

The other was a man in the middle of the journey, of medium height, robust and muscular. His skin had the honeyed tinge of the golden tobacco of Havana, of the choice cinnamon of Ceylon. His eyes were living pools of coffee, dark and depthless. His features were full-fleshed, and his beard, iron of hue, sparse and coarse, was neatly trimmed to form a goatee. His hot land lay athwart the sun-drenched confines of the South. And so he bore the sonorous title of King of the South. His real name, however, was just Melchior.

The third, the last, was one of those persons whose age is hard to define, who seemed young, but who was probably older than he looked. His skin was the color of old vellum or of burnt ivory, and his thick, straight hair had the bluish black hue of ebony. Short rather than tall, heavy-set, with enigmatic dark, slanting, almond-shaped eyes, and beardless. His kingdom stretched along the immense reaches of the East. And so he was called Emperor of the Orient. As such he was known, even though at birth his parents had named him Gaspar.

So, once upon a time, there were these three—kings among

kings—lords of their vast domains; and, besides, they were re-
nowned—all three of them—as great and learned wise men,
skilled in numbers and versed in letters, interpreters of signs and
portents, nightly scanners of the stars. Perhaps because they were
so wise and so deep-seeing, they were, above everything else, three
generous men.

This wisdom and generosity were the only links between the
three. Everything else separated them. For even though each of
them had, from time to time, received vague word of the other
two, none had laid eyes upon the others, nor had they any hope of
meeting, or talking together, or coming to understand one another.
And the fact that each of them was the ruler of powerful and
dissimilar nations separated them even more than distance.

The nation that gave allegiance to Gaspar was a great nation
with a history stretching back to antiquity. But it was, above all, a
nation of unshakable Faith. During its long existence, as it acquired history, it could not escape, at the same time, accumulating
suffering. But it also accumulated cruelty. And this icy passion—
the thing that harmed it most—often perverted its unique gift of
redemption, blighting the blessing and the ripening of the firm fruit
of its Faith. It was like frost striking the lemon trees in flower, and
with its needles and pincers of ice checking the flow of the life-
giving sap to the tender shoots, blasting the now sterile bloom.

The people governed by Balthasar lived on Hope. This gave them
dreams and confidence. It bore them up in disaster. It sustained
them in hours of trial. Thanks to it, and to it alone, they endured.
But ever prone to forget this, they all too often let pride become
their master. And this barren passion destroyed the innate grace of
their own Hope, the ever-flowing spring, the fountainhead of life
for them. Then it was like a consuming drought that turned the
fields of wheat to straw and chaff before the grain could fill the
ears.

The people who followed Melchior as their supreme leader were
a good people. It was a people disposed—predisposed—toward
sweetness, light-heartedness, candor. The essence of their spirit
was Charity, a wondrous perfumed flower, like no other, that
bloomed and bloomed again on the desolate waste of an old, deep-
rooted discouragement. But because of this discouragement which
gnawed at their stout hearts, bruised of soul, wanting in Hope,
barren of life-giving Faith, they were quick to fall victim to terror

and panic. As a result, they were often seized by sudden wrath, by unpredictable explosions of rage frequent in the disheartened and frustrated. When this happened, this volatile and violent passion blinded them. Like a blood-red bolt of lightning it deprived them of the clear, kindly light of their fructifying Charity. It was like the furious blast of the tropical hurricane, which passes in roaring flight, leveling the crops, snapping the tall palms, ripping the rustling banana, deracinating the coffee groves, mutilating the proud trunks of the mightiest trees.

Thus, each of the three peoples had one unique and supreme quality—each different from the other—which heartened and sustained it, which made existence bearable, fruitful, even magnificent at times. It was the never-failing consolation for all their failures. It was the divining rod that discovered the spring of their vitality; the magic key which opened the vein of the simple human condition hidden in the animal vitals. But each people also possessed its peculiar capital defect, its dominant passion, which was its greatest vice and the thing which did it most harm. And lacking the two virtues which were the ornament and distinction of the other two nations, this shortcoming denatured, perverted, and undermined—when difficulties arose—the very virtue each possessed. And then horror, stupidity, brutality slipped their chains.

And those three famous leaders of their peoples, Melchior, Gaspar, and Balthasar, wise men though they were, were unable to discover the reason for such things or to find a remedy for these tribulations. Perhaps they themselves did not abound in what their countrymen needed, and could not give it. But as the three of them were exceptionally generous, they spared no effort to supply the lack. They loved their peoples, and wanted to see them healthier and happier, nobler and better. This unremitting, never satisfied concern gave them a sad air.

But it came to pass one day that the three of them—remote and distant each from the other—all smiled at the same time. They smiled without knowing why. That night the Star appeared for the first time. It was a new, unaccountable Star that hung motionless halfway between the spreading horizon and the peak of the zenith. The new Star shone and glittered with a light that cast an irresistible spell, at once eloquent and unutterable.

The three wise kings beheld it, and they marveled. In the calm night, in the midst of the silence, the Star spoke, calling them without sound and without words in the mute, gentle, sincere language that only the heart can understand. And the three of them understood. They were men of good will.

First of all they had to make ready for a long journey, following that hidden secret of the heavenly light. At the end of the journey the veil of the mystery would be torn asunder.

All night long the Star gleamed, fixed, steady, with a rare light shimmering blue and gold rays. The wise men watched it. The more they observed it, the clearer and more directly they felt its all-powerful, portent-filled spell. Dawn found them lost in contemplation of the wonder.

Three successive nights the Star appeared in the same place on the firmament, always with its same alluring spell. The three wise men spent the three nights in vigil, and, on the fourth they set out upon the route leading to the unknown spot of the Earth the Star was pointing to with its rays.

Each of the wise kings traveled completely alone, without retinue or attendants, not even grooms to look after the animals they were riding. Nor were they armed. Only the exceptional quality of their mounts, the pomp of their robes, and the richness of garb and trappings revealed the fact that they were lords and monarchs. The reason for such display was that the three knew that they were setting out in search of a Personage of high rank, and they hoped thus to do him fitting honor, coming before him with all show of outward respect as an earnest of the inner fervor which moved them. In their wise innocence they believed this indispensable.

As they observed the Star, during the three successive nights they kept vigil, they came to understand many things, but not all. They knew that, for their own good and that of their peoples, they had to seek the presence of a certain unknown exalted Personage, one who was lord and master of harmony and prince of peace; the monarch of three magnificent invisible empires: King of Concord, Comradeship, and Brotherhood.

Before they set out the three wise kings sought the most beautiful and richest jewel of their kingdoms to take with them as a simple token of their homage.

They spent two full days seeking and choosing among their

manifold treasures. Nothing pleased them, nothing satisfied them, neither the rich cloth so skillfully woven, nor the rarest of gems, nor the most delicate examples of the goldsmith's art.

On the third day, therefore, they decided to appeal to their peoples. They made known the need and difficulty which confronted them; and in no time at all a host of magnates, merchants, and artists came forward with riches beyond number. But to no avail. Until finally as the afternoon shadows of the third day were falling there came before Melchior a poor man, a beggar, ragged and unshod.

And he said to him, "I will give you the most valued treasure of this nation. Give me a vessel of cork, with a cover of the same rough material, unadorned. I will fill it with the finest dust. It will be gold dust, the incomparable gold of Charity."

So he did, and good Melchior was happy with his gift of fine gold.

On the same day, and at the same vesper hour, there came before Gaspar an old anchorite, gaunt and feeble, almost blind.

And he spoke after this wise: "I know the jewel of greatest price of this land. I have it and I will give it to you. Give me a clay flask with a stopper made of clay, too. I will place the jewel in the flask. What I bring to you are crystalline pearls of the purest incense, of the fragrant incense of Faith."

As he had promised so he did, taking the gift from his bosom. And Gaspar accepted it and was pleased and satisfied with his aroma-laden incense.

At the same twilight hour Balthasar was timidly approached by a pale-cheeked girl, a friendless orphan, on the threshold of maidenhood.

All confusion, she murmured gently, "If you would give me a little box of pine wood I would return it to your hands filled with a treasure, the finest and most precious to be found in our land. Because I bring you here these grains of myrrh, new gathered and odorous, delicate and stimulant, the restoring, imperishable myrrh of sweet Hope."

And immediately Balthasar saw that what she said was true, and he thanked her and received her gift. And he was happy with his fine myrrh.

The three kings thanked, to the best of their ability, the three donors. And at once, without loss of time, they ordered their mounts to be made ready and saddled. When night had fallen and the Star once more appeared in the sky they mounted and set out, each following his own road, all by himself, toward the unknown.

Balthasar was mounted on a spirited horse, jet-black in color and with a mane of fire. It was a beautiful creature, many hands high, fleet of limb, broad of chest, head carried proud. Its curbed impatience gave elegance to its movements.

Gaspar was riding a white dromedary with golden hoofs. Its slender legs were firm, high, and sinewy as befits a nomad wanderer. It carried its delicate head high, and its eyes and lashes were those of a blonde maiden. Its bearing was at once inquiring and haughty. The eager rhythm of its swift gait as it moved revealed an exotic grace.

Melchior was seated upon a solid, docile elephant of a rare shade of gray, a bluish silver. The handsome animal, noble of appearance and stock, had a knowing eye, a bellowing trumpet, huge tusks. There was great majesty in its firm, measured tread.

Thus each pursued his own way until the three met at a crossroads. Three greetings sounded in unison.

"Well met, gentlemen."

"Your health, noble travelers."

"Welcome, brothers."

They had never seen one another before. But they soon learned, all three, who the other two were. And they learned of the journey each was making, and the similar motive which had impelled the three. And they rejoiced. For that reason, they traveled the rest of the road together, following that Star, in good company.

Afternoons followed mornings, and mornings afternoons; hours of sunlight succeeded hours of darkness. Until one frosty dawn, on the outskirts of a little village, the Star came to rest at last above a rustic stable. The three wise travelers realized that they had come to the end of their strange adventure.

In the vague light of daybreak Melchior, Gaspar, and Balthasar dismounted. With great courtliness they asked permission at the stable door to enter. A humble workman received them warmly. An odor of pine gum, cedar, cypress, satinwood emanated from his person. One had only to look at him to see that he was a just man, a good man. But definitely he was not the lofty Personage they were seeking. An inner conviction assured them of that.

They stood hesitant in the doorway, bewildered, not knowing what to say. They were afraid they might have made a mistake.

Suddenly, amidst the shadows of the stable, the presence of a babe in a manger, haloed by the tenuous blues and pale golds of the Star's light, was revealed to them. A mule and an ox were warming him with their steaming breath. And a beautiful gentle young woman caressed him.

It was a newborn babe, almost naked, helpless, weak. Yet now there could be no doubt. From perplexity the three kings passed to amazement. That newborn babe, he, he was the lofty Personage they were seeking. There could be no mistake. The light of an inner assurance told them so. They entered with firm tread.

With bows and obeisance they laid before him the gifts they had brought. And the three spoke brief and identical words.

"I bring the only thing worthy of you in my land, the most precious treasure we possess. I offer it to you in the name of my people."

Melchior laid the vessel of rude cork containing the pollen of gold beside the manger; Gaspar, his flask of clay with the pearls of incense; and Balthasar, his wooden box holding the grains of myrrh.

Asleep in the straw of the manger, the babe smiled, smiled. . . .

And making new obeisance and bows the three wise kings departed from the stable. Happy, they set out for their respective lands.

The day was breaking. Shepherds from far-off approached singing carols:

> Scatter jasmine petals
> And orange blossoms white
> On the crystal maiden
> Who gave birth tonight.
>
> Long live cinnamon
> And honey of gold;
> The silken petaled lily
> And carnation flower bold.

Once more, homeward bound, the three wise kings reached the crossroads where their paths divided. They had taken leave of one another with embraces and protestations of friendship, with a sincere display of brotherly love.

Each set his face toward home. But suddenly the three halted. Out of the East came an old, purblind hermit. A tattered beggar was approaching from the South. And from the West, a pale young girl. They were the donors of the incense, the gold and the myrrh which the kings had borne. They came looking for their princes, urged on by keen impatience and deep curiosity.

They wanted to settle their doubts, to learn whether the gift had been fitting, adequate. To make sure of the acceptability, the happy choice of the offering chosen. To learn the details of all that had taken place.

Beneath the afternoon sun still blazing and reverberant, the girl, the hermit, and the beggar arrived with one accord. The kings dismounted from their beasts and hurried forward to meet them. They stood, an animated group, at the intersection of the crossroads. That meeting point of remote highways came alive with questions and exclamations.

The generous wise men wished to give the new arrivals some refreshment first, but they refused.

"Give us, before anything else, the grace and favor of the word," spoke the hermit.

The girl and the beggar made a gesture of assent. The hermit continued, "At least answer these questions: What have you brought back with you? What did you set out to find? And what did you receive in return for your gifts?"

It fell to Balthasar, as the oldest, to make reply, "It is plain that we set out to seek nothing. We wished only to enter the presence of the Prince of Peace. We did not go to seek anything. On the contrary, we wanted to give—as well you know—the best we had. We bring back nothing but a gentle rejoicing. The mighty Hierarch we sought was a newborn babe who smiled in his dreams . . ."

Silence followed. And all stood thoughtful. Even the dromedary, the elephant, and the horse seemed to be reflecting.

After a long pause, Melchior employed the drawn-out moment to take from his hampers provisions to offer the recent arrivals.

Gaspar began to pull mats, rugs, and pillows from his fardels to serve as seats and cloths. Balthasar remembered that the three weary travelers were his guests, too, and he reached into his saddlebags.

It was then that the miracle took place. In full view of all.

Each of the wise men found in his luggage the very same gift he had left in the stable. In addition, all three found an exact replica of the gift of each of the other two. Now each of them had a bowl filled with *that* gold, a box filled with *that* myrrh, and a flask of *that* incense.

The three kings thought of their peoples and were filled with joy. They rejoiced at the thrice multiplied grace which, on their return, they would give back to all the people. They made room on the haunches of the elephant, the dromedary, and the horse for the beggar, the hermit, and the maiden. And with all haste they set out for home.

The journey back seemed to them long, so very long, endlessly long. . . .

From what I have been told, they are still on the way. They have not yet arrived.

But in the air crystalline voices from afar sing on high:

"Peace on earth!"

"Good will to men!"

TRANSLATED BY HARRIET DE ONÍS

Dutch Section

INTRODUCTION

IF some giant were to toss a stone far up the arc of the Lesser
Antilles, it might fall near Saba—itself a five-square-mile volcanic
rock—St. Eustatius, or that third of Sint Maarten that is Dutch.
The larger islands of the Netherlands Antilles—Curaçao, Aruba,
and Bonaire—lie off the coast of Venezuela and are, as is that
country, sustained largely by *black gold, oil.* Surinam, on the continent of South America, one of the three Guianas, is by far the
largest country on the Atlantic under Dutch influence. Though
there had been Dutch colonization there as early as 1624, the area
underwent the usual exchanges of ownership until, in 1677, at the
Peace of Breda, the English ceded their then colony to the Dutch
in exchange for New Amsterdam, better known as New York.

Here again, as all through the islands, to fill the gap left after the
banning of the slave trade, a great variety of people were brought
in. To the basic unit of the Dutch were added, after the Negroes,
Portuguese, Indians (both Moslem and Hindu), Indonesians, Jewish families of British nationality, Syrians, and countless more. A
Surinamer might be, then, of almost any origin, and the composite
Surinamer is indeed an international man.

The problem of communication has, for Surinam especially, but
also for all the islands, been a considerable one. All these varied
people had to be able to make themselves understood, to buy, sell,
barter, and work out the myriad details of life. As with pidgin
English, that *lingua franca* of Far Eastern ports which is
spoken by some forty million people, the West Indies too have
developed their several vernaculars. Even in Barbados, which is
one of the few islands with a continuity of language, the dialect is
rich and varied, many words current in eighteenth century England, for instance, being still in use. On the other hand, many
more are slang, amusing inventions, illiteracies, portmanteau
words which add imaginative depth to the language. Some examples, from Frank Collymore's *Notes for a Glossary of Words*

and Phrases of Barbadian Dialect, are as follows: *"peradventure.* This word, now archaic in Standard English, is still used locally." *"blam* is a portmanteau word formed from slam and bang, as, *The door just blammed."* And *"birdspeed.* Very fast. *He went down the road birdspeed."* And *"dontcarish.* A very useful compound," writes Mr. Collymore, "for which it is difficult to find an exact synonym." And one more example: *"downalong.* (adj.) Applied to anyone from the other British West Indian islands. *But listen to she and she downalong talk!"*

In the islands and that section of the mainland under Dutch control, at least two dialects are prevalent. Papiamento, a dialect based on Spanish, is spoken on the islands; in Surinam, Taki-taki or Sranan-Tongo, a dialect based on English, is not only spoken but written as well; newspapers and literary magazines both carry stories in Sranan-Tongo as well as in Dutch. Ivan T. Sanderson, in an interesting essay on Surinam, gives an example of a proverb in Taki-taki: *"Sekrepatoe no habi wiwiri, a kari hen wefi kisi loso,"* which, put another way, comes out to be "The turtle has no hair, but he calls his wife to delouse him." He adds that "one has to know that *sekrepatoe* is an Amerindian name for water-tortoise, that hair is considered in Africa to be wiry, and that the ticks which adhere to tortoises are called kiskisi."

In Haiti, though French is spoken for formal occasions, that product of the linguistic melting pot, Creole, is generally used; in Martinique and Guadeloupe a patois is spoken, as is a dialect in Cuba, while a variety of new words and special pronunciations are added in Puerto Rico. One of the wonders of the islands is that so great a measure of communication has been achieved.

And in another way, all these stories, from these very different peoples and places, speak back and forth to each other. For instance, put Pedro Juan Soto's story alongside of Austin Clarke's; or note the sophistication of mind behind the stories of Albert Helman, say, and Pierre Duprey. All in all, the imaginative works collected together here form a kind of anthological magic lantern which sheds, I hope, through its many facets, a many-colored light on the green islands of the Antilles.

Cola Debrot

THE GAUCHO

THE sultry wind
strokes the dry lips
of the gaucho,
plays with the mane
and tail of his horse.
Three weeks long the animals have grazed,
quenched their thirst,
day after day
without caring.
Three weeks long,
but now the herd has broken up.
It can no longer
restrain its fury.
The herd in stampede
charges toward an unknown goal.
The animals rush onwards
life steams from their nostrils.
How alike
are these animals
with one or two exceptions
that stare from the corners
of their glassy eyes,
the evil eye
as is said
when later they speak,
much later,
of the catastrophe.
The gaucho holds his whip ready
The horse has become indifferent flesh
Without intent
with instincts numbed
The gaucho stares into the distance

at the visible setting of the sun
that triples itself
between drab green lanes of cloud.
He hesitates between murmurings
and memories.
Murmurings
of the Virgin del Valle
of the Virgin de Coromoto.
Memories
of the willingness
of the putas of the llano.
The virgins and the putas,
the maidens and the whores,
they have the same names
Maria Margareta Magdalena
Perhaps I won't make it tonight
They have the same nice names
They sing with angel throats
or warble in the brothels
The clouds are hunting in space
What does it matter,
They warble and they caress
It is ominously quiet on earth
Pray for us
Pray for the gaucho. Amen.

TRANSLATED BY ESTELLE REED DEBROT.

Albert Helman

MY MONKEY WEEPS

Somehow I just can't remember what day it was that the hunter came to my door and sold me the monkey. He carried in his basket the fresh-killed game, still warm. His laugh was full and loud as he lifted the cover to display the blood-dripping flesh. All this I remember, but I don't know any more whether there was sunshine or rain that day.

On the hunter's shoulder sat the monkey he had caught with one quick grasp, without a blow or a shot. He had kept it as a dumb companion, and he brought it on his errant passings through the city—for cities are lonely and empty to a hunter who is at home with the dangers of the jungle and the swamp.

There were two qualities in the monkey that had attracted me— his contorting face and his tail. Between these poles pulsed his whole being. His grimace began at the flat, stuck-out nose, then expanded and circled round the two ears that were ridiculous miniatures of human ears.

Through his grimace his white teeth twinkled timidly, and a net of fine wrinkles formed around his sly little eyes. When I looked more closely I saw that the contortion of his face went further, spreading from the corners of his mouth toward his long arms; the thin, mobile fingers were the fringe of his grimace. His whole body was a grimace, held together by his small middle.

But the marvel of the monkey lay in the blend of tragic seriousness and aimless contortion. The seriousness was his tail. Whenever the tail was still it curved in a line so elegant that it might be either an ornament or a purpose of existence. But suddenly he would become like a fool seeking to understand a profound phrase; he achieved a stable contradictoriness.

The tail could move with the slow menace of an accusing finger pointed at an adulterous wife; it could swing back and forth like a lash in a monastic penance. But the tail held my attention most when it was curled in a little noose around a post or around one of his legs. When I looked at the tail I forgot the vacuous contortions of his grimace.

The tail was the seat of his understanding, the tail strove toward wisdom, the tail was his will, the instrument of his desires, the pendulum of his balance, the sorrow of his homesickness for the forest. It was through his tail that the monkey acquired a resemblance to man. But if I suddenly looked at him it was the grimace that I saw first; then he was a stupid beast, with exaggerated movements, an idiot creature showing amusement at things he could not understand. His contortions made me forget to look at his tail. While I wondered at this antithesis in my monkey the curling tail snaked up to the grimace of his head.

When the hunter saw my interest in the monkey he wanted to sell it to me on the spot. For a hunter is anything but sentimental and his first concern is profit despite his daily contact with nature and nature's unselfishness, with herbivorae, dicotyledons, and the like. But I was sentimental enough to want to forget what I paid for my monkey, for I saw him as a priceless treasure.

It didn't work out as I wanted. It was just because of my wish to forget about the price that I remember to the cent how much I paid. I handed over to the hunter exactly nine and a half guilders in two hard rijksdaalders, four guilders, and two kwartjes. He put the coins in a little green crocheted purse which he pulled out from under the pheasants in his basket. But, strangely enough, I can't remember any more the sort of day it was when I bought the monkey.

The animal made absolutely no objection to coming into my possession, and this came as a disappointment to me, for we are all too accustomed to the classic example of the faithful dog and the fable of the lion. I had bargained hard with the hunter and I had knocked down the price by half, and if the monkey had had the slightest understanding or intuition he would have seen that I did not value him highly or think much of my status of ownership. But the thoughtless indifference he showed at becoming my property proved that he postured more with his smirk than he reasoned with his tail. This disposition epitomized the essence of his monkey existence.

Man poses often enough, but a monkey poses all the time. Man reflects; a monkey never. Yet the combination of these two truths is common to both—in man by chance, in the monkey by nature.

The hunter went away, out of my ken, leaving me the happy owner of a gray-brown animal as big as a dog, with a leering smirk as big as a man and a tail as long as the whole world.

But no. The curl of his tail was like an eye, a mean little eye through which a ragged philosopher peered at the world; the tail, the sixth sense, curved like a perverse orchid, cone-shaped like an artfully stylized anus. Everything would have been fine but for the monkey's inanity and his complete indifference as to who was his master and who and what his new master was.

But his interest did not go beyond what was immediately in front of him, or any object that came by chance in contact with his tail.

So it was that he saw not much more of mankind than trouser legs or flesh-colored stockings. Considered from a human viewpoint he lived in a state of hysteria or restricted consciousness, and from this condition all his conflicts derived.

The monkey capered round the house just as if he had been at home there for years. This annoyed me and his witlessness kindled a resentment in me. At that moment I would have sold him for any reasonable offer. But there just wasn't any offer.

The first further development of our association came, of course, when I had to feed him. At first this was a problem. Should the monkey—who was now in a human sphere, and thus must live as a domestic animal—be given human food, in human quantity and with human regularity? Then, thinking of his natural environment, I wondered whether I should compromise in the all too difficult process of adapting his jungle nature to our established mores and habits and feed him rather on food that would conform near enough to his original diet. It was something of a quandary.

All sorts of possibilities occurred to me—from Nutricia's baby food to a rare sort of sapodilla fruit that grows only in the interior of Guiana.

Still at a loss, I went to the cupboard to take out the leftover scraps from my lunch; but I stopped, feeling a sadist. Why should we, who are so concerned with preserving ourselves as we are,

demand of an animal—that has God knows what sort of feeling—
that it disavow its own nature for our pleasure? So that settled
it—no lunch leftovers.

I went into the garden to pick lettuce and half-ripe fruit for him.
I stopped for a moment to look at the chrysanthemums I had
planted. By the time I came back the monkey had stolen all the
remains of my lunch and was licking the bowl dry. His mouth was
opened in a happy leer, and in his paws he held the last crust of
bread. My first reaction of anger passed as I began to realize that
the monkey had shown more wisdom than myself—for I had not,
after all, taken into account the irrepressible primitive urge of
hunger, which he could not in any way subdue, and which is one of
the four elements in each world war. At the same time I was glad
that a solution had been found to the problem. From now on the
monkey would eat exactly what I ate; just think what that
means—he would have to taste whatever I tasted, he would be
committed to the same physical functions as I was. It was an
affirmation of equality, a process of assimilation which degraded
me to the same extent as it enhanced him.

Later the thought struck me that the taking of the lunch scraps
from the cupboard was, in fact, a theft. But this fruit of Calvinistic
atavism proved too foolish, for my monkey had already shown
beyond any doubt that he had no powers of reasoning. And those
who are bereft of reason cannot be sinners, not even before the
law.

The consequences of the situation were clear. From now on I
would have to forgive the monkey for all his misdeeds, and obviously we would only be able to get on together provided I was
prepared to expect anything. It was a lot that he was asking from
me. I felt a little anxious at being committed now to constant
vigilance. Meanwhile, my monkey sat with his hands on his
stomach digesting his meal.

My mother noticed him at once when she came home in the
evening. She went over to him in the corner, and smiling, stroked
his head.

"A monkey is just like a mirror," she said. "In a monkey we can
see our own folly."

Then she asked, "Have you given him something to eat?"

I told her of the monkey's theft, but she smiled again, under-standingly. She came and sat opposite me by the window behind a little forest of geraniums. The monkey crept slowly toward her and lifted up his right paw.

"Look, what a little hand he has," my mother said.

And already he had sprung up on her lap, sniggering in his most stupid manner. I went to get a book, and when I came back he was lying by her side like a baby. She let him play with her finger, just as a young mother does with a child. I could see myself lying there, just like that, a little gurgling bundle being caressed playfully by its mother.

It annoyed me a little to think that the monkey was lying there just as I had done, absorbed by the same unthinking pleasure in nothing. I was annoyed to see my mother's attention centered on him, even for a moment.

"How can you bear to touch the beast? They're filthy," I said.

She answered, seeming to divine my thoughts, "So were you in those days when I played with you."

I forced myself to look at my book, but I couldn't read. My eyes kept turning back to the monkey. The presence of the animal obsessed me, and with a sudden gesture I pitched the Tauchnitz edition at his head. My mother smoothed her dark skirt, and looked at me, a vague sympathy in her glance. Then she smiled again, a smile I can still see.

After that we were alone, the monkey and I—no, it must be I and the monkey. With long strides I crossed over to him and looked down at him, from the height of my human stature, from the eminence of my thinking head, with all the contempt I could bring myself to feel. Miserable, misshapen beast. That sluggish body, that big flat head, those dangling long arms, that twisted rubber hose of a tail. How in the name of God could anyone . . . ?

With a swift leap he was up on my shoulder, and there he squinted at me, his face twisted in its widest grimace. Then he tapped his little hand against my head. His face crinkled up like the face of an aged Negro. His tail hung over my coat like a stole. Next, he stood up on my shoulders and peered over my head at my mother as she came into the room again.

"Be careful," she said, "you'll get hair from the beast all over your coat."

My monkey understood and knocked down a vase from the mantelpiece; then he went and sat sulking in a corner. I was angry without knowing exactly why.

But then, I didn't understand this first revelation of the humanism of the ages to come.

For days I hadn't looked at him, but now, in the sad, wet afternoon, the house was a prison and he was sharing my cell. He had crawled up into the curtains as if to cloak himself in a gigantic mantle. The gray-brown of him against the dull red of the fabric was drearily morbid in the rainy gloom.

It was damp and chilly, and not being in the mood to go out, I paced to and fro in the room. The monkey sat still, looking through the folds of the curtain. He sat there bent forward as if deep in thought and gazed at the far end of his tail. He didn't move. I hardly saw him—only when I walked in his direction. Then I tensed, waiting to see if he would look up. I passed close to him. He didn't move; he only drew his tail a little nearer to him, afraid I might tread on it. He did not even notice me; for him I didn't exist. And by this attitude he forced me to look at him.

More and more clearly I discerned the substance of his calm and the power of his impassivity. He grew to the size of a lion, and still larger, immense as a sphinx, as a terrible stone monster that could break me and smash me.

So it had been through the millennia that with this same awful spell, animals had become the gods of men. The very presence of the monkey sucked all will from me; in the thrall of this gigantic totem I did not dare to move. In terror I stared at the dark hollow of his belly. The cigarette dropped out of my hand.

That was what he had been waiting for. He grabbed it with his paws and examined it from every angle. Then the smoke made him sneeze. I knew now that I had conquered him this time, through my fear—like some Pharaoh who had sat in his pyramid meditating until he realized that no animal could be a God—and echoed faintly the shy laugh of the Horus statue in Memphis. Yet this fear triumphant was but chance and thus, in spite of victory, a nothingness. Outside, the rain was falling in a slow drizzle, the wetness dripped through the limp foliage. My monkey was no longer interested in the cigarette end, and he was sitting hunched up staring

now at the heap of ash on the floor. I ground out the butt with the
toe of my slipper. His eyes stayed fixed.

Then, with my walking stick, I rained blow after blow on him
until he slunk away on his hands and feet, moaning. His crazy tail
slid after him like a leash. But the footsteps of a passerby brought
me to my senses. What the hell . . . It was my own animal that I
was beating, the creature that was here by my own will in this
room. Or had I struck him only because his power was greater
than mine?

My monkey sat timorous in a dark corner, his paws thrown over
his head. His mouth was resting against his belly. Every now and
then he was shaken by a short tremor of pain.

He calmed down, and sat picking his nose. I felt ashamed of my
indiscreet boldness, just like a schoolboy who has been cheating
and is afraid of being found out.

I couldn't look at him again without a feeling of vague guilt. And
he too seemed not to have forgotten the blows, for now he had
completely finished with all familiarity. It wasn't that he avoided
me; in his usual animal fashion he would jump around me, be-
sporting himself with quick movements of his arms and legs and
the rhythmic waving of his tail. But he didn't climb up on my
shoulder anymore, nor did he ever sit quietly staring. If I was near
he found it always necessary to perform a repertoire of stupid
monkey antics.

Sometimes when I went out and the sun was shining he came
along. I would tie a strap around his belly—what did he know of a
biblical symbol?—and put a cord on the strap, and he would run
behind me like a young dog. Note that he observed the world from
the quadruple viewpoint of hands and feet. His whole body was
turned toward the ground, but his tail circled high in the
air—for us, like a living question mark. For him, his tail was the
organ of perception which, like a man, looked upright at the world.
It was a barometer of understanding, a sundial of affection. Once,
on one of our walks, I noticed that a small black line of hair ran
from his head to his tail. My monkey was, indeed, nothing more
than a tail, a tail with four paws and a head for taking in food.

He preferred most of all to go with me into the open countryside. As soon as we were a little out of the city he began to dart

here and there, springing about without any fear of landing in the
barbed wire through his capers.

I knew that as he tumbled he looked at me stealthily, but I took
no notice. For conscious clownery is always tragic and we are
living too late for tragedy.

Besides, in spite of the painters, I do not believe in animal
tragedy. An animal lives its life to the full in the circumstances of
each moment. What man or what woman does that? Without
moral quality there is no aspect of tragedy. Man is naturally tragic;
an animal, never.

Yet it was really I who was the dupe—a man wandering with
his monkey through the outskirts of the city, obviously because he
cannot find anything in the city's center. O reasoning man, you
who are of stature erect, you, with hands stretched to seize the
heavens, with a mind seeking to encompass what is beyond the
heavens, tell, if you can, what it is we seek but never find. But it is
better left to the poets, this precious problem of the tragic.

My monkey had found a couple of acorns that were lying along
the road. Now he was rolling them in front of him, like a boy
playing marbles and trying to break them on a stone so he could
eat them. He is smirking already at the thought of it. Then we
come to where the fields lie open and the thickets begin. My
monkey is elated, and turns a somersault. How wonderfully the
world spins over for him. Just for a second he strides against the
sky. It makes me sad, for my monkey is clownish, but I am—
worse still, alas—tragic.

The difference between a male monkey and a female monkey is
slight. This is the apex of instinctive happiness. My monkey was a
friendly creature, not averse to mixing with people, and so he was
all at once good friends with the girl from the moment she came in.
The tale is about my monkey, and not about my amours, so there
is no need for a description of the girl. Moreover, the erotic interest has long since passed.

It is enough to say that the girl was pretty and sweet. Now
"pretty" and "sweet" are, in combination, two dangerous qualities,
not only because each is essentially the antithesis of the other
("pretty" is *"n'y touchez pas"* and "sweet" is "pluck me, pluck
me, I'll be good every day") but also because those who possess

these qualities are always in serious difficulties (take the films and novels), especially with me, since they are never able to feel the subtle affection existing between me and my monkey. A parson once said that excessive love of animals is a form of misogyny, and for this statement he was dismissed, and he ended up as the most detested sexton in the land. Well, I maintain that excessive hatred of animals, or rather, every sort of hatred of animals is a lack of affection for mankind.

Now, all those who are "pretty" and "sweet" are completely devoid of all capacity for self-sacrifice or affection for humanity, otherwise they would not be "pretty" and "sweet" at the same time. Thus, all who are "pretty" and "sweet" have the accompanying characteristic of excessive hatred of animals. I am going to prove this with the example of the monkey and the girl.

She stroked his back and rubbed him on the neck, her slender, white fingers slid fondly over his head. As I watched her, I smiled happily, thinking again: How sweet she is, how pretty she is! Like the woman with the unicorn—also biblical, I think—she enfolds the monkey with the warmth of her kindness.

"What is he called?" she asked all of a sudden.

"Called? He hasn't got a name. Just 'monkey.'"

"Isn't that just like you. 'Monkey' . . . just 'Monkey' . . . no feeling, so cold . . . not the least bit of poetry."

"I could call him 'monk' if you like," I said, still smiling although I was disturbed by her question.

"That isn't any good either, is it, my little one?" she whispered to the monkey. "Why don't you call him Rex, or Ikhnaton, or Henkie, or Anatole?"

"But these are all names for men . . . not for an animal . . . so how . . ." I began to explain, but I stopped short in the middle of the sentence.

Oh, this perfidy. She fondles the animal and rejects the fact of his animalness. She gives him an endearing name that characterizes and caricatures before the whole world the very nature of his beast being, and she herself is happy and pretty and sweet and poetic. How could I suddenly be filled with hatred for the white hand that had, but a moment before, been stroking his hair? Had she ever given me a name too? O, yes, a name that was a monkey name, and for my crest a monkey tail. I became impatient for her to go. I couldn't stand any more.

"Oh, what a treacherous little beast! He nearly bit me," she cried out, and gave him a soft kick with her suede-clad foot.

"Don't go so near him then," I told her.

My monkey spat on the floor, contemptuously; and the angry flash of that little foot stayed in my memory.

Now I will prove that he had a notion of sex, for this is necessary to explain the rest of the story.

One day little Marie came to visit us. She is only five, and under her short skirt her knees are too big, and her hands above her skirt are too small. When she saw the monkey for the first time she was frightened and hid behind her mother. But after a while she was curious and looked at him attentively. The next time she came she clapped her hands for joy at the sight of him.

Apparently she had thought about him after she had got home, for on another visit she brought a flower and some peanuts for him. The poets will think naturally that my monkey would take the flower first, and the humanists will, of course, think it was the nuts. But he didn't look at either the flower or the nuts; instead he caressed little Marie, touching her knees, and her small hands.

"Is he dangerous?" she asked.

"No, he won't hurt you."

"Will he bite?"

"Only if you tease him."

We who have read Dostoevsky's novels, and lots of other books (especially those by Herbart), we know that this situation is, in miniature—in miniature, of course—perfectly analogous to many grave themes recorded in the world's literature. So much so that if our readers had more understanding, our best novels would not need to be longer than a dozen words. But as the human race is not by nature given to reflection, we who write furnish mankind with reflections as material for thought. We compose thick volumes only to explain all things to the unenlightened.

So my monkey caressed little Marie and ignored the gifts she had brought him. He esteemed as such the being that she was far more than her actions and expressions of feeling. With a sour regret I recalled that he accepted everything I gave him as a matter of course without ever having shown any special attachment toward me. The inference was clear. He had a notion of sex. This was his downfall.

For a few days I had been really concerned over him. It seemed that he had fallen sick—all the spirit, all the life was gone from him. He sat hunched up, silent, in a corner, inert, his hands dangling over his caved-in stomach. His face had taken on an even grayer hue from the pale red of his eyes, and his tail was thin and tremulous.

Nothing at all interested him. I wore myself out cajoling him; I tempted him with the tastiest food, but he hardly touched it. I spoke enticingly the most flattering phrases, but he hardly raised his apathetic eyes. I didn't know what more I could do. It was just too silly to call in a veterinarian. After all, a monkey is no cow or goat, and I was sure that my monkey wouldn't have put up with this sort of attention.

Completely at a loss, I decided there was nothing I could do and I left him to himself. At times he stretched himself out on the floor—something he had never done before. His head would be slumped on one arm, his other forepaw resting on his head. Now and then he flexed the soft flesh of his belly in jerky movements like the throat of someone swallowing; then he would flick his leg convulsively. The room, the whole house, became oppressive and dismal from it. And the worst of it all was that he lay there—so stupid and listless, his eyes bleary, sickness stamped on his foolish face—unable to make known what it was he needed. I opened the window, for the room was too eerie and close for me. Then it happened. In the garden there is a big cherry tree in which a flock of crows often come to perch. One of them fluttered down to the windowsill, and the instant my monkey saw it he jumped up. He ran his hand over his head and beckoned the crow. But the bird flapped its wings, gave a short caw, and flew off. Exhausted, my monkey slumped back in the corner.

Now I knew what it was. He was in love. So that was it, he was in love. Stupid of me not to have realized it earlier, but I hadn't known then that he had a notion of sex. We, who understand so little of one another, what can we understand of a monkey? Nature must ever take its course. Men fall in love, animals fall in love, whether they are in their natural element or not.

One day or another they are afflicted with a strange sort of longing, and then they are in love. My poor monkey. I had thought him wiser; I had thought everything he saw left him unmoved, and now he was so pitiably hurt. . . .

Oh well, we have, all of us, been in love once. Of course, but in another way, in a human fashion. There's no comparison. Nevertheless, there was my monkey lovesick, and I, I was secretly gripped by fear.

Martha (she was another one, not "the girl") had been sitting with me for half an hour without having noticed him. Nor had I given him a thought, for Martha has a delicate, finely chiseled profile. Her quiet, rich voice gave me the vision of a blue bowl full of shining black cherries. Her face was delineated sharply in the vista of my life. I have never told her, but I know that her voice takes on a special lilt when she speaks to me. She noticed he was there when she heard him groan softly.

"What's this? You've got a monkey now?"

"Yes, for as long as he holds out. He won't last long. He's sick and he hardly eats anything."

"Don't you know what is wrong with him?"

Martha went over and knelt beside him and looked at him carefully.

"Yes, I think so. I'll tell you. He's in love, and it's got him down."

Martha opened wide her eyes as if to say: What have you thought up now?

"He's in love with one of the crows from our cherry tree."

Martha burst out laughing; she almost doubled up.

"What an imagination you have." She was still laughing. Then suddenly she said seriously, "How is that possible? A monkey in love with a crow? A monkey in love with a monkey—that I can imagine. But with a crow! Do you really believe that?"

I nodded, a little embarrassed, but at the same time not displeased, for it is always entertaining to talk with an attractive woman about love.

She was right. How could I have really believed such a thing?

There were the laws of nature that decreed that animals of one species might mate only with others of the same species, and that man could only pair with woman. That is to say, marry. But then was his sickness something else?

"Shall I tell you what is wrong with him?" Martha asked. "You don't know a thing about animals. They have a sort of periodic being in love as it were. This is called the mating phase. During this period they must be in their natural surroundings or they become restless and ailing. They must find a mate so they can bring forth their young as their instinct urges them. But it is only a phase and soon passes. Don't worry. He'll be over it in a week or so."

Martha had stood up. She was elegant and well-proportioned, with broad hips and firm breasts, young and full. Martha was twenty-seven and had a degree in law. She didn't like children. Possibly she liked me nevertheless.

My monkey groaned again as she stood up. He had one paw stretched out like the hand of a beggar.

"Shall we go outside?" she asked. "The weather is wonderful."

My monkey lay alone, moaning. Martha and I walked together in the sunshine.

However, he didn't get better as quickly as we had thought he would. Each day saw him still listless and brooding, although he did occasionally stir himself to move around. Mostly he sat sulking in his corner, huddled down between his legs, his tail hidden under his belly.

He had, in the meantime, become a little bigger, for he was still not full grown when I bought him. But his outward appearance was unchanged, except that sometimes he seemed to have got thinner.

One afternoon he had found his way into my study. I came home earlier than usual and surprised him there in the midst of a heap of papers he had thrown on the floor. A volume of Goethe lay flung half open in a corner.

I shouted at him, but I didn't hit him for he was still weak and thin. I was going to put him out of the room and leave it at that when I noticed he was holding a crumpled sheet of paper in his right paw. As I tried to take it from him, he jumped away with an agility I hadn't seen in him for weeks. I went after him through the room.

"Come here! Give it to me!"

But he dodged every move I made. I began to get angry. Again and again he darted past me and, when I suddenly stumbled and realized the ridiculousness of the situation, my anger rose to a blind rage. I hurled my ruler at him, then my blotter. A glass paperweight thudded against his chest with a dull smack, like a boat knocking against a pier, and I flinched myself at the violence of the blow. He didn't move anymore, but he held the paper tightly in his black paw. I pulled it out; it was a photo. When I smoothed it out I saw, to my astonishment, that it was a photo of Martha, the girl with a clear-cut profile, a photo that was always on my table even though I hardly ever looked at it. Now it was creased and torn. Useless.

In my anger I would have kicked him if he hadn't lain there so motionless. Probably I would have finished him off, for I was more than inclined to kill him then and there. But I couldn't have faced the other members of the household—my mother and the rest, who would ask: "Where is your monkey?" Then I would be called a vicious brute—an indignity to be avoided at any cost.

I sprinkled water over his head, and forced some into his mouth. He was still alive; I could see his chest moving. I waved my handkerchief over him, the way they do to revive a groggy boxer. He drew in the paw that had held the photo. As he opened his eyes again he saw that his paw was empty. Then slowly he dragged himself away to totter down the stairs back to his corner.

I stared after him, puzzled and bewildered. What could be the meaning of all this?

He never got over the blow I had given him with the paperweight. I had broken two of his ribs, and from then on he lived in a languishing stupor. My mother had given him a basket with a cushion in it and there he lay, pining, a shriveled-up lump, with his tail over his head.

Martha came to see me again, only a few days later, and she asked if he was any better. I didn't dare to mention that I had beaten up the monkey—women have always such an exaggerated sympathy for animals that they take a distorted view of human

22

conduct. So I just lied, "No, he is still in love, or in his mating phase, as you call it."

Martha looked at him. "I didn't know that it had got him down as much as all that," she said. "Maybe an operation or something like that isn't so cruel as you might be inclined to think. You'd spare him a lot of bother and misery."

"I don't like anything unnatural," I answered. "It would probably be best to get another monkey to keep him company."

"That won't help. It doesn't make any difference if they're not in their natural environment. At least the human species is better off. These difficulties can usually be got over fairly easily."

"Maybe that's not quite right, Martha. Isn't it a question of whether there doesn't linger in the mind, in the deepest, most secret feelings, a sense of incompleteness, of unfulfillment, a result of not having known all that life can offer?"

"Oh, you're making it too profound."

"Not really. Let us take what we might call his being in love. He could only have become conscious of this through an instinctive feeling of unfulfillment."

"You're raising the issue to a purely human level," Martha objected. "Don't forget it's only a monkey."

In these words I sensed a self-aggrandizement, an arrogance that pained and irritated me.

"Nevertheless, he has fallen well and truly in love, just like anyone else," I insisted.

"But then you have to find out who he is in love with."

"That, I know already. The other day I nearly killed him because he had stolen a piece of paper. That piece of paper was your photo. It's you that he's in love with." I felt shocked at what I had said when I saw how pale Martha had turned.

"You're disgusting!" she screamed. "How revolting you are!"

With the flat of her hand she slapped me in the face, hard. At this my monkey was on his feet, baring his teeth at her in a snarl. His hair stood up like a brush on his back from anger, his tail was erect and as stiff as a flagpole.

I laughed nervously. "Are you annoyed over a silly joke like that?"

Martha was abashed. She blushed and made up to me. But the same afternoon it so happened that we quarreled over the validity of the verdict in an appeal hearing in Apeldoorn. This quarrel has never been patched up even though I still meet Martha often. My monkey stuck out his tongue at her as she left and I smiled to myself sarcastically.

Not long after that I met Dr. Schneider in a bar. At that time, before he compromised himself with a hairdresser's assistant, he was still a famous gynecologist. The moment he saw me, he said, "I hear from Martha that you have a rather eccentric monkey. I'd like very much to see it. Monkeys, you know, are remarkable fetishists, and with many women pregnancy seems to cause a curious ambivalent fear of them. Have you ever noticed this?"

"Our house isn't a clinic," I said.

"Oh, but there are a lot of such cases. Only recently I heard a story about a monkey. It was sickly and pining. But as soon as he found a woman's silk stocking he would liven up and begin to unravel all the threads until there was nothing but a heap of silk. Then he would lie on it and go to sleep. When he died they found in his cage enough silk for ten pairs of stockings."

"Your stories aren't exactly suitable for babies," I commented.

"I'm not for babies myself," Schneider answered, not at all perturbed, and, bending toward me as if he wanted to tell a secret, he whispered, "Martha is in love with you, I believe."

"Hardly—she takes more interest in my monkey than in me. That I know for sure."

"Ah, but that's just it, don't you understand? She has an infantile fixation on the monkey, but it's you all the time."

"Your idea sounds like a lot of nonsense. In any case, I find it anything but flattering to me."

"It's not as remarkable as it seems. Quite usual in fact. Quite common. I know of a case of a man who had a mania for collecting postage stamps. But he wouldn't look at any from Nyasaland. Because they had a giraffe on them." He broke off with a short laugh. "In his youth he had heard someone say that all mothers-in-law are just like giraffes. This came back to him only after he had had an altercation with his own wife in front of the giraffe enclosure at the zoo."

"You hear some curious things at your clinic, Dr. Schneider."

"Yes," he said, "psychiatry really interests me more than gynecology. And animals have a special significance. There has been so little attention given to animal psychiatry although there is a lot that can be done. And then aren't some mental patients just like animals? I came across one who thinks that he is a cockchafer . . ."

"Oh, no more of these gruesome stories, Doctor, *bitte sehr*."

"Well, I can stick to my clinic, that's enough. You know, if we observe human animalphobia, we can discover so much more about the animal psyche."

"To tell the truth, I had always thought that no animal could have what we understand as a psyche."

"And the emotional reactions and the instincts of an animal? Just watch your monkey. No doubt he could teach you a lot. I should like to make a study of him."

"Come and have a look at him if you want to," I said.

"Good, and I'll bring Martha with me."

"As you like . . . I mean . . . certainly, by all means."

Dr. Schneider didn't get the chance to see my monkey, for it was only shortly after our meeting that, as I mentioned, he compromised himself and he left the country.

Although I found all his theorizing pure drivel, his talk had, however, made such an impression on me that my thoughts were more than ever centered on the monkey. In spite of myself I began to regard him, from then on, as an embodiment of the utmost degeneration. Just in the same way that we always wonder what secret sins animals hold hidden from our knowledge. It is not by mere coincidence that, in man, moral corruption often goes with an aggressive affection for animals.

And I, I was tormented by a question I couldn't answer. Why had Martha spoken to Dr. Schneider about my monkey; and did she perhaps associate in her mind Dr. Schneider and the monkey?

I have no respect for the babble of the learned. And yet in the end no one else saw through the monkey as clearly as my brother—despite his first-year-high-school wisdom. He came in while the monkey sat drooling over his breakfast in a corner of the room.

"He's not getting any better, the poor monkey," my brother said.

"Do you really know what a monkey is?" I asked him, only to annoy him.

"Of course," he answered, "we have just learned it at school. Monkeys are mammals of the highest order. There are two groups—monkeys of the Old World and monkeys of the New World. The difference lies in the breadth or thinness of the septum, and in the dental formula. The monkeys of the Old World have no tail, or only a short one. The monkeys of the New World mostly have a long tail and prehensile feet."

"You forget something," I pointed out. "They have an opposable thumb like us. You must know not only the differences but the similarities as well."

My brother thought for a moment. "Yes," he recalled, "there is also something of the sort about the facial angle. But it's all rot. There's this search for a link between man and monkey, but the link isn't likely to be found. The power of reasoning you see . . ."

"Haven't you heard of the Pithecanthropos Saman and the Homo Heidelbergensis?" I asked.

"Our teacher said none of that could hold water."

I looked at my brother. He stood by the window, placid, looking at the children in the street playing on their way to school. Only then did I notice that his shoulders were broadening, that his face was taking on a certain hardness. A false manhood in his voice irritated me.

There was a clatter. My monkey had let his bowl slip out of his hands. The noise made us both look round to see what he was doing. He moved himself unsteadily on his hands and feet, stumbling over the remains of his meal to get to the bowl. When he reached it he lay down and curled up again, inert.

"I wish the filthy beast would go ahead and die," I said, "It's getting on my nerves, all this."

"Oh, he's sure to get better soon," my brother asserted, "He's probably only caught a chill."

"These animals never catch a cold in their natural state. So why now?"

"Just look at him. It's just as if he were human," my brother said, and he carefully laid his rumpled handkerchief over the monkey.

I knew what that meant. He had suddenly seen that my monkey

was naked. Naked in a human likeness. And he had forgotten the missing link, and the earlier link to the Homo Heidelbergensis.

My monkey moved his black eyes like an invalid grateful for attention.

I forgot about my brother, lost in bewildered contemplation of the new problem—the humanness of my monkey.

On one of those tedious Sunday afternoons, when you feel how slowly and emptily life goes by, I was sitting by the window with a book by Strindberg. The book was *Der Vater,* in deference to the many church-minded passersby. But I couldn't read. The sky had a jaded pallor and the sultry heat was almost suffocating. My monkey crawled sluggishly through the room—one movement every half-hour.

Then I heard the sound of brisk footsteps on the path—that could only be Martha. It was the unexpected treat of this dismal afternoon—something like cool lemonade offered in a thick, coarse restaurant glass. I was pleased; it would have been an unbearable torture to watch that lethargic apery hour after hour.

On no account could I let Martha have the chance of fussing with the monkey; that would only cause another quarrel and irritation, and the stupid animal would annoy me even more. I pushed open the window and called my monkey, "Quick, into the garden."

But with his sick, stupid head he had somehow recognized Martha's step, and he lay, ignoring my call, as if he was unconscious.

"Poxy little beast," I hissed.

I grabbed him by the neck to let him slide down the wall into the garden. But at that moment the door opened, and with a yell of pain I let him loose. He had sunk his teeth into my wrist and the blood spurted over my hand and my sleeve. Martha stood at the door, pale, her dark eyes open wide. Through the pain, through the red of the blood on my hand, I saw the beauty of her.

"God, what has happened?" she gasped. "You're bleeding to death."

"It's not that serious," I assured her, and I wrapped a handkerchief around my wrist. Her hand trembled a little as she helped me tie the knot; I savored the warmth of her flesh on my arm.

"How did it happen?" she asked.

"The monkey again, of course," I said, and pointed toward the window. "I wanted to put him out when . . ."

"What a thing to do! He's sure to have fallen and killed himself, the poor dear, the little darling," Martha lamented.

Her whole attention was focused through the window, but the monkey wasn't to be seen in the garden.

"Why did you have to put him outside?" Martha wanted to know, after we had sat silent for a while. "Was he being a nuisance?"

"No, but I heard you coming, and I was afraid he might annoy you. The last time, you remember, he wasn't exactly friendly toward you."

"So you mean to say it's my fault. You blame me for everything."

She began to cry, and she sobbed out, "I'm going. . . . I don't ever want to see you again."

Angrily, she buttoned up her coat and gave me a curt nod. On the steps she met the monkey who was sitting there huddled up. She petted him, and I heard her say to him something like "My poor little darling."

That evening the weather changed completely. It turned bleak and gray, and a storm blew up, sending a sad, sighing clamor through the shrubbery and trees in the garden. I couldn't go out, I thought too much about Martha, and besides, my wrist was sore. I decided to go to bed early.

Around midnight I woke, aching and restive. I felt feverish, and my wrist throbbed with a stinging pain. My head was heavy, and I vaguely remembered that I had dreamed. Then, as I watched the dark corner between my wardrobe and the wall, the dream came back, yellowed now, and bedraggled, but still clear in its unreal light.

I was wandering in a strange house that was half dark. Inside there were staircases, each with an iron balustrade and ornaments of small glass cubes—like paperweights. I opened one of the doors in a passage. A woman was lying in the room, naked. Her body writhed in spasms and she was moaning loudly. She sighed and screamed, begging me to bring her water. I ran up and down stairway after stairway. There was no water anywhere. Frantic, I ran in and out of the rooms. I wanted to ask where I could find water, but there was no one to ask. I came at last to a courtyard where drooping weeds grew between the flagstones. In the middle of the courtyard there stood on a pedestal a monkey of black basalt. He looked straight at me and seemed to giggle imperceptibly. His tail stood up behind him like a big black question mark. I was desperate and distraught, hearing the groans of the woman resound with long echoes through all the house as she cried, "Water, water."

I saw the snigger of the monkey. I ran at him, wanting to tear him apart. But my fingers slipped off the smooth stone. It was as if my hand had seized wet soap.

Then, with a mad violence, I wrenched one of the flagstones loose. I hurled it with all my might at the monkey image. The head shattered into fragments and became a glowing star, and the star fanned out, then changed into a little fountain from which I caught water in my cupped hands.

Walking carefully I went back to the room where the woman lay. This time it was only a short distance. I wanted to give her the water, but when I touched her head with my hand I saw the skull was smashed, hideously cleft where a gaping wound showed the blood trickling redly against the white brains. And worse horror! On the pillow, between the long tresses of hair, was the stone that I had thrown at the basalt monkey.

I wanted to call out, but I could only stare at the covering over her knees that was moving. The body seemed to be rising slowly, and from between the knees there suddenly wriggled up the head of a monkey which stuck a little red tongue out at me. . . . Then the room was suddenly full of panes of glass, and behind these were a thousand monkeys all poking out their flame-red tongues at me. . . . Everything began to rock and turn, the ceiling fell in, streams of water gushed down over me. . . . Then I woke.

I couldn't get to sleep again. The dream had made me jittery and given me a dull headache. I lay tossing, and then I lay quite still because of the wet compress on my wrist. The clock ticked with a sorrowful regularity, and the sound of the soft pattering of the rain still came from the garden.

I tried to distinguish the sounds. First, a passerby in the street, then another, the clock, the rain, a cat, another clock. Now I heard

a sound I couldn't recognize. It was something between a whispering and a faint crooning. Or perhaps a distant piano. No . . .
not that either. It was more of a moaning . . . and it came from
somewhere nearby . . . a frightened child . . . My youngest brother
must have got out of bed and not been able to find his way back.

I got up and went to his room. He was sleeping peacefully, his
little fist above the blanket. I listened. The singing went on, a slow
dolorous song, intoned in a stifled voice. It was even nearer now. I
had to find out what it was, this sound, so sorrow-laden, almost
inhuman. I padded down the stairs, stealthily so as not to wake the
others. In the passage I put the light on.

There, in front of me, was a sight I never will forget, even if I
live for a thousand years, though I may see men slaughtered like
beasts and women slit open like dead sausages. For not with death
or with pain does the danger of memory lie, but deep, deep in the
secrets that we are loath to unveil.

The moment the light went on I saw him sitting in his basket,
my monkey. Sitting straight up like a child. He was weeping long
tears, and sobbing, sobbing pitiably. Like a woman, like a mother
in pain, like a child who knows he will soon die, like a man who,
for the first time, finds the strength gone from his muscled arms. It
was a weeping that came from some unknowable anguish. The
tears rolled down his black face onto his wet chest; with his little
hands he dried them, but he couldn't hold in the sobs that racked
his whole body.

A dizziness seized me. There was within me an unbearable urge
to shout: "My monkey weeps! Look, my monkey is weeping!" But
fear pressed down the shout, and I shuddered.

In the dark of the night, in the lonely, rain-dreary night, when
everyone was sleeping, I squatted down beside him. Humbly, I
loosened the strap around his stomach, and there I was taking him
in my arms. I stroked his head gently, and I kissed him. Inside
myself I felt a tightening of infinite compassion coupled with fear.
And I whispered to him that we are all like that—frightened animals in God's arena. In the iron cage of His laws we beat against
the bars, bruising and tearing our hands that would reach ever
upward, striving higher and higher, because we are strong, and a
strange untamable passion drives us on. But our loins are clamped
in shackles of His fashioning and He has tethered us fast with

chains. What can we do but weep in the depth of the night, when we think that He sleeps.

Yet, we are, in turn, each of us, a god. A god who dominates inexorably. A god who creates his ideas, his impregnable *Welt* (world) as *Wille* (will) *und Vorstellung* (imagination), so as to thrust these on the monkeys that he owns.

I sat squatting beside my monkey, now, for the first time, as both his master and his equal. He quivered still with little shudders, and he looked frightened like a child. Finally he closed his eyes and slept. It was almost morning when I went back upstairs, stiff and cold.

Mother was in a bad mood at breakfast. The monkey had made a mess over the whole ground floor of the house during the night and had stolen everything edible in the cupboard.

"He just can't stay here," she said. "It's too much nuisance in a busy house. And besides, he's upsetting everyone with his silly whims and his sickness. You've hardly been bearable yourself for weeks, and now there's never a happy word from you."

"So it's the monkey once again. . . ." I broke in.

"Yes, and if it hadn't been for thinking of you, I'd have got rid of the dirty little pest long ago."

"I'm rather attached to him," I said ironically.

"You just don't know yourself how you run after him."

"Say, did you come downstairs last night?" my brother asked as if he had suddenly remembered something.

I answered him with an evasion, "It was just the right weather for getting out of bed."

"Then I must have imagined it. I thought someone came down the stairs."

"For a little boy at school you think too much," I snapped.

But my brother came back at me, "Maybe you came down to get your beloved monkey a hot-water bottle."

"Get a move on, snotty nose, it's time for school," I jeered at him, irked that this thrust had hit the mark.

"See, you can't even take a joke any more," my mother said.

And when I had got up angrily from the table she stopped me by the door and asked softly, "Is anything wrong?"

Irritated, I shook my head impatiently and went out. As I

stopped in the passage to take my hat from the rack the monkey sidled up to me. A sun ray, streaming through the windowpane, fell yellow across his back. My anger flared to a rage. Was it because of this yellow light? I lashed at him with my foot.

Outside it was still damp, but there was a warmth in the air. I walked aimlessly, on and on, through the desolate outskirts, past the scruffy gardens in front of the houses.

My mother was right. He was to blame for everything. Everything was his fault. It was almost pathological—that a mere monkey could, in a couple of weeks, make a complete neurasthenic of you! It was as if you had to live in a house where there was nothing else but portraits of yourself, like a museum filled with Pictures of Dorian Gray. And no anchorage anywhere. It all comes to the same thing. Every book is a self-portrait. Every object. Whatever path you follow there is the ever present I. You never get beyond yourself—you never look further than yourself. The treacherous teaching of Delphi said: "Know thyself." But what else do we know but Self, that little presuming Self, this demon that possesses us. My mother, my brother, Martha, the monkey. Again and again myself, each a travesty of my real self. Oh, if I ever found the Other, then I could love and be happy.

My reflections brought me to a final decision. In some way the animal must be eliminated. And the elimination must be drastic— thus, there was no question of selling him. Anyway, who would want to buy a worn-out, sick monkey?

From my friend the goldsmith I got a flask of cyanide "for mounting butterflies." I brought it home hidden away deep in my pocket. The monkey shuddered when he saw me come in.

I had his favorite meal prepared—sweet rice with peanuts— saying that perhaps this would pick him up. No one could notice the blue traces of the cyanide in the bowl I put before him.

I wanted to go away, but an inexplicable curiosity held me—the curiosity we all have for the end of something—to behold the far horizons that will fall away and the new infinities that are created.

I sat down opposite him. He chewed slowly with his dry jaws, biting with a little vigor only when he found a nut. Then, indifferent, he pushed the bowl away, and tilted his head to look up at me.

He looked up at me for a long time; it was as if he understood. The wrinkles were gone from his face; his expression had something of a dull humanness, a sort of sad bewilderment; his tail was curled round him as in a statue of Mithra.

Then his expression changed; his flat mouth curved into a smile, and, pulling the bowl toward him abruptly, he began to eat in a frenzy of greed.

Had there come to him, so shortly before his dying, an awareness of his approaching death? Was he enticed with those same distant, twilight cadences that we hear in our quietest hour? For then, he would inflict on mankind the supreme humiliation by dying a human death, and with the dignity of a Socrates. And would I be the Plato who must write his *Phaedo?* That, I could never endure. Die he would, but not as a man dies. Was this, our ultimate, most sacred mystery, Death—the final secret that is ours at the cost of everything—to be parodied by a monkey? That, I would never endure. And now it came to me how I hated him with a hate that had grown in me since my tenderest years. I had hated him with a deadly hate right from the moment I saw him. And now I must devise for him a manner of dying so cruel and inhuman that his death would be other than the mere passing away of life. A manner of dying so exquisite as to be beyond the imagination of either Roman or cannibal.

But I had to be quick, for the cyanide was taking effect. He was dying already, and how could I stage his exit?

Upstairs I went to get my bassoon. Again I sat opposite him and played a slow, slow music with dark, thick notes heavy like fat bubbles that swell up and burst on the surface of a swamp. Red notes I blew out of the wooden tube; they splattered on his head like overripe tomatoes and the red juice dripped along his nose toward an empty echo.

His paws shook; he was terrified; he shriveled up from fear until he was as small as a black marmot. His eyes were fixed on the shining bassoon. Relentless, I blasted out the notes in the deepest bass, and then again higher. Like a juggler I blew out notes that were spinning colored balls—green and blue. He pulled himself across the floor with his weak, trembling paws; he rolled himself over on his back and hit the ground with his head. The room was pale now and vast, a white temple of Baal, and I sat there, big and strong, with the ecstasy of a high priest who carries out the sacrifice for a new ritual. The bassoon was pressed against me like a weapon ... no ... like a woman by whose side you are mighty, a conqueror of all worlds.

The monkey lay on his back, hands and feet spread out, as if bound to an X-shaped cross. His tail lay under him, the shaft of his head. His rump had shrunk out of sight. His stomach arched convulsively, and under his ribs the convulsion rose up to his throat. Strange folds came on his face; his tongue hung out on one side, bluish red. From the bassoon I blew out every note up to the highest register.

Then I turned my thoughts to music that is tender and lovable and bound to the joyousness of the earth.

I played a melody of Mozart, so touching, with all the yearning of spring, pale and pink as the heart of a camellia, mysterious as the petals of a hyacinth, ill-omened as a fading orchid.

The melody ended. A tremor flickered through his arms and legs. Motionless my monkey lay, stiff, his tail pointed like a dagger. He was dead.

With the toe of my shoe I pushed him into a corner and locked the door for the night.

And when my mother asked, "Where is the animal?" I said, *"Mein Affe ist heute an Schwermut gestorben"* ("My monkey died today of melancholia"), for we are all of us actors.

Yet my words grieved me, since with this tenderness I was unjust and ungrateful toward my mother, who did not know Strindberg because Thomas à Kempis was enough for her. But at the same time I was glad with a new and youthful gladness, for good and evil, joy and pain had mingled for one indivisible moment.

INTERMEZZO

And because the aged always have a wisdom that they must pass on to us, my grandmother said—after the monkey had been buried by my brother under a balsam bush in the garden—"I know a very old story about monkeys that the Indians have told for centuries."

"There was once a king who possessed great forests and many

gardens. In one of the gardens stood many coconut trees with fruit hanging so high that no one could pick it. A great drought fell on the land, and the king desired to drink the juice of the coconuts. So he sent a message to all corners of his domain announcing that whoever could pick the fruit would win his only daughter, the princess, as a bride.

Many came to try but none succeeded. The trees were too slender and the trunks were too smooth. The climbers stopped halfway, either tired or fearing to go higher. One morning there came a strange, ugly little man who said he would climb the highest tree and pick all the fruit for the king.

With his clothes on he clambered up the tree as fast as another would walk on the ground and went right up to the cluster of leaves where the coconuts hung and threw the fruit down, two at a time. Everyone was surprised to see that before noon he had plucked all the fruit from the tree. And when he had finished the king said, "Come, my son, I will give you my daughter."

The stranger refused at first, but the king was eager to have such a brave son-in-law, and used every kind of flattery to persuade him to stay. The king promised there would be a great wedding feast and named all the rich spices and fine drinks to be brought for the celebration. But only when the king mentioned peanuts did the stranger agree to stay.

Within a few days he was married and he lived in the palace. The princess had become pale and wan and would speak to no one. She was afraid and sad, for each morning, long before sunrise, her new husband went off to bathe in the garden by the wood. No matter how she pleaded, he would never let her come with him, and each day she became paler and sadder from frightened curiosity.

At last her old nurse decided to follow the prince early one morning. And what did she see?

Hardly had he reached the pond than he threw off his clothes as quickly as he could and stood there, naked and shaggy, by the water. Then he lifted his arms and began to sing a song:

> " 'Na mi'okro bia graman
> 'Na mi'okro bia graman
> Graman kari mi'okro bi."

And directly there came from all sides out of the trees about fifty monkeys, chattering and tumbling, to join the prince, who was also a monkey, for he had a long tail and hair on his back.

They jumped through the branches frolicking gaily. They threw fruit seeds at each other and splashed around in the pond. But as soon as the first red beams of the sun appeared over the water, all the monkeys scurried back into the wood while the prince pulled on his clothes and sauntered back to the palace just like a man.

Trembling, the old nurse sought out the king and whispered to him what she had seen. But no one believed the tale she told.

That afternoon, as he was strolling with his son-in-law by the pond, the king stepped behind the prince and sang the song:

> " 'Na mi'okro bia graman
> 'Na mi'okro bia graman
> Graman kari mi'okro bi."

At once the prince began chattering and prancing and he threw off all his clothes. The other monkeys came tumbling out of the wood to join him and they jumped around in the trees. But the king took his bow and arrow and shot his son-in-law dead, right through the heart. So it was that from then on all monkeys were hated in that land."

"Yes, by everyone except perhaps the princess," I said skeptically, but softly.

One morning not long after all this the hunter came by again. He carried in his bag the fresh-killed game that was still warm. His laugh was loud and free as he showed the blood-dripping flesh, but I don't remember any more whether it was sunny that day or raining.

When he saw me there came on his face a strange smile.

"How is the monkey?" he cried.

"Oh, hunter," I answered, "I know that you are my friend, and a mighty killer of beasts you are, so I can tell you. I have killed my monkey."

The hunter straightened his hat and crossed his arms over his chest. "Why?" he asked, looking me straight in the eye.

"I killed my monkey out of hate and anger," I said, "and in order to free myself."

"Yes, we dare not face the simple truth that to whatever extent we are not different from a monkey we are identical with it."

"Hunter, this is a dreadful truth."

"And yet it is not. For in one respect we differ greatly. God has made us far more cruel than the animals. We are able to kill ourselves too, the self within us. Herein lies our power and, at the same time, our distinction. You have won for yourself the reality of man's being by destroying this, your own likeness."

The hunter gripped the wild game that hung by his side and lifted it up high to let me see the rich booty.

"And what am I to do now?" I asked. "For life has become so oddly different for me. I am estranged from all the others—from my mother, my brother, from Martha."

"Do as I do," replied the hunter. "You must hunt. Go and hunt day after day through the thickest forests. Only in hunting and killing can you find the wildest joys of real cruelty. The scent of danger is more fragrant than the finest cigar. Fearing you, all the animals will hold you in awe. Amongst mankind you will be alone, you who know the paths they have never trodden. Be then a hunter as I am."

I heard the hunter's words and I embraced him; and I breathed in his jacket the air of forest and swamp.

"Hunter, my friend, my only friend," I said, "I will go with you wherever you go. I'm saying farewell to this flat dreary town with its houses and gardens, its petty-minded females and their smug and pallid consorts, with its dogs and chickens, with its zoo and its parks. Hurrah! Hurrah! I'll go with you."

A hat with a waving feather the hunter has given me, and a rifle that never misses. Now I'll go and shoot all the monkeys I can find. And any that I can catch, I'll take and sell to people in the city. The first one is for Martha.

TRANSLATED BY ALEX BROTHERTON

Tip Marugg

from WEEKEND PILGRIMAGE (a novel)

THERE is a country house which plays a prominent part in the memories of my youth. It lay on a low hill, like most of the country houses in Curaçao, and it had many arched windows. From a distance it looked as if the entire building consisted of white arches, there were so many of them. It had many large rooms too, and three long corridors. When you walked along one of those corridors the heels of your shoes made a high, ringing noise on the hard stone floor. But that didn't often happen, for you were usually barefooted when you walked through the big house. You even sat down to dinner without shoes on.

On the right-hand side of the house, between the living quarters and the old outbuildings, lay an enclosed courtyard, a shady patio where it was always lovely and cool because the sun never penetrated there. For in the middle of the little patio stood an enormous oleander, whose long and widely spreading branches covered it completely. When that tree was in flower a soft, sweet perfume was diffused over the entire house, right through to the kitchen at the other end. And when you looked down on to the tree from one of the windows on the upper floor, the whole courtyard was hidden under a white roof of oleander blossoms. You hardly even saw the green leaves anymore, because they, too, were overwhelmed and ousted by the white flowers.

When I was a little boy, I once said, in a company of grown-ups, that I would like to be buried under such a flowering oleander. Little boys can make such strange pronouncements! Of course, everyone laughed at me. And yet, although that was many years ago, I still don't find it was such a silly idea.

Even then the house was already in a more or less tumbledown condition. We children were strictly forbidden to go up into the attic; people were afraid we might get one of the loose tiles down on our skulls. But of course we went there just the same, for to us the attic was the most fascinating part of the whole house. From time to time fragments of dried plaster were liable to fall down on your head, but—provided you walked carefully over the loose planks—nothing worse happened. It was that plaster which usually gave us away, for when we sat down at the table and the grown-ups noticed the white stuff in our hair, they knew at once that we had been up in the forbidden attic. But such a thing only happened once or twice; after that we always went to the kitchen when we'd been on a journey of discovery in the attic, and Ia, the cook, carefully cleaned us up before we went in to dinner. Ia was a good soul. She always had some choice tidbit for me. I loved her very much in those days, though I suspected her of drinking quite a lot in secret. I figured that she did that because she was very unhappy; for, some time before, her husband had fallen down the well and been drowned, early in the morning, before it was properly light. Nobody saw him fall down the well, and an intensive search was made for him for two whole days. People were already beginning to assume that he had taken to his heels for some reason or other and had secretly gone to Venezuela or Colombia on board a schooner, when his body was discovered in the well. I was there when they pulled him out. The police stepped in, too, and interrogated both Ia and the other workers on the plantation for hours.

We children liked best to go up to the attic just before sundown, for at that hour the bats began to emerge from their hiding places. Each of us would be armed with a slingshot, and we had our trouser pockets full of small flat stones which we had collected on the beach, during the day, especially for the purpose. There were generally three of us, my two cousins and I; and on some days we shot down more than a hundred bats among us. But the supply never ran out. Every time, there were just as many as before. One of my cousins, Wim's his name, he's now a member of the church council, always felt remorseful when we piled all the dead bats in a heap in order to count them. He always said then that it was cruel of us to have killed those inoffensive little creatures, and that he'd never come up to the attic with us any more. But when the next time came, he was there all right. I never had any feelings of guilt about killing bats. I found them dirty animals, and I could kill thousands of them with pleasure. But there *were* creatures I never could bear to kill—such as, for instance, those shy little birds with gray wings and a yellow belly. They have no proper name; "yellowbellies," everyone says, and you know at once what bird they mean. I've never fired my slingshot at a yellowbelly.

Sometimes, though, I went up to the attic on my own; sometimes even when it was already quite dark. Now I come to think of it, that was odd, for there were hundreds of small things I was frightened of in those days, or which I didn't dare to do alone; but I was never frightened in that big dark attic. When I went there by myself, I usually lay on one of the big window seats and gazed outside. If there was a moon, the sight could be marvelous. Then I would gaze at the gleaming sea in the distance; it really looked as if there were stars in the black water, too, gathered together in a broad path of light that reached from the coast to the horizon and then climbed up along the sky, right up to the moon. Or I would look at the waving, rustling treetops, or at the mysterious will-o'-the-wisps which moved at such lightning speed from one place to another. Sometimes, too, I would close my eyes and listen to the wind. I had never paid any attention to it before, but I discovered then that the wind could make a thousand different sounds.

Even now, I still like listening to the wind, at silly moments. The wind's a part of the island. It's a wind which never gets tired, and which blows over Curaçao like a stimulating breath, fresh and thin in the cool rainy period, languid and hot in the warm September days, heavy and strong in the hurricane season. The wind which makes the tough acacia and divi-divi trees bow their heads in defeat; which takes on its wings the small boats laden with fruit and makes them cleave the waves; which sometimes sweeps the heat away like a great invisible broom and drives the coolness of the sea onto the land in its stead; the wind which catches the cotton-covered seeds that burst from the oblong pods of the kapok tree and sends them floating like little brown birds above the croton shrubs.

. . . It's the same wind you listened to when you were still a boy and lay in bed in that big house on the hill and felt so lonely. The wind which murmured mysteriously at night between the sleeping blossoms of the oleander in the courtyard. Or which tossed restlessly in the crowns of the flamboyant trees, and made their flat woody pods clack anxiously, like chattering teeth, and which then climbed up the white wall and opened an attic window and slipped into the house like a thief and slammed the window shut behind him. You heard the floor creak softly under his light tread, and you heard a bat flutter away, which he had startled into wakefulness. And then you heard him come down the stairs; they creaked one by one. Then he was on the veranda, and flew out again through one of the side arches, back to the oleander in the patio, and from there to the coconut palms at the foot of the hill.

Once, when you were out of sorts and couldn't get to sleep, he crossed the veranda and entered the corridor. He paused outside your bedroom door, and you heard his hurried breathing! A great terror seized you, for you realized he meant mischief. He opened the bedroom door and came in. But it was the wind no longer, it was a woman, a terrifying Negress: the wind had concealed itself in the shape of Ia, the cook, who always had all kinds of tidbits for you in the kitchen.

Ia came nearer, and called you her darling, and asked whether you were still feverish. But you were scared to death, and dared not answer her, and pretended to be asleep. She climbed into bed beside you, and you felt her heavy black body pressing down on you, but her face was different, it wasn't Ia's face, it wasn't the friendly, smiling Ia from the kitchen. You wanted to shout, to call for help, but Ia's face, that distorted mask, was too close, the distance between your face and hers was too small to let any sound through. You felt a heavy hand which stroked your hair so fiercely that it began to scorch; and a thick, warm breath of white rum struck your right eye. The burning hairs on your head fell down, over your face, your chest, your stomach and your legs, and the smell of burning from the stinging wounds over your whole body mingled with the nauseating stench of white rum. You tried to hold your breath in order not to inhale that noxious vapor, but you didn't succeed. You sucked the repulsive stench in through your nostrils, through your mouth, through all your pores. It was as if a thousand sharp cactus needles were tearing your skin open and penetrating deep into your body to find a place in which to empty the stupefying liquor.

You closed your eyes and you knew then that you were climbing a cactus column. You felt the razor-sharp spines ripping open the skin of your thighs, but the pain no longer bothered you; you only had eyes now for that proud, lofty column you had to climb—higher, ever higher. Then you were at the top, and a tremendous flash of lightning split the sky outside, and lit up the plantation, the house and your room. The column shuddered, and with it the whole house.

You glanced swiftly downward, to see the boy you had left at the foot of the column, but you saw nothing. All was dark.

Then came the rain. The great ice-cold drops fell and trickled down the green grooves in the cactus column, and you let yourself slide down with them. And the column bent over like a weary acacia tree that slowly bows to the ground its head, grizzled by the sun.

You looked about you to see all the new things, but everything was just as it had been: the same ugly cracks in the white walls of the goat stalls; the same sweet perfume from the oleander blossoms; the same bats shunning the light in the attic; the same monotony of sun and wind.

Everything was just as it had been. Except that Ia, the cook, always called you "sir" after that night.

TRANSLATED BY ROY EDWARDS

Boeli van Leeuwen

from THE ROCK OF OFFENSE (a novel)

FOR as long as I can remember it was said of Aunty Da: *"Jesus e tun bon hende!"* ("God, what a good soul she is!") Her father said it when the young men came to wait upon her on the veranda, "My daughter is much too good for those louts who prey upon her. She must wait until the right man comes along and carries her to paradise." And so he chased off all the suitors and sat with her on the porch in the setting sun.

When Da was thirty her mother died and Papachi attached himself to the good Da, who spoilt him like a child while he lay fractiously in bed and ordered her about; she sat for hours next to his bed when he could not sleep and stroked his fleshy hand.

She grew fat and wore plain cotton dresses which she bought from the Poles on the Dempel. She twisted her hair into a nondescript coil behind her neck and trudged about the house in slippers.

When her father had a stroke, Da had to bathe and dress the heavy man, who had become completely childlike, and help him back into bed again. He could no longer talk: he could only say her name when he needed her. He uttered a melancholy sound which much resembled a foghorn. He lay the whole day in the gloom of his bedroom with his powerless hands on the sheet and his eyes followed her continually as she moved about the room. Now and then he bleated plaintively, "Daaa, Daaa."

The family naturally felt very sorry for her and said, *"Da ta un pan di Dios, Jesus e pober ta un bon hende."* ("Da is a good soul, God, what a good soul she is.") But in bed at night the husbands and wives told one another, "Today or tomorrow Da will break out, of course; a young woman cannot stand such an unnatural life for long! But then, Papachi is wedded to her, the old egoist, and no one can come between."

Then her father had a second stroke: his mouth lolled open and his eyelids hung in flabby folds over his pupils, while his hands trembled continually. He dirtied his bed three or four times a day, so that flies danced in swarms about his body. Da toiled continually from the bathroom to the bedroom to nurse her father, who had become a will-less plant.

When, one evening, he gave a shriek and rolled dead from the bed, she felt relieved at first; then she was overcome by a pitiable feeling of grief. In a couple of weeks streaks of gray shot through her hair and thick pouches grew under her eyes; she wept continually and blew her nose absentmindedly in the hem of her underslip. She upset food on her skirt and did not notice that she was beginning to smell stale.

The family was very concerned about her and often invited her to come for Sunday dinner; they made forced lively conversation until Aunty Da began to cry into the soup, with her red nose snuffling over her plate and her red-rimmed eyes screwed up. The children would then scrape their feet under the table in embarrassment until they got the order to go and play, after which their parents tried to comfort her.

It was then decided that Da would move in with a brother who had seven children and help with the housekeeping in return for food and lodging.

After a while she became very attached to the children, particularly to the youngest; when the child had to be punished, Da locked herself in the bathroom in order not to hear its cries and rested her forehead against the cool side of the basin. She would do anything for the children; she stole cigarettes for the older ones and made dolls for the younger ones.

One day, a man who worked somewhere in the harbor came to live in a neighboring house. He was a big ugly Hollander with red hair and good-natured eyes. He had dirty nails and spoke with a flat Hague accent, through which infiltrated the echo of that city's slums. Since he was fond of children, sometimes, when he met Da, who was out walking with the youngest child in front of the house, he stood and stroked the child's head with his rough hand. Then Da looked down at his square neck, always rather grimy from lubricating oil, and smiled. And gradually they began to talk to each other, she greatly embarrassed because of her inner thoughts, he stiff as only a man of forty can be when he pays court.

He told her about his father, who was a cycle repairer in the old part of The Hague, and about his brothers, who worked for the municipality. He himself had always wanted to leave Holland and finally ended up in Curaçao; it was no life for a bachelor really, no company and he thought sometimes: damn it, Karel, what have you let yourself in for? But he had made his bed and he had to lie in it, didn't he?

And she told him of her father, who had lain helpless in his bed in his last years and watched her as she walked about the room and called her in the night and could not say why he had called her.

She bought a corset and a lovely mauve dress in the Herenstraat and went walking with the children on Sunday afternoons under his window, while she looked out of the corner of her eye to see whether he had seen her. And he bought three Arrow shirts and a jar of pomade, great lumps of which he smeared on his red head and then tried furiously to bring his hair under control. He shaved himself so closely on Sunday afternoons that there was blood on his razor, and he scraped under his fingernails with a penknife to get out the workman's dirt. Then they went walking together, the workman from The Hague and Aunty Da from Curaçao, while the child ran ahead of them. Sometimes he took her pliant tropical hand in his horny fingers and she lowered her head like a young girl, blushing with embarrassment.

One day he bought her a bunch of flowers and said hesitantly that he was in love with her and wanted to marry her. He was only a simple workman, but he could earn his bread, for he was a first-class tradesman, there was no better welder on Curaçao. Hadn't they brought him from the Isla when the new welding equipment broke down? And he wiped the sweat from his forehead and inserted his finger behind his collar, which seemed to be restricting his breathing.

Aunty Da said she was well aware she was not beautiful and that she had never had a young man because her father had always chased them away from the porch. When he became ill she had no time or inclination for courting. But if he would have her she would marry him, for she loved him too and she very much wanted to have children. But he would have to speak to her brother, as that was the custom on Curaçao. And so it came about that Karel sat one Saturday evening in Alfred's living room, in his best suit, looking at a yellowed engraving of a dejected Napoleon in exile. Next to the portrait of Napoleon hung a peeling painting of a battle—a confused heap of horses and riders with flags and muskets stumbled over one another, while, in the distance, white plumes of smoke represented cannon fire. Karel sweated freely and wiped his palms on his trousers. A couple of children came in and, without giving a greeting or beginning a conversation, stood looking at the red-headed man. At last Alfred came and classified the suitor at a glance: *macamba* (Dutchman on Curaçao) and, moreover, a *pletter* (working-class Dutchman).

They engaged in small talk and drank a whisky-and-soda. Large sweat stains appeared on Karel's chest and his Adam's apple went spasmodically up and down; now he had to come forward with his request. But the brother gave him no opportunity; he said what a beautiful country Holland was and described everything he had done in Amsterdam and The Hague on his last leave.

When it was dinnertime, Karel stood on the porch bewildered and a little befuddled from the strong whisky-and-sodas and cursed because he had not had a chance to make his request. The next time, damn it, he would not let himself be fobbed off by that fellow, who spent the whole time reminiscing about his leave. What would he say to Da?

But he did not have to say anything to Da, for her brother had already decided that Da could not marry a *pletter*. Just imagine, a rough workman with dirty nails, who thought he could marry Da for the asking! No good would come of it anyway. And the same evening Alfred spoke to Da on the porch.

"Listen, Da, when our poor father died, we, your next of kin, had the responsibility for your welfare. We have taken you into our home and the children love you as much as they do their own father and mother. And, because we have your welfare in mind, we don't think you ought to go out with that *macamba* anymore. He is only an ordinary workman, a welder or something, a *pletter* who, in Holland, would live on the third floor of one of those houses where the washing hangs behind the windows. As long as Karel is on Curaçao it won't be so bad, but imagine if he should decide today or tomorrow to return to Holland and take you with him, what then? Would you be happy in a cramped house among workers who sing about Sien, Sien, beautiful Sien, when they are drunk, and slap one another's wives on the behind? You have seen for yourself at the party at the Asiento club how rough and crude that sort is when they have had a drink. No, you must understand that, in your own interest, I advise you not to go out with Karel any more."

And so he went on; he insisted that she should stop seeing him. If she would not listen to him, who had only her best interests at heart, then he could no longer . . .

Aunty Da, crimson and deeply hurt, looked at her hands and thought of Karel's good-natured face and his awkward affection for her. She thought of the dreams which had come to her in her sleep, of a house where she could be alone with a husband who would fill his pipe after the evening meal and read the "Stock Exchange and News Reports," shaking his head over political affairs and the knife fights in the Punda.

And she thought of a cradle in which her child would lie with its little fist in its mouth and grasp Karel's forefinger with its other hand. But she realized at once that she would never have the courage to defy her brother.

When she met Karel again, he gazed at his feet in embarrassment and did not dare look at her. And at that moment she felt a great love for the red-headed man surge through her; she took his head in her arms and kissed him on his eyes and his mouth.

Then Karel said, "Why don't you let that brother of yours go to hell? When all is said and done, you are an adult and what that dirty egoist wants is a cheap nurse for his children. Let them all go to hell, and marry me. For the present we can rent a room somewhere until I have saved some money, and then we will furnish a little house. What do you say, Da?"

But she started to cry and said, "Ai, no Karel, I can't do that! Not only my brother, but the whole family will be against me if I don't do as he wishes. All my uncles and aunts and cousins will avoid me and the two of us would not be happy here in Curaçao."

That evening her brother said, "Nechi van Denden has told me that she has seen you talking with that *macamba* of yours. Remember what I told you! If a woman loses her name on a small island, she is lost completely. Think of your good name and of your poor father, who isn't long dead. Do you think it right that a woman of your age should stand smooching on the street corner with a foreigner, where any passerby can see her? I won't have you going round with that man any more. I forbid you! Remember that."

And so began for Da and Karel a period of secret meetings in the dusk, of hurried conversations, where they both looked over their shoulders to see if anyone saw them.

When she was with Karel in the car, she lay half stretched out on the front seat so that her head could not be seen through the side window. Sometimes she slipped into the cinema, where she would meet him in the back row. She always waited until the film had begun, but in the semidarkness she saw heads turning and it sometimes happened during the interval that she looked right into the face of a cousin who was sitting with her husband. On such evenings she went home trembling, for she knew that there would be a mighty scene the next day at the breakfast table, when her brother would work himself up and use language such as Karel had never dreamed of. She grew thin and nervous and felt herself followed by the eyes of all. Wherever she went she imagined that people were watching her and laughing ironically, and that the whole island population was gossiping about her conduct.

One evening, after devising a plan employing all her feminine cunning, she drove with Karel to Westpunt. She sat next to him in the old Ford with her hand on his knee, the intimate gesture of a woman in love. There was a thin sickle of moon in the sky and Karel grasped the steering wheel with the intensity of those who have learned to drive only late in life. They parked the car behind a tree and walked along the beach, where nobody was to be seen. The edge of the sea lay like a silver line at their feet and they crushed brittle shells as they walked. The rocks around the bay projected menacingly in the semidarkness and the little fishing boats smelled of salt and decaying fish.

Then they lay in the sand and embraced. And in the roar of the surf Da was drawn along by a passion so consuming and irresistible that Karel was overwhelmed. When he fell back exhausted on the sand, she held his head against her breast and rocked him with great tenderness to and fro. Lines of phosphorescence shot along the water where fish disturbed the surface with their tails. On the rocks above their heads the cacti stood outlined darkly against the sky and a soft wind caressed their heated bodies.

And slowly a suffocating fear descended upon Aunty Da: she knew that nothing could remain hidden on Curaçao. She trembled at the thought of returning home again and facing her brother. She began to weep; Karel sat helplessly next to her and let the sand slip through his fingers. Then they dressed and began the return journey. She sat upright next to him in the car, stiff with fear, and said nothing during the whole of the drive from Banda Row. Karel, who thought that she was angry, clutched discomfited at the steering wheel and stared into the light of the headlights as it picked out the narrow road.

When they arrived at the house, she ran quickly up the steps without taking leave of him and turned the handle of the door; but the door would not open. She ran to the back in order to get in by the kitchen door; but that door was locked too. Then she sat on a box by the steps and covered her face with her hands.

When her brother let her in the next morning, he said nothing. She ran to her room and closed the shutters. Then she sat on the edge of the bed and thought: they saw me on the beach and tomorrow all Curaçao will know what happened. And she crept under the sheet and hid her head under the pillow. For three weeks she lay thus: she ate nothing and drank only a little milk now and then. She became as thin as a skeleton and her skin hung in unnatural folds over her joints; her hair dried out and looked like coconut matting; her bloodless lips quivered continually.

When she came out of her bedroom again, she was changed; she giggled at her brother and pulled her dressing gown over her limbs with a demure gesture. Then she combed her hair with a green comb and looked at herself in a hand mirror which she unwrapped from a handkerchief. She sighed and giggled like a child who has sampled some jam and suddenly discovers that there is still a smear on his mouth.

The family looked with horror at the gruesome woman who walked around prudishly in a dressing gown and suddenly stopped coquettishly to comb her hair. Her brother sent for the doctor, who spoke with her in her room. He stayed for two hours and the family heard her occasional laugh and then the deep growl of his voice in reply. When he reappeared, her brother asked, *"Kiko dokter ta kere di e caso?"* ("What does the doctor think of the case?")

And the doctor looked at him with eyes filled with such contempt that her brother took a step back and tugged defensively at his trousers.

"Your sister is very ill, Alfred," he said, "she is very ill and we must only hope that she can still be cured." Then he walked off without any leave-taking.

That night Alfred's wife was awakened by Aunty Da, who stood tugging at her foot. After she got over the fright she went with Da. Behind the bedroom door Da whispered, "I have something very serious to tell you, Vilma. When I get undressed at night, Alfred stands in the garden behind my shutters and watches me. And yesterday, when I took a bath, he stood at the bathroom window looking at me. You mustn't tell him I know, but see to it that he leaves me alone, for a lady must look after her reputation. I am a respectable woman and I do not care to have a man see me naked in the bath." And she giggled with her hand in front of her mouth and brought out her comb.

After a couple of weeks the family grew used to the new Da and they could smile again at *e cos di pasa nan cu tante Da ta hasi* (the silly behavior of Aunty Da). The oldest son always said when he saw her, *"Tante Da, mi ta mira bo saja"* ("Aunty Da, I can see your petticoat"), at which she pulled her skirts closer round her legs with a shriek and ran to her room. When she took a bath, her brother sometimes thumped good-naturedly on the door and cried, *"Cuidow, Da, mi ta miraboe"* ("Look out, Da, I can see you") and smiled, shaking his head at her startled cries.

So Aunty Da gradually became completely mad and was gradually accepted as such by everyone: a thin little woman, who always giggled behind a handkerchief and continually drew a green comb through her stiff hair. One evening, when Alfred came home a little drunk from the club, he found her naked in the sitting room with a knife in her hand; there was foam on her lips and her eyes were yellow with hate and dementia. She screamed and sprang at him like a wild animal; and she stabbed him twice in the arm with the knife. Then she was taken to Monte Cristo, where I go to visit her when I am on the island.

TRANSLATED BY R.R. SYMONDS

René de Rooy

THE PRECIOUS STONES
OF UNCLE BRINK

"An American was here to see you," my wife said when I came home one afternoon. "He asked if he could take a look at those stones of yours, 'the rough gems,' but I told him to come back tomorrow, when you'd be free, and he said he would. We talked for a while and he seems very much interested in all kinds of minerals."

"What kind of fellow was he?" I asked.

"Oh, a thin man in khaki trousers and sport shirt. A weather-beaten face. He's an independent prospector who now and then hikes inland. Besides, he's a buyer of all kinds of precious stones, so he says. Rudi Bartels told him you have a few stones you might be willing to sell. In any case, he'll be back tomorrow; then you can see for yourself if those emeralds and diamonds of yours are worth anything. I just hope you'll be able to sell them, for we need the money. . . ."

She need not have reminded me of that; for it was a week ago, just as I was trying to think of a way to lay my hands on an extra hundred guilders, that Rudi popped in and I had shown him Uncle Brink's stones. Rudi has a cousin who works somewhere on a gold placer on the upper Surinam, from whom he now and then gets rough crystals for his collection. Those stones of mine, about which my wife spoke with some ridicule, were glued to a rectangular piece of black lacquer—a large green one, about the size of a sapodilla pit, and a few small white ones, which were scattered at random around it, as if they had been scraped from a piece of paper onto the warm lacquer and pressed down next to the green.

I'd had the piece of lacquer, with its stones, for years. Sometimes I forgot all about it. Once it popped up in a box of rubbish in the closet, and then, late one night, I discovered it in the drawer of my desk. I set it before me and sat for a long time fascinated, watching the glittering lights in the dull green, glowing in the dust. Often, after moving, I had to make a real search, for I had become very much attached to my Uncle Brink's old stones. But if I could get a good price, I was willing to sell. Maybe the American would pay a hundred guilders; that would solve our immediate problem. Nevertheless, I would miss them. For though I am someone who can part easily with possessions, I regarded those stones as a point of contact with my youth and its fading memories, which like a row of trees on the horizon disappears during the rainy season behind the gray-steadily-thickening haze. Of the scattered palm trees that remains only an unrecognizable blot. And the bare solitary cancan tree, in whose grotesque branches I imagined all sorts of figures, melts away in the silver mist of a horizon that is yet close.

But when I, in a quiet moment, watched the sparkling of the stones, the thought of this time, so nearly lost in memory, revived. And once again I smelled the scent of jasmine in the morning hedgerows covered with dew. And once again the city became white with joy to me, as when I encountered Anette under the bright flamboyants of Gravenstraat, where as a dreamy boy of twelve I had gone walking one afternoon, and returned at dusk to the parental home in the Combé with a happy heart.

Saturday was always for us boys a wonderful, unbridled day in the house or in the Palmenlaan. Then we were allowed to romp to our heart's content in the vast garden. We played soccer with a ball made from old stockings, and *batenball* on the forbidden *tiekpauw,* and we filled our hungry stomachs with green *manjas* and *goejaves.* Unfortunately, quite often my father would call me away from a game, or out of the tree in which I sat like a monkey, to send me on an errand downtown. Mostly I had to go to the post office, and this I very much disliked, since my father always expected more letters than I brought back, and inquired suspiciously after a business letter from Curaçao, which unfortunately had not been handed to me over the counter. Or he sent me with a note to one of his old friends, asking how they were doing. I thought this concern of his superfluous and blamed it on the noise and shouting in the garden, whose tone I usually dominated. Once in a while, though, if he had been lucky in a game of *piauw*, of which according to him he had made a study, I was sent to his old friend, our Uncle Brink, with a few guilders, depending on the number of "eyes" that had come up at the drawing of Bank 18.

In the beginning I classified Uncle Brink as one of the boring old people to whom I was sent in order to keep the games in the back yard within limits. My dislike, however, changed gradually to pleasure, when Uncle Brink became more communicative, and made me—possibly as bringer of my father's saving gifts—a partner in his adventures inland.

He lived near the end of the still, quiet Wagenwegstraat, on the right side of that shady alley with its long double rows of mahogany trees, which aroused in my sensitive boy's heart the same feeling that much later was to fascinate me in Milan on coming from the sunny square upon the mysterious, Gothic cathedral.

When I knocked carefully on the copper door knocker of the unpainted little house, Uncle Brink's old "Missie"—I have never known what his relation to her was—shuffled out on the veranda. She let me into the small living room full of Austrian bentwood chairs and small bracket tables with copper basins on high decorated legs.

"Sit down; your Uncle will come right away," she would say, and shuffle back to her dark storeroom. Alone, I started looking around at the framed portraits: a fat brown woman in a long-sleeved dress with lace at the collar. Opposite, in a large oval, was a man also unknown to me, with a buttoned-up coat and stiff collar like the one my father had worn before he went to Curaçao. The painted face observed me severely over a wide mustache which was curled to a point. Then the door across from the entrance opened and the long skinny figure of my Uncle Brink entered. With one hand he held his pajama trousers together, and stretched out the other toward the guilders in my father's folded envelope; this he would stuff away in his pocket unopened.

"Thank your father for me. Yes, Rudolf is one of the few friends who still think of me." Then he was silent, and with bony hands stroked his hollow cheeks, which were covered with a silver stubble. "All my friends have deserted me. Only Bado has remained faithful," he added, musing, as if his thoughts had wandered back to better days.

I asked about his old friends who had given my father the
nickname "Ba Doffie," which soon became Bado among his
equals. And Uncle Brink explained, he described their old school-
mates. Some of them were now in Cuba, in Venezuela, Holland or
the Dutch East Indies. One was a telegraph operator like my father, others a chemist, a planter and a doctor, but he never saw
them any more. He complained that they did not answer his letters,
and spoke of the lasting bad times. Sometimes he read me those
letters. They were written on long sheets covered with graceful
erect characters and all the additional flourishes, but his friends
never responded. Evidently they no longer cared to be bothered
with his endless plans and projects, which, according to their cre-
ator, would surely succeed if only he had the necessary capital.

"Capital, capital, my boy! That's all we need to exploit all the
treasures which are waiting to be picked up in the interior." This
discussion would be interrupted by Missie, who entered with a box
of cookies, and Uncle Brink changed the subject.

"What did you learn about geography in school this week?" he
asked.

"Toemoek Hoemak Mountains," I said. "Surinam is bounded
on the north by the Atlantic Ocean and on the south by Brazil."
Beautiful-sounding words, I thought, and added, glad to be able to
air my knowledge, "Marowijne River, Commewijne River, Coran-
tijn . . ."

Missie had shuffled out again, and Uncle Brink stared over
my head out the window. "The mountains are beautiful," he
mumbled. "He who is willing to brave the rapids and wild animals
will be rich, very rich." Then he raged. "They don't teach you a
thing in school, not a thing!" and started describing the preparation
for an expedition.

At night I would dream about it. Far behind Paramaribo, farther than the wobbly train ever penetrated, stretched the forest of
gold. Placer mines fallen into decay and unexploited fields lay
waiting for the intrepid bushrangers. During the day they perched
in long slender canoes, rushing at great speed over the rapids
foaming between rocks, till the water was calm again and a peaceful scene unfolded before their eyes. Hundreds of curious monkeys
were swinging in the trees on the river banks, following the adven-
turers. Laughing, one of the men aims a double-barreled rifle, and

a large howling monkey, the leader of the troop, tumbles scream-ing from the branches. Later, the bushrangers lie in their ham-mocks around the fire listening to the long-drawn-out sounds of evening and of night. In the darkness, one can trace glowing eyes circling the camp, and in the morning, when the thin mist rises—tracks of tigers.

At long last, after several days by boat, they cut a way with razor-edged machetes through the impenetrable verdure. Giant boa constrictors cross their path, but they leave them be. Then the forest becomes less dense and the savanna stretches out before them to the foot of a hill. At long last, the deserted gold placer mine. Drenched with sweat they work for weeks with spade and pickax. The ore is washed in the long tom, and then among the chunks of earth and rubble one lucky day—the discovery! Nuggets as big as stones gleam dim but unmistakable in the damp gravel.

Then, with the spoil of tens of kilos of gold, comes the fast trip back to civilization. In a native village where they stop there is dancing and drinking. And then on downstream to the city. At night the rower's singing resounds over the moonlit sheet of water. Finally the nuggets are weighed and turned into cash. Well-being is the order of the day. A few are rich. Others quench their thirst and smoke expensive cigars, which they light with banknotes. Who cares about the money going up in smoke? Won't there be a new season, more profitable expeditions?

Always new expeditions, some of which fail through a variety of setbacks; the death of a friend from snakebite, or from lingering malaria, whose delirium makes a man cry out unintelligible words.

I was too young to realize that Uncle Brink, too, was such an adventurer, who had fallen sick and had failed and was no longer taken seriously. Did he cling still to the vanity that was his golden dream, this old man, who apparently wanted to instill in me his passionate love for the secrets concealed in the interior?

I well remember the afternoon—he had been talking for a long time and the light had faded between the trunks of trees in the alley—when he took a small box out of a chest under his bed and carefully unlocked it. I could not see everything it contained, but he extracted a faded document, which he unfolded with trembling fingers.

"Listen well, my boy," he said in a solemn tone, his tired eyes resting insistently on me. He hesitated, as if to formulate as well as he could what he was going to say. "You know what I've so often told you. Here is everything. . . . I can't do it anymore. . . . Neither can your father, but you boys, you'll be able to find it. . . ." And his bony old hands moved over a mysterious map, which looked strange with its crosses and dotted lines, on which neither the Toemoek Hoemak Mountains nor the Atlantic Ocean were placed as they were in school. When Uncle Brink continued, I had the feeling he was already thinking ahead, entangled unconsciously in his dreams.

"Here it is . . . this river. Remember it well, my boy. Four days by boat past the last village . . . on the right bank, an enormous basralocus tree. . . . you can't miss it. . . . a solitary giant, close to the edge. *There* it is. *There* you must disembark, cut a path in a straight line to the foot of the mountain . . . the Northern slope, you hear. . . . *There* you'll find them . . . like these . . . I kept them for you. . . ."

And the old man grasped the box with both hands, upon which the lid fell open. In the late light of the fading afternoon, before my own eyes—wide-open with astonishment—were the first rough gems I had ever seen. So *that's* what he wanted to tell me. In me he saw his successor, who must find the treasure that he had given up after many hardships and fruitless trips and a persistent fever. My brain reeling, I walked back home that evening the wealthy heir to dreams as mysterious as that deep blue sky in the treetops where the bluebirds were singing with fervor.

With the worries of his last years weighing on him, my father paid no attention to my story about Uncle Brink's precious stones. At most, he shrugged his shoulders compassionately. Financial troubles multiplied day by day, and in the course of his efforts still to leave us something, he died even before I had finished school. An unreal period of sorrow settled down over the big house in the Combé, which now we were forced to leave; a period which kept everything and everybody in its sad grip.

I can still see my stepmother, her eyes red with crying, wandering through the house—and I doing my homework, climbing the manja tree once again, walking along the cove to school and returning home. We live on, and gradually the voices of my younger brothers and sisters ring through the house again, and the atmosphere relaxes at the prospect, pleasant for the children at least, of moving to another place. I help my mother empty the cupboard. For the first time she is able to touch my father's things without bursting into tears. We go over his papers and take out what should be burned. Love letters in French to his first wife, my mother; an expired policy; old clothes.

From among the books, family portraits and correspondence, suddenly appears a small box that makes my heart beat faster: Uncle Brink's legacy. My mother wants to throw this rubbish away, but I hide it among my things. Later on, when I am alone, I nervously open the box, and there under his old letters to my father are the precious stones of Uncle Brink. But the map, which I would now be able to understand, is gone. . . .

Next day the American came—my wife's description of him was accurate, as usual—and I talked with him politely. First, he offered me twenty-five dollars and, when I refused, was willing to make it forty, even though my "rather worthless stones" were not, in truth, worth much. However, I explained that I would prefer not to sell them, "for sentimental reasons," and he took his leave, obviously disappointed.

Indeed no, I was neither willing nor able to sell him these precious stones—that rubbish of Uncle Brink. As a true son of Surinam, I still cherish the vague dream—doubtless merely a chimera—of the existence of hidden treasure in the interior, but it is a dream with which I have grown up, and which is closely interwoven with love for my native soil. I'd far rather live in poverty, and die sick and senile, like my uncle, in a shack, than sell this green glittering dream for a few worthless cents to just any American . . . or to anyone else.

TRANSLATED BY HUBERT VAN DEN BERGH

BIOGRAPHICAL NOTES

ABELARDO DÍAZ ALFARO. Born in the town of Caguas, Puerto Rico, in 1920. After studying at the University, he taught in rural schools and came to know much about the problems of the lives of the farmers. A series of sketches of rural life, *Terrazo*, was his first literary success.

EMILIO S. BELAVAL. Born in Fajardo, Puerto Rico, in 1903. A lawyer as well as a writer, he has published a number of books, among them *Cuentos para fomentar el turismo*, in which this present story appeared.

TOMÁS BLANCO. Born in San Juan, Puerto Rico, he has studied medicine in the United States, traveled extensively in Europe, and is the author of several books of essays, short stories and novels.

JUAN BOSCH. Born in La Vega, the Dominican Republic, in 1910. Well-known as a political leader and writer, he was President of the Dominican Republic after the overthrow of the Trujillo dictatorship; seven months later, he was himself overthrown, and now lives in Puerto Rico. He is the author of several volumes of short stories, among them *La Muchacha de la Guaira*, 1955, from which the work here included was taken.

LYDIA CABRERA. Born in Cuba in 1900, she lived for many years in Paris; while there she collected Negro stories and legends she had heard in her childhood in Cuba. These first appeared in French, and subsequently in Spanish in two volumes: *Cuentos negros de Cuba* (1940) and *Por qué* (1948). She now resides in Florida.

LINO NOVÁS CALVO. Born in Spain in 1905, he was taken to Cuba as a child. A leading figure in Cuban literature, he has published, among other books, *La luna nona y otros cuentos* (1942) and *No sé quién soy* (1945). He has a wide knowledge of American literature and has translated a number of books into Spanish. Currently he lives in New York.

ALEJO CARPENTIER. Born in Cuba in 1904, has lived much abroad, but is at present in Cuba. He is also a musicologist, an interest reflected in his books. His first novel, *Ecué-Yamba-O,* appeared in 1933. Since then several others have appeared, including *The Lost Steps,* published here in 1956, for the French version of which he received the Prix du Meilleur Livre Étranger in 1956.

AIMÉ CÉSAIRE. Born in Martinique, he was editor in Fort-de-France of the literary magazine *Tropiques.* Two books of his poems are: *Les Armes Miraculeuses* (1946) and *Cahier d'un Retour au Pays Natal* (1947). The latter will soon appear in an English translation. Probably the greatest French poet of Negro origin, his work has been widely hailed. He now lives in Paris.

GILBERT DE CHAMBERTRAND. Born in Guadeloupe, he has had a wide interest in the arts, being at once artist, novelist, poet, astrologer, playwright, and journalist. His book of short stories, *Titine Grosbonda,* was published in Paris in 1948.

AUSTIN CLARKE. Born in Barbados, he has lived for some time in Canada, where he works for the C.B.C. His first novel, *Survivors of the Crossing,* has recently been published in England.

FRANK A. COLLYMORE. Born in Barbados and for long a teacher of English, he has, as well as writing short stories and editing the literary magazine *Bim,* had a lively interest in the theater, and has appeared in a number of plays. Aside from occasional trips abroad, he resides in Barbados.

COLA DEBROT. Born on the island of Bonaire in 1902. He received degrees in both law and medicine, and for a time edited the literary magazine *Criterium.* Among other works, he is the author of *My Sister the Negro,* a novella which appeared in 1935. He is currently Governor of the Netherlands Antilles.

ELISEO DIEGO. Born in Havana, Cuba, in 1920. He has traveled widely in Europe and the United States, and has a broad knowledge of English literature. In addition to poetry, he has published works of prose, including the volume of short stories *Divertimentos* (1946). He lives at present in Cuba.

PIERRE DUPREY. Born in 1911 in Fort-de-France, he studied in Paris and traveled widely. He has worked as a journalist, and is currently technical adviser on information for the government of the Ivory Coast. His novel *Bli* appeared in 1950, and more recently a history of the people of the Ivory Coast.

A. N. FORDE. Born on the island of Grenada, he was for many years assistant at the Grenada Grammar School. Since 1959, he has been an editor of *Bim,* residing in Barbados, and is currently employed in the Government Secretariat.

NICOLAS GUILLÉN. Born in Camagüey, Cuba, in 1904, he studied law at the University of Havana. He brought the *son,* the local Cuban folk song, into literature, and made African folklore popular as artistic material. There is a strongly political note in his work. Among his books of poetry is *Motivos de Son* (1930).

JOHN HEARNE. Born in Jamaica, he served in the R.A.F. during the war. His first novel, *Voices under the Window,* was published by Faber & Faber in 1955. Since then, he has published several other novels. At present he lives in Jamaica, and is Resident Tutor in the Department of Extra Mural Studies, at the University College of the West Indies in Jamaica. His work has also been published in this country.

ALBERT HELMAN. Born in Paramaribo in 1906, he spent his youth in Surinam. He is the author of a novel, *Zuid Zuid-West,* among other works, and is currently Minister Plenipotentiary at the Royal Netherlands Embassy in Washington. Albert Helman is a pseudonym; his real name is Dr. L. A. M. Lichtveld.

DANIEL SAMAROO JOSEPH. Born, I believe, in Trinidad, he has continued to live in Port of Spain, but no accurate information is forthcoming.

ISMITH KHAN. Born in Trinidad, and now residing in the United States, he had his first novel, *The Jumbie Bird,* published in London in 1961. He worked as a reporter for the *Trinidad Guardian,* and later studied at Michigan State University and at the New School for Social Research in New York. He is at present employed by the New York Public Library.

GEORGE LAMMING. Born in Barbados in 1927, he taught in Trinidad, and in 1950 went to London. Since then he has been active in the B.B.C., broadcasting a weekly program of reviews of books and films. His first novel, *In the Castle of My Skin,* was published here in 1953, and additional novels have followed. He lives currently in London.

BOELI VAN LEEUWEN. Born in the Netherlands Antilles, he is the author of *The Rock of Offense,* of which this story is a part.

MAGLOIRE-SAINT-AUDE. Born in Haiti, he is well known as a poet and novelist. Among his works are *Dialogue de mes Lampes* (1941), *Tabou* (1941), *Parias* (1949), and *Ombres et Reflets* (1952). He lives at present near Port-au-Prince.

ROGER MAIS. Born in Jamaica, he published three novels, *The Hills Were Joyful Together* (1953), *Brother Man* (1954), and *Black Lightning* (1955), as well as short stories, poems and plays. His early death was a great loss to West Indian literature.

TIP MARUGG. Born in Curaçao, he has traveled extensively, but prefers his native island. He is editor of a monthly magazine, *De Passaat,* and has published poems as well as the novel from which this excerpt was taken.

CARLOS MONTENEGRO. Born in Spain of Cuban parents, he later emigrated to Cuba. He lived for a time in Argentina, and in the United States, where he worked in an arms factory; subsequently he spent some years at sea. Jailed after a night of street fighting, he remained in prison nineteen years. Toward the end of this period he wrote a short story for the magazine *Carteles,* for which he won first prize and the interest of his fellow writers, which led subsequently to his release. Among his works are a novel, *Hombres sin mujer,* and various volumes of short stories. The story included in this volume appeared before 1952.

FLORETTE MORAND. Born in Guadeloupe, she has lived in France, and traveled extensively. Her writings include *Chanson pour ma Savane,* a book of poems; *Biguines,* short stories; and *Doudou,* a novel. At present she is living in France.

V. S. NAIPAUL. Born in Trinidad of parents of East Indian origin, he now lives in London. He has written several novels, among which are *The Mystic Masseur,* winner of the John Llewellyn Rhys Memorial Prize, and a volume of short stories, *Miguel Street,* which won the Somerset Maugham Award.

ST.-JOHN PERSE. Born on an island off Guadeloupe, St.-John Perse is the pseudonym for Alexis St. Léger Léger. Educated in Paris, he subsequently entered the diplomatic service and lived for some time in China. From this period came the long poem *Anabase.* An earlier book of poems, *Eloges,* was first published in 1911. He left the diplomatic service in 1940, for voluntary exile in the United States. Since then he has published several more volumes of poetry. In 1940, he received the Nobel Prize in Literature.

V. S. REID. Born in Jamaica in 1914, his first novel, *New Day,* was published in this country in 1949. He started out as an accountant, and later switched to journalism. He is the author also of a second novel, *The Leopard,* and numerous short stories.

CLÉMENT RICHER. Born in Fort-de-France, Martinique, in 1914, he attended college in Moulins, France, and studied subsequently at the Sorbonne. His first novel appeared in 1937, and in 1951 *Ti-Coyo and his Shark* appeared in this country. He has been awarded numerous literary prizes, among them the Prix Paul Flat in 1941 and again in 1948. At present he lives in Belgium.

RENÉ DE ROOY. Born in Surinam, he now lives in Curaçao. Poet, sculptor and storyteller, he writes in Dutch, Papiamento, and Sranan-Tongo, and is one of the founders of *Simadan,* a literary review.

KARL SEALY. Born in Barbados, he has written a number of short stories, many of which have appeared in *Bim.*

SAMUEL SELVON. Born in Trinidad of Indian parents in 1924, he now lives in London. During the war he served for five years on a minesweeper. He is the author of several novels and books of short stories, and was awarded a Guggenheim Fellowship in 1955.

PEDRO JUAN SOTO. Born in Catano, Puerto Rico, in 1928. He studied at Long Island University (B.A., 1950) and at Columbia Teachers College (M.A., 1953). He has written several short stories, novels, and plays, among them *Spiks,* published in 1956.

He lives at present in Puerto Rico, and is, among other things, an editor of the *San Juan Review*. Since 1954 he has been preparing film scripts and educational booklets for the Division of Community Education.

RAPHAËL TARDON. Born in Fort-de-France, Martinique, in 1911, he studied subsequently in Paris, taking degrees in law and in letters. As a Specialist in Information, he has been Attaché to the High Commissioners in Madagascar and Senegal, and more recently was Director of the Information Service in Guadeloupe. He is the author of a number of books, among them *Starkenfirst* which won the Grand Prix des Antilles in 1949.

PHILIPPE THOBY-MARCELIN. Born in Port-au-Prince, Haiti, in 1904, he lived for some time in France and now makes his home in the United States. He was actively connected with the *Revue Indigène* (1927-1928). Author of several volumes of verse he also wrote three novels of Haitian life with his brother, Pierre Marcelin, one of which, *Canapé-Vert*, won the Second Latin American Literary Prize Contest.

DEREK WALCOTT. Born in St. Lucia in 1930, he published his first book, *Poems*, at nineteen. In 1961 he was chosen for a Guinness Award for poetry. He also received a fellowship from the Rockefeller Foundation. His *Selected Poems* has recently appeared in this country.

JOSEPH ZOBEL. Born in Martinique, he has published several novels, among them *Diab'là* and *Les Jours Immobiles*. He is currently Cultural Adviser at Radio Senegal in Dakar.